Psychological and Physical Aggression in Couples

Psychological and Physical Aggression in Couples

Causes and Interventions

Edited by
K. Daniel O'Leary
and Erica M. Woodin

American Psychological Association
Washington, DC

Chapter 2 was coauthored by an employee of the United States government as part of official duty and is considered in the public domain.

Published by
American Psychological Association
750 First Street, NE
Washington, DC 20002
www.apa.org

To order
APA Order Department
P.O. Box 92984
Washington, DC 20090-2984
Tel: (800) 374-2721; Direct: (202) 336-5510
Fax: (202) 336-5502; TDD/TTY: (202) 336-6123
Online: www.apa.org/books/
E-mail: order@apa.org

In the U.K., Europe, Africa, and the Middle East, copies may be ordered from
American Psychological Association
3 Henrietta Street
Covent Garden, London
WC2E 8LU England

Typeset in Goudy by Stephen McDougal, Mechanicsville, MD

Printer: United Book Press, Inc., Baltimore, MD
Cover Designer: Watermark Design Office, Alexandria, VA
Technical/Production Editor: Devon Bourexis

The opinions and statements published are the responsibility of the authors, and such opinions and statements do not necessarily represent the policies of the American Psychological Association.

Library of Congress Cataloging-in-Publication Data

Psychological and physical aggression in couples : causes and interventions / edited by K. Daniel O'Leary and Erica M. Woodin. — 1st ed.
    p. cm.
  Includes bibliographical references and index.
  ISBN-13: 978-1-4338-0453-3
  ISBN-10: 1-4338-0453-0
  1. Family violence—United States. 2. Passive-aggressive personality—United States.
I. O'Leary, K. Daniel, 1940– II. Woodin, Erica M.

  HV6626.2.P79 2009
  362.82'92—dc22
                                                2008046652

British Library Cataloguing-in-Publication Data
A CIP record is available from the British Library.

Printed in the United States of America
First Edition

CONTENTS

CONTRIBUTORS

Julia C. Babcock, PhD, University of Houston, Houston, TX

Monique Clinton-Sherrod, PhD, RTI International, Research Triangle Park, NC

Christopher I. Eckhardt, PhD, Purdue University, West Lafayette, IN

Miriam K. Ehrensaft, PhD, John Jay College of Criminal Justice, New York, NY

William Fals-Stewart, PhD, University of Rochester Medical Center, Rochester, NY

Vangie A. Foshee, PhD, University of North Carolina at Chapel Hill

Claudia Garcia-Moreno, MD, MSc, World Health Organization, Geneva, Switzerland

L. Kevin Hamberger, PhD, Medical College of Wisconsin, Milwaukee

Denise A. Hines, PhD, Clark University, Worcester, MA

Amy Holtzworth-Munroe, PhD, Indiana University, Bloomington

Anita Jose, MA, Stony Brook University, Stony Brook, NY

Keith Klostermann, PhD, University of Rochester Medical Center, Rochester, NY

Tracii S. Kunkel, MA, Northern Illinois University, DeKalb

Jennifer Langhinrichsen-Rohling, PhD, University of South Alabama, Mobile

Heidi Lary Kar, MHS, MA, Stony Brook University, Stony Brook, NY

Eric E. McCollum, PhD, Virginia Tech Northern Virginia Center, Falls Church

Heathe Luz McNaughton Reyes, MPH, University of North Carolina at Chapel Hill

Laura A. Meis, PhD, Veterans Affairs Medical Center, Minneapolis, MN

Jared D. Michonski, BA, University of Houston, Houston, TX

Candice M. Monson, PhD, Veterans Affairs National Center for Posttraumatic Stress Disorder and Boston University School of Medicine, Boston, MA

Christopher M. Murphy, PhD, University of Maryland, Baltimore County, Baltimore

K. Daniel O'Leary, PhD, Stony Brook University, Stony Brook, NY

Alan Rosenbaum, PhD, Northern Illinois University, DeKalb

Kimberly J. Saudino, PhD, Boston University, Boston, MA

Sandra M. Stith, PhD, Kansas State University, Manhattan

Casey T. Taft, PhD, Veterans Affairs National Center for Posttraumatic Stress Disorder and Boston University School of Medicine, Boston, MA

Erica M. Woodin, PhD, University of Victoria, Victoria, British Columbia, Canada

Sarah C. Wyckoff, MPH, University of North Carolina at Chapel Hill

Psychological and Physical Aggression in Couples

INTRODUCTION

K. DANIEL O'LEARY AND ERICA M. WOODIN

The field of partner aggression research has come a long way since the late 1970s and early 1980s, when the initial books and articles on violence against women and family members were published. The latest findings from this growing body of work illustrate the complexity of couples' experiences with psychological and physical aggression and point to the need for a more complex, multifaceted approach to understanding the development and treatment of aggression against intimate partners. Fortunately, some of the very significant progress in the partner aggression field is well documented by the authors of the chapters in this book.

This book is designed to provide readers with a comprehensive understanding of the prevalence, causes, and treatment of psychological and physical aggression in intimate relationships. The chapters are authored by well-regarded researchers who specialize in these topics. Each chapter contains a synthesis of cutting-edge empirical evidence along with a roadmap for applying these findings in clinical settings. In many cases, the authors present significant new insights into the partner aggression field that challenge existing conceptualizations of how to understand and treat aggression between intimate partners.

The focus of this book encompasses both physical and psychological aggression against partners because there is a substantial need in the field to attend to the interaction between these two forms of aggression. As documented in the book *Psychological Abuse in Violent Domestic Relations* (O'Leary & Maiuro, 2001), psychological aggression is much more common than physical aggression in intimate relationships and almost always precedes acts of physical aggression. Moreover, the effects of psychological aggression on individual and family functioning can often be as devastating as physical aggression. Clinicians working with couples and families may believe that partner aggression is not something they are likely to encounter; however, this book makes clear that most couples seeking therapy have perpetrated or experienced some form of psychological aggression in their intimate relationships. Further, although therapists may not expect that their clients will have experienced physical aggression, this book documents how common physical aggression is in close relationships.

This book is intended for use in a range of academic, clinical, and research contexts. It can serve as a useful text for a variety of general courses in psychology, sociology, and family studies, as well as advanced courses in clinical psychology, social work, family counseling, and marital and family therapy. Because each chapter specifically addresses the clinical implications of a given topic, clinicians working with couples and families will find this book accessible. Finally, the state-of-the-art empirical focus and implications for future research make this an important compendium for researchers in the family violence field.

The three parts of this book address prevalence, etiology, and interventions. The parts are designed to examine partner aggression from a broad and multifaceted perspective with the goal of answering three questions: How common is partner aggression? Why does it occur? How can it be prevented and treated?

Across chapters, partner aggression is approached from a range of theoretical perspectives, including biological, psychological, and social viewpoints. Some chapters review well-established areas of research with extensive empirical evidence, whereas others represent cutting-edge new directions in the partner aggression field. Across chapters, the authors review and critique the state of existing theory and empirical evidence and discuss appropriate clinical implications in light of existing research. We now provide an overview of the themes and significance of each part.

PREVALENCE

Approximately 10% of men and women in representative samples in the United States report being the victims of physical aggression by their partners in the past year (e.g., Straus & Gelles, 1990). Physical aggression occurs in approximately 35% to 60% of couples seeking therapy for relationship problems (e.g., O'Leary, Vivian, & Malone, 1992). Although physical aggression by men and women is often similar in frequency, rates of injury and murder of women are often much higher than for men (e.g., Archer, 2000; Cascardi, Langhinrichsen, & Vivian, 1992). The vast majority of physical aggression in representative samples, however, does not cause injury; it is engaged in by both partners and is sometimes called *common couple violence* (M. P. Johnson, 1995). *Battering*, in contrast, consists of physically aggressive behaviors that are used in the context of fear and intimidation tactics. A significant percentage of couples presenting for therapy are characterized by severe physical aggression and sometimes a pattern of intimidation (e.g., Simpson & Christensen, 2005).

Psychological aggression is now also being examined as well because of the significant overlap with physical aggression and implications for victim mental health functioning. Serious and frequent psychological aggression is the most important predictor of physical aggression (e.g., White, Merrill, & Koss, 2001). Further, in some populations of abused women, psychological aggression is reported as having similar or even greater impact on victims than physical aggression (e.g., Dutton, Goodman, & Bennett, 2001).

Jose and O'Leary (chap. 1) open this book with an overview of the prevalence of various forms of psychological and physical aggression in both community and clinic couples. The authors discuss similarities and differences between community and clinic samples, with particular attention to gender differences and injury rates. They highlight the high frequency of aggression, particularly in clinic samples, as well as the detrimental impact of aggression on individuals and relationships. Finally, Jose and O'Leary provide data on the prevalence of partner aggression in same-sex relationships. Given the high prevalence of partner aggression, especially in couples seeking therapy, the authors emphasize the importance of assessing psychological and physical aggression victimization and perpetration in treatment-seeking populations.

Aggression of a sexual nature is an important but often unrecognized factor in many intimate relationships. Monson, Langhinrichsen-Rohling, and Taft (chap. 2) provide evidence on the prevalence of sexual assault in the United States and discuss the historical divide between the study of sexual aggression and other forms of partner aggression. Although psychological and physical aggression are much more common than sexual aggression and coercion in intimate relationships, recent findings suggest that sexual and nonsexual forms of aggression frequently co-occur. Monson et al. examine the commonalities and distinctions between sexual and nonsexual aggression and the ways in which the two fields may be thought of in a more integrated manner. The authors discuss clinical implications regarding the presence or history of sexual coercion and aggression in treatment-seeking couples. Finally, they emphasize the importance of inquiring about sexually coercive and assaultive behaviors during clinical assessment and treatment.

Physical aggression against women appears to be nearly culturally universal, and Lary Kar and Garcia-Moreno (chap. 3) show that rates of physical aggression against female partners are considerably higher in developing countries compared with the United States and other industrialized nations. Moreover, the authors show that in some countries, acts of violence against women begin in utero and continue through adolescence and adulthood with female trafficking and dowry killing of young married women. The authors discuss the prevalence of physical, psychological, and sexual aggression in a number of countries, with emphasis on the frequency and impact of aggressive behaviors cross-culturally. Finally, they discuss the clinical and public policy issues in identifying and reducing aggression in developing countries.

ETIOLOGY

Many factors are likely to influence the development of partner aggression, and it seems clear that it is time to move beyond any one single explanation. As we and others have documented in multivariate analytic studies, power and control factors are important correlates and sometimes precursors to partner physical aggression (e.g., O'Leary, Smith Slep, & O'Leary, 2007); however, they are not the only factors that contribute. Partner aggression is also likely influenced by a range of variables, including genetic predisposition, psychophysiology, family background, personality, psychopathology, and relationship factors.[1] Thus, this part reflects a multifaceted approach to understanding the etiology of partner aggression.

An understanding of the role of psychopathology in partner aggression perpetration is important from both the etiological and intervention perspectives. Hamberger and Holtzworth-Munroe (chap. 4) discuss several important psychopathological predictors of male partner aggression, including anger dysregulation, substance abuse, antisocial personality disorder, and borderline personality disorder. The authors also review three subtypes of aggressive men—family-only, borderline/dysphoric, and generally violent/antisocial—and the possible antecedents and intervention approaches most suitable for each type. Finally, the authors explore the clinical implications of treating aggressive individuals with co-occurring psychopathology.

Ehrensaft (chap. 5) summarizes the role of familial factors such as exposure to parental violence, childhood maltreatment, and parental antisocial behavior in predicting partner aggression in adulthood. The author discusses marital discord between adult partners as placing couples at risk for psychological and physical aggression, and in turn, partner aggression may also adversely affect marital satisfaction and stability. Ehrensaft provides excellent

---

[1]Although beyond the scope of this book, cultural factors are also important in understanding the etiology of partner aggression. For a more comprehensive review, we suggest the excellent books *Physical Violence in American Families: Risk Factors and Adaptations to Violence in 8,145 Families* (Straus & Gelles, 1990) and *Violence Against Women: An International Perspective* (H. Johnson, Ollus, & Nevala, 2007).

longitudinal evidence from several studies regarding the link between the development of antisocial behavior and intimate partner violence for both men and women and also discusses the controversial issue of assortative mating for antisocial characteristics. Finally, she discusses psychological aggression, and particularly controlling behavior, in the context of physically abusive relationships.

There is a growing body of research showing that psychophysiological indexes, and particularly increased autonomic reactivity during conflict, are associated with risk of relationship deterioration. Michonski and Babcock (chap. 6) discuss emerging findings about the role of psychophysiology as a predictor of physical aggression in couples. They explore the role of autonomic reactivity, in particular, as an explanation for the intriguing finding that some antisocial individuals escalate to severe forms of partner aggression whereas others do not. Although the immediate clinical implications of these findings remain unclear, the authors speculate about possible moderators and mediators of autonomic reactivity as targets of change.

Finally, Hines and Saudino (chap. 7) introduce the behavioral genetic perspective to explain the intergenerational transmission of partner aggression. They point out that social learning theory relies solely on shared family environment to explain the widely recognized cross-generational transmission of partner aggression. Because families share both genes and environment, however, the pattern of familial resemblance could also be attributed to shared genes. Using twin populations, the authors discuss the relative influence of genetic heritability, shared environments, and nonshared environments in predicting the use of physical and psychological aggression. The authors also point out that genetic influences are probabilistic, not deterministic, and discuss the role of environmental factors in shaping genetic predispositions.

Overall, the etiological research to date clearly illustrates the need to be aware of the different forms and severity levels of psychological and physical aggression. A person who slaps a partner once and is not highly psychologically aggressive is quite different in many ways from someone who has beaten a partner repeatedly and controls a partner through fear and intimidation tactics. Failure to take into account these varying forms and functions of aggression is shortsighted and potentially harmful. Moreover, failure to take into account the form and function of aggressive behaviors by both men and women is also shortsighted if the goal is to understand, prevent, and ultimately intervene successfully with partner aggression.

INTERVENTIONS

From the accumulating etiological evidence, one message comes through loud and clear: One size does not fit all. That is, one should not expect to find an intervention or treatment approach for partner aggression that works for everyone. The field has reached the point where there is a need for open minds and new conceptualizations of partner aggression, not least of which because the batterer intervention efforts used thus far have not proved to be much more successful than court monitoring alone (Babcock, Green, & Robie, 2004).

One major possible inroad to address the problem of partner aggression is to intervene before the problem exists or is still in the early stages. Foshee, McNaughton Reyes, and Wyckoff (chap. 8) take the position that to prevent adult partner aggression, society needs to prevent the psychological and behavioral precursors to partner aggression that develop during infancy, childhood, adolescence, and young adulthood. The authors describe a variety of approaches to the primary prevention of partner aggression, including intervening with parents to decrease the likelihood that children will observe violence, preventing and reducing bullying, intervening with children exposed to family violence, providing dating abuse prevention programs for adolescents, developing premarital education and counseling programs, and establishing sexual assault prevention programs on college campuses. They also explore the strengths and limitations of existing prevention programs and highlight several areas that demonstrate particular promise.

Treatment for more entrenched forms of aggression may take many forms depending on the characteristics of the aggressive individual. Group treatments have long been the most common option available for male batterers who are court ordered to treatment, and Rosenbaum and Kunkel (chap. 9) describe the development of batterer intervention programs (BIPs) over the past 30 years. The authors discuss common emphases across programs, including a focus on batterer accountability, the effects of violence on women and children, sociocultural attitudes toward gender roles and male dominance, power and control issues, time-out procedures and anger management strategies, attention to beliefs associated with violence and oppression of women, and education regarding the link between substance abuse and violence in intimate relationships. Given the lack of evidence about the effectiveness of different types of BIPs, the authors also explore the need to document the utility of such programs over and above the effects of court monitoring alone.

Murphy, Meis, and Eckhardt (chap. 10) point out that statewide program guidelines in the United States almost exclusively recommend standardized group treatments for male batterers, despite their lack of demonstrated effectiveness and high dropout rates. The authors propose an individualized treatment alternative that addresses diversity in factors such as readiness to change, motivations for abusive behavior, personality problems, and comorbid difficulties such as substance abuse and trauma symptoms. Although the efficacy of the proposed individualized approach remains to be demonstrated, the authors suggest that it is time to develop and test alternative interventions and that ignoring the need for new approaches would be a grave disservice to victims of partner aggression.

Couples therapy may also have a place in partner aggression treatment in certain cases. Historically, couples treatment for physically aggressive couples was often discouraged because of concern that conjoint treatment may place victims at risk. However, couples often request conjoint treatment, and roughly half of couples presenting to couples therapy are physically aggressive. Stith and McCollum (chap. 11) discuss the feasibility of conjoint treatment for partner aggression. The authors have been developing a couples-based intervention for more than 10 years called Domestic Violence Focused Couples Treatment. In this chapter, they provide a summary of their solution-focused treatment model and review empirical evidence supporting the efficacy of a couples-based approach based on their own and others' research.

Finally, the evidence now suggests that assessment and treatment of substance abuse is one of the most important methods to reduce or eliminate partner aggression. Fals-Stewart, Klostermann, and Clinton-Sherrod (chap. 12) explore the historically controversial topic of the role of substance abuse in partner aggression. Although many studies have documented an association between partner aggression and substance abuse, until recently it remained unclear whether substance abuse actually plays a causal role in partner aggression perpetration. The authors review several recent, well-designed longitudinal and treatment studies with appropriate temporal ordering that have provide important information about the role of substance abuse in incidents of partner aggression. They also discuss the importance of these findings for substance abuse and partner aggression treatment approaches, with particular attention to the need for coordinated services for co-occurring partner aggression and substance abuse.

TERMS USED IN THIS BOOK

A final and important note is in order regarding the terms used in this book. The authors of each chapter have chosen to use different terminology to describe the phenomena under question, as have we as the editors of this volume. *Aggression, violence, abuse, battering, coercion, rape, assault,* and many other terms are used throughout this book to describe a cluster of harmful physical and verbal behavior patterns between intimate partners. Unfortunately, despite significant advances, the field does not have a consistent vocabulary to describe the behaviors that constitute psychological and physical aggression. There are many reasons why uniformity may be so difficult to come by, including different clusters of behaviors under question or different backgrounds and agendas of the researchers and advocates creating the definitions.

The Centers for Disease Control and Prevention has advocated for the use of the term *intimate partner violence*, which encompasses psychologically, physically, and sexually violent behavior toward a current or past intimate partner, and several authors in this book have adopted this recommendation. We have chosen to use the term *partner aggression* in the book title and in our own writing because there are various forms of psychological and physical aggression that few would consider to be violent in nature. In ordinary English, the term *violent* refers to severe or uncontrolled forces or activities (*Merriam-Webster's Collegiate Dictionary*, 2003). The term *aggression* is more encompassing in our view, as we believe that the milder forms of psychological and physical aggression are also important to understand, prevent, and treat in a couples context. The chapters in this book thus encompass the full gamut of aggressive behaviors, from relatively mild to severe forms of psychological and physical aggression between partners.

REFERENCES

Archer, J. (2000). Sex differences in aggression between heterosexual partners: A meta-analytic review. *Psychological Bulletin, 126*, 651–680.

Babcock, J. C., Green, C. E., & Robie, C. (2004). Does batterers' treatment work? A meta-analytic review of domestic violence treatment. *Clinical Psychology Review, 23*, 1023–1053.

Cascardi, M., Langhinrichsen, J., & Vivian, D. (1992). Marital aggression: Impact, injury, and health correlates for husbands and wives. *Archives of Internal Medicine, 152*, 1178–1184.

Dutton, M. A., Goodman, L. A., & Bennett, L. (2001). Court-involved battered women's responses to violence: The role of psychological, physical, and sexual abuse. In K. D. O'Leary & R. D. Maiuro (Eds.), *Psychological abuse in violent domestic relations* (pp. 177–195). New York: Springer.

Johnson, H., Ollus, N., & Nevala, S. (2007). *Violence against women: An international perspective*. New York: Springer.

Johnson, M. P. (1995). Patriarchal terrorism and common couple violence: Two forms of violence against women. *Journal of Marriage & the Family, 57*, 283–294.

Merriam-Webster's collegiate dictionary (11th ed). (2003). Springfield, MA: Merriam-Webster.

O'Leary, K. D., & Maiuro, R. D. (Eds.). (2001). *Psychological abuse in violent domestic relations*. New York: Springer.

O'Leary, K. D., Smith Slep, A. M., & O'Leary, K. D. (2007). Multivariate models of men's and women's partner aggression. *Journal of Consulting and Clinical Psychology, 75*, 752–764.

O'Leary, K. D., Vivian, D., & Malone, J. (1992). Assessment of physical aggression against women in marriage: The need for multimodal assessment. *Behavioral Assessment, 14*, 5–14.

Simpson, L. E., & Christensen, A. (2005). Spousal agreement regarding relationship aggression among treatment-seeking couples. *Psychological Assessment, 17*, 423–432.

Straus, M. A., & Gelles, R. J. (1990). How violent are American families? Estimates from the National Family Violence Resurvey and other studies. In M. A. Straus & R. J. Gelles (Eds.), *Physical violence in American families: Risk factors and adaptations to violence in 8,145 families* (pp. 95–112). New Brunswick, NJ: Transaction.

White, J. W., Merrill, L. L., & Koss, M. P. (2001). Prediction of pre-military courtship violence in a Navy recruit sample. *Violence and Victims, 16*, 910–927.

I

PREVALENCE

1

PREVALENCE OF PARTNER AGGRESSION IN REPRESENTATIVE AND CLINIC SAMPLES

ANITA JOSE AND K. DANIEL O'LEARY

Mental health professionals ignored the phenomenon of partner aggression until the past few decades. In the past, researchers did not assess partner aggression in any systematic manner, thinking it to be relatively nonexistent in mental heath clinics and rare in general or representative populations. However, as this chapter documents, psychologists now know that physical aggression occurs in approximately one third or more of young married couples. Further, evidence shows that physical aggression occurs in approximately half of all couples attending university marital clinics.

The major aim of this chapter is to review research on the prevalence of physical aggression and psychological aggression in nationally representative samples and clinic samples of heterosexual couples. Where possible, we use victim reports of overall aggression in the tables, although the text may describe aggression rates in a variety of ways (e.g., perpetrator reports, compos-

The chapter authors thank Jaslean Lataillade, PhD, and Lorelai Simpson, PhD, for providing data on the prevalence of partner violence.

ite reports, severe aggression only, mild aggression only) to allow the reader a more nuanced understanding of this information.

A second aim of this chapter is to provide a brief discussion of possible reasons for discrepant rates across samples. Specifically, we discuss the reason behind differing prevalence rates for different representative and community samples.

Finally, we briefly describe other issues relevant to partner aggression at the end of this chapter. These issues include the rates and effects of injury in relationship violence and the prevalence rates of aggression in same-sex couples, as well as the possible reasons for different rates of aggression between men and women.

In terms of physical aggression, we present statistics for male-to-female and female-to-male physical aggression separately, because perpetration rates may differ by gender (Archer, 2000). We use only victim reports of physical aggression, as they may be less biased by denial or minimization than perpetrator reports. Because the prevalence literature for psychological aggression is somewhat less extensive than research on physical violence, we use composite or perpetrator reports of violence when victim reports are unavailable.

Because the Conflict Tactics Scale (CTS; Straus, 1979, 1990) and Revised Conflict Tactics Scale (CTS2; Straus, Hamby, Boney-McCoy, & Sugarman, 1996) are the most commonly used measures of aggression and have been psychometrically validated, this chapter reviews only studies using the original or revised CTS or an adaptation thereof. Researchers have used other methodologies and scales (e.g., Follingstad, Rutledge, Berg, Hause, & Polek, 1990; Marshall, 1996), and the interested reader can consult these sources.

To provide context, we first briefly review the mental health effects of partner aggression on victims and perpetrators and the indirect effects on children of observing partner aggression. We then discuss the changing societal attitudes toward partner aggression, as this issue is not covered elsewhere in this book.

MENTAL HEALTH EFFECTS OF PARTNER AGGRESSION

Research has long suggested that women who are the victims of severe aggression by their male partners suffer adverse mental health consequences, such as symptoms of posttraumatic stress disorder (PTSD) and depression, and engage in high-risk behaviors, such as illicit drug and alcohol use (e.g., Cascardi, O'Leary, Lawrence, & Schlee, 1995; Golding, 1999). Male recipients of physical aggression also have negative mental health consequences, such as elevated depressive symptomatology (Cascardi, Langhinrichsen, & Vivian, 1992). Furthermore, aggression is related to physical health in victims; studies have indicated that aggression is related to physical injury for victims, particularly women (Cantos, Neidig, & O'Leary, 1994; Cascardi et al., 1992), and to greater reports of poor current health and history of chronic illness in both men and women (Coker et al., 2002).

Perpetrators of physical aggression are also at greater risk of mental health problems compared with their nonaggressive counterparts. For instance, aggression perpetration has been associated with alcohol problems in men and women arrested for domestic violence (Stuart et al., 2006). In addition to alcohol use, a meta-analysis has indicated that illicit drug use and depressive symptoms are significant predictors of male-to-female aggression (Stith, Smith, Penn, Ward, & Tritt, 2004). Moreover, aggressive men exhibit a higher level of antisocial (Murphy, Meyer, & O'Leary, 1993) and borderline (Hamberger & Hastings, 1991) personality traits compared with controls.

In addition to the direct effect of partner aggression on members of the couple, children are unintended victims of partner aggression; children who observe such aggression may be at elevated risk of later engaging in physical aggression against their own partners. Some studies have found that childhood observation of partner aggression may affect children's attitudes about aggression (Stith & Farley, 1993). Furthermore, a large epidemiological study suggested that women who reported lifetime victimization were significantly more likely to have witnessed parental violence as a child than those who had not been victimized (Thompson et al., 2006).

Clearly, violence in relationships has a significant effect on couples and families, as well as on individual psychological and physical health. Relationship violence subsumes more specific types of aggression, including physical aggression, psychological aggression, sexual aggression, and injury caused by aggression. This chapter focuses on physical and psychological partner aggression and also briefly addresses the injury-related components of partner aggression. A detailed treatment of the issue of sexual aggression can be found in chapter 2 of this volume. Whereas this chapter centers on aggression in the United States, chapter 3 of this volume discusses aggression in a cross-cultural context.

CHANGING SOCIETAL VIEWS OF PARTNER AGGRESSION

As mentioned at the start of this chapter, societal views of aggression have changed significantly over time. Partner aggression began to be seen as a social problem in the late 1970s and early 1980s, as illustrated by *Bruno v. Codd* (1977) in New York, which stipulated that cases of domestic violence should be treated by police like any other misdemeanor or felony assault case (Bush, 1992). In other words, partner aggression came to be seen as part of the purview of law enforcement, rather than a private family issue. The outcome of this case had a beneficial effect on American society, as it led citizens to regard aggression as relevant to all citizens, not just the poor population or members of minority or other marginalized groups (Peter, 2006). This destigmatization of reporting partner aggression may also have been a springboard for the perception of partner aggression as a policy issue with major social repercussions.

Government policy has in fact reflected a greater focus on domestic violence in the past few decades. For instance, the Violence Against Women Act, whose genesis was in the 1980s with grassroots efforts on behalf of abused women, was passed in 1994 (Roe, 2004). This bill set aside $1.8 billion to be used between 1995 and 2000 to fund programs aimed at reducing violence against women. A new version of the bill drafted in 1999 increased funding for these programs to $3.3 billion between 2000 and 2005. The slight decrease in male-perpetrated domestic violence between 1975 and 1985 (Straus & Gelles, 1986) has been interpreted as a response to the increased government focus on this issue, leading to greater funding for research and interventions to protect women against violence within the home (Bergman & Brismar, 1993).

Despite a considerable amount of policy change and research on this topic, particularly since the 1980s, disseminating information to clinicians is still a challenge. Some clinicians may be interested in better understanding the data on the occurrence and frequency of aggression; others may be interested in better understanding possible reasons behind discrepant rates. The remainder of this chapter discusses rates of relationship aggression with the overarching goal of presenting a general background for clinicians.

REPRESENTATIVE SAMPLES: MARRIED AND COHABITING COUPLES

Quite a few research studies on partner aggression focus on couples within the community, particularly married or cohabiting adults. Generally, studies of aggression include either large-scale samples that are representative of the nation (e.g., Straus & Gelles, 1990a; Tjaden & Thoennes, 2000) or state (Weinbaum, Stratton, Roberson, Takahashi, & Fatheree, 2006) or nonrepresentative community samples that do not necessarily reflect the demographic makeup of the community from which they are drawn. The initial emphasis of this chapter is on representative sample studies, in an effort to draw conclusions about the prevalence of partner aggression in the general population.

Prevalence of Physical Aggression: Male-to-Female Violence

The classic research studies addressing aggression within the family use results from the National Family Violence Surveys. Straus and Gelles (1990a) used data from the 1985 National Family Violence Resurvey to calculate the

TABLE 1.1
Annual Rates of Physical Aggression in Various Samples

Perpetrator	Sample type	Reported by	Prevalence (%)	Reference
Male	Representative	Female victim	11.9	Straus and Gelles (1990a)[a]
		Female victim	9.8	Schafer, Caetano, and Clark (1998)
		Female victim	1.3	National Center for Injury Prevention and Control (2003)[b]
		Female victim	5.1–6.4	Weinbaum, Stratton, Roberson, Takahashi, and Fatheree (2006)
	Clinic	Female victim	54.0	Cascardi, Langhinrichsen, and Vivian (1992)
		Female victim	58.0	Holtzworth-Munroe et al. (1992)
		Female victim	53.0	O'Leary, Vivian, and Malone (1992)
		Female victim	54.0	Murphy and O'Farrell (1994)
		Female victim	36.3	Simpson and Christensen (2005)[a]
		Female victim	51.0	Epstein and Werlinich (2003); LaTaillade, Epstein, and Werlinich (2007)[a]
Female	Representative	Male victim	12.2	Straus and Gelles (1990a)[a]
		Male victim	10.6	Schafer et al. (1998)
		Male victim	0.6	Tjaden and Thoennes (2000)
	Clinic	Male victim	57.0	Cascardi et al. (1992)
		Male victim	37.4	Simpson and Christensen (2005)[a]
		Male victim	48.0	Epstein and Werlinich (2003); LaTaillade et al. (2007)[a]

[a]The data presented were based on the publication referenced, but the prevalence rates were obtained directly from the study author and/or the data set used by the study author to provide victimization rates for overall physical and psychological aggression.
[b]According to the Centers for Disease Control and Prevention (CDC) publication (National Center for Injury Prevention and Control, 2003), the male-to-female annual aggression victimization rate is 1.3%. However, according to Tjaden and Thoennes (2000), the male-to-female annual aggression victimization rate is 1.1%. This table presents the CDC rates.

incidence and prevalence of partner physical aggression. These researchers contacted 6,002 families (including both married and unmarried cohabiting couples) using random digit dialing and assessed the 1-year prevalence of partner aggression, among other variables. They found that physical aggression had occurred in 16.1% of couples in the United States in the prior year. However, the prevalence rate of 11.6% (3.4% severe) they reported for male-to-female violence was based on the entire sample and therefore is a composite measure of male perpetration and female victimization rates. (Data independence was ensured, as only one family member from each household participated in the survey.)

Because this chapter presents data in terms of victimization rates (see Table 1.1), we calculated the prevalence of male-to-female violence using data only from the 2,952 women who were married or cohabiting at the time of the survey. Of these women, 11.9% reported having been victimized by their partners in the past year. (A somewhat lower proportion of men in the study [10.5%, $N = 2,303$] reported having perpetrated male-to-female aggression in the past year.)

Schafer, Caetano, and Clark (1998) conducted a more recent study of partner aggression using the representative U.S. sample obtained from the ninth National Alcohol Survey. The researchers used data collected beginning in the spring of 1995 from a sample of 1,635 participating married or cohabiting couples who were interviewed face to face in their homes. They presented the results in terms of male and/or female reports that a physically aggressive behavior occurred, yielding four groups: both partners agree on occurrence, only female partner states behavior occurred, only male partner states behavior occurred, and both partners agree on nonoccurrence. We combined occurrence rates for any physical violence endorsed by the female partner (e.g., both partners agree on occurrence or only female partner states behavior occurred). Based on this calculation, the 1-year prevalence rate of male-to-female aggression was 9.8% in this sample.

This estimate is similar to the rate Straus and Gelles (1990a) found. Schafer and colleagues' (1998) slightly lower rate may be due to the study's smaller sample size, as well as a difference in methodology: The National Family Violence Resurvey interviews were conducted over the phone, whereas Schafer and colleagues' interviews were conducted face to face in respondents' homes; some participants may have viewed the face-to-face method as less anonymous, leading to an underestimate in aggression rate.

Tjaden and Thoennes (2000) published a large-scale representative study of partner aggression in American couples, part of which informed a 2003 Centers for Disease Control and Prevention (CDC) report on the costs of intimate partner violence against women (National Center for Injury Prevention and Control, 2003). They analyzed data from 5,655 women who were married or cohabiting with an opposite-sex partner, from a larger pool of 8,000 women recruited for the National Violence Against Women Survey (NVAWS) in 1995 and 1996.

According to the CDC report, 1.3% of married or cohabiting female participants reported having been victimized by their partner in the past 12 months (National Center for Injury Prevention and Control, 2003). Women who reported any physical aggression by their partners were victimized an average of 3.4 times within the previous year. The CDC also presented the prevalence data in terms of lifetime prevalence rates; 22.1% of women who were married or had cohabited with a romantic partner in their lifetime ($N =$ 7,278; Tjaden & Thoennes, 2000) also reported having been victimized by a current or former partner (National Center for Injury Prevention and Control, 2003).

Although well known and widely cited in the field, the information provided in the NVAWS sample is clearly discrepant from previous prevalence estimates by Straus and Gelles (1990a) and Schafer and colleagues (1998). This may be because, as Straus (1999) discussed, the NVAWS study was presented as a study of "personal safety, injury, and violence." He noted that the context in which the study was presented could have taken precedence over the specific instructions to include all assaults, and participants may have perceived that the study was concerned only with violent or criminal assaults. In short, the presentation of the study may have led to underreporting, yielding the very low rates of partner aggression found in the NVAWS compared with the other representative samples described in this chapter.

The California Women's Health Survey (CWHS) is a sample of women 18 years or older who reside in California and who are randomly selected and recruited annually via telephone surveys. The information provided here was taken from CWHS data obtained between 1998 and 2001. Surveys are conducted in English or Spanish and ask a variety of questions related to women's health, including those related to partner aggression (Weinbaum, 2006). The telephone survey includes items modified from the CTS (Straus, 1979, 1990) and asks for a yes-or-no response when assessing the occurrence of eight physical aggression items in the previous year. This study measures only victimization rates. Annual prevalence rates ranged from 5.1% (for the 2001 survey) to 6.4% (for the 1999 survey). According to the 2000 survey, which also reported lifetime physical aggression, 41.1% of survey respondents reported being victimized by a romantic partner in their lifetime (Weinbaum et al., 2006).

Overall, data from two representative samples of U.S. couples indicate that up to 10% of women report having been physically victimized by their partners in the past year (Schafer et al., 1998; Straus & Gelles, 1990a), whereas data from a third study indicate a prevalence of over 5% (Weinbaum et al., 2006). Finally, a fourth study suggested that over 1% of women are victimized (National Center for Injury Prevention and Control, 2003; Tjaden & Thoennes, 2000). Annual prevalence estimates of violence against women are often much lower than lifetime estimates; even the conservative annual estimates of the Tjaden and Thoennes (2000) study yielded lifetime victimization rates suggesting that close to one quarter of women who had ever been in a relationship had been physically victimized by their partners. These numbers highlight the significant impact of physical aggression on women in the United States.

Prevalence of Physical Aggression: Female-to-Male Violence

The three representative studies on the prevalence of male-perpetrated physical aggression (i.e., Schafer et al., 1998; Straus & Gelles, 1990a; Tjaden & Thoennes, 2000) also provided data on female-perpetrated aggression. To begin with, Straus and Gelles (1990a) indicated that in the past year, the rate of any female-to-male physical aggression in the full sample was 12.4%, and the rate of severe physical female-to-male violence was 4.8%. In an effort to separate victimization and perpetration rates, we reexamined data from the National Family Violence Surveys discussed in the section on male-to-female violence to provide information on the occurrence of physical aggression in married and cohabiting couples. Of the 2,303 men included in the survey, 12.2% reported having been victimized by their partner in the previous year. Similarly, 12.1% of the 2,952 women who participated reported having perpetrated violence against their partner in the preceding year.

Schafer and colleagues (1998) also studied rates of physical aggression in U.S. couples using a sample of 1,635 couples who were interviewed face to face using items modified from the CTS. To calculate men's victimization rates, all data in which men had reported any female-to-male violence occurring were summed. Seven percent of men agreed with their partners that any physical violence had occurred in the past year, and an additional 3.6% of men stated that physical violence had occurred in the past year, although their partners stated that no violence had occurred. Overall, 10.6% of men in this sample reported being physically victimized.

Tjaden and Thoennes (2000) also assessed rates of female-to-male aggression using data from the NVAWS. Of the total sample of 8,000 men, 5,982 reported being in a married or cohabiting relationship at the time of interview, and 0.6% of this sample reported having been the victim of physical aggression in the past year. Furthermore, 6,934 men reported having been married or having cohabited at some point in their life; 7% of those men reported having been victimized in their lifetime. Similar to estimates of male perpetration, these estimates of female perpetration are significantly lower than the annual prevalence estimates provided by Straus and Gelles (1990a) and Schafer and colleagues (1998).

The reader may notice that the prevalence rates of female-to-male aggression in the representative samples are slightly higher than the prevalence rates of male-to-female aggression. A possible explanation for the relatively high published rates of female-to-male aggression is that female-perpetrated aggression may be less injurious or painful than male-perpetrated aggression (Cantos et al., 1994; Straus & Gelles, 1990b). As male victims may suffer less injury, pain, or fear than female victims, it may be that male victims of aggression are less likely to identify and/or report female aggressive behaviors as acts of aggression. We discuss gender differences in relationship violence and the role of injury in violence later in this chapter.

Prevalence of Psychological Aggression

Although the prevalence of psychological aggression[1] has not been researched to the extent that physical aggression has been, some research studies have addressed this issue; Table 1.2 summarizes the results. Prevalence research, including the studies described in this section, suggests that psychological aggression may be relatively normative in community couples. However, research has also highlighted the presence of a link between psychological and physical aggression—specifically, empirical evidence indicates that past psychological aggression is one of the biggest predictors of current physical aggression (e.g., Murphy & O'Leary, 1989).

Stets (1990) analyzed data on psychological aggression using a nationally representative sample of 1,461 married men and 1,909 married women who completed the CTS (Straus, 1979, 1990) during phone interviews conducted as part of the 1985 National Family Violence Resurvey. Seventy five percent of men and 80% of women in the sample reported perpetrating psychological aggression within the home, but most aggressive behaviors were relatively minor (e.g., sulking, refusing to talk about a conflict issue, insulting the partner).

Although studies assessing the prevalence of psychological aggression are not as numerous as those examining physical aggression within the community, it is clear that psychological aggression rates are extremely high within representative community couples. These results suggest this may be a normative way that couples manage conflict in U.S. households.

SAMPLES FROM THE CLINIC

As demonstrated by the studies discussed in the previous section, both physical and psychological aggression occur in a relatively high proportion of relationships (findings by Tjaden & Thoennes, 2000, are a notable exception). However, couples who participate in psychotherapy often have more severe and distressing problems than are found in a representative sample. Marital clinic samples may thus provide information about the prevalence

---

[1]Although some studies describe this construct as *verbal aggression*, we refer to it as *psychological aggression* throughout this chapter because all the studies included here use the Psychological Aggression subscale of the Conflict Tactics Scale (Straus, 1979, 1999), Revised Conflict Tactics Scale (Straus et al., 1996), or modified Conflict Tactics Scale (Pan, Neidig, & O'Leary, 1994) to measure this construct.

TABLE 1.2
Annual Rates of Psychological Aggression in Various Samples

Perpetrator	Sample type	Reported by	Prevalence (%)	Reference
Male	Representative	Male perpetrator	75.0	Stets (1990)
	Clinic	Female victim	76.1	O'Farrell and Murphy (1995)
		Female victim	94.9	Simpson and Christensen (2005)[a]
Female	Representative	Female perpetrator	80.0	Stets and Straus (1990)
	Clinic	Male victim	69.3	O'Farrell and Murphy (1995)
		Male victim	94.9	Simpson and Christensen (2005)[a]

[a]The data presented were based on the publication referenced, but the prevalence rates were obtained directly from the study author and/or the data set used by the study author to provide victimization rates for overall physical and psychological aggression.

of partner aggression in a population of people often characterized by greater relationship distress, greater subjective distress, and more co-occurring pathology.

Data on agreement for dyadic events suggest that interpartner agreement is lower in more distressed relationships and when the behaviors being assessed are more negative or less socially acceptable—as with partner aggression (O'Leary & Williams, 2006). Therefore, it is possible that reported rates of relationship aggression in clinic samples may generally underestimate the true frequency of the behavior for a variety of reasons (e.g., memory decay, different perceptions of the event, social desirability), especially if only one partner's report of the event is used (Archer, 1999; Heyman & Schlee, 1997; O'Leary & Williams, 2006). The estimates reported in this section, though compelling, may underestimate the true prevalence of aggression in clinic couples.

Prevalence of Physical Aggression: Male-to-Female Violence

This chapter reviews the prevalence of male-to-female aggression in clinic samples using data from six research studies incorporating eight separate samples. All but one study recruited participants as couples; Holtzworth-Munroe et al. (1992) reported one study that included a sample of 211 women who were recruited without their partners for a phone screen. Sample sizes for the studies ranged from 20 couples (from one of the samples described in Holtzworth-Munroe et al., 1992) to 290 couples (e.g., the sample described in Epstein & Werlinich, 2003, and in LaTaillade, Epstein, & Werlinich,

2007). In addition, most of the samples described in this section were recruited from among couples seeking marital therapy (Cascardi et al., 1992; Epstein & Werlinich, 2003; Holtzworth-Munroe et al., 1992; LaTaillade et al., 2007; O'Leary, Vivian, & Malone, 1992; Simpson & Christensen, 2005). One study recruited a more specialized treatment sample, namely, couples interested in marital therapy for men recovering from alcoholism (Murphy & O'Farrell, 1994). Finally, one study recruited participants using advertisements to conduct a phone-based survey of women's experiences of partner violence (Holtzworth-Munroe et al., 1992).

The data discussed here come from a variety of locations within the United States, including California (Simpson & Christensen, 2005), Indiana (see Holtzworth-Munroe et al., 1992), Massachusetts (Murphy & O'Farrell, 1994), Maryland (Epstein & Werlinich, 2003; LaTaillade et al., 2007), New York (Cascardi et al., 1992; O'Leary et al., 1992), and Washington State (see Holtzworth-Munroe et al., 1992; Simpson & Christensen, 2005).

We obtained prevalence data directly from the manuscripts of the studies (Cascardi et al., 1992; Murphy & O'Farrell, 1994; O'Leary et al., 1992), with three exceptions. Specifically, we obtained aggression data from the Simpson and Christensen (2005) study directly from Dr. Simpson and data for Epstein and colleagues' sample (discussed in Epstein & Werlinich, 2003; LaTaillade et al., 2007) directly from Dr. LaTaillade. Finally, as Holtzworth-Munroe and colleagues' (1992) article included five studies (three of which are discussed in this chapter because they dealt directly with female reports of victimization), we calculated an overall prevalence rate for the three studies together, weighted to account for differences in sample size.

As Table 1.1 illustrates, rates of aggression ranged from 36.3% (Simpson & Christensen, 2005) to 58.0% (Holtzworth-Munroe et al., 1992) in the samples we review here. For the most part, aggression rates were similar across the clinic samples; Cascardi et al. (1992), Epstein and Werlinich (2003), Holtzworth-Munroe et al. (1992), LaTaillade et al. (2007), Murphy and O'Farrell (1994), and O'Leary et al. (1992) reported that at least half of the women in their samples had been the victims of relationship aggression. However, Simpson and Christensen's (2005) data indicated a somewhat lower prevalence rate for male-to-female aggression than the other studies. Those authors suggested that one possible reason for this lower rate was that participants were asked to complete the CTS2 (Straus et al., 1996) at home, which could have led to low reported rates of aggression compared with the other studies described here. Participants may have completed the measures together, or they may have been concerned about partner access to their responses.

When comparing Simpson and Christensen's (2005) research with Cascardi and colleagues' (1992) study, methodological differences (e.g., use of different versions of the CTS2) or sample-based differences (e.g., geographic location, sample size) may be responsible for differences. Additionally, Cascardi and colleagues classified *perpetrators* as mildly or severely aggressive, whereas Simpson and Christensen classified *behaviors* in terms of minor or severe aggression. This difference qualifies any comparison that can be made about mild or minor versus severe aggression across the two studies. Overall, research on male-to-female physical aggression in clinic samples indicates a much higher prevalence of violence than in nonclinic samples, with most results indicating that women are victimized by their partners in more than half of couples presenting for therapy.

Prevalence of Physical Aggression: Female-to-Male Violence

Although much of the reported prevalence information in clinic couples' aggressiveness focuses on male-to-female aggression, some information is available on female-perpetrated aggression within these samples. In this chapter, the information on female-to-male violence in clinic samples is based on data from three of the research studies described in the previous section. Cascardi et al. (1992), Epstein and colleagues (Epstein & Werlinich, 2003; LaTaillade et al., 2007), and Simpson and Christensen (2005) recruited couples for marital therapy. These studies took place in four different states (New York, Maryland, and California/Washington, respectively) and ranged in sample size from 93 couples (Cascardi et al., 1992) to 290 couples (Epstein & Werlinich, 2003; LaTaillade et al., 2007).

As seen in Table 1.1, rates for female-to-male aggression ranged from 37.4% to 57.0% in the three studies examined here. Reflecting the pattern in male-to-female violence, Simpson and Christensen's (2005) sample reported a much lower rate of aggression than the other studies. As described earlier, this can be interpreted as underestimation due to reports of aggression being completed at home rather than in the lab, where they might have been more confidential.

Although there is less research on male physical victimization in clinic samples than on female victimization, the studies reviewed here suggest that female-to-male aggression occurs in a substantial proportion of couples presenting for couples therapy. The dearth of research on female-perpetrated violence in clinic couples suggests that further exploration of the occurrence and frequency of this type of aggression, as well as insight into the mechanisms underlying this problem, would be a fruitful avenue for further research.

Prevalence of Psychological Aggression in Males and Females

Evidence presented earlier in this chapter clearly indicates that psychological aggression may be normative in community populations. However, it has also been examined in a variety of clinic-based samples. This section highlights some research addressing the prevalence of psychological aggression in clinic samples (see Table 1.2).

Two studies (O'Farrell & Murphy, 1995; Simpson & Christensen, 2005) reported rates of psychological aggression in clinic couples. Simpson and Christensen gathered data from a sample of 273 couples recruited to participate in marital therapy study in California and Washington. O'Farrell and Murphy (1995) also recruited couples, but from a slightly different population; they recruited 88 men who reported co-occurring alcohol and marital problems and their partners. For both studies, the researchers measured psychological aggression at pretreatment using victim reports.

Based on victim reports, 94.9% of women in Simpson and Christensen's (2005) sample reported that their partners had been psychologically aggressive in the previous year, and 96.3% of their partners reported perpetrating any male-to-female psychological aggression in the past year. However, considerably fewer men (36.6%) than women (43.6%) reported severe male-to-female psychological aggression in this sample. Simpson and Christensen also found high rates of female-to-male psychological aggression, reporting a prevalence of 94.9% for male victimization and 95.5% for female perpetration. However, women reported perpetrating a much lower rate of severe aggression (37.4%) compared with their husbands' reported severe victimization rates (48.0%).

O'Farrell and Murphy (1995) found that 76.1% of women and 69.3% of men reported that their partners had engaged in clinically significant levels of psychological aggression in the previous year. The authors conceptualized clinically significant levels of verbal aggression as scores at the 75th percentile or above compared with nationally normative levels (based on the National Family Violence Resurvey; Straus & Gelles, 1990a). Therefore, the overall prevalence of psychological aggression in this study may be higher than the reported rates.

Clearly, rates of psychological aggression found in these studies suggest that, as in community-based samples, psychological aggression is highly prevalent in clinic samples. However, O'Farrell and Murphy's (1995) rate is considerably lower than Simpson and Christensen's (2005) estimate; this is likely due to their sampling methodology, in that the prevalence statistic included only couples who reported engaging in psychological aggression to the same degree as the highest quartile of couples in a nationally representative sample.

ADDITIONAL ISSUES

This section addresses other relevant issues related to partner aggression, including the prevalence of physical aggression in same-sex relationships, the prevalence of injury, and gender differences in relationship aggression.

Prevalence Rates in Same-Sex Relationships

Aggression in same-sex relationships has begun to receive researchers' attention only recently (McClennen, 2005). However, much of the data published to date indicate that aggression in same-sex relationships is an important issue. For instance, a study by Turrell (2000) indicated that 55.0% to 58.0% of women in same-sex relationships ($N = 250$) and 44.0% of men in same-sex relationships ($N = 213$) reported that physical aggression had occurred in a past or present relationship. Although high, these are lifetime, rather than annual, rates of relationship aggression. In addition, the survey created for the study did not have normative data and may not be comparable with the CTS (Straus, 1979, 1990) or CTS2 (Straus et al., 1996).

Burke and Follingstad (1999) described results from various studies of aggression in same-sex relationships. For instance, Gardner (1988) studied reports of physical violence in the previous year among a sample of 125 heterosexual, lesbian, or gay couples. This study assessed aggression using either partner's report on the CTS (Straus, 1979, 1990). Gardner found that 48.0% of lesbian couples and 38.0% of gay couples reported the occurrence of physical aggression in the previous year. The study also found that 28.0% of heterosexual couples reported aggression; a 3 (heterosexual vs. lesbian vs. gay) × 2 (violent vs. nonviolent) χ^2 analysis yielded no significant difference in the occurrence of aggression as a function of sexual orientation.

Because, on the basis of these reports, aggression rates in same-sex relationships seem at least as high as those in heterosexual relationships, an important future direction would be to test the CTS and other aggression measures in same-sex couples. If these measures seem appropriate for measuring aggression in this context, additional psychometric information relevant to these populations would be valuable. If not, the creation of a standard, empirically sound assessment of aggression that is appropriate for use in same-sex couples is necessary. More research should be conducted on the role of various risk factors for aggression in gay and lesbian relationships as they may differ from precipitants of aggression in heterosexual relationships.

Rates of Injury

Injury rates are an important outcome measure in violence research because the same aggressive behavior may have differential outcomes as a function of the perpetrator's and victim's gender. Women may suffer more severe physical consequences of aggression than men, even though women are at least as likely as men to perpetrate aggression against their partners. Stets and Straus (1990) addressed this question using data from the NFVS and found that 3.0% of female victims and 0.4% of male victims in this nationally representative sample reported seeking medical care after an incident of aggression occurred, suggesting that women were more likely than men to seek medical attention. When analyzing minor and severe incidents separately, the difference between men's and women's visits to health care providers was nonsignificant for minor incidents but remained significant for cases of severe aggression.

Simpson and Christensen (2005) found the injury rate to be quite high in a clinic sample. Specifically, 11.7% of wives reported experiencing injury as a result of conflict with their partner in the year before attending therapy. Husbands' reports of injury perpetration were considerably higher; 18.3% of men reported injuring their partner. In terms of female-to-male injury, 15.4% of husbands in Simpson and Christensen's sample experienced injury as a result of relationship conflict. Wife self-reports of perpetration were slightly higher, indicating an overall injury rate of 17.9%.

Simpson and Christensen (2005) also analyzed potential gender differences in other proxy variables relating to physical injury due to victimization (time off from work, number of days spent in bed because of illness). Although nonsignificant, both analyses suggested a trend such that women seemed marginally more likely than men to take time off from work and lose at least 1 day of work because of illness after an assault.

Simpson and Christensen's (2005) findings may underreport the true injury rate in a clinic sample because participants' completion of the measures at home may have led them to minimize aggression. This study provides evidence, however, that injury rates are high in clinic samples and that women perpetrate more overall, minor, and severe injury against their partners when comparing victims' reports. However, a comparison of men's and women's self-reports of their own injury perpetration indicate that men report slightly higher total injury perpetration than women do.

Stets and Straus's (1990) assessment of injury rates in a representative sample reflects the conclusions of a recent meta-analysis (Archer, 2000). Archer sampled individuals in a variety of romantic relationship types and found that the female partner sustained most (62%) of the injuries reported due to violence, indicating that women may generally run a higher risk of injury due to violence than men do.

Although the excellent psychometric properties of the CTS suggest it is an appropriate measure to assess partner violence, these findings highlight the importance of assessments that further examine the consequences and context of violence, particularly in terms of injury rates. Additionally, the discrepancy between Simpson and Christensen's (2005) and Stets and Straus's (1990) results indicates that the rate and distribution of injuries among partners clearly differ in clinic and community samples and that future research on this topic is warranted.

Gender Issues in Physical Aggression

Culturally and historically, physical aggression research in the United States has focused on the effect of violence on women. However, the data on physical aggression discussed in this chapter reflect a finding typical in the relationship violence literature—that is, in representative samples, the prevalence of physical aggression is similar in men and women. However, prevalence rates do not provide a full picture of partner aggression. As indicated in the previous section on injury, women in representative and clinic samples sustain more physical injury than men as a consequence of relationship violence. This conceptualization of the role of injury in violence is supported by independent studies on clinic (Cantos et al., 1994; Cascardi et al., 1992) and representative (Stets & Straus, 1990) samples, as well as findings from meta-analytic research (e.g., Archer, 2000).

Furthermore, research suggests that despite similar physical aggression perpetration for men and women, women report greater fear of their partner than women in nonviolent relationships. For instance, Cascardi and colleagues (1995) found that women who reported aggression in their relationships indicated greater fear of their partner than distressed–nonviolent and community controls. Stith et al. (2004) also reported that fear was significantly associated with women's victimization in their meta-analysis.

Fear of partner has also been found to be higher in women compared with men in a variety of settings. A study of military couples by Langhinrichsen-Rohling, Neidig, and Thorn (1995) mandated for marital violence treatment found that women were more likely than their partners to report fear during the last marital conflict. Jacobson and colleagues (1994) found that compared with nonviolent couples, women (but not men) in violent couples showed behavioral cues indicating fear. This result in itself indicates that, by objective observer reports of couple behavior, fear of the partner occurs differentially in violent and nonviolent relationships and in male and female partners.

CONCLUSION AND FUTURE DIRECTIONS

Violence within romantic relationships is not uncommon, with about 1% to 12% of women and less than 1% to just over 12% of men in representative community samples reporting having been physically victimized by their partners. Because the unusually low aggression rates obtained using data from one representative sample (National Center for Injury Prevention and Control, 2003; Tjaden & Thoennes, 2000) may be due to underreporting, the annual prevalence of partner aggression is most likely to be in the 10% to 12% range or higher. Research conducted in marital clinic samples indicates that between 36% and 58% of women are victimized by their partners; many samples indicate that about half of all couples presenting for marital therapy have engaged in physical violence in the previous year.

Male victimization in clinic samples has been less widely studied, but estimates range from about 37% to 57%. Clearly, physical aggression is a significant issue for both men and women in couples presenting for therapy.

Notably, although men and women engage in physical aggression at similar rates in community and clinic samples, rates of injury are much lower than rates of aggression for both men and women. In community samples, less than 0.5% of men and 3% of women reported injury in the previous year. In clinic samples, about 12% of women and over 15% of men reported injury. These data also suggest that injury is more common for women in community samples but is a more prevalent issue for men in clinic samples.

Research described in this chapter indicates that violence in relationships is a relevant issue in both same-sex and heterosexual relationships. Furthermore, highly distressed couples seem significantly more likely to engage in physical aggression, as demonstrated by much higher prevalence rates for aggression in clinic samples compared with representative samples. The importance of marital distress in the occurrence of aggression was mirrored in a report by Holtzworth-Munroe and colleagues (1992) suggesting that in surveys using the CTS (Straus, 1979, 1990), approximately 20% of nondistressed husbands and 11% of nondistressed wives reported male-to-female aggression in the previous year. In distressed samples, 43% to 46% of husbands and 38% to 62% of wives reported aggression, indicating that distressed husbands were about twice as likely to report aggression and distressed wives were up to 5.5 times more likely to report aggression compared with their nondistressed counterparts.

About 75% of men and 80% of women in representative samples engaged in psychological aggression against their partners. Additionally, close to 95% of men and about 95% of women in clinic samples were psychologically aggressive toward their partners. Clearly, psychological aggression is a normative occurrence in many relationships, but substantially more psychological aggression occurs in couples being treated in a clinic. One would also expect that the intensity and frequency of psychological aggression would be much greater in clinic than nonclinic couples.

Future research exploring whether type or frequency distinguish the experience of representative community couples and clinic couples could further research on relationship violence. Specifically, a focus on patterns of psychological aggression that differentiate clinic and community samples, patterns that differentiate psychologically aggressive individuals who do and do not engage in other types of aggression (e.g., physical violence, sexual violence), and patterns of psychological aggression that may temporally predict other types of aggression would be an important place to begin.

Violence within the family is clearly an important issue in the United States, and additional research may be aimed at understanding the context and frequency of partner aggression, the correlates and predictors of physical aggression (e.g., psychological aggression, sexual aggression), and the outcomes of aggression (e.g., injury rates, financial costs, susceptibility to mental health, behavioral health, physical health problems) separately for men and women and for representative and marital clinic samples.

Additionally, it is crucial that future research be conducted on aggression in same-sex couples to better determine the contextual factors surrounding violence in gay and lesbian relationships. It would be a mistake to assume that the context of aggression in same-sex relationships is either wholly similar to or wholly dissimilar from the context of aggression in heterosexual relationships.

REFERENCES

Archer, J. (1999). Assessment of the reliability of the Conflict Tactics Scales: A meta-analytic review. *Journal of Interpersonal Violence, 14*, 1263–1289.

Archer, J. (2000). Sex differences in aggression between heterosexual partners: A meta-analytic review. *Psychological Bulletin, 126*, 651–680.

Bergman, B., & Brismar, B. (1993). Assailants and victims: A comparative study of male wife-beaters and battered males. *Journal of Addictive Diseases, 12*, 1–10.

Bruno v. Codd, 396 N.Y.S.2d 974 (Sup. Ct. Special Term 1977).

Burke, L. K., & Follingstad, D. R. (1999). Violence in lesbian and gay relationships: Theory, prevalence, and correlational factors. *Clinical Psychology Review, 19*, 487–512.

Bush, D. M. (1992). Women's movements and state policy reform aimed at domestic violence against women—A comparison of the consequences of movement mobilization in the United States and India. *Gender and Society, 6*, 587–608.

Cantos, A. L., Neidig, P. H., & O'Leary, K. D. (1994). Injuries of women and men in a treatment program for domestic violence. *Journal of Family Violence, 9*, 113–124.

Cascardi, M., Langhinrichsen, J., & Vivian, D. (1992). Marital aggression: Impact, injury, and health correlates for husbands and wives. *Archives of Internal Medicine, 152*, 1178–1184.

Cascardi, M., O'Leary, K. D., Lawrence, E. E., & Schlee, K. A. (1995). Characteristics of women physically abused by their spouses and who seek treatment regarding marital conflict. *Journal of Consulting and Clinical Psychology, 63*, 616–623.

Coker, A. L., Davis, K. E., Arias, I., Desai, S., Sanderson, M., Brandt, H. M., & Smith, P. H. (2002). Physical and mental health effects of intimate partner violence for men and women. *American Journal of Preventive Medicine, 23*, 260–268.

Epstein, N. B., & Werlinich, C. A. (2003, November). *Assessment of physical and psychological abuse in an outpatient marital and family therapy clinic: How much abuse is revealed, under what conditions, and with what relation to relationship distress?* Paper presented at the meeting of the Association for Advancement of Behavior Therapy, Boston, MA.

Follingstad, D. R., Rutledge, L. L., Berg, B. J., Hause, E. S., & Polek, D. S. (1990). The role of emotional abuse in physically abusive relationships. *Journal of Family Violence, 5*, 107–120.

Gardner, R. A. (1988). Method of conflict resolution and correlates of physical aggression and victimization in heterosexual, lesbian, and gay male couples (Doctoral dissertation, University of Georgia, 1988). *Dissertation Abstracts International, 50, 746.*

Golding, J. M. (1999). Intimate partner violence as a risk factor for mental disorders: A meta-analysis. *Journal of Family Violence, 14,* 99–132.

Hamberger, L. K., & Hastings, J. E. (1991). Personality correlates of men who batter and nonviolent men: Some continuities and discontinuities. *Journal of Family Violence, 6,* 131–147.

Heyman, R. E., & Schlee, K. A. (1997). Toward a better estimate of the prevalence of partner abuse: Adjusting rates based on the sensitivity of the Conflict Tactics Scale. *Journal of Family Psychology, 11,* 331–338.

Holtzworth-Munroe, A., Waltz, J., Jacobson, N. S., Monaco, V., Fehrenbach, P. A., & Gottman, J. M. (1992). Recruiting nonviolent men as control subjects for research on marital violence: How easily can it be done? *Violence and Victims, 7,* 79–88.

Jacobson, N. S., Gottman, J. M., Waltz, J., Rushe, R., Babcock, J., & Holtzworth-Munroe, A. (1994). Affect, verbal content, and psychophysiology in the arguments of couples with a violent husband. *Journal of Consulting and Clinical Psychology, 62,* 982–988.

Langhinrichsen-Rohling, J., Neidig, P., & Thorn, G. (1995). Violent marriages: Gender differences in levels of current violence and past abuse. *Journal of Family Violence, 10,* 159–176.

LaTaillade, J. J., Epstein, N. B., & Werlinich, C. A. (2007). *Conjoint treatment of intimate partner violence: A comparison of cognitive–behavioral and other systemic approaches.* Manuscript in preparation.

Marshall, L. L. (1996). Psychological abuse of women: Six distinct clusters. *Journal of Family Violence, 11,* 379–409.

McClennen, J. C. (2005). Domestic violence between same-gender partners: Recent findings and future direction. *Journal of Interpersonal Violence, 20,* 149–154.

Murphy, C. M., Meyer, S., & O'Leary, K. D. (1993). Family of origin violence and MCMI—II psychopathology among partner assaultive men. *Violence and Victims, 8,* 165–176.

Murphy, C. M., & O'Farrell, T. J. (1994). Factors associated with marital aggression in male alcoholics. *Journal of Family Psychology, 8,* 321–335.

Murphy, C. M., & O'Leary, K. D. (1989). Psychological aggression predicts physical aggression in early marriage. *Journal of Consulting and Clinical Psychology, 57,* 579–582.

National Center for Injury Prevention and Control. (2003). *Costs of intimate partner violence against women in the United States.* Atlanta: Centers for Disease Control and Prevention.

O'Farrell, T., & Murphy, C. (1995). Marital violence before and after alcoholism treatment. *Journal of Consulting and Clinical Psychology, 63,* 256–262.

O'Leary, K. D., Vivian, D., & Malone, J. (1992). Assessment of physical aggression against women in marriage: The need for multimodal assessment. *Behavioral Assessment, 14,* 5–14.

O'Leary, K. D., & Williams, M. C. (2006). Agreement about acts of aggression in marriage. *Journal of Family Psychology, 20,* 656–662.

Pan, H. S., Neidig, P. H., & O'Leary, K. D. (1994). Male–female and aggressor–victim differences in the factor structure of the Modified Conflict Tactics Scale. *Journal of Interpersonal Violence, 9,* 366–382.

Peter, T. (2006). Domestic violence in the United States and Sweden: A welfare state typology comparison within a power resources framework. *Women's Studies International Forum, 29,* 96–107.

Roe, K. J. (2004). *The Violence Against Women Act and its impact on sexual violence public policy: Looking back and looking forward.* Retrieved April 14, 2007, from http://www.nrcdv.org/docs/Mailings/2004/NRCDVNovVAWA.pdf

Schafer, J., Caetano, R., & Clark, C. L. (1998). Rates of intimate partner violence in the United States. *American Journal of Public Health, 88,* 1702–1704.

Simpson, L. E., & Christensen, A. (2005). Spousal agreement regarding relationship aggression among treatment-seeking couples. *Psychological Assessment, 17,* 423–432.

Stets, J. E. (1990). Verbal and physical aggression in marriage. *Journal of Marriage and the Family, 52,* 501–514.

Stets, J. E., & Straus, M. A. (1990). The marriage license as a hitting license: A comparison of assaults in dating, cohabiting, and married couples. In M. A. Straus & R. J. Gelles (Eds.), *Physical violence in American families: Risk factors and adaptations to violence in 8,145 families* (pp. 227–244). New Brunswick, NJ: Transaction.

Stith, S. M., & Farley, S. C. (1993). A predictive model of male spousal violence. *Journal of Family Violence, 8,* 183–201.

Stith, S. M., Smith, D. B., Penn, C. E., Ward, D. B., & Tritt, D. (2004). Intimate partner physical abuse perpetration and victimization risk factors: A meta-analytic review. *Aggression and Violent Behavior, 10,* 65–98.

Straus, M. A. (1979). Measuring intrafamily conflict and violence: The Conflict Tactics (CT) Scales. *Journal of Marriage and the Family, 41,* 75–88.

Straus, M. A. (1990). The Conflict Tactics Scale and its critics: An evaluation and new data on validity and reliability. In M. A. Straus & R. J. Gelles (Eds.), *Physical violence in American families: Risk factors and adaptations to violence in 8,145 families* (pp. 49–73). New Brunswick, NJ: Transaction.

Straus, M. A. (1999). The controversy over domestic violence by women: A methodological, theoretical, and sociology of science analysis. In X. B. Arriaga & S. Oskamp (Eds.), *Violence in intimate relationships* (pp. 17–44). Thousand Oaks, CA: Sage.

Straus, M. A., & Gelles, R. J. (1986). Societal change and change in family violence from 1975 to 1985 as revealed by two national surveys. *Journal of Marriage and the Family, 48,* 465–479.

Straus, M. A., & Gelles, R. J. (1990a). How violent are American families? Estimates from the National Family Violence Resurvey and other studies. In M. A. Straus & R. J. Gelles (Eds.), *Physical violence in American families: Risk factors and adaptations to violence in 8,145 families* (pp. 95–112). New Brunswick, NJ: Transaction.

Straus, M. A., & Gelles, R. J. (1990b). Societal change and change in family violence from 1975 to 1985 as revealed by two national surveys. In M. A. Straus & R. J. Gelles (Eds.), *Physical violence in American families: Risk factors and adaptations to violence in 8,145 families* (pp. 113–132). New Brunswick, NJ: Transaction.

Straus, M. A., Hamby, S. L., Boney-McCoy, S., & Sugarman, D. B. (1996). The revised Conflict Tactics Scale (CTS2): Development and preliminary psychometric data. *Journal of Family Issues, 17,* 283–316.

Stuart, G. L., Meehan, J. C., Moore, T. M., Morean, M., Hellmuth, J., & Follansbee, K. (2006). Examining a conceptual framework of intimate partner violence in men and women arrested for domestic violence. *Journal of Studies on Alcohol, 67,* 102–112.

Thompson, R. S., Bonomi, A. E., Anderson, M., Reid, R. J., Dimer, J. A., Carrell, D., & Rivara, F. P. (2006). Intimate partner violence: Prevalence, types, and chronicity in adult women. *American Journal of Preventive Medicine, 30,* 447–457.

Tjaden, P., & Thoennes, N. (2000). Prevalence and consequences of male-to-female and female-to-male intimate partner violence as measured by the National Violence Against Women Survey. *Violence Against Women, 6,* 142–161.

Turrell, S. C. (2000). A descriptive analysis of same-sex relationship violence for a diverse sample. *Journal of Family Violence, 15,* 281–293.

Weinbaum, Z. (2006). Executive summary. In Z. Weinbaum & T. Thorfinnson (Eds.), *Women's health: Findings from the California Women's Health Survey, 1997–2003* (pp. i–iii). Sacramento: California Department of Health Services, Office of Women's Health.

Weinbaum, Z., Stratton, T., Roberson, S., Takahashi, E. R., & Fatheree, M. S. (2006). Women experiencing intimate partner violence, California, 1998–2002. In Z. Weinbaum & T. Thorfinnson (Eds.), *Women's health: Findings from the California Women's Health Survey, 1997–2003* (pp. 12.1–12.6). Sacramento: California Department of Health Services, Office of Women's Health.

2

SEXUAL AGGRESSION IN INTIMATE RELATIONSHIPS

CANDICE M. MONSON, JENNIFER LANGHINRICHSEN-ROHLING, AND CASEY T. TAFT

Until the late 1970s, clinicians, researchers, and legal scholars wrote little about the occurrence of sexual aggression within intimate relationships. One significant factor contributing to this lack of attention was that rape by a spouse was a legal impossibility in most states until the mid-1980s (Small, & Tetreault, 1990). In addition, theory and research on sexual and nonsexual/physical[1] aggression has tended to unfold in relatively independent streams, and each stream has minimally addressed sexual aggression within committed relationships. Thus, until relatively recently, mental health professionals have not fully appreciated the approximately 10% lifetime prevalence of sexual assault of a woman by an intimate partner and its accompanying consequences (e.g., Bachman & Saltzman, 1995; Basile, 2002).

This chapter was coauthored by an employee of the United States government as part of official duty and is considered to be in the public domain. Any views expressed herein do not necessarily represent the views of the United States government, and the author's participation in the work is not meant to serve as an official endorsement.

[1]The terms *physical violence* and *nonsexual violence* are used interchangeably throughout the chapter.

This chapter reviews and integrates the literatures on marital rape and intimate partner physical aggression to provide a better understanding of the relationships among these forms of aggression that can, and often do, co-occur in dysfunctional intimate relationships. We first briefly review the legal history that has influenced the study of intimate sexual aggression and discuss some important definitional issues related to nonsexual and sexual aggression. We then discuss prevalence rates of intimate partner aggression and describe an approach to integrating information about perpetrator heterogeneity in understanding differences in the various forms of violence that are perpetrated in intimate relationships.

It is important at the outset for us to delineate the specific types of aggression that will be the focus of this chapter. We limit our discussion to aggression that occurs within the context of an established, otherwise committed intimate relationship, whether the partners in that relationship are legally married or not. This definition excludes the majority of existing literature on acquaintance or date rape in which the two individuals have not established an ongoing intimate relationship with one another when the sexual aggression occurs. We have also chosen to use the term *intimate partner* versus *marital* as a descriptor of the various forms of aggression to reflect greater inclusiveness of same-sex, as well as unmarried, cohabiting heterosexual couples. However, we use the term *marital rape* when the authors did so in their writings.

As discussed later in this chapter, minimal research has been conducted on sexual violence within committed same-sex couples. In addition, only a few studies have been conducted about female sexual perpetration, and most of these have not focused on women who perpetrate sexual aggression against their intimate partners. Thus, our considerations are almost exclusively based on research and theory about married heterosexual couples. The degree to which these findings generalize to other types of couples is an important focus of investigation (Brownridge & Halli, 2000; Ratner, Johnson, & Shoveller, 2003; Rose, 2003).

LEGAL HISTORY OF THE MARITAL RAPE EXEMPTION AND ALLOWANCES

Historically, husbands could not be prosecuted for raping their wives. The origins of these marital rape "exemptions" to sexual assault laws have been traced back to a 17th-century English chief justice, Lord Matthew Hale (1736). These exemptions prototypically defined *rape* as occurring when a "man engaged in intercourse with a *woman not his wife* [italics added], by force or threat of force; against her will and without her consent" (Russell, 1982b, p. 17). Traditional legal arguments for the decriminalization of marital rape included the notion that husbands and wives merged into a single entity with marriage (*unity theory*), that women were property of their husbands, and that marriage was a legal contract providing for mutual sexual exchange.

More modern justifications have included the need for deterrence against fabricated claims of rape that could function as a weapon for vindictive wives in divorce and custody proceedings, the importance of protecting the institution of marriage, and the existence of alternative criminal (e.g., prosecution under assault and battery statutes) and civil (e.g., orders of protection) remedies for victims of this form of aggression (Augustine, 1991; Sitton, 1993). Currently, the federal government and all 50 states have removed marital rape exemptions from their criminal statutes (National Clearing House for Marital and Date Rape, 2005).

In spite of progress in the legal arena over the past 30 years, it is important to note that sexual assault statutes and their application differ across the United States according to written definitions about what constitutes sexual assault or aggression, sentencing guidelines, and the extent of discretion by prosecutors to prosecute these cases. Thus, although there are no longer exemptions, there continue to be some marital rape "allowances" (Monson & Langhinrichsen-Rohling, 1998). Allowances detail when it is not against the law for a husband to rape his wife. Examples of such allowances include the degree of physical force used in the assault or the ability of the wife to give consent. As of 2005, 30 states had marital rape allowances in their sexual assault statutes. Five states (i.e., Connecticut, Delaware, Iowa, Minnesota, and West Virginia) treat cohabiting couples as married couples. The remaining 20 states and the District of Columbia treat rape by a spouse (or cohabiting partner in the state of Connecticut) as similar to rape by any other type of perpetrator (National Clearing House for Marital and Date Rape, 2005).

DEFINITIONAL AND RELATED ASSESSMENT ISSUES

Physical violence or the threat of physical violence is often thought of as a necessary, but insufficient, requirement for more severe forms of sexual aggression. For example, *sexual assault* is prototypically defined by researchers and lawmakers as a nonconsensual sexual act obtained by force through the threat of bodily harm or when the victim is incapable of providing consent. The definition of rape generally includes the additional requirement of penetration of a victim's orifice, and rape is considered to be a severe form of sexual assault (DeGue & DiLillo, 2005; Finkelhor & Yllo, 1985). The inclusion of force or threat of force as part of the topographical definition of sexual assault automatically, and perhaps artificially, creates a relationship between sexual and nonsexual intimate violence. According to this definition, it would be extremely rare for severe forms of sexual aggression to occur in the absence of physical violence, except in those instances when the intimate perpetrator somehow incapacitates the victim through nonviolent means (e.g., administration of a hypnotic medication like flunitrazepam (Rohypnol).

This definition is too limited because there is a spectrum of sexually aggressive acts that includes other types of problematic behavior, such as unwanted sexually suggestive or coercive verbal behavior and/or sexual harassment without fondling or penetration and that has been characterized as "sexual coercion" (DeGue & DiLillo, 2005). Sexual coercion shares definitional overlap with traditional definitions of *psychological aggression* or *interpersonal control*. For example, a husband may berate his wife or threaten her physically if she does not engage in sexual relations. Using these coercive methods to achieve victim acquiescence to sexual acts is similar to how psychological aggression has been defined (Murphy & Cascardi, 1999) and assessed on many standardized instruments (e.g., Murphy & Hoover, 1999).

The perpetrator's intention when using psychological and physical violence is perhaps the most important consideration in understanding the intersection between sexual and nonsexual forms of violence. For example, if the perpetrator is using psychological or physical aggression as a means to achieve sexual access, then these behaviors would be considered as part of the topography of sexual aggression. For some perpetrators, these types of aggression (sexual, nonsexual/physical, and/or psychological) are interchangeable methods of establishing dominance or control. In addition, some sexual aggression may occur as a result of defective attempts to make up for the deleterious effects of previously occurring physical or psychological aggression (i.e., unwanted "make-up sex").

There were no items related to sexual aggression on the original Conflict Tactics Scale (CTS), an often-used set of scales to assess interpersonal violence experiences (Straus, 1979). With the inclusion of a sexual aggression scale in the Revised Conflict Tactics Scale (CTS2; Straus, Hamby, McCoy, & Sugarman, 1996), there has been more recognition of, and reporting on, the prevalence of this type of aggression. However, both the CTS and CTS2 were designed to measure violence topographically, or by indicating the frequency with which certain types of behavior were experienced or perpetrated. It has been argued that this measurement method fails to recognize the context surrounding the episode(s), the intent of the perpetrator, and the perception of risk and fear of potential bodily harm, which play a role in the response of victims (Browne, 1993; Dobash, Dobash, Wilson, & Daly, 1992; Kurz, 1993). In addition, there have been inconsistent findings about the degree of congruence between intimate partners about the violence that has been perpetrated or experienced in their relationship (e.g., Langhinrichsen-Rohling & Vivian, 1994; Moffitt, Caspi, Krueger, Magdol, & Margolin, 1997).

Although incongruence between partner self-reports has been minimally studied, at least two recent studies suggest that this incongruence may be particularly pronounced when spouses are asked to reveal the occurrence of acts of sexual aggression (O'Leary & Williams, 2006; Simpson &

Christensen, 2005). Given these reporting concerns, we consider topographical self-report measures alone to be inadequate to fully understand the role of sexual aggression in intimate relationships. Instead, we recommend that clinicians also learn to routinely and directly ask intimate partners whether they have had these experiences, and if so, the clinician needs to carefully examine the context and functionality of all types of violent behavior that have occurred. This examination may best be accomplished by conducting a multilevel functional analysis of the aggression. Langhinrichsen-Rohling, Huss, and Rohling (2006) outlined a flexible battery of assessment for aggression that takes into account these multiple levels. Others have used similar approaches to derive structured or actuarial strategies to assess sexual aggression (e.g., Sexual Violence Risk Appraisal Guide; Quinsey, Harris, Rice, & Cormier, 1998).

PREVALENCE OF INTIMATE PARTNER SEXUAL AGGRESSION

It is important to preface a review of the prevalence rates of intimate partner sexual aggression with a discussion of the sample biases found in this area (see Martin, Taft, & Resick, 2007, for a more extended discussion of sampling issues and a thorough review of existing marital rape studies used to estimate prevalence). The literature on the prevalence of intimate partner sexual aggression is largely based on convenience or clinical samples—for example, clients of battered women shelters and individuals seeking therapy. Researchers have argued that samples of identified victims of intimate partner physical violence or maritally dissatisfied spouses will yield especially high prevalence rates of intimate partner sexual aggression for two reasons: (a) The comorbidity of violence experiences is high (Hanneke, Shields, & McCall, 1986; Kilpatrick, Best, Saunders, & Veronen, 1988; Meyer, Vivian, & O'Leary, 1998), and (b) marital distress is an important correlate of physical aggression (Stith, Smith, Penn, Ward, & Tritt, 2004). Other demographic characteristics, such as age and poverty, have also been associated with perpetrating and experiencing violence (Stith et al., 2004), and these characteristics are not usually representative in convenience samples (Johnson & Sigler, 2000; Tjaden & Thoennes, 2000). Bearing in mind the relatively few studies of intimate partner sexual aggression, we focus on the prevalence rates found in nationally representative samples, random community samples, and well-delineated community/clinical samples (see Table 2.1).

Random National Samples

The National Institute of Justice and the Centers for Disease Control and Prevention jointly funded the National Crime Victimization Survey (NCVS; Bachman & Saltzman, 1995) in 1992 and 1993 and the National

TABLE 2.1
Prevalence of Women's Intimate Sexual Victimization, by Sample Type

Type of sample	Authors	Prevalence
National, random (NCVS)	Bachman and Saltzman (1995)	26% of all sexual assaults perpetrated by intimate partner
National, random (NVAWS)	Tjaden and Thoennes (2000)	7.7% lifetime rape
		0.3% yearly rape
National, random	Basile (2002)	34% lifetime sexual coercion or assault
		13% current partner sexual assault
		9% current partner sexual coercion
Community, random	Russell (1982a)	14% lifetime rape
Community, random	Finkelhor and Yllo (1985)	10% lifetime rape
Community/clinical	Hanneke, Shields, and McCall (1986)	9% most recent partner sexual assault
		34% current partner rape
Community/clinical	Meyer, Vivian, and O'Leary (1998)	Treatment-seeking couples: 36%/35% sexual coercion past year, 5%/0.5% sexual assault past year [a]
		Community couples: 14%/23% sexual coercion past year, 0%/0% sexual assaults past year
Clinical	Simpson and Christensen (2005)[b]	49% sexual coercion past year
		11% sexual assault past year
Community	Marshall and Holtzworth-Munroe (2002)[b]	50% sexual coercion past year
		10% sexual assault past year

Note. NCVS = National Crime Victimization Survey; NVAWS = National Violence Against Women Survey. [a]Percentages are based on women's and men's reports, respectively. [b]Percentages are based on combined couple report.

Violence Against Women Survey (NVAWS; Tjaden & Thoennes, 2000) in 1995 and 1996. The NCVS data indicated that 26% of all rapes and sexual assaults were committed by an intimate partner, with 10% of those rapes and sexual assaults committed by a spouse or ex-spouse. The NVAWS estimated that 7.7% of women are raped in their lifetime by an intimate partner. According to the NVAWS, 3.2 in 1,000 women are raped by an intimate partner each year.

Studying only intimate partner sexual aggression, Basile (2002) conducted a national random telephone survey of 1,108 female residents who were 18 years and older. Thirty-four percent of all women sampled were victims of some type of sexual coercion or aggression by a husband or an intimate partner during their lifetime. Thirteen percent of the currently married women reported that they had been physically forced or threatened with force to obtain sexual intercourse by their husbands (rape). Nine percent of the women indicated that they had experienced unwanted sex with a current partner or spouse because the partner had said things to bully them into it (sexual coercion).

Random Community Samples

Russell (1982a) conducted one of the first random community sample studies on marital rape with a sample of 930 women who were 18 years and older and living in San Francisco. Using a conservative definition of *completed rape*, she found that 14% of the married women had experienced rape by a husband or ex-husband during their lifetime. Similarly, Finkelhor and Yllo (1985) used an area-probability methodology sampling of 326 mothers of school-age children in the Boston area. They found that 10% of the women had experienced attempted or completed rape by a husband or cohabiting partner in their lifetime. In these random samples, marital rape was reported to occur 3 to 4 times more often than rape by a stranger. The number of attacks by a husband or ex-husband was also 3 times more frequent than the number of attacks experienced by the next most frequent category of perpetrator (i.e., romantic acquaintance). Thus, wives who are victims of intimate partner rape are more likely to experience multiple traumatic episodes than victims raped by strangers.

Community/Clinical Samples

Hanneke et al. (1986) used questionnaire- and interview-based strategies to assess the prevalence rate of marital rape in two different samples. They used the questionnaire-based strategy to assess a sample garnered from a university, a family planning agency, and respondents to a newspaper survey, and they used the interview-based strategy with a sample from agency referrals, self-referrals through advertisements, and letters sent to women who had filed for protection orders against their partners. The questionnaire sample revealed that approximately 9% of the women reported that their current intimate partner had used physical force to engage in sexual acts with them. The interview sample indicated that 34% of the women reported experiencing this sexual aggression in their current relationship.

In one of the few studies to assess both husbands' and wives' reports of husbands' intimate partner sexual perpetration, Meyer et al. (1998) investigated 252 discordant couples seeking marital therapy and matched these couples with a community control group of 53 couples. This study used an expanded version of the Sexual Experiences Survey (SES; Koss & Oros, 1982) to measure sexual aggression during the past year. In the treatment-seeking group, 36% of wives and 35% of husbands reported that the husband had perpetrated any act of sexual coercion in the past year. In contrast, in the community sample, 14% of women and 23% of men reported that the husband had perpetrated any act of sexual coercion in the past year. Five percent of the women and 0.5% of the men in the treatment-seeking sample reported that the husband had used force or the threat of force to obtain sex in the past year. None of the community sample reported this severe type of sexual aggression in the past year.

Using data from a large randomized trial of participants in conjoint therapy (Christensen et al., 2004), Simpson and Christensen (2005) examined the prevalence of men's and women's reported aggression on the CTS2 at baseline. They combined the men's and women's reports and found that 49% of the couples reported minor sexual coercion (e.g., insisted on or threatened physical force for sex), and nearly 11% reported that severe sexual coercion (e.g., used force to make partner have sex) had occurred in their relationship.

Marshall and Holtzworth-Munroe (2002) recruited a nonclinical sample of community couples. They used both the CTS2 and the SES to evaluate the existence of sexual coercion and threatened/forced sex in these couples. Between one third and one half of the spouses reported that the husband had engaged in sexual coercion in the past year, and 5% to 10% of the spouses reported that the husband had engaged in threatened/forced sex in the past year. Overall, the SES identified more husbands as sexually aggressive in the past year than did the CTS2.

Female Perpetration

The prevalence and quality of female-perpetrated aggression remains largely unaddressed. Several authors have asserted, and crime statistics data have generally confirmed (Bureau of Justice Statistics, 2006), that the sexual assault of men by women is either very rare or nonexistent (e.g., Abbey, Zawacki, Buck, Clinton, & McAuslan, 2004; Browne, 1993). Rape of men by women is particularly rare. For example, in a community sample, only 0.3% of men reported being raped by a female intimate partner at any point in their lifetime (Tjaden & Thoennes, 2000). In keeping with this notion, theories of sexual offenders and reviews of sexual offender treatment have assumed that the perpetrator was a man (e.g., Abracen & Looman, 2004).

Other researchers, however, have highlighted the importance of explicitly assessing and theorizing about women's sexual perpetration. For example, cross-sectional studies of dating couples have shown that although women report being sexually victimized more often than men, between 1% and 5% of women report perpetrating sexual acts against their boyfriends that would meet the definition of *rape* (e.g., Monson & Langhinrichsen-Rohling, 1998; Pirog-Good, 1992). Moreover, a recent review of the research on female sexual perpetrators (Johansson-Love & Fremouw, 2006) indicates that some risk factors may be specific to female sexual perpetration. These include a higher than expected probability of being the victim of childhood sexual abuse and a family history of psychological problems. Finally, unlike male sexual perpetrators, women are more likely to sexually offend in the presence of a male coperpetrator. When this occurs, their victims are often other women, rather than men.

Comorbidity of Intimate Sexual Aggression and Other Forms of Intimate Aggression

There has been relatively minimal analysis of the associations among the types of violence experiences in large epidemiological samples. Instead, most of the data on the co-occurrence of intimate sexual aggression with other forms of intimate aggression has come from convenience samples. For example, in studies of battered women residing in shelters, 33% to 59% of the women reported experiencing marital rape in addition to their experiences of physical violence. Moreover, the severity of physical aggression these women experienced was associated with the co-occurrence of more severe and more frequent sexual aggression (Bowker, 1983; Campbell, 1989; Frieze, 1983; Hanneke et al., 1986; Pagelow, 1984; Walker, 1984). Likewise, in a sample of individuals who had experienced physical violence in their same-sex intimate relationship, Heintz and Melendez (2006) found that 41% of the victims reported that their partners had also forced them to have unwanted sex.

Consistent with the definitional issues that we outlined previously, Meyer et al. (1998) found that husbands' sexual coercion was associated with their perpetration of psychological aggression, whereas husbands' threatened/forced sex was related to their perpetration of both moderate and severe physical aggression. Compared with non–physically abused and mildly or moderately physically abused wives, severely physically abused wives reported the highest rates and greatest frequency of experiencing both sexual coercion and threatened/forced sex. Similarly, Marshall and Holtzworth-Munroe (2002) found that perpetrating psychological and physical aggression was associated with perpetrating both sexual coercion and threatened/forced sex in the marital relationship.

A DIMENSIONAL APPROACH TO INTIMATE SEXUAL VIOLENCE PERPETRATORS

The ability to predict the occurrence of intimate physical aggression has been found to be better based on perpetrator than victim characteristics (see Schumacher, Feldbau-Kohn, Smith Slep, & Heyman, 2001). Thus, to aid conceptualization of why intimate partner sexual violence occurs and what interventions are most likely to be successful, researchers have focused on risk factors associated with the perpetration of sexual aggression. To further an understanding of all types of violence within intimate relationships, both the intimate partner violence and sexual offender literatures have moved beyond simply comparing perpetrators to nonperpetrators. Instead, in many current studies of intimate partner aggression, the focus is on understanding and accounting for the heterogeneity among perpetrators and comparing subtypes of perpetrators to one another (e.g., Holtzworth-Munroe & Stuart, 1994; Knight, 1999).

Chapter 4 of this volume covers different proposed subtypes of intimate aggressors in greater detail. One perpetrator typology, outlined by Monson and Langhinrichsen-Rohling (1998), integrates typologies put forth for sexual perpetrators (Finkelhor & Yllo, 1985) and intimate relationship aggressors (Holtzworth-Munroe & Stuart, 1994). The typology identifies four different perpetrator types: family-only, dysphoric/borderline, generally violent/ antisocial, and sexually obsessive. Two empirical studies have provided at least partial support for the typology in male college students (Monson & Langhinrichsen-Rohling, 2002) and community men (Marshall & Holtzworth-Munroe, 2002).

There is a growing trend, however, to embrace dimensional rather than categorical taxonomies for understanding psychopathology (e.g., Krueger, Watson, & Barlow, 2005; Trull, Tragesser, Solhan, & Schwartz-Mette, 2007). Specific to intimate partner violence perpetrators, research is accumulating to suggest that a strictly categorical approach may not best capture the heterogeneity manifested among these perpetrators.

In a longitudinal study testing their original typology, Holtzworth-Munroe, Meehan, and Herron (2000) found an additional type of perpetrator (i.e., low-level antisocial) at initial assessment, and they also reported instability in the subtype categorizations of their husband perpetrators up to 3 years later (Holtzworth-Munroe, Meehan, & Herron, 2003). These findings suggest that measuring the degree of antisociality the perpetrator exhibits may have more clinical utility than using an arbitrary cut-point on an antisocial scale to determine category membership. As we mentioned, Holtzworth-Munroe et al. (2000, 2003) found only partial support for their integrated typology. Others have also failed to replicate various proposed categorical typologies of intimate violence perpetrators (Babcock, Green, Webb, & Graham, 2004; Meehan, Holtzworth-Munroe, & Herron, 2001; Waltz, Babcock, Jacobson, & Gottman, 2000; White & Gondolf, 2000). Similarly, rapist classification systems have undergone several revisions to better capture the heterogeneity among these perpetrators (Knight, 1999).

It now appears best, for clinical assessment and treatment purposes, to conceptualize intimate partner aggression from a multidimensional perspective and to include the environmental, relationship-specific, and situational contexts in which the aggression is occurring (Langhinrichsen-Rohling et al., 2006). The primary dimensions to assess should include the type and severity of various aggressive behaviors each partner has perpetrated, including co-occurring psychological and physical aggression. Additional important dimensions are the generality of aggression, negative affectivity and/ emotional dysregulation, the degree of antisociality or psychopathy, and the presence or absence of a variety of proximal factors, including the use of alcohol or drugs.

Type and Severity of Aggression

If an individual reports being the victim of sexual coercion or aggression, clinicians should consider the likelihood of co-occurring physical and psychological aggression. Assessing for sexual violence experiences should occur routinely in every battered women's shelter, conjoint or marital therapy case, and public health screening about violence in the country. Such assessment is particularly important in light of emerging evidence that the severity of sexual violence that physically abused women experience explains a unique portion of the variance in symptoms of posttraumatic stress disorder (PTSD), above and beyond the variance explained by the severity of physical violence they have endured (Bennice, Resick, Mechanic, & Astin, 2003).

Co-Occurring Psychological Aggression

We and others have made a distinction between sexual behavior achieved through psychological coercion versus sexual behavior that is garnered via threats of force or the actual use of force. Psychological sexual coercion is important to consider because, as previously noted, it is frequently reported and has deleterious effects. Research on the impact of psychological aggression, as compared with the impact of physical aggression, suggests that psychological aggression can be as harmful as, if not more so than, physical aggression (O'Leary, 1999). Further research is needed to parcel the sequelae attributable to experiencing sexual coercion with or without the co-occurrence of sexual aggression.

Admittedly, there is some gray area when differentiating between persuasion and coercion within an established intimate relationship, particularly if that relationship has a history of consensual sex. Differences in obtained prevalence rates highlight this gray area. For example, Basile (2002) found that 24% of the married women in her sample reported complying with their husbands' demands for sex because they believed intercourse was expected after their husbands spent money on them, even though the sexual act was unwanted.

It is also important to note that an ultimately successful perpetrator may not ever have to use or continue to use severe forms of psychological or physical aggression to achieve desired sexual contact. For example, in a sample of women who had experienced unwanted sex with their husband or intimate partner, Basile (1999) found that 20% of the women who had prior experiences with forced sex reported later acquiescence in their ongoing efforts to avoid another episode of forced sex.

Co-Occurring Physical Aggression

Threat of physical force or the actual use of physical force is the central component in defining *physical aggression*. In the case of sexual assault or sexual aggression, physical force or the threat of it is imbued with sexual motivations. In most studies, threat of physical force and the use of physical force for the express purpose of obtaining sexual access within an intimate relationship have rarely been separated from threats of force and use of force for other purposes. Moreover, studies of sexual aggression have not always separated perpetrators who actually used physical force from those who threatened to use force but did not. This may have happened because threatened force without some episode involving actual force has been shown to be rare (e.g., Basile, 2002; Russell, 1982b). Practically speaking, however, the distinction may be important for understanding victim and perpetrator perceptions, implementing risk reduction strategies, and treatment planning.

Research on sexual offenders, and sexual sadists in particular, suggests that the risk of further offending, treatment prognosis, and treatment recommendations should be different based on the characteristic use of physical threats only versus the actual use of physical force before or during intimate sexual exchanges (e.g., Doren, 2002; Russell, 1982b). For risk assessment and treatment purposes, it is important to discern whether the perpetrator and/or victim experiences sexual gratification related to the intermingled physical and sexual aggression. If so, the risk of continued, and perhaps escalating, aggression is increased.

Generality of Aggression

The generality of all forms of aggression, including sexual aggression, is important for appreciating the possible situational variables associated with perpetration, as well as the stability and pervasiveness of the aggressive behavior. With regard to sexual aggression, we have previously postulated that sexually obsessive perpetrators would be most likely to perpetrate sexual aggression both within and outside of the intimate relationship. We theorized that these perpetrators are defined by their sexual fixation and that their sexual fantasies, arousal, and behavior are more deviant in general. The availability of an intimate partner likely makes for more opportunities for the desired sexual gratification with less risk.

Research on sexual deviance suggests that when an individual exhibits some form of aberrant sexual behavior, he or she is likely to exhibit some other sexual deviance or paraphilia (Dunsieth et al., 2004). Consequently, the range of sexually deviant behaviors should be assessed when intimate partner sexual aggression or sexual coercion is found to occur within a relationship. In addition, greater generality of deviant behavior increases the risk of reoffending, the potential for negative consequences for the victim, and the need for sex-specific and intensive treatment.

Negative Affectivity and Emotional Dysregulation

In perpetrator typology efforts, researchers have differentiated offenders on the basis of whether they had primary affective disturbances or personality disorders marked by emotional regulation problems (e.g., borderline/dysphoric) versus antisocial personality characteristics. This distinction maps onto the traditional distinction between "instrumental" or "proactive" versus "impulsive" or "reactive" types of aggressors (Chase, O'Leary, & Heyman, 2001; Tweed & Dutton, 1998). Recent research, however, suggests that these categories may not be mutually exclusive. For example, psychometric studies of personality disorders suggest that borderline, narcissistic, histrionic, and antisocial personality disorders are interrelated (see Kraus & Reynolds, 2001) and, in fact, are considered to form a cluster of problematic personality characteristics (i.e., Cluster B) according to the *Diagnostic and Statistical Manual of Mental Disorders* (4th ed., text rev.; American Psychiatric Association, 2000). Moreover, typology studies of offenders suggest that individuals who evidence antisocial personality traits and behaviors have mood disorder and regulation problems and vice versa (Waltz et al., 2000). Thus, we advise that clinicians consider the emotional dysregulation and antisocial characteristics of perpetrators simultaneously in risk assessment and treatment planning.

If a clinician believes that a mood disturbance is related to violence perpetration, including sexual violence, treatment specifically targeting increased self-regulation and decreased sensitivity to rejection would ostensibly decrease violence. Consistent with this assertion, greater mood symptomatology has been associated with more severe sexual offending (Dunsieth et al., 2004). Moreover, the propensity toward and strength of jealousy experienced in the intimate relationship should be specifically assessed because they relate to sexual violence perpetration (Levy, Kelly, Jack, Mikulincer, & Goodman, 2006). A number of interventions for intimate aggression perpetrators are predicated on the notion that poor affect management is related to the aggression (Murphy & Scott, 1996; Rosenbaum & Leisring, 2002), and these interventions may be appropriate for cases involving sexual aggression. As we discuss in the next section, this recommendation might depend on the level of the offenders' level of psychopathy.

Antisociality and Psychopathy

Antisocial attitudes and beliefs have been associated with more frequent and severe forms of sexual aggression (see Knight, Guay, & Patrick, 2006, for a review). Antisocial traits can be further differentiated from psychopathy, seen in individuals who use charm, manipulation, intimidation, and violence to control others and to satisfy their own selfish needs. Psychopathic individuals generally lack conscience and empathy for others and have a minimal sense of guilt or regret when they violate social norms (Hare,

Abracen, J., & Looman, J. (2004). Issues in the treatment of sexual offenders: Recent developments and directions for future research. *Aggression and Violent Behavior, 9*, 229–246.

American Psychiatric Association. (2000). *Diagnostic and statistical manual of mental disorders* (4th ed., text rev.). Washington, DC: Author.

Augustine, R. (1991). Marriage: The safe haven for rapists. *Journal of Family Law, 29*, 559–590.

Babcock, J. C., Green, C. E., Webb, S. A., & Graham, K. H. (2004). A second failure to replicate the Gottman et al. (1995) typology of men who abuse intimate partners and possible reasons why. *Journal of Family Psychology, 18*, 396–400.

Bachman, R., & Saltzman, L. E. (1995). *National Crime Victimization Survey: Violence against women: Estimates from the redesigned survey* (Report No. NCJ 154348). Washington, DC: U.S. Department of Justice.

Basile, K. C. (1999). Rape by acquiescence: The ways in which women "give in" to unwanted sex with their husbands. *Violence Against Women, 5*, 1036–1058.

Basile, K. C. (2002). Prevalence of wife rape and other intimate partner sexual coercion in a nationally representative sample of women. *Violence and Victims, 17*, 511–524.

Bennice, J. A., Resick, P. A., Mechanic, M., & Astin, M. (2003). The relative effects of intimate partner physical and sexual violence on posttraumatic stress disorder symptomatology. *Violence and Victims, 18*, 87–94.

Bowker, L. (1983). *Beating wife beating*. Lexington, MA: Lexington Books.

Browne, A. (1993). Violence against women by male partners: Prevalence, outcomes, and policy implications. *American Psychologist, 48*, 1077–1087.

Brownridge, D. A., & Halli, S. S. (2000). "Living in sin" and sinful living: Toward filling a gap in the explanation of violence against women. *Aggression and Violent Behavior, 5*, 565–583.

Bureau of Justice Statistics. (2006). *Criminal victimization in the United States: 2005 statistical tables* (Report No. NCJ 215244). Washington, DC: U.S. Department of Justice.

Butcher, J. N., Dahlstrom, W. G., Graham, J. R., Tellegen, A., & Kaemmer, B. (1989). *Minnesota Multiphasic Personality Inventory (MMPI–2)* (2nd ed.). Minneapolis: University of Minnesota Press.

Campbell, J. C. (1989). Women's responses to sexual abuse in intimate relationships. *Health Care for Women International, 10*, 335–346.

Chase, K. A., O'Leary, K. D., & Heyman, R. E. (2001). Categorizing partner-violent men within the reactive–proactive typology model. *Journal of Consulting and Clinical Psychology, 69*, 567–572.

Christensen, A., Atkins, D., Berns, S., Wheeler, J., Baucom, D., & Simpson, L. E. (2004). Traditional versus integrative behavioral couple therapy for significantly and chronically distressed married couples. *Journal of Consulting and Clinical Psychology, 72*, 176–191.

Coker, A. L., Smith, P. H., & McKeown, R. E. (2000). Frequency and correlates of intimate partner violence by type: Physical, sexual, and psychological battering. *American Journal of Public Health, 90*, 553–559.

DeGue, S., & DiLillo, D. (2005). "You would if you loved me": Toward an improved conceptual and etiological understanding of nonphysical male sexual coercion. *Aggression and Violent Behavior, 10,* 513–532.

Dobash, R. P., Dobash, R. E., Wilson, M., & Daly, M. (1992). The myth of sexual symmetry in marital violence. *Social Problems, 39,* 71–91.

Doren, D. M. (2002). *Evaluating sex offenders: A manual for civil commitments and beyond.* Thousand Oaks, CA: Sage.

Dunsieth, N. W., Nelson, E. B., Brusman-Lovins, L. A., Holcomb, J. L., Beckman, D., Welge, J. A., et al. (2004). Psychiatric and legal features of 113 men convicted of sexual offenses. *Journal of Clinical Psychiatry, 65,* 293–300.

Finkelhor, D., & Yllo, K. (1982). Forced sex in marriage: A preliminary research report. *Crime & Delinquency, 28,* 459–478.

Finkelhor, D., & Yllo, K. (1985). *License to rape: Sexual abuse of wives.* New York: Free Press.

Finkelhor, D., & Yllo, K. (1988). Rape in marriage. In M. B. Straus (Ed.), *Abuse and victimization across the life span* (pp. 140–152). Baltimore: Johns Hopkins University Press.

First, M. G., Gibbon, M., Spitzer, R. L., & Williams, J. B. (1996). *Structured Clinical Interview for DSM–IV (SCID).* New York: Biometrics Research Department, New York State Psychiatric Institute.

Frieze, I. H. (1983). Investigating the causes and consequences of marital rape. *Signs: Journal of Women in Culture and Society, 8,* 532–553.

Hale, M. (1736). *Historia placitorum coronae: The history of the pleas of the crown.* London: Gyles, Woodward, & Davis.

Hanneke, C. R., Shields, N. M., & McCall, G. J. (1986). Assessing the prevalence of marital rape. *Journal of Interpersonal Violence, 1,* 350–362.

Hare, R. D. (1993). *Without conscience: The disturbing world of the psychopaths among us.* New York: Simon & Schuster.

Hare, R. D. (2003). *Hare Psychopathy Checklist—Revised* (2nd ed.). Toronto: Multi-Health Systems.

Heintz, A. J., & Melendez, R. M. (2006). Intimate partner violence and HIV/STD risk among lesbian, gay, bisexual, and transgender individuals. *Journal of Interpersonal Violence, 21,* 193–208.

Holtzworth-Munroe, A., Meehan, J. C., & Herron, K. (2000). Testing the Holtzworth-Munroe and Stuart (1994) batterer typology. *Journal of Consulting and Clinical Psychology, 68,* 1000–1019.

Holtzworth-Munroe, A., Meehan, J. C., & Herron, K. (2003). Do subtypes of maritally violent men continue to differ over time? *Journal of Consulting and Clinical Psychology, 71,* 728–740.

Holtzworth-Munroe, A., & Stuart, G. L. (1994). Typologies of male batterers: Three subtypes and the differences among them. *Psychological Bulletin, 116,* 476–497.

Huss, M. T., Covell, C. N., & Langhinrichsen-Rohling, J. (2006). Clinical implications for the assessment and treatment of antisocial and psychopathic domestic violence perpetrators. *Journal of Aggression, Maltreatment, and Trauma, 13*, 59–85.

Huss, M. T., & Langhinrichsen-Rohling, J. (2000). Identification of the psychopathic batterer: The clinical, legal, and policy implications. *Aggression and Violent Behavior, 5*, 403–422.

Johansson-Love, J., & Fremouw, W. (2006). A critique of the female sexual perpetrator research. *Aggression and Violent Behavior, 11*, 12–26.

Johnson, I. M., & Sigler, R. T. (2000). Forced sexual intercourse among intimates. *Journal of Family Violence, 15*, 95–108.

Kilpatrick, D. G., Best, C. L., Saunders, B. E., & Veronen, L. J. (1988). Rape in marriage and in dating relationships: How bad is it for mental health? *Annals of the New York Academy of Sciences, 528*, 335–344.

Knight, R. A. (1999). Validation of a typology for rapists. *Journal of Interpersonal Violence, 14*, 303–330.

Knight, R. A., Guay, J.-P., & Patrick, C. J. (2006). The role of psychopathy in sexual coercion against women. In C. J. Patrick (Ed.), *Handbook of psychopathy* (pp. 512–532). New York: Guilford Press.

Koss, M. P., & Oros, C. J. (1982). Sexual Experiences Survey: A research instrument investigating sexual aggression and victimization. *Journal of Consulting and Clinical Psychology, 50*, 455–457.

Kraus, G., & Reynolds, D. J. (2001). The "A-B-Cs" of the Cluster Bs: Identifying, understanding, and treating Cluster B personality disorders. *Clinical Psychology Review, 21*, 345–373.

Krueger, R. F., Watson, D., & Barlow, D. H. (2005). Introduction to the special section: Toward a dimensionally based taxonomy of psychopathology. *Journal of Abnormal Psychology, 114*, 491–493.

Kurz, D. (1993). Physical assaults by husbands: A major social problem. In R. J. Gelles & D. Loseke (Eds.), *Current controversies on family violence* (pp. 88–103). Thousand Oaks, CA: Sage.

Langhinrichsen-Rohling, J., Huss, M. T., & Rohling, M. L. (2006). Aggressive behavior. In M. Hersen (Ed.), *Clinician's handbook of adult behavioral assessment* (pp. 371–395). San Diego, CA: Elsevier.

Langhinrichsen-Rohling, J., & Vivian, D. (1994). The correlates of spouses' incongruent reports of marital aggression. *Journal of Family Violence, 9*, 265–284.

Langton, C. M., Barbaree, H. E., Harkins, L., & Peacock, E. J. (2006). Sex offenders' response to treatment and its association with recidivism as a function of psychopathy. *Sexual Abuse: A Journal of Research and Treatment, 18*, 99–120.

Levy, K. N., Kelly, K. M., Jack, E. L., Mikulincer, M., & Goodman, G. S. (2006). Sex differences in jealousy: A matter of evolution or attachment history? In M. Mikulincer & G. S. Goodman (Eds.), *Dynamics of romantic love: Attachment, caregiving, and sex* (pp. 128–145). New York: Guilford Press.

Marshall, A. D., & Holtzworth-Munroe, A. (2002). Varying forms of husband sexual aggression: Predictors and subgroup differences. *Journal of Family Psychology, 16*, 286–296.

Martin, E. K., Taft, C. T., & Resick, P. A. (2007). A review of marital rape. *Aggression and Violent Behavior, 12,* 329–347.

Meehan, J. C., Holtzworth-Munroe, A., & Herron, K. (2001). Maritally violent men's heart rate reactivity to marital interactions: A failure to replicate the Gottman et al. (1995) typology. *Journal of Family Psychology, 15,* 394–408.

Meyer, S. L., Vivian, D., & O'Leary, K. D. (1998). Men's sexual aggression in marriage: Couples' report. *Violence Against Women, 4,* 415–435.

Millon, T., Millon, C., & Davis, R. (1994). *Millon Clinical Multiaxial Inventory—III manual.* Minneapolis, MN: National Computer Systems.

Moffitt, T. E., Caspi, A., Krueger, R. F., Magdol, L., & Margolin, G. (1997). Do partners agree about abuse in their relationship? A psychometric evaluation of interpartner agreement. *Psychological Assessment, 9,* 47–56.

Monson, C. M., & Langhinrichsen-Rohling, J. (1998). Sexual and nonsexual marital aggression: Legal considerations, epidemiology, and an integrated typology of perpetrators. *Aggression and Violent Behavior, 3,* 1–21.

Monson, C. M., & Langhinrichsen-Rohling, J. (2002). Sexual and nonsexual dating violence perpetration: Testing an integrated perpetrator typology. *Violence and Victims, 17,* 403–428.

Murphy, C. M., & Cascardi, M. (1999). Psychological abuse in marriage and dating relationships. In R. L. Hampton (Ed.), *Family violence: Prevention and treatment* (2nd ed., pp. 198–226). Beverly Hills, CA: Sage.

Murphy, C. M., & Hoover, S. A. (1999). Measuring emotional abuse in dating relationships as a multifactorial construct. *Violence and Victims, 14,* 39–53.

Murphy, C. M., & Scott, E. (1996). *Cognitive–behavioral therapy for domestically assaultive individuals: A treatment manual.* Unpublished manuscript, University of Maryland, Baltimore County, Baltimore.

National Clearing House for Marital and Date Rape. (2005). *State law chart.* Retrieved January 15, 2008, from www.ncmdr.org

O'Leary, K. D. (1999). Psychological abuse: A variable deserving attention in domestic violence. *Violence and Victims, 14,* 3–23.

O'Leary, K. D., & Williams, M. C. (2006). Agreement about acts of aggression in marriage. *Journal of Family Psychology, 20,* 656–662.

Pagelow, M. D. (1984). *Family violence.* New York: Praeger.

Pirog-Good, M. A. (1992). Sexual abuse in dating relationships. In E. C. Viano (Ed.), *Intimate violence: Interdisciplinary perspectives* (pp. 101–110). Washington, DC: Hemisphere.

Quinsey, V. L., Harris, G. T., Rice, M. E., & Cormier, C. A. (1998). *Violent offenders: Appraising and managing risk.* Washington, DC: American Psychological Association.

Ratner, P. A., Johnson, J. L., & Shoveller, J. A. (2003). Non-consensual sex experienced by men who have sex with men: Prevalence and association with mental health. *Patient Education and Counseling, 49,* 67–74.

Rice, M. E., Harris, G. T., & Cormier, C. A. (1992). An evaluation of a maximum security therapeutic community for psychopaths and other mentally disordered offenders. *Law and Human Behavior, 16,* 399–412.

Rose, S. M. (2003). Community interventions concerning homophobic violence and partner violence against lesbians. *Journal of Lesbian Studies, 7,* 125–139.

Rosenbaum, A., & Leisring, P. A. (2002). Group intervention programs for batterers. *Journal of Aggression, Maltreatment & Trauma, 5,* 57–71.

Russell, D. E. (1982a). The prevalence and incidence of forcible rape and attempted rape of females. *Victimology, 7,* 81–93.

Russell, D. E. (1982b). *Rape in marriage.* New York: Macmillan.

Schumacher, J. A., Feldbau-Kohn, S., Smith Slep, A. M., & Heyman, R. E. (2001). Risk factors for male-to-female partner physical abuse. *Aggression and Violent Behavior, 6,* 281–352.

Shields, N., & Hanneke, C. R. (1983). Battered wives' reactions to marital rape. In D. Finkelhor, R. J. Gelles, G. T. Hotaling, & M. A. Straus (Eds.), *The dark side of families: Current family violence research* (pp. 132–148). Thousand Oaks, CA: Sage.

Shields, N., & Hanneke, C. R. (1988). Multiple sexual victimization: The case of incest and marital rape. In G. T. Hotaling, D. Finkelhor, J. T. Kirkpatrick, & M. A. Straus (Eds.), *Family abuse and its consequences: New directions in research* (pp. 255–269). Thousand Oaks, CA: Sage.

Simpson, L. E., & Christensen, A. (2005). Spousal agreement regarding relationship aggression on the Conflict Tactics Scale—2. *Psychological Assessment, 17,* 423–432.

Sitton, J. (1993). Old wine in new bottles: The "marital" rape allowance. *North Carolina Law Review Association, 72,* 261–289.

Small, M. A., & Tetreault, P. A. (1990). Social psychology, "marital rape exemptions," and privacy. *Behavioral Sciences and Law, 8,* 141–149.

Stith, S. M., Smith, D. B., Penn, C. E., Ward, D. B., & Tritt, D. (2004). Intimate partner physical abuse perpetration and victimization risk factors: A meta-analytic review. *Aggression and Violent Behavior, 10,* 65–98.

Straus, M. A. (1979). Measuring intrafamily conflict and violence: The Conflict Tactics (CT) Scales. *Journal of Marriage and the Family, 41,* 75–88.

Straus, M. A., Hamby, S. L., McCoy, S. B., & Sugarman, D. B. (1996). The Revised Conflict Tactics Scales (CTS2): Development and preliminary psychometric data. *Journal of Family Issues, 17,* 283–316.

Tjaden, P., & Thoennes, N. (2000). *Extent, nature, and consequences of intimate partner violence: Findings from the National Violence Against Women Survey* (Report No. NCJ 181867). Washington, DC: U.S. Department of Justice.

Trull, T. J., Tragesser, S. L., Solhan, M., & Schwartz-Mette, R. (2007). Dimensional models of personality disorder: *Diagnostic and Statistical Manual of Mental Disorders* fifth edition and beyond. *Current Opinion in Psychiatry, 20,* 52–56.

Tweed, R. G., & Dutton, D. G. (1998). A comparison of impulsive and instrumental subgroups of batterers. *Violence and Victims, 13*, 217–230.

Walker, L. A. (1984). Battered women, psychology, and public policy. *American Psychologist, 39*, 1178–1182.

Waltz, J., Babcock, J. C., Jacobson, N. S., & Gottman, J. M. (2000). Testing a typology of batterers. *Journal of Consulting and Clinical Psychology, 68*, 658–669.

White, R. J., & Gondolf, E. W. (2000). Implications of personality profiles for batterer treatment. *Journal of Interpersonal Violence, 15*, 467–488.

3

PARTNER AGGRESSION
ACROSS CULTURES

HEIDI LARY KAR AND CLAUDIA GARCIA-MORENO

Violence against women is increasingly recognized as an issue of critical importance on the global women's agenda in human rights, public health, peace and security, and development overall. It is sometimes called *gender-based violence* because much of this violence is rooted in unequal gender power relations, particularly in societies that see women as subordinate to men and as deserving of male chastisement or discipline (Archer, 2006; Heise, Ellsberg, & Gottemoeller, 1999). This chapter addresses violence against women by their male partners, or intimate partner violence (IPV). It reviews existing data on abuse by intimate male partners, whether physical (e.g., shoving, kicking, burning, beating), sexual (obtaining sex through use of force or intimidation), or psychological–emotional. Although we recognize that between one half and two thirds of murders of females (femicide) are perpetrated by intimate partners, this chapter does not cover femicide (Bachman & Saltzman, 1995).

Violence by an intimate partner is only one of many forms of violence that many women around the world encounter in their lifetime. The life

The views expressed in this chapter are those of the authors and do not necessarily reflect World Health Organization policy.

cycle model of violence against women illustrates the many different types of violence that women and girls may experience in different stages of their life: infancy (e.g., female infanticide, neglect), childhood (e.g., child abuse, female genital mutilation,), adolescence (e.g., forced prostitution, trafficking, forced early marriage), reproductive age (e.g., honor killing, dowry killing, intimate partner violence, rape and other forms of sexual violence), and old age (e.g., intimate partner violence, institutional elder abuse). Understanding the interconnectedness of different forms of violence against women is vital to establishing a solid framework from which to conceptualize the underpinnings of partner violence prevention (Watts & Zimmerman, 2002).

CROSS COUNTRY RESEARCH ON PREVALENCE

Nearly 80 population-based studies spanning 50 countries address IPV. International research has demonstrated that a woman is more likely to be assaulted, injured, raped, or killed by a current or former intimate partner than by anyone else (Garcia-Moreno, Jansen, Ellsberg, Heise, & Watts, 2005). Collectively, international data indicate that partner violence perpetrated by men is widespread, albeit with some variation, but until recently, researchers' differing definitions of violence and research methods have made comparisons across studies very difficult. Studies have differed regarding the specific population studied (e.g., all women, ever-married women, ever-pregnant women), types of violence assessed (e.g., physical, sexual, *psychological–emotional*), time period covered (e.g., ever experienced, experienced in the past year), specific questions used, and measures taken to ensure confidentiality and privacy of subjects, all of which have been shown to affect women's willingness to report violence (Ellsberg, Heise, Pena, Agurto, & Winkvist, 2001). As such, cross-study comparisons must be interpreted with caution.

Recently, researchers have made efforts to develop instruments and protocols that can be used across populations, allowing for culturally specific adaptations. The majority of the data presented in this chapter emanate from multicountry population-based surveys, in particular the World Health Organization (WHO) Multi-Country Study on Women's Health and Domestic Violence. We selected the studies discussed in this chapter because they used a standardized instrument across countries, thereby providing the best basis for cross-country comparison of male partner violence prevalence rates. However, because studies spanned different countries with differing samples and measures, comparisons within studies remains easier than comparisons across studies.

Dedicated Violence Against Women Surveys

Information on violence against women until recently came from questions added to surveys on other topics, such as reproductive health or women's health more broadly. More recently, there have been surveys dedicated exclusively to understanding the magnitude, nature, causes, and consequences of violence—known as "dedicated violence against women surveys." These surveys are considered to provide the most reliable estimates of prevalence.

International Violence Against Women Survey

The International Violence Against Women Survey (IVAWS) collected data using telephone interviews with nationally representative samples, mainly in industrialized countries (e.g., Australia, Czech Republic, Denmark, Hong Kong, Lithuania, Poland, Switzerland), but also in Costa Rica, Mozambique, and the Philippines. The specific population of women surveyed (e.g., by age, partner status, child status) varied across country site. The questionnaire assessed for lifetime physical and sexual violence victimization by a male perpetrator (i.e., partners and former partners, friends, acquaintances and other known men, and strangers) since the age of 16. The victimization screening sections included 12 questions that started broadly, asking about lifetime victimization, and then were followed by detail-gathering processes that focused on prevalence and incidence by perpetrator (Johnson, Ollus, & Nevala, 2007).

Worldsafe Study

In the Worldsafe study, researchers collected partner violence data using face-to-face interviews from six sites within four countries: Chile, Egypt, India, and the Philippines. Data were gathered via population-based household surveys with women between 15 and 49 years who had at least one child. Physical violence was assessed as the presence of any of four behaviors—slap (open hand), hit or punch (closed fist), kick, or beat (hit repeatedly)—across two time frames—lifetime ("ever") and current—during the previous 12 months (Sadowski, Hunter, Bangdiwala, & Muñoz, 2004).

The World Health Organization Multi-Country Study on Women's Health and Violence Against Women

The WHO Multi-Country Study on Women's Health and Violence Against Women used local research teams across 15 sites in 10 countries (Bangladesh, Brazil, Ethiopia, Japan, Namibia, Peru, Samoa, Serbia and Montenegro, United Republic of Tanzania, and Thailand). In each country, the teams conducted cross-sectional, population-based household surveys with women between 15 and 49 years of age in one or two settings. In half of the countries (i.e., Bangladesh, Brazil, Peru, United Republic of Tanzania, and Thailand), surveys were conducted in (a) the capital or a large city and (b) one province or region, usually containing both urban and rural populations and selected to be representative. The study did not attempt to measure national prevalence but rather looked in more depth at two sites reflecting an urban–rural mix (Garcia-Moreno, Jansen, Ellsberg, Heise, & Watts, 2006).

Although this study took a population approach with regard to sampling in each site, it is not possible to extrapolate the findings to the country's entire population. A single rural setting was surveyed in Ethiopia, and a single large city was used in Japan, Namibia, and Serbia and Montenegro. In Samoa, the whole country was sampled. Researchers gathered data about IPV by asking women about their experience of physical, sexual, and psychological–emotional violence ever and in the last year, as well as the frequency and timing of violent events. In addition, the researchers asked about violence during pregnancy and about violence (physical and sexual) by perpetrators other than intimate partners (Garcia-Moreno et al., 2006).

International Health Surveys Addressing Violence Against Women

Two international household surveys, the Demographic and Health Surveys (DHS), supported by Macro International and the U.S. Agency for International Development, and the International Reproductive Health Surveys (RHS), supported by the Centers for Disease Control and Prevention (CDC), have contributed to understanding IPV and its associations with some health aspects. The DHS collected data in Cambodia, Colombia, Dominican Republic, Egypt, Haiti, India, Nicaragua, Peru, and Zambia (Kishor & Johnson, 2004). RHS data provided the first national-level data on violence against women in Eastern Europe and the Caucasus, providing country data from Azerbaijan, Georgia, Moldova, Romania, Russia, and Ukraine (CDC & ORC Macro, 2003).

These surveys interviewed a representative sample of households in each country on a wide range of reproductive and other health topics and included also few targeted questions assessing for IPV. The DHS surveys in Cambodia, Colombia, Dominican Republic, Haiti, and Nicaragua included a separate IPV module that included questions similar to those used in the WHO study and assessed for physical, sexual, and emotional–verbal violence. One possible explanation for the lower rates emanating from the RHS data, based on our understanding of methodology, is that asking only a few IPV questions is likely to have elicited lesser reporting than using a full module, as in the DHS.

COMPARING PREVALENCE DATA ACROSS COUNTRIES

Although the studies mentioned here provide data from a range of countries, it is still problematic to compare results across studies, as they used different frameworks. In addition, each study focuses on different forms of intimate partner violence, providing a partial picture of a complex phenomenon: The IVAWS examines sexual and physical violence, Worldsafe examines physical violence only, and the WHO study, DHS, and RHS look at physical, sexual, and emotional violence.

Physical Violence

The lifetime prevalence of physical violence by an intimate partner among women across most studies is between 10% and 62% (Johnson et al., 2007). The WHO study, the DHS, the IVAWS, and other recent studies include questions about specific acts of physical abuse by a current or former partner, such as "slapped or threw something" at her; "pushed," "shoved," "kicked," "dragged," "beat her up"; "hit her with a fist or object"; "choked or burned her"; or "threatened or used a gun, knife, or other weapon against" her. Some of their results are presented in this chapter.

The WHO study found prevalence rates of physical partner violence ranging from 13% in the Japan city to 62% in the Peru province (see Figure 3.1). The most commonly reported acts of physical violence by a partner in the WHO study sites were being slapped and being struck with a fist, although the country-specific percentages differed substantially.

The WHO study categorized *severe physical violence* as one of the following acts: being hit with a fist, kicked, dragged, or threatened with a weapon or having a weapon used against one. According to this definition, the percentage of ever-partnered women experiencing severe physical violence ranged from 4% of women in Japan to 49% in the Peru province, with most countries falling between 13% and 26%. In almost all sites, between half and two thirds of women who had ever experienced physical partner violence were likely to have experienced severe violence. In only three countries— Bangladesh, Japan, and Serbia and Montenegro—had a greater proportion experienced only moderate violence than had experienced severe violence (Garcia-Moreno, Jansen, et al., 2005).

The IVAWS found prevalence rates of lifetime IPV of between 6% in Hong Kong and 36% in Mozambique. The study also found that Mozambique had significantly higher 1-year rates of IPV (Johnson et al., 2007). In the WHO study, the prevalence of IPV in the last 12 months varied between 19% and 34% in all sites, with the exception of Japan, Serbia and Montenegro, and the Brazil city, where it was between 4% and 9% (Garcia-Moreno, Jansen, et al., 2005). One possible explanation for the lower rates is the difference in resources and opportunities available to women in those locations to leave violent partners and seek separation or divorce.

In the DHS countries where the survey included expanded domestic violence sections (Cambodia, Colombia, Dominican Republic, Haiti, and Nicaragua), physically violent acts included being pushed, shaken, slapped, or targeted with a thrown object or having one's arm twisted. Prevalence rates of any physical partner violence ever ranged from 16% to 40% for ever-married women (see Figure 3.2). Types of physical violence reported ranged

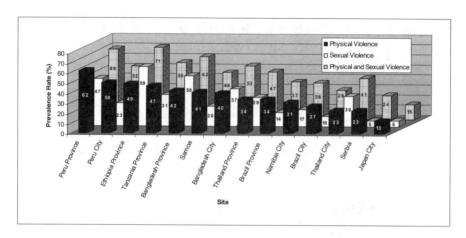

Figure 3.1. Findings of the World Health Organization study on physical and sexual violence. From "Prevalence of Intimate Partner Violence: Findings From the WHO Multi-Country Study on Women's Health and Domestic Violence," by C. Garcia-Moreno, H. Jansen, M. Ellsberg, L. Heise, and C. Watts, 2006, *The Lancet, 368,* p. 1264. Copyright 2006 by Elesevier. Adapted with permission.

from "physical mistreatment" by a partner to "being beaten" by a partner (Kishor & Johnson, 2004).

The Worldsafe study found prevalence rates for lifetime physical violence of 25% in Chile, 11% in Egypt, 31% to 43% across sites in India, and 21% in the Philippines (Hassan et al., 2004). Country-specific RHSs conducted in Azerbaijan, Georgia, Moldova, Romania, Russia, and Ukraine found that between 5% in Georgia and 29% in Romania of ever-married women 15 to 44 years of age reported ever experiencing physical partner abuse and that 2% and 10%, respectively, reported experiencing physical abuse in the past year.

Sexual Violence

Sexual violence and coercion affect women in many different situations, including within intimate partnerships. Sexual coercion entails a lack of choice in engaging in sexual activity and severe physical, social, or economic consequences if the woman resists sexual activity (Jewkes, Sen, & Garcia-Moreno, 2002). In many settings, men, and even women, believe that sexual violence and coercion cannot occur within marriage or cohabiting partnerships because sex with a partner is seen as a right of marriage, irrespective of the woman's wishes. Because of this perception and the privacy and/or shame that sexual matters are usually afforded, many women have difficulty reporting or are unable to discuss or question the sexual abuse they experience in intimate partnerships.

The DHS measured rates of sexual violence by asking women whether a partner had ever threatened her to force her to have sexual intercourse,

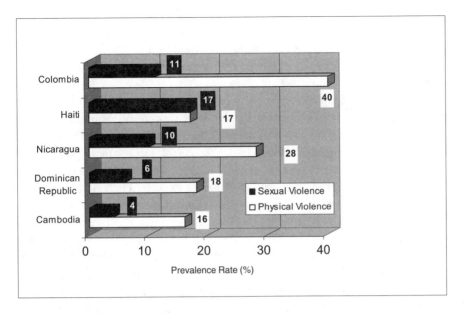

Figure 3.2. Findings of the Democratic and Health Surveys on physical and sexual intimate partner rates among ever-married women ages 15 to 49 years. From *Profiling Domestic Violence—A Multi-Country Study* (pp. 15–16), by S. Kishor and K. Johnson, 2004, Calverton, MD: ORC Macro. In the public domain. Adapted with permission of S. Kishor.

physically forced her to have sexual intercourse, and/or forced her to perform other types of sexual acts she did not want to perform. Reported lifetime prevalence of sexual violence by an intimate partner ranged from almost 4% in Cambodia to 17% in Haiti (Figure 3.2).

The WHO sexual violence questions were the same and included whether the respondent had been physically forced to have intercourse, had intercourse out of fear, and/or had been forced to do something sexual she found degrading or humiliating. In the WHO study, the range of reported lifetime prevalence of sexual violence by an intimate partner was between 6% (Japan city, Serbia and Montenegro city) and 59% (Ethiopia province), with most sites falling between 10% and 50% (Figure 3.1). Although in most settings intimate partner sexual violence was considerably less frequent than physical violence, sexual violence was more frequent in the Bangladesh province, the Ethiopia province, and the Thailand city. The IVAWS found prevalence rates of sexual violence by an intimate partner of between 3% (Philippines, Switzerland) and 15% (Costa Rica).

Patterning of Partner Abuse

One major contribution of the WHO study has been explicating information on the patterning of abuse across countries. The WHO data showed that the vast majority of women physically abused by partners experienced acts of violence more than once, and sometimes frequently, which reflects a pattern of continuing abuse. Over half of the women who had experienced a nonsevere violent act in the past 12 months had experienced that act more than once. This finding was true across all sites.

The data also showed that physical violence and sexual violence tend to co-occur in many relationships. However, this pattern is not always found across sites or studies, and in some settings, perpetration of sexual violence in isolation has also been documented (WHO, 2002). For example, WHO data from both the city and province sites in Thailand suggested that a proportion of women who experienced partner violence experienced only sexual violence. In Bangkok, 44% of women who reported some type of partner violence reported only sexual violence. Twenty-nine percent of women in the Thailand province reported the same. Similarly, 32% of women in the Bangladesh province and 31% of women in the Ethiopia province reported experiencing only sexual violence. In the IVAWS study, women in Costa Rica experienced sexual violence by intimate partners at a rate higher than in other countries (15%), twice the rate for women in Australia (8%) and Denmark (6%; Johnson et al., 2007).

Psychological–Emotional Violence

Arriving at an operational definition and standard set of criteria for *psychological–emotional violence* that is relevant across cultures is a challenge, in part because different cultures view and conceptualize the psyche and emotions very differently (Wierzbicka, 1986). Anthropological research has demonstrated that different cultures give more weight or credence to certain emotions than to others, and people from different cultures have been found to experience emotions differently depending on whether they have an "independent" or "interdependent" sense of the self (Markus & Kitayama, 1991). Evaluating constructs like "emotional abuse" across cultures is no simple task and, most would agree, is much more complicated than assessing for distinct physical types of violent behavior. Few studies of intimate partner violence have therefore attempted this so far.

The WHO study's criteria for emotionally abusive acts by a partner included being insulted or made to feel bad about oneself, being humiliated in front of others, being intimidated or scared on purpose, and being threatened directly or through a threat to someone the respondent cares about. Between 20% and 75% of women across sites had experienced one or more of these acts. The most frequently mentioned types of emotionally abusive actions were insults, belittling, and intimidation. Although threats of harm were reported less frequently, nearly one in four women in the Brazil and Peru provinces reported receiving threats from a partner. Two thirds of all women who reported an act of emotional abuse reported experiencing the behavior more than once. Data were also collected about partners' controlling behaviors, such as routinely attempting to restrict a woman's contact with her family or friends, insisting on knowing where she is at all times, and controlling her access to health care. Significantly, the number of controlling behaviors by the partner was associated with the risk of physical or sexual violence or both (Garcia-Moreno et al., 2006).

The sexual and emotional violence data, both quantitative and qualitative, suggest that types and situations of intimate partner violence are not the same across contexts; therefore, it is important not to generalize findings from one area or population to another. Although there is relative agreement internationally on how best to measure physical violence, the measurement of sexual and emotional violence needs to be developed further.

ACCOUNTING FOR DIFFERENCES ACROSS COUNTRIES AND ACROSS SITES

As evidenced by the prevalence data previously presented, substantial differences in reports of partner violence experience exist across studies and across sites. Reasons for these differences can stem from three major sources: differing methodologies used across studies, community factors that either increase vulnerability to abuse by intimate partners, or protect women from such abuse, and differing social norms about masculinity and what is acceptable in terms of violent behavior. An ecological model being used to explain causality considers factors at the individual, family, community, and societal levels and how they interact (Kruge et al., 2002).

Methodological Issues

Until recently, it was unclear whether the variation in prevalence rates reflected true differences in violence experience or whether the differences represented an artifact of nonstandard data gathering methods. Questions regarding the vast differences in prevalence rates across countries have prompted experts to try to standardize instruments and methodologies used in order to increase the likelihood of comparability. In addition, there is growing agreement on ethical and safety standards for these kinds of studies to ensure that women are not put at risk by the study and that those who need care and support can be referred as needed (Ellsberg et al., 2001; WHO, 2001). The WHO study attempted to achieve this standardization in methodology and still elicited very different prevalence rates across types of abuse and across populations, suggesting that prevalence and types of violence do vary across contexts and cultures, even within the same country.

Even when standardization is attempted, however, it may be difficult to achieve in practice. For example, in the DHS, difficulties in meeting ethical standards in some of the early surveys and research may have affected prevalence results (Ellsberg et al., 2001). Similarly, partner violence questions in some countries were asked only of women who had ever been married, whereas other countries surveyed all women over a certain age (Kishor & Johnson, 2004). These differences in methodologies necessarily affect the prevalence rates of reported partner violence across settings. Data from the Romanian RHS, which included men, verified that men reported inflicting abuse about as often as women reported being abused, confirming women's own reports of violence experiences (CDC & ORC Macro, 2003). This consistency is substantiated by studies in India (Martin et al., 1999) and South Africa (Abrahams, Jewkes, Hoffman, & Laubsher, 2004), which documented men's reports of use of violence on their wives or partners.

Community Factors Affecting Prevalence

At the community level, poverty and associated factors have been found to increase women's vulnerability to IPV (Harvey, Garcia-Moreno, & Butchart, 2007); such factors include overcrowding, an environment supportive of IPV, and lack of institutional support or of community sanctions against such violence. Levinson's (1989) aggregated analysis of 90 societies suggested that several community-level factors related to wife beating include male control of wealth and property, male dominance in family decision making, restrictions on female divorce choices, and the absence of exclusively female work groups, including women's village associations, sex-segregated work teams, and female traders.

The WHO study also provided information on community-level factors affecting the prevalence of partner violence. The overall levels of violence across countries varied widely. Although WHO has not yet reported a comprehensive multiple regression analysis of all factors considered, some preliminary findings can be noted. In all countries where an urban and a provincial (usually more rural) site were included, higher levels of IPV were found in the more rural sites. Age, education, and partnership status did not fully explain the differences in prevalence, although certain patterns emerged.

Although older women clearly experienced partner violence, a much larger proportion of partnered 15- to 24-year-olds reported experiencing violence in the past year across most sites. This finding is consistent with the literature, which generally identifies young age as being associated with both victimization and perpetration of IPV (Harvey, Garcia-Moreno, & Butchart, 2007). Another pattern was that women who reported higher educational levels reported a lower lifetime prevalence of partner violence in general than those with less or no educational history. Other individual-level factors identified as increasing vulnerability for women included witnessing or experiencing violence as a child, heavy use of alcohol and other drugs, and having a higher education level than the partner.

Societal Perceptions of Violence and Acceptable Aggression

Perceptions of what constitutes violent behavior and whether that behavior is acceptable vary by country, context, and reason for violence. Despite differing definitions and contextual backgrounds, however, representative data across the world using behaviorally specific questions illustrate that violence against women by intimate partners is a nearly universal *phenomenon*.

The reasons behind how and why people develop differing perceptions of violence and the reasons for it are complex and deeply embedded in social and cultural constructions of gender, power relationships, and the ways masculinity and femininity are conceptualized, sustained, and enforced by social norms. Because the sociocultural acceptability of violence may influence perceptions of what people define as constituting violence or not, there has been a move toward asking about the experience of specific acts rather than asking about the experience of *abuse, violence,* or *rape,* all of which are terms open to interpretation. Use of terms like *abuse* may lead to gross underestimations of the level of IPV. For example, in the United States, a study showed that if one initially asked women attending a clinic for treatment of marital problems if they had been physically abused by their partner in the past year, only 6% of women reported they had. However, if they then were asked to check off whether their husband had engaged in specific acts of physical aggression in the past year, such as pushing, slapping, kicking, hitting, or beating, approximately 60% of the women reported having experienced such an act (O'Leary, Vivian, & Malone, 1992).

Some concepts are easier to break down into distinct, concrete behaviors than are others. For example, respondents in the United Republic of Tanzania, when asked to report whether they had ever forced a partner to have sex, interpreted that phrase as "holding down your partner to have intercourse" (Lary, Maman, Katebalila, & Mbwambo, 2004). That discrete behavior is not comprehensively representative of the concept of forced sex, which includes nonphysical types of force such as threat, intimidation, and economic pressure. Thus, it is very important to conduct initial, formative research at the outset of any instrument development to understand how best to phrase questions to ensure that items are valid (Ellsberg & Heise, 2005; Garcia-Moreno, Jansen, et al., 2005).

More evidence of differences in perceptions of abuse came from Malley-Morrison (2004), who asked subjects in 25 countries to define the concept of abuse. The definitions varied widely according to the social environment and, specifically, the culture and context with which respondents identified. In Saudi Arabia, a country whose political system and cultural identity are based on Islamic principles, many respondents defined *abuse* in terms of any transgression against Islam. In Somalia, 25% of a 40-person sample listed specific physical abuse behaviors like "hitting," "slapping," and "punching," but 15% gave answers related to not taking care of personal or familial responsibilities. Other responses included "not keeping one's word" and "not teaching children to respect others."

Although the focus of this chapter is not on the etiology of partner violence, it is important to note that global research findings show that in some contexts, violence is condoned and encouraged by societal concepts of masculinity. For example, Archer (2006) demonstrated that countries scoring low on measures of gender empowerment are more likely to have higher rates of intimate partner violence. Indeed, in some places, physical violence by a husband against his wife is expected and viewed as a necessary disciplinary method, even by women themselves (Jewkes et al., 2002). In many areas of the world, expectations that women be submissive and obedient toward their husbands allow for men to punish and "correct" their partners for wrongdoing (Ellsberg & Heise, 2005). Cross-cultural research also suggests that partner violence is often more pervasive in societies in which other types of violence are more common, such as in societies involved in military conflict or political struggles (Levinson, 1989).The WHO study assessed women's views on the acceptability of partner abuse. Women were given six situations and asked whether the man was justified in beating his wife. Respondents who considered the beating acceptable gave widely varying reasons, with the most accepted being the woman's infidelity and the second being her disobedience of the husband. Wide variation also existed as to whether the respondents felt that violence was ever justified. The starkest variation was between urban and rural settings: More than 75% of women in the urban settings of Brazil, Japan, Namibia, and Serbia and Montenegro agreed that no reason justified abuse by a partner in contrast to only a quarter of women in Bangladesh, Ethiopia, Peru, and Samoa (Garcia-Moreno, Jansen, et al., 2005). This acceptance of male IPV has been documented in other studies (Kishor & Johnson, 2004).

In almost all settings in the WHO study and across all reasons, abused women tended to report higher tolerance of violent behavior than did nonabused women. Explanations for this finding could be that either women who are in violent situations learn to accept violence as part of life or that women who perceive violence as normal may be more willing to enter or remain in relationships that include violence. Future analyses of the data will explore, among other things, whether levels of violence are higher in communities in which violence against women is more widely accepted (Garcia-Moreno, Jansen, et al., 2005).

WHO respondents also were asked about the acceptability of several reasons why a woman could refuse sex (e.g., the partner mistreats her, she is sick, he is drunk, she does not want to engage in sex). More responded that a woman could refuse sex when she was ill or when the partner was drunk or abusive than when the woman preferred not to have sex. Between 10% and

20% of women in the Bangladesh province, Ethiopia, the Peru province, Samoa, and the United Republic of Tanzania province did not feel women had the right to refuse sex under any of the circumstances (Garcia-Moreno, Jansen, et al., 2005).

CONCLUSION AND RECOMMENDATIONS FOR FUTURE EFFORTS

Although comparative analyses of rates of partner violence across countries indicate that some countries and communities have lower prevalence rates than others, any prevalence of partner violence is unacceptable and should be addressed. Existing data show violence against women by male partners to be a pervasive and global problem that is both a human rights violation and a public health problem. All countries should develop a multisectoral, multiagency response to IPV that gives priority to issues of primary prevention—that is, stopping the violence from happening in the first place. Primary prevention is critical to realistically tackle the problem in the long term, and health care providers, among others, can play a critical role in advocating for such efforts. More research is needed to identify and document effective interventions and strategies at all levels. Promising interventions currently exist and need to be promoted and evaluated to increase our understanding of how to effectively prevent and respond to this problem. In high prevalence settings, more focus may be needed on changing norms around masculinity and the acceptability of violence. In all situations, prevention and intervention strategies must be tailor made to the community and social context to be effective.

Development of public policy (in addition to law reform) is often seen as an endpoint in using research findings to make a difference. It is known, however, that simply creating policy or changing laws will not effect change in a society. Enforcement of that law and practical implementation of that policy are vital, and community members, as well as the police, judges, doctors, educators, clergy, and others, must understand the issues involved, challenge existing attitudes, and break the silence and stigma surrounding IPV. Attitude change among community members is often necessary before women and their families feel comfortable enough to come forward with concerns about IPV. The role of male leaders in this process is critical.

An important priority for future public policy efforts and for research is prevention, , and there are several promising areas for intervention. Early childhood interventions have been developed with children who witness or are themselves victims of violence, and school-based programs are available that promote social and emotional intelligence, build self-esteem, and teach nonviolent ways of resolving conflict (Gamache & Snapp, 1995; Jaffe, Wolfe, Crooks, Hughes, & Baker, 2004; Sudermann, Jaffe, & Hastings, 1994; Wolfe, Wekerle, & Scott, 1997).

Another set of promising interventions focus on changing cultural norms around masculinity and gender relationships. Mass media interventions have included soap operas and radio programs, such as Puntos de Encuentro in Nicaragua (see http://www.puntos.org.ni/English). Peer groups are another intervention method; examples are Promundo's Program H in Brazil (Barker, Nascimento, Segundo, & Pulerwitz, 2000), Tuelimishane in the United Republic of Tanzania (Lary, Maman, Mbwambo, & Katebalila, 2004), Stepping Stones in South Africa (Welbourn, 1995), and the Jovem para Jovem (Guy to Guy) project in Rio de Janeiro (Nascimento, Barker, & Marcondes, 2002). Most of these interventions have yet to be evaluated in a rigorous way. It is important to support action research that will develop the evidence base for more concerted and effective action in this field. Other strategies focus on women's empowerment, financial and otherwise; for example, the IMAGE study demonstrated a 50% reduction in IPV following an intervention with microfinance and a 10-hour gender training curriculum (Sisters for Life) in South Africa (Pronyk et al., 2006).

Designing effective interventions for such a multifaceted issue as IPV is complex. Interventions that prove successful in one situation or community may be ineffectual or even deleterious in another. An example can be found in applicability of microcredit intervention programs designed to help women increase their financial autonomy with the downstream goal of reducing IPV from their partners. Conflicting studies in Bangladesh have demonstrated a complicated relationship between IPV rates and women's membership in savings and credit groups, with some studies demonstrating decreasing levels of domestic violence among women who are members and other studies demonstrating increases (Rahman, 1999; Schuler, Hashemi, & Badal, 1998).

Increased support of research in this area is needed urgently. All sectors (e.g., health, education, legal, finance), disciplines, and actors have a role to play. It is important that clinicians and researchers take action based on what they know now as they continue to build an understanding of the factors that may increase vulnerability to or be protective against IPV and of the effectiveness of different interventions. Clinicians must continue to respond to the victims now, but they also need to strengthen efforts to prevent this violence from happening at all.

Violence against women, and IPV in particular, is now well recognized as both a global women's health concern and a human rights violation. Global initiatives to enhance women's status and health are critical in addressing IPV around the world; such initiatives include access to education, safe and well-remunerated employment, contraception, and access to health care, as well as equality under the law. Working with men and boys to challenge and change norms that promote a model of masculinity based on the exercise of power and abuse is equally important. All society needs to engage and address this issue as not just a women's concern, but one that affects all sectors of society.

REFERENCES

Abrahams, N., Jewkes, R., Hoffman, M., & Laubsher, R. (2004). Sexual violence against intimate partners in Cape Town: Prevalence and risk factors reported by men. *Bulletin of the World Health Organization, 82*, 330–337.

Archer, J. (2006). Cross-cultural differences in physical aggression between partners: A social–structural analysis. Personality and Social Psychology Review, 10, 133–153.

Bachman, R., & Saltzman, L. E. (1995). *National Crime Victimization Survey: Violence against women: Estimates from the redesigned survey* (Report No. NCJ 154348). Washington, DC: U.S. Department of Justice.

Barker, G., Nascimento, M., Segundo, M., & Pulerwitz, J. (2000). *How do we know if men have changed? Promoting and measuring attitude change with young men: Lessons from Program H in Latin America*. Washington, DC: Oxfam.

Centers for Disease Control and Prevention & ORC Macro. (2003). *Reproductive, maternal and child health in Eastern Europe and Eurasia: A comparative report*. Atlanta, GA: Author.

Ellsberg, M., & Heise, L. (2005). *Researching violence against women: A practical guide for researchers and activists*. Washington, DC: World Health Organization and Program for Appropriate Technology in Health.

Ellsberg, M., Heise, L., Pena, R., Agurto, S., & Winkvist, A. (2001). Researching domestic violence against women: Methodological and ethical considerations. *Studies in Family Planning, 32*, 1–16.

Gamache, D., & Snapp, S. (1995). Teach your children well: Elementary schools and violence prevention. In E. Peled, P. J. Jaffe, & J. Edleson (Eds.), *Ending the cycle of violence: Community responses to children of battered women* (pp. 209–231). Thousand Oaks, CA: Sage.

Garcia-Moreno, C., Heise, L., Jansen, H., Ellsberg, M., & Watts, C. (2005, November 25). Public health: Violence against women. *Science, 310*, 1282–1283.

Garcia-Moreno, C., Jansen, H., Ellsberg, M., Heise, L., & Watts, C. (2005). *WHO Multi-Country Study on Women's Health and Domestic Violence Against Women and initial results on prevalence, health outcomes and women's responses*. Geneva, Switzerland: World Health Organization.

Garcia-Moreno, C., Jansen, H., Ellsberg, M., Heise, L., & Watts, C. (2006, October 7). Prevalence of intimate partner violence: Findings from the WHO Multi-Country Study on Women's Health and Domestic Violence. *The Lancet, 368*, 1260–1269.

Harvey, A., Garcia-Moreno, C., & Butchart, A. (2007). *Primary prevention of intimate partner violence and sexual violence: Background paper for WHO expert meeting May 2–3, 2007*. Available at http://www.who.int/violence_injury_ prevention/publications/violence/IPV-SV.pdf

Hassan, F., Sadowski, L. S., Bangdiwala, S. I., Vizcarra, B., Ramiro, L., De Paula, C. S., et al. (2004). Physical intimate partner violence in Chile, Egypt, India and the Philippines. *Injury Control and Safety Promotion, 11*, 111–116.

Heise, L., Ellsberg, M., & Gottemoeller, M. (1999). *Ending violence against women*. Available at http://www.infoforhealth.org/pr/l11edsum.shtml#contents

Jaffe, P., Wolfe, D., Crooks, C., Hughes, R., & Baker, L. (2004). The fourth R: Developing healthy relationships through school-based interventions. In P. Jaffe, L. Baker, & A. Cunningham (Eds.), *Protecting children from domestic violence: Strategies for community intervention* (pp. 200–218). New York: Guilford Press.

Jewkes, R., Sen, P., & Garcia-Moreno, C. (2002). Sexual violence. In E. Krug, L. Dahlberg, J. Mercy, A. Zwi, & R. Lozano (Eds.), *World report on violence and health* (pp. 149–181). Geneva, Switzerland: World Health Organization.

Johnson, H., Ollus, N., & Nevala, S. (2007). *Violence against women: International perspectives*. New York: Springer.

Kishor, S., & Johnson, K. (2004). *Profiling domestic violence—A multi-country study*. Calverton, MD: ORC Macro.

Lary, H., Maman, S., Katebalila, M., & Mbwambo, J. (2004). Exploring the association between HIV and violence: Young people's experience with infidelity, violence, and forced sex in Dar es Salaam, Tanzania. *International Family Planning Perspectives, 30*, 200–206.

Lary, H., Maman, S., Mbwambo, J., & Katebalila, M. (2004). Working with young men to address violence and HIV in young women: A community-based intervention study in Dar es Salaam, Tanzania. *Sexual Health Exchange*. Available at http://www.kit.nl/frameset.asp?/ils/exchange_content/Default.asp&frnr=1

Levinson, D. (1989). *Violence in cross-cultural perspective*. Newbury Park, CA: Sage.

Malley-Morrison, K. (Ed.). (2004). *International perspectives on family violence and abuse: A cognitive ecological approach*. Mahwah, NJ: Erlbaum.

Maman, S., Mbwambo, J., Campbell, J., Hogan, M., Kilonzo, G., Weiss, E., & Sweat, M. (2002). HIV-1 positive women report more lifetime experiences with violence: Findings from a voluntary HIV-1 counseling and testing clinic in Dar es Salaam, Tanzania. *American Journal of Public Health, 92*, 1331–1337.

Markus, H., & Kitayama, S. (1991). Culture and the self: Implications for cognition, emotion, and motivation. *Psychological Review, 98*, 224–253.

Martin, S., Kilgallen, B., Tsui, A., Maitra, K., Singh, K., & Kupper, L. (1999). Sexual behaviors and reproductive health outcomes: Associations with wife abuse in India. *JAMA, 282*, 1967–1972.

Nascimento, M., Barker, G., & Marcondes, W. (2002, July). *Guy to guy project: Engaging young men in gender violence prevention and STI/AIDS* (Abstract no. E11676). Paper presented at the International AIDS Conference, Bangkok, Thailand.

O'Leary, K., Vivian, D., & Malone, J. (1992). Assessment of physical aggression against women in marriage: The need for multimodal assessment. *Behavioral Assessment, 14*, 5–14.

Pronyk, P. M., Hargreaves, J. R., Kim, J. C., Morison, L. A., Phetla, G., Watts, C., et al. (2006, December 2). Effect of a structural intervention for the prevention of intimate-partner violence and HIV in rural South Africa: A cluster randomized trial. *The Lancet, 368*, 1973–1983.

Rahman, A. (1999). Micro-credit initiatives for equitable and sustainable development: Who pays? *World Development, 27*, 67–82.

Resnick, H., Acierno, R., & Kilpatrick, D. (1997). Health impact of interpersonal violence: Medical and mental health outcomes. *Behavioral Medicine, 23*, 65–78.

Rhodes, K., & Levinson, W. (2003). Interventions for intimate partner violence against women. *JAMA, 289*, 601–605.

Rodriguez, M., Bauer, H., McLaughlin, E., & Grumbach, K. (1999). Screening and intervention for intimate partner abuse: Practices and attitudes of primary care physicians. *JAMA, 282*, 468–474.

Sadowski, L., Hunter, W., Bangdiwala, S., & Muñoz, S. (2004). The world studies of abuse in the family environment (WorldSAFE): A model of a multi-national study of family violence. *Injury Control and Safety Promotion, 11*, 81–90.

Schuler, S., Hashemi, S., & Badal, S. (1998). Men's violence against women in rural Bangladesh: Undermined or exacerbated by microcredit programmes? *Development in Practice, 8*, 148–156.

Sudermann, M., Jaffe, P. G., & Hastings, E. (1994). A.S.A.P.: A school-based anti-violence program. *Women's Voices: Journal of Women in Educational Administration, Ontario, 1*(1).

Wathen, N., & MacMillan, H. (2003). Interventions for violence against women. *JAMA, 289*, 589–600.

Watts, C., & Zimmerman, C. (2002, April 6). Violence against women: Global scope and magnitude. *The Lancet, 359*, 1232–1237.

Welbourn, A. (1995). *Stepping Stones: A training package in HIV/AIDS, gender issues, communication and relationship skills.* Oxford, England: Strategies for Hope.

Wierzbicka, A. (1986). Human emotions: Universal or culture-specific? *American Anthropologist, 88*, 584–594.

Wolfe, D., Wekerle, C., & Scott, K. (1997). *Alternatives to violence: Empowering youth to develop health relationships.* Thousand Oaks, CA: Sage.

World Health Organization. (2001). *Putting women first: Ethical and safety recommendations for research on domestic violence against women.* Geneva, Switzerland: Author.

World Health Organization. (2002). *World report on violence and health.* Geneva, Switzerland: Author.

II

ETIOLOGY

4

PSYCHOPATHOLOGICAL CORRELATES OF MALE AGGRESSION

L. KEVIN HAMBERGER AND AMY HOLTZWORTH-MUNROE

Intimate partner violence (IPV) has been a topic of great concern to social scientists, public health professionals, policymakers, clinicians, and battered women's advocates beginning with the focus of community activists as part of the early women's movement in the 1970s (Tjaden, 2004). One early analysis of the cause of IPV, particularly violence against women, focused on feminist analysis of sociopolitical factors that supported male domination and oppression of women (e.g., Schechter, 1982; Walker, 1979).

Related to male domination, a number of other sociopolitical factors have also contributed, directly or indirectly, to support of woman abuse. These include cultural systemic factors that have served to subordinate women; examples include entertainment forms that objectify women as sex objects, religious institutional beliefs and practices that subordinate women in both the family and society at large, and employment practices that condone unequal pay for equal work. Health care systems (including mental health care) historically rendered abuse victims invisible and/or pathologized victims with diagnostic labels suggesting victim blaming (e.g., masochism; e.g., Martin, 1987) rather than supporting victims in assessing their options and finding safety. Further, the criminal justice and family court systems also tradition-

ally failed to account for IPV and deliver appropriate consequences to perpetrators while providing relief to victims. It is against this backdrop that we
examine psychological characteristics of IPV perpetrators.

Early analyses suggested that abusive men were primarily gender war-
riors on the front lines of societal attempts to control women (e.g., Gondolf,
1987) and that abusive men were not different from other men, except for
their use of physical violence to control their partners (Saunders, 1987).
However, another analytic focus emerged from the psychotherapy and psychiatry fields and examined what it was about the man's psychological makeup
that would prompt him to batter his partner (e.g., Elbow, 1979), as researchers asked, "Who are these guys?" (Gondolf, 1988). While discussion of the
debate about the relative contributions of sociopolitical forces versus psychopathology to the etiology and maintenance of intimate partner violence
is often quite heated and would be interesting (e.g., Dutton, 1996; Dutton &
Nicholls, 2005), it is beyond the scope of the present chapter. Instead, we
focus on the psychopathological characteristics of men who perpetrate IPV.

Early reports of batterer characteristics were based primarily on clinical
observation of select patients who sought some form of psychotherapy (Elbow, 1979) or battered women's descriptions of their male partners' characteristics (Gondolf, 1988; Rosenbaum & O'Leary, 1981). One reason abusive
men initially were not studied directly is they were not readily available. Few
communities required arrest of domestic violence perpetrators, and few clinical
programs for treating abusive men existed until the late 1980s. Furthermore,
abusive men did not often volunteer for studies or treatment (Hamberger &
Hastings, 1986a). However, with the development of programs specializing
in the treatment of men who batter their female partners, such men became
increasingly available for study. The implementation and proliferation of
mandatory arrest laws for domestic violence resulted in even more men being court mandated to specialized batterer treatment programs (Hamberger
& Arnold, 1990). The increased availability of abusive men opened the door
for in-depth study of their characteristics.

Recent research with large community and national databases of
nonclinical samples, along with longitudinal cohort studies of nonclinical
samples, has begun to offer the field much information on the etiology and
risk factors for IPV. We agree with Straus (1999) that data from community
and national representative samples probably underrepresent clinical populations and thus have greater value for the development of prevention programs and policy. Given our interest in findings most likely to have direct
clinical implications for providers of direct services to batterers, as well as for
those who would develop innovative abuse abatement programs, we focus
primarily on studies of abusive individuals in clinical settings, such as batterer
treatment programs. We label these individuals *batterers*, not merely aggressive individuals. Also, our focus is on men, as too little research has been
conducted on partner-abusive women in clinical samples to draw meaning-

ful conclusions about the role of psychopathology in their use of partner violence.

Hamberger and Lohr (1989) and others (Dutton, 1996; Murphy & Eckhardt, 2005) have argued that study of psychological processes and psychopathology among battering men is a legitimate approach, as battering is a complex behavior governed by principles of learning and amenable to behavioral analysis and psychotherapeutic change processes. Study of psychopathology and psychological processes does not excuse the batterer for bad behavior. Rather, it may increase professionals' understanding of abuse and ways to prevent and end it. Indeed, as far back as 1989, Hamberger and Lohr discussed the value of conducting a psychological analysis of abusive behaviors and abusive persons for purposes of identifying appropriate targets of intervention while holding perpetrators responsible for their actions and for changing them, because abusive behaviors are self-generated. Perpetrators must assume responsibility for the legal, social, and relational consequences of their battering behaviors. By doing so, psychological analyses also invalidate personal excuses for abusive behaviors (e.g., the depression did not "make" him do it). Moreover, given that abusive men are born and develop in the sociopolitical matrix noted previously, it is understood that such behaviors develop within that context, leading to the need to address the problem of IPV in a holistic manner, working to change society while simultaneously working to help individual abusers change their behaviors.

In this chapter, we describe and discuss psychological characteristics of men who batter their intimate female partners. In the first section, we describe research that attempts to differentiate abusive men from nonabusive men in an effort to highlight those psychological characteristics that are related to abuse perpetration. In the second section, we describe and discuss research that seeks to highlight the heterogeneity of male batterers by reviewing research on batterer typologies. We then review selected large sample and longitudinal cohort studies that have sought to isolate risk factors in the etiology of IPV. We conclude the chapter by proposing mechanisms by which psychopathology leads to IPV, and associated clinical implications.

PSYCHOLOGICAL CHARACTERISTICS OF MEN WHO BATTER THEIR PARTNERS

Study of the psychological characteristics of male IPV perpetrators has proceeded along two primary paths. One approach has been to compare cohorts of abusive men with comparison groups of nonviolent men who are in either distressed or nondistressed relationships. This case comparison approach helps answer the question of whether and how abusive men differ from nonviolent men but typically does not highlight the heterogeneity of the violent men. A second approach has attempted to highlight the diversity and heterogeneity of abusive men by identifying different "types" or subgroups based on psychological and/or behavioral variables. Using these two approaches, researchers have learned a considerable amount about abusive men that can help to determine risk factors for intimate partner abuse.

Case Comparison Studies of Abusive and Nonabusive Men

In the first line of research on abusive men, researchers have compared abusive men with nonviolent men to elucidate characteristics that are unique to, or at least more typical of, abusive men. Such studies have been conducted along a variety of dimensions of psychopathology, including (a) anger and hostility and (b) alcohol and drug abuse as two primary examples.

Anger and Hostility

Several early studies on batterer characteristics showed that some men who batter their partners, though not all, struggle with anger and hostility. Therefore, the conclusions one can reach about anger problems among batterers are not as simple as one might expect based on a general notion that aggressive people are also angry people (Murphy & Eckhardt, 2005). For example, in some studies, abusive men also scored higher than nonabusive men on measures of state anger (i.e., anger at the moment) and trait anger (i.e., the tendency to become angry; e.g., Barbour, Eckhardt, Davison, & Kassinove, 1998). In contrast, other studies have revealed low levels of anger in men who batter compared with nonviolent controls (e.g., Hastings & Hamberger, 1988). In addition, other study findings suggest that only some batterers evidence anger problems (e.g., Hamberger & Hastings, 1986a; Hamberger, Lohr, Bonge, & Tolin, 1996) or that certain types of violent men, particularly those with borderline personality characteristics (e.g., Dutton, Starzomski, & Ryan, 1996; Hamberger & Hastings, 1986b; Holtzworth-Munroe, Rehman, et al., 2000; Tweed & Dutton, 1998) or antisocial personality characteristics (Holtzworth-Munroe, Rehman, et al., 2000) have the highest levels of anger. Finally, some researchers find differing patterns of anger experiences within samples of violent men. For example, Hershorn and Rosenbaum (1991) showed that batterers experienced and expressed anger and hostility in different ways. Men with undercontrolled hostility were more frequently violent with their partners and more violent generally in their lives. Men with overcontrolled hostility showed less frequent episodes of violence, but the episodes were more severe and confined to their intimate relationships.

Despite these complexities in the findings across studies, recent reviews and a meta-analysis reached the conclusion that overall, among men, there is an association between anger and physical aggression toward a partner (see Eckhardt, Norlander, & Deffenbacher, 2004; Holtzworth-Munroe & Clements, 2007; Stith, Smith, Penn, Ward, & Tritt, 2004). In addition, case comparison studies have also shown that abusive men are more hostile than nonviolent men. Abusive men show levels of hostility similar to those exhibited by generally violent men but higher than nonviolent men (Maiuro, Cahn, Vitaliano, Wagner, & Zegree, 1988). Further, batterers show different types of hostility compared with nonviolent men. For example, compared with criminally violent men who are not maritally violent, abusive men exhibit higher overall hostility but lower suspicion (Barnett, Fagan, & Booker, 1991). Compared with nonviolent men, abusers are more likely to exhibit hostility directed at themselves and toward others and lower anger control (e.g., Barbour et al., 1998).

Although indirectly related to anger and hostility, a number of studies have begun to investigate the types of attributions abusive men make, compared with nonviolent men, in situations related to relationship conflict. This research provides insight into how an abusive man labels and interprets partner behavior that may lead to highly negative feelings, including anger. Holtzworth-Munroe and Hutchinson (1993) reported that compared with nonviolent men, abusive men are more likely to attribute negative wife behaviors to the wife's negative intent. Moreover, compared with nonabusive men, abusive men tend to attribute negative partner behavior as attributable to her selfishness and blameworthiness (Tonizzo, Howells, Day, Reidpath, & Froyand, 2000). Other research has shown that abusive men tend to make these hostile attributions regarding partner intent in situations that are moderately provocative. In highly provocative situations, nonabusive men also make such negative attributions. Hence, in situations where "anybody would be upset," both violent and nonviolent men make similar types of attributions. But in less intense situations, abusive men continue to react as though their partner "did it on purpose," whereas nonviolent men do not (Moore, Eisler, & Franchina, 2000).

Alcohol and Other Drug Abuse

In a review of the literature on the relationship between alcohol use and battering, Conner and Ackerley (1994) found that alcohol abuse was observed among men who batter their partners at rates approaching 60% to 70%, and in their meta-analyses, Stith et al. (2004) found a strong effect size for the relationship between male IPV offenders and both alcohol and drug use. More recently, Foran and O'Leary (2008) reported on a meta-analysis of the relationship between alcohol use and intimate partner violence. The authors reported that overall, there is a significant relationship between alcohol and IPV. This observed relationship holds across different methods of aggression measurement and levels of aggression (i.e., mild/moderate or severe). Binge drinking and heavy drinking were more highly related to IPV than drinking frequency. In addition, studies that compared clinical samples and nonclinical samples showed the largest effect sizes of the role of alcohol in IPV. Foran and O'Leary speculated that the methodology of comparing extreme ends of the continuum of IPV results in a stronger association than would be expected from the general population as a whole. Nevertheless, these findings are consistent with findings reported in chapter 10 of this volume that the percentage of men who had been drinking when aggressive differed markedly between community and clinical samples.

Heyman, O'Leary, and Jouriles (1995) discovered, from longitudinal research, that the role of alcohol in predicting partner violence changes over the course of the relationship. From premarriage to 6 months after marriage, alcohol use was positively associated with serious partner violence. After 18 months of marriage, alcohol use interacted with aggressive personality style to predict level of marital violence. Fals-Stewart (2003) reported, in another longitudinal study, that on days when abusive men were drinking, the odds of them perpetrating partner violence were 8 times higher than on days they did not drink alcohol. The odds of severe marital violence on drinking days were even higher—11 times higher than on days of no drinking—suggesting that among abusive men, episodes of drinking increase the risk of a violent event.

Other research suggests that it is the man's expectations of aggression following drinking that mediate the relationship between alcohol use and partner violence (e.g., Field, Caetano, & Nelson, 2004). Specifically, expectations that aggressive behavior will follow alcohol consumption increased the odds of partner violence by a factor of 3.2. Recent research with clinical samples of abusive men has also shown the complex relationship between problem drinking and IPV. For example, Snow, Sullivan, Swan, Tate, and Klein (2006) observed that abusive men who were problem drinkers used more avoidance coping strategies and fewer problem-solving strategies than abusive men who were not problem drinkers. Furthermore, use of avoidance coping strategies was directly related to greater physical and psychological abuse, which was, in turn, associated with higher levels of injury to female victims.

Typologies of Abusive Men

A second line of research has served to identify and highlight the variability among abusive men along various dimensions of personality and psychopathology. A number of typologies of abusive men have been advanced, including those based on violence profiles, such as family-only versus general violence (Shields, McCall, & Hanneke, 1988) or proactive versus reactive violence (Chase, O'Leary, & Heyman, 2001) and those based on psychopathology (Hamberger & Hastings, 1986b). In the present chapter, we focus on the typology Holtzworth-Munroe and Stuart (1994) described, because it helps describe the relationship between type of violence and psychopathology. Holtzworth-Munroe and Stuart reviewed batterer typology research and determined three main subtypes— borderline/dysphoric (BD) batterers, generally violent/antisocial (GVA) batterers, and family-only (FO) batterers. Holtzworth-Munroe, Meehan, Herron, Rehman, and Stuart (2000) provided empirical support for this typology, as have others (e.g., Hamberger et al., 1996).

Borderline/Dysphoric Batterers

Across studies, BD batterers have been described as negativistic/dependent (Hamberger et al., 1996) or schizoidal/borderline (Hamberger & Hastings, 1986b), with their psychopathology probably reflecting the continuum of borderline personality organization more than a particular diagnostic category (Dutton & Starzomski, 1993). Such men are capable of appearing pleasant if brooding, at times charming and effusive. They can quickly and intensely establish an intimate level of relating. Their partners frequently comment on how, on first meeting, the couple spent hours, long into the night, discussing their lives and experiences, leading the woman to believe that he was a man in touch with his feelings. Sometimes, such men also appear to be lost and enlist the aid of the woman. These men typically appear dependent on their intimate partners for a sense of identity but experience tremendous conflict between their dependence and their fear of being "taken over" or engulfed by her. Others may view these men as unpredictably moody—clingy and fawning one moment and angry and rejecting the next. Their partners frequently describe these men as having a "Dr. Jekyll–Mr. Hyde" personality.

BD men are typically hypersensitive to subtle interpersonal slights that others would not notice. For example, a BD man may interpret his partner's absence from the house when he returns from work as "proof" of her "screwing around." The batterer's experience of rejection can result in a spectrum of emotions, including anger and rage. These men constituted about 18.5% of a clinical sample of batterers studied by Hamberger et al. (1996).

BD batterers exhibit a number of other features. Among the batterer subtypes, BD batterers commit fairly high levels of violence toward their partners, significantly higher than nonpathological, FO batterers (e.g., Hamberger et al., 1996; Holtzworth-Munroe, Meehan, et al., 2000). Tweed and Dutton (1998) described the violence of BD batterers as more impulsive than that of GVA batterers. BD batterers also show fairly high rates of annual police contact for a variety of law violations.

BD batterers have been observed to have higher rates of alcohol and drug abuse than FO batterers, although they may (e.g., Hamberger et al., 1996) or may not (e.g., Holtzworth-Munroe, Meehan, Herron, Rehman, & Stuart, 2003) differ from GVA batterers on such measures. BD batterers appear to be the most depressed and suicidal and are likely to suffer high levels of anger proneness. Cognitively, these batterers tend to express a high need for approval, jealousy, and pessimism about their ability to change negative behavior patterns. They may have fearful and/or preoccupied attachment styles (e.g., Dutton, Saunders, Starzomski, & Bartholomew, 1994; Holtzworth-Munroe, Meehan, et al., 2000). Hence, BD batterers appear to enter intimate relationships with concerns about rejection and abandonment, feel highly anxious, and look to their intimate partners to provide them with a sense of self-worth, validation, and stability, while simultaneously fearing being engulfed and controlled. BD batterers report having witnessed more parental violence than did FO batterers. Further, compared with other subtypes, BD batterers report high rates of experiencing abuse as a child (Hamberger et al., 1996; Johnson et al., 2006), from both mother and father (Holtzworth-Munroe et al., 2000) and experiencing more rejection by their parents and less parental warmth than did FO batterers (Dutton et al., 1996).

Despite a great deal of interest in recent years in understanding borderline personality processes in men who batter their partners (e.g., Dutton & Starzomski, 1993; Dutton, Starzomski, & Ryan, 1996; Tweed & Dutton, 1998), it should be noted that there are some differences across specific typologies in their exact characterization of the BD batterer. For example, some of Dutton's (2006) characterizations of the BD batterer overlap with those given here for the FO batterer. At the other end of the spectrum, some recent evidence suggests that BD batterers may not significantly differ from GVA batterers on key personality and pathology variables. For example, Waltz, Babcock, Jacobson, and Gottman (2000) were unable to discern unique types consisting of GVA batterers and BD batterers. Although some overlap between these two subtypes is expected (e.g., both GVA and BD men should score high on measures of impulsivity and related problems, such as substance abuse), in theory there should be significant group differences on other variables (e.g., BD men should be distinguished by attachment problems). Resolution of such issues awaits future research.

Generally Violent/Antisocial Batterers

Despite some recent debate regarding whether antisocial and narcissistic batterers are separate clusters (Johnson et al., 2006), past studies with larger samples suggest it is appropriate to focus on the GVA batterer subtype. A primary characteristic of the GVA batterer is antisocial and aggressive behavior. On a psychological level, these men are characterized as being self-centered, self-absorbed, and lacking in empathy. They may also view others, including intimate partners, essentially as objects, possessions to be used for the gratification of the perpetrator's needs and ends. For example, after his partner left him, one GVA batterer commented, "I finally got rid of her. No big deal. I can just go out and get me another one."

The GVA batterer may exhibit reciprocity and mutuality, but for his own benefit rather than for the benefit of the relationship or another person. Hence, he may buy his potential partner expensive gifts to impress her with his generosity and status, not as a sign of his affection. Such individuals are typically seen as charming and interesting in superficial interactions. To a potential intimate partner, the GVA man appears confident and exciting. He may impress his potential partner as protective and caring, particularly if she is vulnerable. As the relationship progresses, the GVA batterer often manipulates and imposes his values and perceptions on his partner. He sets the rules, feels entitled to have them complied with, and claims the right to determine and mete out punishment when they are violated. Hamberger et al. (1996) observed that GVA batterers composed 26.5% of their clinical batterer sample.

GVA batterers commit high levels of violence toward their partners, often equal to or more severe than BD batterers, and considerably more severe than FO batterers. Further, GVA batterers commit more severe sexual battery toward their partners than the other two subgroups. As implied in the subgroup name, in comparison with the other subgroups, GVA batterers exhibit more general violence outside of intimate relationships. Further, GVA batterers experience significantly more arrests than the other subtypes. GVA men also report having more criminally deviant friends than the other batterer subtypes, especially FO batterers.

GVA batterers experience high levels of substance abuse. They may exhibit fairly low levels of depression, although the findings are mixed (e.g., Hamberger et al., 1996; Tweed & Dutton, 1998). On measures of irrational cognitions, GVA batterers appear to view their emotional problems and negative emotional reactions as the fault of, and as controlled by, external sources, such as other people doing things they do not like (Lohr, Hamberger, & Bonge, 1988). Holtzworth-Munroe, Meehan, et al. (2000) found GVA batterers to exhibit a dismissing attachment style, especially compared with FO batterers, and lower levels of spouse-specific dependency than BD batterers. Although findings are mixed (Hamberger et al., 1996), in some studies GVA men were found to have high levels of anger (e.g., Holtzworth-Munroe, Rehman, & Herron, 2000).

Family-Only/Nonpathological Batterers

Across studies using different measures of psychopathology, a group of nonpathological batterers has been observed (Holtzworth-Munroe & Stuart, 1994). *Nonpathological* batterers are typically labeled so not because their violence is "normal" and not deviant, but because they rarely show evidence of psychopathology on psychological measures. Nonpathological batterers are the stereotypical "man next door." They live conventional lives, blend into their community's fabric, and casually appear to be normal.

A variation among nonpathological batterers is men who show elevated scores on measures of passive dependency or compulsive personality features. Such batterers typically have low self-esteem and engage in passive and ingratiating ways. They may lack assertive skills for setting boundaries or negotiating conflict. Thus, such a man may subordinate his rights in conflicts to "keep the peace" while building internal resentments that occasionally erupt in aggressive, rebellious outbursts of hostility and physical aggression. The batterer with a compulsive personality style also typically lacks confidence in self-assertion but has adapted by developing adherence to a set of rules. Although they may view themselves as disciplined and reliable, others may see them as rigid, rule-bound, and unexpressive, though highly conventional, predictable, polite, and respectful.

The challenge for such a man is coping with the inherent differences between partners in intimate relationships. For example, the man might hold the belief that after work, everyone should stay home and engage in "family" activities. If his partner belongs to organizations that meet in the evening, he might view his partner's behavior as violations of the rules, resulting in his feelings of anger and anxiety. Such men use violence to reduce their immediate sense of anxiety and develop a pattern of violence and coercion to maintain control over others as a means of adhering to their "rules." The violence may escalate to the point of police intervention and referral to batterer treatment. Hamberger et al. (1996) observed that nonpathological batterers composed 41.9% of their clinical sample.

Compared with the other two batterer subgroups, FO batterers appear to confine their violence mainly to their intimate relationships and families, and their levels of partner violence are lower than those observed among BD and GVA batterers. Compared with the other groups, FO batterers engage in the lowest amounts of general violence and criminal behavior. Further, FO batterers show the lowest levels of depression, suicidal thoughts or attempts, anger, jealousy, and alcohol and drug abuse.

Typology Summary

Typology research has an advantage in highlighting the heterogeneity of characteristics of abusive men. Relevant to this chapter, much of that heterogeneity exists in psychological characteristics and types of psychopathology. The approach, however, has limitations. Many typologies have been offered, and the details of descriptions of the main subtypes often differ across typologies (e.g., see Dutton, 2006, for some different characterizations of BD batterers); some of these differences reflect theoretically different constructions of batterer subtypes, whereas others may result from variations in the samples examined and measures used across studies. In addition, although little data exist on the issue, there is some concern about the stability of typologies; this issue requires further examination in future research (Holtzworth-Munroe & Meehan, 2004). Also, typology research categorizes men based on features such as individual characteristics and violence, but such features may occur, in nature, along a continuum. Importantly, despite some promise for the clinical utility of batterer typologies (Lohr, Bonge, Witte, Hamberger, & Langhinrichsen-Rohling, 2005), they have so far had limited clinical application.

RISK FACTOR PREDICTION OF
INTIMATE PARTNER VIOLENCE BY MEN

Researchers have increasingly begun to examine how the many variables previously elucidated may combine to allow predictive statements about risk of perpetrating IPV. Many of these studies have included large community-based samples or developmental cohorts, but not clinical samples. Thus, it may be impossible to generalize directly from such community samples to clinical populations (Straus, 1999). Some of the community samples, however, have included individuals who perpetrated severe levels of partner violence (Danielson, Moffitt, Caspi, & Silva, 1998; Pan, Neidig, & O'Leary, 1994) or subgroups that are involved in "clinical" levels of partner violence (Ehrensaft, Moffitt, & Caspi, 2004). For example, in a randomly selected community sample of parents, 14% of the men were severely physically aggressive toward their partners (Smith Slep & O'Leary, 2005). Thus, we briefly review a few such example studies.

Hanson, Cadsky, Harris, and Lalonde (1997) found that abuse was associated with high levels of violence victimization during childhood, antisocial personality disorder, personal distress, marital distress, impulsivity, and positive attitudes toward violence against women. Furthermore, Hanson et al. reported a linear relationship between the latter variables and severity of violence. In a study of more than 15,000 members of the U.S. Army, Pan et al. (1994) observed that both moderate and severe IPV was predicted by lower income, alcohol problems, marital discord, and depression. Similar to the observations of Hanson et al., Pan et al. found that severe IPV was predicted by the lowest income levels, the most marital discord, and the highest levels of depression. In addition, severe IPV was predicted by perpetrator drug abuse.

Using a developmental cohort sample, Danielson and colleagues (1998) also observed that partner violence was related to *psychopathology*, defined as some type of diagnosable psychiatric disorder. In particular, the authors reported that nearly half of all participants involved in *domestic violence*, defined as any physical violence as measured by the Conflict Tactics Scale (Straus, 1979), had a psychiatric disorder, and one third of those with a psychiatric disorder were involved in domestic violence. Specifically, perpetrators and nonperpetrators of partner violence had a psychiatric diagnosis prevalence of 58.5% and 34.2%, respectively. For severe violence, the prevalence rate for diagnosis was 88.0% for perpetrators versus 36.3% for nonperpetrators.

Several research groups investigating the role of childhood, adolescent, and adult psychopathology in predicting adult partner violence using community and developmental cohort samples have reported consistent findings. From such studies, we have learned that intimate partner violence is predicted by anxiety and depression (Danielson et al., 1998; Ehrensaft, Moffitt, & Caspi, 2006); substance use, including alcohol abuse (Ehrensaft et al.,

2006); and antisocial personality disorder (Andrews, Foster, Capaldi, & Hops, 2000; Danielson et al., 1998; Ehrensaft et al., 2006).

RELATIONSHIP OF PSYCHOPATHOLOGY TO PSYCHOLOGICAL AND PHYSICAL AGGRESSION

The data reviewed in this chapter show that men who batter their partners are a heterogeneous group. Although abusive men cannot be characterized by a particular profile, many of them do show clear signs of diagnosable psychopathology, including both disordered personality styles and pathology related to depression, anxiety, anger dysregulation, and substance abuse. Nevertheless, unless the observed psychopathology can be related to dimensions of abuse and violence, such descriptions, although interesting, may be clinically useless. Fortunately, a number of long-term developmental studies have begun to investigate the relationship between early childhood and adolescent experiences and risk factors for domestic violence (see chap. 5 of this volume for a review of these background factors).

In general, men who use aggression against their intimate partners are more likely than nonviolent men to have grown up in homes with aversive family communication (Andrews et al., 2000), parental violence (Ehrensaft et al., 2003), incompetent or punitive parenting (Capaldi & Clark, 1998; Ehrensaft et al., 2003), and abuse and maltreatment (Ehrensaft et al., 2003; Kessler, Molnar, Feurer, & Appelbaum, 2001). Such individuals often exhibit behavior problems in childhood (Ehrensaft et al., 2003), as well as adolescent antisocial disorder or other disinhibitory and personality deviance (Andrews et al., 2000; Capaldi & Clark, 1998; Ehrensaft et al., 2004; Giordano, Millhollin, Cernkovich, Pugh, & Rudolph, 1999) and adolescent psychiatric disorder (Ehrensaft et al., 2006). These characteristics, in turn, predict adult domestic violence, yielding a variety of individual risk factors related to psychopathology for male perpetration of IPV. In their recent meta-analysis, Stith et al. (2004) listed the following such variables as having strong effect sizes (listed here in decreasing order of strength): use of emotional–verbal abuse and forced sex, illicit drug use, attitudes condoning violence, traditional sex role ideology, anger and hostility, history of partner abuse, alcohol use, depression, and jealousy.

Dutton and colleagues have studied the relationship between specific aspects of psychopathology among male batterers and abusive behavior (Dutton et al., 1996; Dutton & Starzomski, 1993). Although Dutton used cross-sectional research methods, thus limiting our understanding of causation, his findings are nevertheless instructive. For example, these researchers demonstrated that compared with nonviolent men, abusive men reported growing up in homes characterized by paternal rejection, lack of maternal warmth, and abuse. As adults, compared with nonviolent men, abusive men scored higher on measures of borderline personality organization, anger, fearful attachment style, and trauma symptoms. Dutton referred to this complex of characteristics as the *abusive personality*.

Dutton et al. (1996) also observed the latter characteristics to be significantly correlated with measures of physical and emotional abuse. For example, components of borderline personality organization and anger accounted for 50% of the variance in wives' reports of their partners' use of dominance or isolation tactics and 35% of the variance in the husbands' use of emotional abuse. Dimensions of anger and borderline personality organization accounted for 18% of the variance in measures of physical violence. Hence, psychopathology predicts forms and severity of psychological and physical abuse.

As reviewed earlier, researchers have demonstrated and catalogued the various forms of psychopathology among batterers. However, we do not yet understand how such psychopathology, at the level of the individual, is translated into violent actions in specific dyadic situations. As one example of a possible mechanism, social information processing models suggest that psychopathology leads to misinterpretations of wife behavior, which may escalate a marital conflict situation into violence (Holtzworth-Munroe, 2000). For example, borderline personality characteristics may lead a man to be hypervigilant to criticism and rejection, resulting in his misperceiving his wife's actions as threats to the relationship and as having been inflicted with hostile intent. Given such interpretations, a man with borderline personality characteristics might react to such situations with violence, perhaps as a result of emotional dysregulation. More careful testing of models that help to translate gross-level descriptions of psychopathology into specific situational and interaction level explanations of violence awaits future research attention, but seems likely to be a fruitful direction.

PRACTICE IMPLICATIONS

Despite the large amount of research conducted describing the psychological characteristics of men who batter their partners, little work has been done applying the knowledge gained to clinical intervention strategies to end partner violence. A few studies have attempted to link psychopathology to treatment outcome measures such as recidivism and premature termination. For example, Hamberger and Hastings (1990) found that self-report of substance abuse and narcissistic personality style predicted violence recidivism within 1 year of treatment completion. A number of researchers have found that borderline personality traits and alcohol and drug abuse predict treatment dropout (Daley & Pelowski, 2000).

Considering typologies, an example study by Eckhardt, Holtzworth-Munroe, Norlander, Sibley, and Cahill (in press) found that BD and GVA batterers were the most likely to drop out of treatment (91% of GVA and 62% of BD men, vs. 23% of FO men, dropped out) and to commit new acts of partner violence or be arrested after beginning treatment. Gondolf and co-workers have studied and reported on predictors of treatment outcome from a large, multisite evaluation of batterer treatment (e.g., Gondolf & Jones, 2001; Jones & Gondolf, 2001). Key findings are that psychopathology, generally, and *alcohol abuse*, defined as drunkenness during the follow-up interval in which violence occurred, significantly predicted violent recidivism (Jones & Gondolf, 2001). Further, Gondolf and Jones (2001) reported that psychopathology predicted premature dropout from batterer treatment. Moreover, while program completion was found to decrease rates of reassault, the effect of program completion was greatest for men with no psychopathology and very small and inconsistent for men with psychopathology (Jones, D'Agostino, Gondolf, & Heckert, 2004). Thus, psychopathology seems to play a role in the effectiveness of batterer treatment. As Snow et al. (2006) pointed out, one implication of these findings is that abusive men with coexisting psychopathology may need different treatment approaches to assist them in ending their violent and abusive behaviors.

It would seem natural that elucidation of psychopathology among batterers would lead directly to treatments designed to reduce such pathology. However, this has not happened consistently in the batterer treatment field. Reasons have been advanced for this seeming disconnect between batterer psychopathology and batterer treatment. For example, the research on batterer psychopathology has not demonstrated a functional, cause–effect relationship between pathology and partner violence. Some work has been done attempting to integrate partner violence treatment with alcohol and drug abuse treatments. Because most substances are not viewed as causing partner violence, however, prevailing thinking in the field, particularly among those who take a sociopolitical view of partner violence, is that substance abuse treatment, by itself, is insufficient to adequately and effectively treat partner violence.

The idea that men's violence against their partners is driven, in part, by psychopathology and that its amelioration should include therapy that targets the psychopathology has similarly met with resistance. Dutton and Nicholls (2005) described the controversy between feminist advocates and proponents of including psychological analysis in our understanding of partner violence. Thus, treatment has continued to focus on social control of batterers and providing psychoeducational programs to help them take responsibility for their violent and abusive behavior, understand the gender-related power dynamics of their use of physical and psychological violence, and develop skills and strategies for creating a safe, nonsexist, egalitarian relationship with their partners.

Unfortunately, there is little evidence for the effectiveness of the predominant model of partner violence treatment, characterized by profeminist analysis of abuse and development of nonabusive cognitive and behavioral relationship skills. Two meta-analyses of batterer treatment outcome research have shown treatment to have a low effect size (Babcock, Green, & Robie, 2004; Feder & Wilson, 2005). Indeed, Babcock et al. (2004) concluded that, on average, batterer treatment results in a 5% decrease in recidivism. Feder and Wilson (2005) used more conservative criteria for their meta-analysis and concluded that current batterer treatment models are ineffective.

The consistent finding that men who batter their partners are a heterogeneous group, with varying levels of psychopathology, calls for a move away from "one size fits all" treatment approaches to models that emphasize pretreatment evaluation of therapy needs and development of individualized treatment plans. Although little work has been done in this area, Murphy and Eckhardt (2005) described a model for conducting in-depth individual assessments, developing individual case conceptualizations, and executing individualized treatment plans, primarily from a cognitive–behavioral perspective. A major challenge to taking such an approach is development of a sufficient workforce to meet the needs of batterers. Alternatively, the challenge will be to develop methods that emphasize the attainment of individual treatment goals within the context of group treatment settings.

CONCLUSION

Over the past 2 decades, a considerable amount of work has been done to elucidate psychological characteristics that differentiate men who batter their partners from those who do not. Such research has focused on personality characteristics, psychopathology, alcohol and drug abuse, family of origin experiences, and violence profiles. Virtually all of these variables differentiate abusive from nonabusive men, with abusive men typically showing more problems, higher levels of pathology, and poorer premorbid functioning. Furthermore, abusive men appear to be a heterogeneous group, as research has repeatedly demonstrated that there is no single "batterer profile." Nevertheless, these variables seem to be related to forms and frequency of domestic violence.

The role of psychopathology in the causes and maintenance of domestic violence remains to be further elucidated. Some recent longitudinal studies are beginning to show how developmental processes that lead to deviant personality processes also predict adult domestic violence. More work needs to be done to further elucidate the mechanisms by which psychopathology translates into partner violence. Finally, more work needs to be done to determine the role of psychopathology and its treatment in the reduction and elimination of domestic violence among perpetrators.

It appears that we presently are at a crossroads in the batterer treatment field, challenged to find new and innovative treatment models that hold promise to effectively treat domestic violence perpetrators. As Hamberger and Hastings (1988) noted nearly 2 decades ago, psychopathology must be viewed as part of the complex, multicausal pathway leading men to batter their partners. It may also be that consideration of psychopathology in treatment of men who batter their partners will be part of the solution.

REFERENCES

Andrews, J. A., Foster, S. L., Capaldi, D., & Hops, H. (2000). Adolescent and family predictors of physical aggression, communication, and satisfaction in young adult couples: A prospective analysis. *Journal of Consulting and Clinical Psychology, 68*, 195–208.

Babcock, J. C., Green, C. E., & Robie, C. (2004). Does batterers' treatment work? A meta-analytic review of domestic violence treatment. *Clinical Psychology Review, 23*, 123–153.

Barbour, K. A., Eckhardt, C. I., Davison, G. C., & Kassinove, H. (1998). The experience and expression of anger in maritally violent and maritally discordant–nonviolent men. *Behavior Therapy, 29*, 173–191.

Barnett, O. W., Fagan, R. W., & Booker, J. M. (1991). Hostility and stress as mediators of aggression in violent men. *Journal of Family Violence, 6*, 217–241.

Capaldi, D. M., & Clark, S. (1998). Prospective family predictors of aggression toward female partners of at-risk young men. *Developmental Psychology, 34*, 1175–1188.

Chase, K. A., O'Leary, K. D., & Heyman, R. E. (2001). Characterizing partner-violent men within the reactive–proactive typology model. *Journal of Consulting and Clinical Psychology, 69*, 567–572.

Conner, K. R., & Ackerly, G. D. (1994). Alcohol-related battering: Developing treatment strategies. *Journal of Family Violence, 9*, 143–155.

Daly, J. E., & Pelowski, S. (2000). Predictors of dropout among men who batter: A review of studies with implications for research and practice. *Violence and Victims, 15*, 137–160.

Danielson, K. K., Moffitt, T. E., Caspi, A., & Silva, P. A. (1998). Comorbidity between abuse of an adult and *DSM–III–R* disorders: Evidence from an epidemiological study. *American Journal of Psychiatry, 155*, 131–133.

Dutton, D. G. (1996). Patriarchy and wife assault: The ecological fallacy. In L. K. Hamberger & C. Renzetti (Eds.), *Domestic partner abuse* (pp. 125–152). New York: Springer.

Dutton, D. G. (2006). *The abusive personality: Violence and control in intimate relationships* (2nd ed.). New York: Guilford Press.

Dutton, D. G., & Nicholls, T. L. (2005). The gender paradigm in domestic violence research and theory: The conflict of theory and data. *Aggression and Violent Behavior, 10*, 680–714.

Dutton, D. G., Saunders, K., Starzomski, A., & Bartholomew, K. (1994). Intimacy anger and insecure attachments as precursors of abuse in intimate relationships. *Journal of Applied Social Psychology, 24*, 1367–1386.

Dutton, D. G., & Starzomski, A. J. (1993). Borderline personality in perpetrators of psychological and physical abuse. *Violence and Victims, 8*, 327–337.

Dutton, D. G., Starzomski, A. J., & Ryan, L. (1996). Antecedents of abusive personality and abusive behavior in wife assaulters. *Journal of Family Violence, 11*, 113–132.

Eckhardt, C., Holtzworth-Munroe, A., Norlander, B., Sibley, A., & Cahill, M. (2008). Readiness to change, partner violence subtypes, and treatment outcomes among men in treatment for partner assault. *Violence and Victims, 23*, 446–475.

Eckhardt, C., Norlander, B., & Deffenbacher, J. (2004). The assessment of anger and hostility: A critical review. *Aggression and Violent Behavior, 9*, 17–43.

Ehrensaft, M. K., Cohen, P., Brown, J., Smailes, E., Chen, H., & Johnson, J. G. (2003). Intergenerational transmission of partner violence: A 20-year prospective study. *Journal of Consulting and Clinical Psychology, 71*, 741–753.

Ehrensaft, M. K., Moffitt, T. E., & Caspi, A. (2004). Clinically abusive relationships in an unselected birth cohort: Men's and women's participation and developmental antecedents. *Journal of Abnormal Psychology, 113*, 258–270.

Ehrensaft, M. K., Moffitt, T. E., & Caspi, A. (2006). Is domestic violence followed by an increased risk of psychiatric disorders among women but not among men? A longitudinal cohort study. *American Journal of Psychiatry, 163*, 885–892.

Elbow, M. (1979). Theoretical considerations of violent marriages. *Social Casework, 58*, 515–526.

Fals-Stewart, W. (2003). The occurrence of partner physical aggression on days of alcohol consumption: A longitudinal study. *Journal of Consulting and Clinical Psychology, 71*, 41–52.

Feder, L., & Wilson, D. B. (2005). A meta-analytic review of court-mandated batterer interventions programs: Can courts affect abusers' behavior? *Journal of Experimental Criminology, 1*, 239–262.

Field, C. A., Caetano, R., & Nelson, S. (2004). Alcohol and violence related cognitive risk factors associated with the perpetration of intimate partner violence. *Journal of Family Violence, 19*, 249–253.

Foran, H., & O'Leary, K. D. (2008). Alcohol and intimate partner violence: A meta-analytic review. *Clinical Psychology Review, 28*, 1222–1234.

Giordano, P. C., Millhollin, T. J., Cernkovich, S. A., Pugh, M. D., & Rudolph, J. L. (1999). Delinquency, identity, and women's involvement in relationship violence. *Criminology, 37*, 17–37.

Gondolf, E. W. (1987). The gender warrior: Reformed batters on abuse, treatment, and change. *Journal of Family Violence, 2*, 177–191.

Gondolf, E. W. (1988). Who are these guys? Toward a behavioral typology of batterers. *Violence and Victims, 3*, 187–203.

Gondolf, E. W., & Jones, A. S. (2001). The program effect of batterer programs in three cities. *Violence and Victims, 16*, 693–704.

Hamberger, L. K., & Arnold, J. (1990). The impact of mandatory arrest on domestic violence perpetrator counseling services. *Family Violence and Sexual Assault Bulletin, 6*, 11–12.

Hamberger, L. K., & Hastings, J. E. (1986a). Characteristics of spouse abusers: Predictors of treatment acceptance. *Journal of Interpersonal Violence, 1*, 363–373.

Hamberger, L. K., & Hastings, J. E. (1986b). Personality correlates of men who abuse their partners: A cross-validation study. *Journal of Family Violence, 1*, 323–341.

Hamberger, L. K., & Hastings, J. E. (1988). Characteristics of male spouse abusers consistent with personality disorders. *Hospital and Community Psychiatry, 39*, 763–770.

Hamberger, L. K., & Hastings, J. E. (1990). Recidivism following spouse abuse abatement counseling: Treatment implications. *Violence and Victims, 5*, 157–170.

Hamberger, L. K., & Lohr, J. M. (1989). Proximal causes of spouse abuse: A theoretical analysis for cognitive–behavioral interventions. In P. L. Caesar & L. K. Hamberger (Eds.), *Treating men who batter: Theory, practice, and programs* (pp. 53–76). New York: Springer.

Hamberger, L. K., Lohr, J. M., Bonge, D., & Tolin, D. F. (1996). A large sample empirical typology of male spouse abusers and its relationship to dimensions of abuse. *Violence and Victims, 11*, 277–292.

Hanson, R. K., Cadsky, O., Harris, A., & Lalonde, C. (1997). Correlates of battering among 997 men: Family history, adjustment, and attitudinal differences. *Violence and Victims, 12*, 191–208.

Hastings, J. E., & Hamberger, L. K. (1988). Personality characteristics of spouse abusers: A controlled comparison. *Violence and Victims, 3*, 31–48.

Hershorn, M., & Rosenbaum, A. (1991). Over- vs. undercontrolled hostility: Application of the construct to the classification of maritally violent men. *Violence and Victims, 6*, 151–158.

Heyman, R. E., O'Leary, K. D., & Jouriles, E. N. (1995). Alcohol and aggressive personality styles: Potentiators of serious physical aggression against wives? *Journal of Family Psychology, 9*, 44–57.

Holtzworth-Munroe, A. (2000). Social information processing skills deficits in maritally violent men: Summary of a research program. In J. P. Vincent & E. N. Jouriles (Eds.), *Domestic violence: Guidelines for research-informed practice* (pp. 13–36). London: Jessica Kingsley.

Holtzworth-Munroe, A., & Clements, K. (2007). The association between anger and male perpetration of intimate partner violence. In T. A. Cavell & K. T. Malcom (Eds.), *Anger, aggression, and interventions for interpersonal violence* (pp. 313–348). Mahwah, NJ: Erlbaum.

Holtzworth-Munroe, A., & Hutchinson, G. (1993). Attributing negative intent to wife behavior: The attributions of maritally violent men versus nonviolent men. *Journal of Abnormal Psychology, 102*, 206–211.

Holtzworth-Munroe, A., & Meehan, J. C. (2004). Typologies of men who are maritally violent: Scientific and clinical implications. *Journal of Interpersonal Violence, 19,* 1369–1389.

Holtzworth-Munroe, A., Meehan, J. C., Herron, K., Rehman, U., & Stuart, G. L. (2000). Testing the Holtzworth-Munroe and Stuart batterer typology. *Journal of Consulting and Clinical Psychology, 68,* 1000–1019.

Holtzworth-Munroe, A., Meehan, J. C., Herron, K., Rehman, U., & Stuart, G. L. (2003). Do subtypes of maritally violent men continue to differ over time? *Journal of Consulting and Clinical Psychology, 71,* 728–740.

Holtzworth-Munroe, A., Rehman, U., & Herron, K. (2000). General and spouse specific anger and hostility in subtypes of maritally violent men and nonviolent men. *Behavior Therapy, 31,* 603–630.

Holtzworth-Munroe, A., & Stuart, G. L. (1994). Typologies of male batterers: Three subtypes and the differences among them. *Psychological Bulletin, 116,* 476–497.

Johnson, R., Gilchrist, E., Beech, A. R., Weston, S., Takriti, R., & Freeman, R. (2006). A psychometric typology of U.K. domestic violence offenders. *Journal of Interpersonal Violence, 21,* 1270–1285.

Jones, A. S., D'Agostino, R. B., Gondolf, E. W., & Heckert, A. (2004). Assessing the effect of batterer program completion on reassault using propensity scores. *Journal of Interpersonal Violence, 19,* 1002–1020.

Jones, A. S., & Gondolf, E. W. (2001). Time-varying risk factors for reassault among batterer program participants. *Journal of Family Violence, 16,* 345–359.

Kessler, R. C., Molnar, B. E., Feurer, I. D., & Appelbaum, M. (2001). Patterns and mental health predictors of domestic violence in the United States: Results from the National Comorbidity Survey. *International Journal of Law and Psychiatry, 24,* 487–508.

Lohr, J. M., Bonge, D., Witte, T. H., Hamberger, L. K., & Langhinrichsen-Rohling, J. (2005). Consistency and accuracy of batterer typology identification. *Journal of Family Violence, 20,* 253–258.

Lohr, J. M., Hamberger, L. K., & Bonge, D. (1988). The nature of irrational beliefs in different personality profiles of spouse abusers. *Journal of Rational Emotive and Cognitive Behavioral Therapy, 6,* 273–285.

Maiuro, R. D., Cahn, T. S., Vitaliano, P. P., Wagner, B. C., & Zegree, J. B. (1988). Anger, hostility, and depression in domestically violent versus generally assaultive and nonviolent control subjects. *Journal of Consulting and Clinical Psychology, 56,* 17–23.

Martin, D. (1987). The historical roots of domestic violence. In D. J. Sonkin (Ed.), *Domestic violence on trial: Psychological and legal dimensions of family violence* (pp. 3–20). New York: Springer.

Moore, T. M., Eisler, R. M., & Franchina, J. J. (2000). Causal attributions and affective responses to provocative female partner behavior by abusive and nonabusive males. *Journal of Family Violence, 15,* 69–80.

Murphy, C. M., & Eckhardt, C. I. (2005). *Treating the abusive partner: An individualized cognitive–behavioral approach.* New York: Guilford Press.

Pan, H. S., Neidig, P. H., & O'Leary, K. D. (1994). Predicting mild and severe husband-to-wife physical aggression. *Journal of Consulting and Clinical Psychology, 62,* 975–981.

Rosenbaum, A., & O'Leary, K. D. (1981). Marital violence: Characteristics of abusive couples. *Journal of Consulting and Clinical Psychology, 49,* 63–76.

Saunders, D. G. (1987, August). *Are there different types of men who batter? An empirical study with possible implications for treatment.* Paper presented at the Third National Family Violence Research Conference, Durham, NH.

Schechter, S. (1982). *Women and male violence: The visions and struggles of the battered women's movement.* Boston: South End.

Shields, N. M., McCall, G., & Hanneke, C. R. (1988). Patterns of family and nonfamily violence: Violent husbands and violent men. *Violence and Victims, 3,* 83–97.

Smith Slep, A. M., & O'Leary, S. G. (2005). Parent and partner violence in families with young children: Rates, patterns, and connections. *Journal of Consulting and Clinical Psychology, 73,* 435–444.

Snow, D. L., Sullivan, T. P., Swann, S. C., Tate, D. C., & Klein, I. (2006). The role of coping and problem drinking in men's abuse of female partners: Test of a path model. *Violence and Victims, 21,* 267–285.

Stith, S. M., Smith, D. B., Penn, C. E., Ward, D. B., & Tritt, D. (2004). Intimate partner physical abuse perpetration and victimization risk factors: A meta-analytic review. *Aggression and Violent Behavior, 10,* 65–98.

Straus, M. A. (1979). Measuring intrafamily conflict violence: The Conflict Tactics (CT) Scales. *Journal of Marriage and the Family, 4,* 75–88.

Straus, M. A. (1999). The controversy over domestic violence by women. In X. B. Arriaga & S. Oskamp (Eds.), *Violence in intimate relationships* (pp. 17–44). Thousand Oaks, CA: Sage.

Tjaden, P. (2004). What is violence against women? Defining and measuring the problem. *Journal of Interpersonal Violence, 19,* 1244–1251.

Tonizzo, S., Howells, K., Day, A., Reidpath, D., & Froyland, I. (2000). Attributions of negative partner behavior by men who physically abuse their partners. *Journal of Family Violence, 15,* 155–167.

Tweed, R. G., & Dutton, D. G. (1998). A comparison of impulsive and instrumental subgroups of batterers. *Violence and Victims, 13,* 217–230.

Walker, L. E. (1979). *The battered woman.* New York: Harper & Row.

Waltz, J., Babcock, J. C., Jacobson, N., & Gottman, J. M. (2000). Testing a typology of batterers. *Journal of Consulting and Clinical Psychology, 68,* 658–250.

5

FAMILY AND RELATIONSHIP PREDICTORS OF PSYCHOLOGICAL AND PHYSICAL AGGRESSION

MIRIAM K. EHRENSAFT

Public health, social, and clinical scientists have long been concerned about the prevalence of intimate partner violence (IPV) and its high potential for physical and psychological injury (Bachman & Saltzman, 1995; Ehrensaft, Moffitt, & Caspi, 2004; Straus, 1999; Tjaden & Thoennes, 1998; Wiist & McFarlane, 1999). This concern extends not only to the millions of women who present to the attention of police and women's shelters each year but also to men and women who are at risk of serious injury and are never identified by these public sources (Ehrensaft et al., 2004; Kessler, Molnar, Feurer, & Appelbaum, 2001; Straus, 1999). Many victims seriously injured and psychologically intimidated by a current or former intimate partner explicitly avoid contact with police, social services, and shelters (Gondolf, 1998) or are not admitted to shelters because of serious psychopathology or substance abuse (Loseke, 1992).

The development of empirically sound preventive interventions for IPV will hinge on identifying major modifiable risks for its perpetration and victimization and sound theoretical models that can explain what remains one of the most complex and intractable public health problems (Dunford, 2000).

Scholars from a wide range of disciplines have devoted their research programs to identifying risks for involvement in abusive relationships (Capaldi & Clark, 1998; Chalk & King, 1998; Ehrensaft, Cohen, et al., 2003; Jouriles, McDonald, Norwood, & Ezell, 2001; Magdol, Moffitt, Caspi, & Silva, 1998; Murphy, O'Farrell, Fals-Stewart, & Feehan, 2001; Wolfe, Wekerle, Reitzel-Jaffe, & Lefebvre, 1998). From the substantial literature on the epidemiology of IPV, a significant emphasis on the importance of family risks has emerged, encompassing both risks based in the family of origin and dyadic (relationship) risks.

This review focuses on three major classes of family of origin risks that increase the risk for subsequent IPV: (a) direct and indirect exposure to interparental conflict and violence, (b) child maltreatment and adverse parenting, and (c) family history of antisocial behavior. Each of these classes of risk may influence the development of behavioral patterns, emotion regulation, and social cognitive competence across the lifespan. Collectively, these risks therefore have broad implications for the capacity to form supportive interpersonal relationships during the school years and healthy opposite-sex relationships in adolescence and during the transition to adulthood. Specifically, in this chapter we detail how the effects of exposure to parental conflict and violence, parent–child relational problems, and parental antisocial behavior may set in motion a developmental course toward risk for both experiencing and perpetrating psychological and physical aggression in adult romantic relationships.

With regard to relationship risks in adults, researchers are increasingly pointing to the significance of specific types of dyadic communication patterns, anger expression, and selective mating among partners with aggressive developmental histories. We will review the existing literature on these risks.

Given the breadth of the literatures focusing on these risk factors, the review of family of origin and dyadic risk factors in this chapter is intended to be representative but not exhaustive. We propose that distal family of origin risks pave the way for the emergence of proximal relationship risks in adolescence and early adulthood.

FAMILY RISK FACTORS FOR PSYCHOLOGICAL AND PHYSICAL AGGRESSION

Direct and Indirect Exposure to Parental Conflict and Violence

Children who have lived in homes with elevated marital or interparent conflict are at risk of problem behavior (Grych & Fincham, 2001). Problem behavior may be conceptualized as undercontrolled or externalizing behavior (such as frequent anger) and/or anxiety and mood problems (e.g., fears, frequent crying, whining; Brook, Whiteman, & Zheng, 2002), both of which have been found to be elevated in children exposed to parental partner conflict (Skopp, McDonald, Manke, & Jouriles, 2005). Early problem behavior is of special concern because conduct problems tend to be moderately stable (Caspi, Henry, McGee, Moffitt, & Silva, 1995) and predictive of subsequent academic, behavioral, and social difficulties (for a review, see Wasserman & Seracini, 2000).

Whereas early research aimed to verify the existence of a link between marital conflict and child adjustment, such as aggression and behavior problems, recent research has led to a search for more sophisticated theoretical models that take into account the overall family context of this conflict on children (Davies & Sturge-Apple, 2007). Among the best developed of a newer generation of theoretical models is the familywide component of the emotional security theory. Emotional security theory proposes that marital conflict increases children's vulnerability to maladjustment by undermining their sense of security in multiple family relationships (Davies & Cummings, 2004). Sustained, intense family conflict may lead to overburdening of children's physiological and emotional resources, resulting in abnormalities in biopsychological systems (Repetti, Taylor, & Seeman, 2002). These processes are thought to increase children's risk of developing psychopathology and problems in social relatedness (Davies, Harold, Goeke-Morey, & Cummings, 2002). Emotional security theory has substantive advantages over many earlier ones because it may be applied broadly to across even the earliest developmental stages due to its focus on emotion regulation processes.

Concerns about children's exposure to physically violent conflict between parents have been of primary importance since the problem of IPV first came to the attention of researchers and clinicians in the 1970s. In the United States alone, 14 million children are exposed to some act of interparent physical violence, more than 6 million are exposed to severe violence (McDonald, Jouriles, Ramisetty-Mikler, Caetano, & Green, 2006), and 1 million seek refuge at domestic violence shelters with their mothers (Jouriles, 2000). In studies of community samples, about 25% recalled seeing or hearing at least one physical fight between their parents, and 14% recalled two or more such fights (Ehrensaft, Cohen, et al., 2003).

Initial theories on adjustment of children exposed to IPV focused almost exclusively on effects of direct and indirect exposure to IPV as the primary explanatory factor for later involvement in partner violence in adolescence and adulthood (see Jouriles, Norwood, McDonald, & Peters, 2000, for a description and critique). The current generation of theories now urges increased sophistication in order to explain the multitude of intertwined variables that interact to predict individual differences in outcomes of children exposed to IPV (Davies & Sturge-Apple, 2007). Thus, theories must go beyond the roles of severity, chronicity, and levels of injury parents experience in violent relationships to identify specific, modifiable psychological processes that mediate or moderate the association of exposure to IPV with children's subsequent behavioral outcomes.

For instance, parental expression of anger, sadness, fear, and threats that occur in the context of partner violence are thought to be important mediators of the effects of parents' IPV on child development (Davies et al., 2002). Children's cognitive representations of IPV, particularly the extent to which children blame themselves for their parents' violence, also play an essential mediating role in the prediction of mental health outcomes (Grych & Fincham, 1990). Emotional security theory has not previously been tested with regard to children's exposure to IPV, but given its focus on the overall family context, it may be particularly well suited to account for the co-occurring effects of other forms of family violence and coercive behaviors on child adjustment (Davies & Sturge-Apple, 2007; Smith Slep & O'Leary, 2005). We now turn to a discussion of these co-occurring forms of family violence.

As a cautionary note, we point to the work of Stith et al. (1998), who have demonstrated that exposure to IPV has an effect size of .22 on child adjustment. Thus, there clearly is a reliable effect of exposure to IPV, but the effects on IPV with a current partner are small. O'Leary, Smith Slep, and O'Leary (2007) showed that the effects of distal variables such as exposure to IPV (a small effect) are less robust than the effects of proximal variables like relationship conflict (large effects). In addition, the study of Skopp et al. (2005) we referred to earlier shows that the majority of children exposed to IPV did not meet criteria for any cutoff on internalizing or externalizing problems. This caution is even more important in light of data from epidemiological studies (e.g., Ehrensaft, Cohen, et al., 2003) finding that 14% of a representative sample reported hearing two or more physical fights between their parents. In other words, research must focus specifically on identifying characteristics of the relatively smaller proportion of children who are exposed to IPV and show clinically significant adjustment problems that are uniquely attributable to that IPV exposure.

Child Maltreatment and Adverse Parenting Practices

A comprehensive understanding of vulnerability to IPV must include a discussion of factors that first emerge in childhood. Principal among these are child maltreatment and negative parenting practices. These distal factors increase the vulnerability to IPV because they increase the odds that children will experience deficits or behavioral patterns that are more proximal predictors of IPV, such as deficits in social learning, emotion regulation, and interpersonal functioning. These factors are reviewed later in this chapter.

Severe parent-to-child violence occurs in 5% of U.S. families (Straus, 1990; Straus, Hamby, Finkelhor, Moore, & Runyan, 1998). Recent research with representative samples found that parent-to-child violence severe enough to meet definitions of *child abuse* occurs in up to 13% of families (Smith Slep

& O'Leary, 2005). However, adverse effects on children's physical, cognitive, and social development are not limited to such severe cases and may occur with more "minor" acts of corporal punishment (Repetti et al., 2002). Scholars of family violence have long been concerned with the effects of child maltreatment and corporal punishment on the risk of subsequent partner abuse perpetration and victimization in adulthood (Straus & Stewart, 1999; Widom, 1989).

Numerous and diverse theoretical perspectives propose a link between child abuse and neglect and subsequent impairments in social functioning over the life course. Many of these theories share an emphasis on effects of maltreatment on children's deviant behavioral development and the cascading effects of disruptive behavior on social development as children age. No single theory can account for the association of child maltreatment with subsequent disruptive behavior, but several theoretical models conjointly explain this link. Each of these theoretical underpinnings suggests that beginning in early childhood, family relations, especially parenting and the relationship between parents, influence the development of emotional and behavioral self-regulation and expectations about the meaning of close relationships (Crittendon & Ainsworth, 1989; Gilliom, Shaw, Beck, Schonberg, & Lukon, 2002; Kopp, 1989; Siegel, 1999; Wasserman & Seracini, 2000; Webster-Stratton, 1997).

Children who have received responsive caregiving develop expectations that their needs will be met in close relationships (Bowlby, 1969) and are likely to cope more adaptively with negative emotions (Carlson & Sroufe, 1995). Children who have experienced parental rejection, abuse, or neglect learn to anticipate and anxiously avoid rejection (Downey & Feldman, 1996) and tend to have hostile attributional biases and social problem-solving deficits (Dodge, Bates, & Pettit, 1990). Social learning theories propose that children who are maltreated by their parents learn aggressive, hostile patterns of social interaction from their families and go on to generalize these outside of the family unit, first to their peer networks and later to intimate partners (Ehrensaft, Cohen, et al., 2003; O'Leary, 1988). Huesmann's (1988) script theory proposes that child abuse leads to the acquisition of aggressive schemas or "stories" about social exchanges. These scripts are stored in memory, are elaborated with repeated parent–child interactions, and are later generalized to social behavior in other relationships.

Empirical research bears up many of these theoretical assumptions. Research on neuropsychiatric development supports psychological theories about the adverse effects of maltreatment on children's reactivity to stress and emotion regulation (Cicchetti & Lynch, 1995; Erickson, Egeland, & Pianta, 1989). These biobehavioral responses to early stress are associated with poor social competence in social environments (Hart, Gunnar, & Cicchetti, 1995). Child maltreatment has repeatedly been linked with poor social functioning in early and middle childhood (Mueller & Silverman, 1989;

Salzinger, Feldman, Hammer, & Rosario, 1993). Compared with nonmaltreated controls, maltreated children are more likely to attribute hostile intentions to their social partners and are more likely to withdraw from or avoid social interactions with peers (Haskett & Kistner, 1991; Mueller & Silverman, 1989).

Early maltreatment appears to have the most detrimental, lasting effects on children's emotion regulation (Gilliom et al., 2002) and social information processing patterns (Dodge et al., 1990), as these patterns are usually formed during the first 8 years of life (Dodge & Price, 1994). Emotion dysregulation predicts social rejection by peers in maltreated children (Shields, Ryan, & Cicchetti, 2001) and thus missed opportunities to observe and rehearse appropriate social behaviors with skilled peers (Bolger, Patterson, & Kupersmidt, 1998; Downey & Feldman, 1996). As a result, maladaptive patterns of problem solving and conflict resolution with peers in the elementary and middle school years are learned, reinforced, and gain stability (Hartup, 1996).

Peer groups are essential to all preadolescent and adolescents for the formation, monitoring, and enforcement of norms regarding acceptable behaviors in the context of romantic relationships, such as the timing of opposite-sex relations and physical intimacy and the pool of acceptable partners (Brown, 1999). Children then apply these norms to early intimate relationships (Connolly & Goldberg, 1999).

Patterns of deviant social behavior and affiliation with deviant, interpersonally aggressive peers severely limit the availability of supportive, prosocial intimate partners (Moffit, Caspi, Rutter, & Silva, 2001; Quinton, Pickles, Maughan, & Rutter, 1993). Thus, unless efforts are made to repair these interpersonal deficits, maltreated youths are more likely to affiliate with deviant peer groups and to enter their first adolescent romantic relationships with inadequate skills to negotiate this critical developmental transition (Feiring & Furman, 2000).

In summary, child abuse may set in motion a lasting pathway to interpersonally deviant behavior across the life-span and associated social impairments. This accrual of deviant social experiences over the course of development has cumulative negative effects on the ability to develop warm, supportive, and trusting relationships with early intimate partners.

Studies investigating the propagation of interpersonal deficits observed in middle childhood and adolescence to adult intimate relationships are few, and almost all are retrospective (Colman & Widom, 2004). But a handful of prospective longitudinal studies support the hypothesis that child maltreatment continues to influence interpersonal functioning in adulthood. Specifically, Colman and Widom followed a sample of youths with substantiated cases of child abuse or neglect, as well as a matched control group, and compared their rates of intimate involvement and relationship functioning in adulthood. Results suggest that both male and female participants with histories of physical or sexual abuse or neglect had higher rates of separation and divorce, perceived their partners as less supportive, and were less likely to be involved in committed romantic relationships, and these findings were not attributable to correlated sociodemographic risks. Using the same prospective design, H. R. White and Widom (2003) found higher rates of IPV among women with a history of child abuse or neglect.

Finally, Ehrensaft, Cohen, et al. (2003) found evidence of higher risk of adulthood IPV perpetration and victimization in children with official records of child abuse compared with those without such records. Cohen, Brown, and Smailes (2001) found increased risk of *Diagnostic and Statistical Manual of Mental Disorders* (4th ed.; American Psychiatric Association, 1994) Clusters A (Odd/Eccentric), B (Dramatic/Erratic), and C (Anxious/Avoidant) personality disorders in maltreated versus nonmaltreated youths. Because personality disorders are in essence disorders of interpersonal functioning, this last finding suggests long-term association of child abuse with maladaptive interpersonal functioning. Subsequent work with this same sample found that the influence of childhood abuse on the risk for partner violence in the early 30s was mediated by personality disorder symptoms measured in the early 20s (Ehrensaft, Cohen, & Johnson, 2006), again underscoring the long-term effects of maltreatment on social functioning.

Numerous studies demonstrate an association of most forms of family violence with maladaptive parenting practices. IPV in the home is associated with parenting practices that are lax, lacking in warmth, hostile, and inconsistent. Such parenting practices are further shown to predict behavioral problems in homes marked by IPV (Holden, Geffner, & Jouriles, 1998). A similar cluster of parenting practices are also elevated in parents of maltreated children, including rejection, withdrawal, hostility, lack of emotional responsiveness, harsh punishment, and inconsistent discipline (Chambless & Ollendick, 2001). Researchers tend to concur that the impact of the IPV exposure and child maltreatment is centrally located in its effect on the quality of parent–child interactions (English, Marshall, & Stewart, 2003; Graham-Bermann & Seng, 2005). However, as Davies and Sturge-Apple (2007) noted, parenting process models of the impact of IPV on family adjustment will require advancement beyond simple cross-sectional empirical tests of association. Longitudinal designs must further unpack the influence of parenting disruptions on specific psychological processes in children that may underlie their subsequent risk for psychopathology, such as affect regulation, stress reactivity, and social information processing.

Significantly, there is substantial co-occurrence of types of family violence, though research on these fields has previously been conducted separately (Appel & Holden, 1998; Holden, Stein, Ritchie, Harris, & Jouriles, 1998; Smith Slep & O'Leary, 2005). Within-perpetrator co-occurrence of severe IPV and child abuse is especially high; for instance, Smith Slep and O'Leary found that 92% of families reporting some sort of severe family aggression reported both severe partner and severe parent-to-child aggression. As a result, clinicians and researchers should pay further attention to the possible influence of one type of family aggression on other forms. These influences may be direct or may be the result of other shared adversities, stressors, and risks that tend to co-occur with all forms of family violence, including poverty, maladaptive parenting practices, poor health, neighborhood violence, and separation and divorce.

In particular, one type of shared risk—a family history of antisocial behavior—may help to explain the co-occurrence of these various forms of violence. This risk has been broadly found to increase all types of interpersonal violence. We turn now to a discussion of this essential vulnerability.

Family History of Antisocial Behavior

Although criminologists have long documented the association of antisocial behavior with interpersonal violence in the family (e.g., Moffitt, Caspi, Rutter, & Silva, 2001; Simons, Wu, Johnson, & Conger, 1995), research in the field of family violence proceeded in nearly complete isolation from this literature until recently (Ehrensaft, Cohen, et al., 2003; Moffitt & Caspi, 2003). Developmental psychopathologists have now taken a particular interest in family violence as a possible mechanism for the intergenerational transfer of antisocial behavior (Ehrensaft, 2007; Moffitt & Caspi, 2003). A host of empirical studies based on prospective longitudinal methods now distinguish a developmental history of antisocial behavior as one of the most robust predictors of IPV for both men and women, even after controlling for other family of origin risks (e.g., Andrews, Foster, Capaldi, & Hops, 2000; Capaldi & Clark, 1998; Ehrensaft, Cohen, et al., 2003; Ehrensaft et al., 2004; Giordano, Millhollin, Cernkovich, Pugh, & Rudolph, 1999; Moffit et al., 2001; Woodward, Fergusson, & Horwood, 2002). These findings come from four different highly regarded epidemiological research programs with distinct community samples. Compounding this risk, there is evidence that antisocial men and women tend to selectively partner, thereby bringing together two partners with antisocial histories; high stress reactivity; and reduced emotion regulation, social competence, and problem-solving skills (Kim & Capaldi, 2004; Krueger, Moffitt, Caspi, & Bleske, 1998; Moffitt et al., 2001).

Because most early research on risks for IPV was cross-sectional and retrospective, early studies failed to take into account a developmental history of antisocial behavior in constructing etiological models. For instance, an assumption of initial theories was that IPV leads to children's behavioral problems. Yet later studies found that interventions for abused women and their children focusing on altering coercive parenting practices in turn led to decreased disruptive behavior symptoms in children (Jouriles et al., 2001). Given the association of IPV with a family history of antisocial behavior, it is thus equally plausible that this maladaptive parenting behavior was already in place before the emergence of IPV. Alternatively, such behavior might well have emerged as part of the expected developmental course of antisocial young adults' use of coercive interpersonal interactions as they cope with the transition to parenthood and their offspring's development (Ehrensaft, Wasserman, et al., 2003; Serbin & Karp, 2003). A history of antisocial behavior is associated not only with physical aggression but also with relational or indirect aggression intended to damage social relationships (Crick & Grotpeter, 1995). Some researchers have suggested that relational aggression among same- and opposite-sex peers in middle childhood and adolescence forms the blueprint for psychological aggression in their subsequent intimate relationships (Wolfe et al., 2001).

RELATIONSHIP RISK FACTORS FOR PSYCHOLOGICAL AND PHYSICAL AGGRESSION

Although substantial controversy surrounds the definition of IPV (see Ehrensaft et al., 2004; Johnson, 1995; Straus, 1999), there is now widespread agreement that the most significantly abusive intimate relationships involve both physical and psychological abuse. O'Leary and Maiuro (2001) defined *psychological abuse* in four dimensions, using a combination of behavioral, motivational, and consequential aspects: (a) denigrating a partner's self-esteem, (b) being passive aggressive (e.g., withholding affection, ignoring, being emotionally distant), (c) engaging in threatening behavior (e.g., overt harm to partner and children, threats of abandonment and infidelity), and (d) restricting personal territory (e.g., social isolation, violation of personal privacy, financial and physical control).

Some intimate relationships may be characterized principally by psychological abuse and others by relatively low levels of physical aggression, yet those considered the most damaging necessarily have comparatively elevated levels of both psychological and physical aggression (e.g., Ehrensaft et al., 2004; Johnson & Ferraro, 2000). Some researchers have found that a constellation of highly controlling behaviors violating an individual's human rights differentiates the most clinically significant abusive relationships (Graham-Kevan & Archer, 2005).

The preponderance of literature on intimate partner abuse has focused on psychological abuse as part of a relationship dynamic in which the male partner seeks to control the female partner's behavior by the use of dominance, isolation, psychological intimidation, and physical violence (e.g., Marshall, 1992; Stets, 1988; Tolman, 1989; Walker, 1989). Interviews with women in battered women's shelters suggest that psychological abuse can be as damaging as and the effects longer lasting than physical violence, in part because of its greater frequency than physical violence (e.g., Marshall, 1992; Walker, 1984).

However, more recent research on this process has involved assessment of both the perpetration and receipt of psychological and physical abuse in both male and female partners drawn from community samples rather than exclusively clinical samples. This research is finding elevated rates of psychological abuse, such as dominance and control, in both male and female partners in highly abusive relationships (Ehrensaft et al., 1999, 2004; Medeiros & Straus, 2007). Psychological abuse appears to be a key predictor of future physical abuse in intimate relationships (O'Leary et al., 2007; J. W. White, Merrill, & Koss, 2001). Moreover, although earlier studies suggested that women used aggression as a means of emotional expression (e.g., communicating frustration and distress resulting from the male partner's abusive behavior), more recent research finds that both men and women in physically aggressive relationships use aggression to instrumentally control a partner (Babcock, Miller, & Siard, 2003) and that both sexes perceive their partners as controlling (Ehrensaft et al., 1999).

Two important caveats to these findings warrant mention. First, the impact of high levels of controlling behavior has important sex differences. In general, the threat of physical consequences is substantially worse for women than it is for men. For example, prospective longitudinal studies have found evidence that women in clinically abusive relationships are more likely to have an increased risk of psychiatric disorders (e.g., posttraumatic stress disorder, major depressive disorder) after controlling for preexisting disorder, whereas no such increased risk was found for men (Ehrensaft et al., 2006). Second, because research on both men's and women's controlling behavior in abusive relationships is sparse, it is premature to conclude that women use controlling behavior in the same fashion and context as men in abusive relationships.

In summary, the extant literature suggests that psychological abuse, particularly controlling behavior, is a hallmark of the most physically abusive relationships. Such behavior may be used by both men and women in abusive relationships. However, the physical and psychological consequences of psychological abuse are more clinically significant for women than they are for men. Further research should attempt to replicate findings on controlling behavior in both men and women in abusive versus nonabusive relationships.

Why is psychological abuse, most specifically controlling abuse, such a central characteristic of the most violent relationships? A particularly elegant explanation comes from Dutton's description of IPV as essentially an "intimacy problem" driven by personality pathology that has roots in the family of origin risks described earlier in this chapter (Dutton, 2003; Dutton & Nicholls, 2005). This perspective coherently integrates findings on a host of relationship risks that impair intimacy and distinguish aggressive from distressed nonaggressive couples. Not only are violent relationships generally more discordant, they also exhibit specific types of dyadic communication.

For instance, numerous studies have found higher levels of "demand–withdraw" communication patterns during videotaped problem-solving interactions, in which the husband demands (e.g., attention, affection) and the wife withdraws (Babcock, Waltz, Jacobson, & Gottman, 1993; Christensen, 1988; Eldridge & Christensen, 2002). In addition, anger expression in both husband and wife, as well as poor problem solving in the husband, predicted aggression (Leonard & Roberts, 1998). Further, members of violent couples appear to be more emotionally reactive to one another's unsupportive behaviors. That is, the association of one individual's behavior toward their partner (e.g., invalidation) with the partner's arousal to that behavior (e.g., reactivity to invalidation by the partner) differentiates violent from nonviolent relationships (Noller & Roberts, 2002; for a review, see Noller & Robillard, 2007). Finally, there appears to be a bidirectional relationship of marital discord with partner violence, where partner violence is an outcome of, as well as a future risk for, relationship dissatisfaction and instability (Lawrence & Bradbury, 2007).

CONCLUSIONS, LIMITATIONS, AND PUBLIC POLICY IMPLICATIONS

This chapter integrates research findings on child development, developmental psychopathology, and romantic relationship functioning to identify family of origin and dyadic risk factors for involvement in abusive relationships. There appears to be substantive support for the proposal that family of origin adversities, including child exposure to interparental conflict and violence, maladaptive parenting practices, and child abuse and neglect, lead to early abnormalities in emotional and behavioral regulation and, in turn, to poor social competence. These difficulties in social competence, including aggressive interactions and difficulties forming close, trusting relationships with others, are rehearsed and reinforced in the peer group. A pattern of antisocial, aggressive behavior may be a shared outcome of many of the family of origin risks described in this chapter. Subsequently, deviant, aggressive social behaviors render the developmental task of establishing intimate relationships far more difficult by the time the youth reaches adolescence and then emerging adulthood.

The occurrence of IPV is an outcome of a long-standing pattern of problems with intimacy, in which the individual approaches relationships with others with emotional oversensitivity, hostility, and avoidance (Dutton, 2003). For the most seriously abusive individuals, these basic intimacy problems are expressed as a combination of physical violence and high levels of coercive control. Contrary to popular belief, there are very few gender differences in risk profiles for involvement in abusive relationships, and this finding is true for psychopathology as well.

It was our aim in this chapter to extend prior reviews of risks for IPV by integrating work on both family of origin and dyadic processes, as reviews of these risks often occur separately. This chapter also has several limitations. We wish to highlight one in particular. Although we have alluded to its great importance, this review has not fully represented the broad literature on neuropsychiatric and genetic risks for aggressive behavior. These risks are worthy of further consideration, though our preventive interventions are certainly lagging in their ability to incorporate these risks into their conceptual frameworks.

An important step for future research would be to develop and pilot experimental interventions targeting specific neuropsychiatric consequences of family of origin insults, such as deficits in hypothalamic–pituitary–adrenocortical axis functioning observed in child maltreatment (Cicchetti & Rogosh, 2001) and other psychobiological abnormalities (DeBellis & Putnam, 1994). Basic research on child maltreatment and other forms of early trauma is working toward establishing mechanisms by which such early stress leads to significant but reversible self-regulation deficits (Kaufman & Charney, 2001). Scholars of IPV would do well to follow their lead in developing preventive interventions for young children at risk for later IPV.

This chapter focuses its review on family and relationship factors that increase vulnerability to aggression; thus, a full discussion of other social contextual factors that may influence the development of aggression is not presented here, most notably socioeconomic disadvantage. Poverty predicts domestic violence, particularly among those living in disadvantaged communities (Benson & Fox, 2004; Browne & Bassuk, 1997; Tolman & Raphael, 2000). Domestic violence may in turn increase the risk of poverty because it is a maternal employment barrier (Lindhorst, Oxford, & Gillmore, 2007) and the effects of domestic violence and poverty may additively amplify the risk of subsequent child adjustment problems (Eunice Kennedy Shriver National Institute of Child Health and Human Development, National Institutes of Health, & Department of Health and Human Services, 2002). Empirical evidence in this area remains impressionistic (Brooks-Gunn & Duncan, 1997; Schechter & Knitzer, 2004), and further investigation is warranted to develop models that can guide public policy for families affected by poverty and domestic violence.

Despite the emergence of children's exposure to IPV and child maltreatment as a key public health problem, scientific resources devoted to furthering basic research on pathways by which such early adversity affects children have become increasingly limited. As a result, the preponderance of services for children affected by family violence continue to be based on clinical hunches rather than empirically informed interventions (Chaffin & Friedrich, 2004). Presently, researchers are at a key juncture; they need to advocate both for continued funds to further basic research on the impact of family violence on children's psychological adjustment and for greater scientific effort to disseminate existing findings to social service agencies serving affected families. In particular, the accruing evidence for gender similarity in risk for IPV is in urgent need of dissemination, as is the role of developmental psychopathology. We urge researchers to take up both of these issues in their scientific endeavors.

REFERENCES

American Psychiatric Association (1994). *Diagnostic and statistical manual of mental disorders* (4th ed.). Washington, DC: Author.

Andrews, J. A., Foster, S. L., Capaldi, D., & Hops, H. (2000). Adolescent and family predictors of physical aggression, communication and satisfaction in young adult couples: A prospective analysis. *Journal of Consulting and Clinical Psychology, 68,* 195–208.

Appel, A. E., & Holden, G. W. (1998). The co-occurrence of child and physical spouse abuse: A review and appraisal. *Journal of Family Psychology, 12,* 578–599.

Babcock, J. C., Miller, S. A., & Siard, C. (2003). Toward a typology of abusive women: Differences between partner-only and generally violent women in the use of violence. *Psychology of Women Quarterly, 27,* 153–161.

Babcock, J. C., Waltz, J., Jacobson, N. S., & Gottman, J. M. (1993). Power and violence: The relation between communication patterns, power discrepancies, and domestic violence. *Journal of Consulting and Clinical Psychology, 61,* 40–50.

Bachman, R., & Saltzman, L. E. (1995). *National Crime Victimization Survey: Violence against women: Estimates from the redesigned survey* (Report No. NCJ 154348). Washington, DC: U.S. Department of Justice.

Benson, M., & Fox, G. (2004). *When violence hits home: How economics and neighborhood play a role* [Research brief]. Washington, DC: National Institute of Justice.

Bolger, K. E., Patterson, C. E., & Kupersmidt, J. B. (1998). Peer relations and self-esteem among children who have been maltreated. *Child Development, 69,* 1171–1197.

Bowlby, J. (1969). *Attachment.* New York: Basic Books.

Brook, J. S., Whiteman, M., & Zheng, L. (2002). Intergenerational transmission of risks for problem behavior. *Journal of Abnormal Child Psychology, 30,* 65–76.

Brooks-Gunn, J., & Duncan, G. J. (1997). The effects of poverty on children. *The Future of Children, 7,* 55–71.

Brown, B. B. (1999). "You're going out with *who?*" Peer group influence on adolescent romantic relationships. In W. Furman, B. B. Brown, & C. Feiring (Eds.), *The development of romantic relationships in adolescence* (pp. 291–329). New York: Cambridge University Press.

Browne, A., & Bassuk, S. S. (1997). Intimate violence in the lives of homeless and poor housed women: Prevalence and patterns in an ethnically diverse sample. *American Journal of Orthopsychiatry, 67,* 261–278.

Capaldi, D. M., & Clark, S. (1998). Prospective family predictors of aggression toward female partners for at-risk young men. *Developmental Psychology, 34*, 1175–1188.

Carlson, E., & Sroufe, A. (1995). Contribution of attachment theory to developmental psychopathology. In D. Cicchetti & D. Cohen (Eds.), *Developmental psychopathology: Vol. 1. Theory and methods* (pp. 581–617). New York: Wiley.

Caspi, A., Henry, B., McGee, R. O., Moffitt, T. E., & Silva, P. A. (1995). Temperamental origins of child and adolescent behavior problems: From age 3 to age 15. *Child Development, 66*, 55–68.

Chaffin, M., & Friedrich, B. (2004). Evidence-based treatments in child abuse and neglect. *Children & Youth Services Review, 26*, 1097–1113.

Chalk, R., & King, P. A. (1998). *Violence in families: Assessing prevention and treatment programs.* Washington, DC: National Academies Press.

Chambless, D. L., & Ollendick, T. H. (2001). Empirically supported psychological interventions: Controversies and evidence. *Annual Review of Psychology, 52*, 685–716.

Christensen, A. (1988). Dysfunctional interaction patterns in couples. In P. Noller & M. A. Fitzpatrick (Eds.), *Perspectives on marital interaction* (pp. 31–52). Philadelphia: Multilingual Matters.

Cicchetti, D., & Lynch, M. (1995). Failures in the expectable environment and their impact on individual development: The case of child maltreatment. In D. Cicchetti & D. J. Cohen (Eds.), *Developmental psychopathology: Vol. 2. Risk, disorder and adaptation* (pp. 32–71). New York: Wiley.

Cicchetti, D., & Rogosh, F. A. (2001). Diverse patterns of neuroendocrine activity in maltreated children. *Development and Psychopathology, 13*, 677–693.

Cohen, P., Brown, J., & Smailes, E. (2001). Child abuse and neglect and the development of mental disorders in the general population. *Development & Psychopathology, 13*, 981–999.

Colman, R. A., & Widom, C. S. (2004). Childhood abuse and neglect and adult intimate relationships: A prospective study. *Child Abuse & Neglect, 28*, 1133–1151.

Connolly, J., & Goldberg, A. (1999). Romantic relationships in adolescence: The role of friends and peers in their emergence and development. In W. Furman, B. B. Brown, & C. Feiring (Eds.), *The development of romantic relationships in adolescence* (pp. 266–290). New York: Cambridge University Press.

Crick, N. R., & Grotpeter, J. K. (1995). Relational aggression, gender, and social–psychological adjustment. *Child Development, 66*, 710–722.

Crittendon, P. M., & Ainsworth, M. D. S. (1989). Child maltreatment and attachment theory. In D. Cicchetti & V. Carlson (Eds.), *Child maltreatment: Theory and research on the causes and consequences of child abuse and neglect* (pp. 432–463). New York: Cambridge University Press.

Davies, P. T., & Cummings, E. M. (2004). Marital conflict and child adjustment: An emotional security hypothesis. *Psychological Bulletin, 116*, 387–411.

Davies, P. T., Harold, G. T., Goeke-Morey, M. C., & Cummings, E. M. (2002). Child emotional security and interparental conflict. *Monographs of the Society for Research in Child Development, 67*(3, Serial No. 270).

Davies, P. T., & Sturge-Apple, M. L. (2007). The impact of domestic violence on children's development. In J. Hamel & T. Nicholls (Eds.), *Family interventions in domestic violence* (pp. 165–189). New York: Springer.

DeBellis, M. D., & Putnam, F. W. (1994). The psychobiology of childhood maltreatment. *Child and Adolescent Psychiatric Clinics of North America, 3,* 663–678.

Dodge, K. A., Bates, J. E., & Pettit, G. S. (1990, December 21). Mechanisms in the cycle of violence. *Science, 250,* 1678–1683.

Dodge, K. A., & Price, J. M. (1994). On the relation between social information processing and socially competent behavior in early school-age children. *Child Development, 65,* 1385–1399.

Downey, G., & Feldman, S. (1996). Implications of rejection sensitivity for intimate relationships. *Journal of Personality and Social Psychology, 70,* 1327–1343.

Dunford, F. W. (2000). The San Diego Navy Experiment: An assessment of interventions for men who assault their wives. *Journal of Consulting and Clinical Psychology, 68,* 468–476.

Dutton, D. G. (2003). *The abusive personality.* New York: Guilford Press.

Dutton, D. G., & Nicholls, T. L. (2005). The gender paradigm in domestic violence research and theory: Part 1. The conflict of theory and data. *Aggression and Violent Behavior, 10,* 680–714.

Ehrensaft, M. K. (2007). Intergenerational transfer of intimate partner violence. In N. Jackson (Ed.), *Encyclopedia of domestic violence* (pp. 390–397). New York: Routledge.

Ehrensaft, M. K., Cohen, P., Brown, J., Smailes, E., Chen, H., & Johnson, J. G. (2003). Intergenerational transmission of partner violence: A 20-year prospective study. *Journal of Consulting & Clinical Psychology, 71,* 741–753.

Ehrensaft, M. K., Cohen, P., & Johnson, J. G. (2006). Development of personality disorder symptoms and the risk for partner violence. *Journal of Abnormal Psychology, 115,* 474–483.

Ehrensaft, M. K., Langhinrichsen-Rohling, J., Heyman, R. E., O'Leary, K. D., & Lawrence, E. (1999). Feeling controlled in marriage: A phenomenon specific to physically aggressive couples? *Journal of Family Psychology, 13,* 20–32.

Ehrensaft, M. K., Moffitt, T. E., & Caspi, A. (2004). Clinically abusive relationships in an unselected birth cohort: Men's and women's participation and developmental antecedents. *Journal of Abnormal Psychology, 113,* 258–271.

Ehrensaft, M. K., Wasserman, G. A., Verdelli, L., Greenwald, S., Miller, L. S., & Davies, M. (2003). Maternal antisocial behavior, parenting practices, and behavior problems in boys at risk for antisocial behavior. *Journal of Child and Family Studies, 12,* 27–40.

Eldridge, K. A., & Christensen, A. (2002). Demand-withdraw communication during couple conflict: A review and analysis. In P. Noller & J. A. Feeney (Eds.),

Understanding marriage (pp. 289–322). Cambridge, England: Cambridge University Press.

English, D., Marshall, D. B., & Stewart, A. J. (2003). Effects of family violence on child behavior and health during early childhood. *Journal of Family Violence, 18*, 43–57.

Erickson, M., Egeland, B., & Pianta, R. (1989). The effects of maltreatment on the development of young children. In D. Cicchetti & V. Carlson (Eds.), *Child maltreatment: Theory and research on the causes and consequences of child abuse and neglect* (pp. 647–684). New York: Cambridge University Press.

Eunice Kennedy Shriver National Institute of Child Health and Human Development, National Institutes of Health, & Department of Health and Human Services. (2002). *Workshop on children exposed to violence: Current status, gaps, and research priorities* (NA). Washington, DC: U.S. Government Printing Office.

Feiring, C., & Furman, W. C. (2000). When *love* is just a four letter word: Victimization and romantic relationships in adolescence. *Child Maltreatment, 5*, 293–298.

Gilliom, M., Shaw, D. S., Beck, J. E., Schonberg, M. A., & Lukon, J. L. (2002). Anger regulation in disadvantaged preschool boys: Strategies, antecedents, and the development of self-control. *Developmental Psychology, 38*, 222–235.

Giordano, P. C., Millhollin, T. J., Cernkovich, S. A., Pugh, M. D., & Rudolph, J. L. (1999). Delinquency, identity, and women's involvement in relationship violence. *Criminology, 37*, 17–40.

Gondolf, E. W. (1998). The victims of court-ordered batterers: Their victimization, helpseeking, and perceptions. *Violence Against Women, 4*, 659–676.

Graham-Bermann, S. A., & Seng, J. (2005). Violence exposure and traumatic stress symptoms as additional predictors of health problems in high-risk children. *Journal of Pediatrics, 146*, 349–354.

Graham-Kevan, N., & Archer, J. (2005). Intimate terrorism and common couples violence: A test of Johnson's predictions in four British samples. *Journal of Interpersonal Violence, 18*, 1247–1270.

Grych, J. G., & Fincham, F. D. (1990). Marital conflict and children's adjustment: A cognitive contextual framework. *Psychological Bulletin, 108*, 267–290.

Grych, J. G., & Fincham, F. D. (2001). *Interparental conflict and child development: Theory, research, and applications.* New York: Cambridge University Press.

Hart, J., Gunnar, M., & Cicchetti, D. (1995). Salivary cortisol in maltreated children: Evidence of relations between neuroendocrine activity and social competence. *Development and Psychopathology, 7*, 11–26.

Hartup, W. W. (1996). The company they keep: Friendships and their developmental significance. *Child Development, 67*, 1–13.

Haskett, M. E., & Kistner, J. A. (1991). The social interactions and peer perceptions of young physically abused children. *Child Development, 62*, 979–990.

Holden, G. W., Geffner, R. A., & Jouriles, E. N. (1998). *Children exposed to marital violence: Theory, research, and applied issues.* Washington, DC: American Psychological Association.

Holden, G. W., Stein, J. D., Ritchie, K. L., Harris, S. D., & Jouriles, E. N. (1998). Parenting behaviors and beliefs of battered women. In G. W. Holden, R. Geffner, & E. N. Jouriles (Eds.), *Children exposed to marital violence: Theory, research and practice* (pp. 289–336). Washington, DC: American Psychological Association.

Huesmann, L. R. (1988). An information processing model for the development of aggression. *Aggressive Behavior, 14*, 13–24.

Johnson, M. P. (1995). Patriarchal terrorism and common couple violence: Two forms of violence against women. *Journal of Marriage and the Family, 57*, 283–294.

Johnson, M. P., & Ferraro, K. J. (2000). Research on domestic violence in the 1990s: Making distinctions. *Journal of Marriage and the Family, 62*, 948–963.

Jouriles, E. N. (2000, April). *Gaps in our knowledge about the prevalence of children's exposure to domestic violence and impact of domestic violence on children.* Paper presented at a meeting of the National Academy of Sciences, Washington, DC.

Jouriles, E. N., McDonald, R., Norwood, W. D., & Ezell, E. (2001). Issues and controversies in documenting the prevalence of children's exposure to domestic violence. In S. A. Graham-Bermann & J. L. Edleson (Eds.), *Domestic violence in the lives of children: The future of research, intervention, and social policy* (pp. 12–34). Washington, DC: American Psychological Association.

Jouriles, E. N., Norwood, W. D., McDonald, R., & Peters, B. (2000). Domestic violence and child adjustment. In J. Grych & F. Fincham (Eds.), *Child development and interparental conflict* (pp. 315–336). Cambridge, England: Cambridge University Press.

Kaufman, J., & Charney, B. (2001). Effects of early stress on brain structure and function: Implications for understanding the relationship between child maltreatment and depression. *Development and Psychopathology, 13*, 451–471.

Kessler, R. C., Molnar, B. E., Feurer, I., & Appelbaum, M. (2001). Patterns and mental health predictors of domestic violence in the United States: Results from the National Comorbidity Survey. *International Journal of Law and Psychiatry, 24*, 487–508.

Kim, H. K., & Capaldi, D. M. (2004). The association of antisocial behavior and depressive symptoms between partners and risk for aggression in romantic relationships. *Journal of Family Psychology, 18*, 82–96.

Kopp, C. B. (1989). Regulation of distress and negative emotions: A developmental view. *Developmental Psychology, 25*, 343–354.

Krueger, R. F., Moffitt, T. E., Caspi, A., & Bleske, A. (1998). Assortative mating for antisocial behavior: Developmental and methodological implications. *Behavior Genetics, 28*, 173–186.

Lawrence, E., & Bradbury, T. N. (2007). Trajectories of change in physical aggression and marital satisfaction. *Journal of Family Psychology, 21*, 236–247.

Leonard, K. E., & Roberts, L. J. (1998). The effects of alcohol on the marital interactions of aggressive and nonaggressive husbands and their wives. *Journal of Abnormal Psychology, 107*, 602–615.

Lindhorst, T., Oxford, M., & Gillmore, M. R. (2007). Longitudinal effects of domestic violence on employment and welfare outcomes. *Journal of Interpersonal Violence, 22,* 812–828.

Loseke, D. R. (1992). *The battered woman and shelters: The social construction of wife abuse.* Albany: State University of New York Press.

Magdol, L., Moffitt, T. E., Caspi, A., & Silva, P. (1998). Developmental antecedents of partner abuse: A prospective–longitudinal study. *Journal of Abnormal Psychology, 107,* 375–389.

Marshall, L. L. (1992). *Psychological abuse: Violation, harassment, battering.* Unpublished manuscript, University of North Texas, Denton.

McDonald, R., Jouriles, E. N., Ramisetty-Mikler, S., Caetano, R., & Green, C. (2006). Estimating the number of American children living in partner-violent families. *Journal of Family Psychology, 20,* 137–142.

Medeiros, R. A., & Straus, M. A. (2007). Risk factors for physical violence between dating partners: Implications for gender-inclusive prevention and treatment of family violence. In J. Hamel & T. Nicholls (Eds.), *Family interventions in domestic violence* (pp. 59–85). New York: Springer.

Moffitt, T. E., & Caspi, A. (2003). Preventing the intergenerational continuity of antisocial behavior: Implications of partner violence. In D. P. Farrington & J. W. Coid (Eds.), *Early prevention of adult antisocial behavior* (pp. 109–129). New York: Cambridge University Press.

Moffitt, T. E., Caspi, A., Rutter, M., & Silva, P. A. (2001). *Sex differences in antisocial behavior: Conduct disorder, delinquency, and violence in the Dunedin longitudinal study.* Cambridge, England: Cambridge University Press.

Mueller, E., & Silverman, N. (1989). Peer relations in maltreated children. In D. Cicchetti & V. Carlson (Eds.), *Child maltreatment: Theory and research on the causes and consequences of child abuse and neglect* (pp. 529–578). New York: Cambridge University Press.

Murphy, C. M., O'Farrell, T. J., Fals-Stewart, W., & Feehan, M. (2001). Correlates of intimate partner violence among male alcoholic patients. *Journal of Consulting and Clinical Psychology, 69,* 528–540.

Noller, P., & Roberts, N. D. (2002). The communication of couples in violent and nonviolent relationships: Temporal associations with own and partners' anxiety/arousal and behavior. In P. Noller & J. A. Feeney (Eds.), *Understanding marriage: Developments in the study of couple interaction* (pp. 348–378). New York: Cambridge University Press.

Noller, P., & Robillard, L. (2007). Couple violence: A new look at some old fallacies. In J. Hamel & T. Nicholls (Eds.), *Family interventions in domestic violence* (pp. 125–144). New York: Springer.

O'Leary, K. D. (1988). Physical aggression between spouses: A social learning theory perspective. In V. B. Van Hasselt, R. L. Morrison, A. S. Bellack, & M. Hersen (Eds.), *Handbook of family violence* (pp. 31–55). New York: Plenum Press.

O'Leary, K. D., & Maiuro, R. D. (2001). *Psychological abuse in violent domestic relations.* New York: Springer.

O'Leary, K. D., Smith Slep, A. M., & O'Leary, S. G. (2007). Multivariate models of men's and women's partner aggression. *Journal of Consulting and Clinical Psychology, 75*, 752–764.

Quinton, D., Pickles, A., Maughan, B., & Rutter, M. (1993). Partners, peers, and pathways: Assortative pairing and continuities in conduct disorder. *Development and Psychopathology, 5*, 763–783.

Repetti, R. L., Taylor, S. E., & Seeman, T. E. (2002). Risky families: Family social environments and the mental and physical health of offspring. *Psychological Bulletin, 128*, 330–366.

Salzinger, S., Feldman, R. S., Hammer, M., & Rosario, M. (1993). The effects of physical abuse on children's social relationships. *Child Development, 64*, 169–187.

Schechter, S., & Knitzer, J. (2004). *Early childhood, domestic violence, and poverty: Helping young children and their families*. Iowa City: University of Iowa, School of Social Work.

Serbin, L., & Karp, J. (2003). Intergenerational studies of parenting and the transfer of risk from parent to child. *Current Directions on Psychological Science, 12*, 138–142.

Shields, A., Ryan, R. M., & Cicchetti, D. (2001). Narrative representations of caregivers and emotion dysregulation as predictors of maltreated children's rejection by peers. *Developmental Psychology, 37*, 321–337.

Siegel, D. J. (1999). *The developing mind: Toward a neurobiology of interpersonal experience*. New York: Guilford Press.

Simons, R. L., Wu, C. I., Johnson, C., & Conger, D. (1995). A test of various perspectives on the intergenerational transmission of domestic violence. *Criminology, 33*, 141–172.

Skopp, N. A., McDonald, R., Manke, B., & Jouriles, E. N. (2005). Siblings in domestically violent families: Experiences of interparent conflict and adjustment problems. *Journal of Family Psychology, 19*, 324–333.

Smith Slep, A. M., & O'Leary, S. G. (2005). Parent and partner violence in families with young children: Rates, patterns, and connections. *Journal of Consulting and Clinical Psychology, 73*, 435–444.

Stets, J. E. (1988). *Domestic violence and control*. New York: Springer-Verlag.

Stith, S. M., Rosen, K. H., Middleton, K. A., Busch, A. L., Lundeberg, K., & Carlton, R. P. (1998). The intergenerational transmission of spouse abuse: A meta-analysis. *Journal of Marriage and the Family, 62*, 640–654.

Straus, M. A. (1990). The Conflict Tactics Scales and its critics: An evaluation and new data on validity and reliability. In M. A. Straus & R. J. Gelles (Eds.), *Physical violence in American families: Risk factors and adaptation to violence in 8,145 families* (pp. 3–16). New Brunswick, NJ: Transaction.

Straus, M. A. (1999). The controversy over domestic violence by women: A methodological, theoretical, and sociology of science analysis. In X. B. Arriaga & S. Oskamp (Eds.), *Violence in intimate relationships* (pp. 17–44). Thousand Oaks, CA: Sage.

Straus, M. A., Hamby, S. L., Finkelhor, D., Moore, D. W., & Runyan, D. (1998). Identification of child maltreatment with the Parent–Child Conflict Tactics Scales: Development and psychometric data for a national sample of American parents. *Child Abuse and Neglect, 22,* 249–270.

Straus, M. A., & Stewart, J. H. (1999). Corporal punishment by American parents: National data on prevalence, chronicity, severity and duration, in relation to child and family characteristics. *Clinical Child & Family Psychology Review, 2,* 55–70.

Tjaden, P., & Thoennes, N. (1998). *Prevalence, incidence, and consequences of violence against women: Findings from the National Violence Against Women Survey* (Report No. NCJ 172837). Washington, DC: U.S. Department of Justice.

Tolman, R. M. (1989). The development of a measure of psychological maltreatment of women by their male partners. *Violence and Victims, 4,* 159–177.

Tolman, R. M., & Raphael, J. (2000). A review of research on welfare and domestic violence. *Journal of Social Issues, 56,* 655–682.

Walker, L. E. (1989). *Terrifying love: Why battered women kill and how society responds.* New York: Harper & Row.

Wasserman, G. A., & Seracini, A. M. (2000). Family risk factors and family treatments for early-onset offending. In R. Loeber & D. P. Farrington (Eds.), *Child delinquents: Development, intervention, and service needs* (pp. 165–189). Thousand Oaks, CA: Sage.

Webster-Stratton, C. (1997). From parent training to community building. *Families in Society: The Journal of Contemporary Human Services, 78,* 156–171.

White, H. R., & Widom, C. S. (2003). Intimate partner violence among abused and neglected children in young adulthood: The mediating effects of early aggression, antisocial personality, hostility, and alcohol problems. *Aggressive Behavior, 29,* 332–345.

White, J. W., Merrill, L. L., & Koss, M. P. (2001). Prediction of premilitary courtship violence in a Navy recruit sample. *Journal of Interpersonal Violence, 16,* 910–927.

Widom, C. S. (1989, April 14). The cycle of violence. *Science, 244,* 160–166.

Wiist, W. H., & McFarlane, J. (1999). The effectiveness of an abuse assessment protocol in public health prenatal clinics. *American Journal of Public Health, 89,* 1217–1221.

Wolfe, D. A., Scott, K., Reitzel-Jaffe, D., Wekerle, C., Grasley, C., & Straatman, A. (2001). Development and validation of the Conflict in Adolescent Dating Relationships Inventory. *Psychological Assessment, 13,* 277–293.

Wolfe, D. A., Wekerle, C., Reitzel-Jaffe, D., & Lefebvre, L. (1998). Factors associated with abusive relationships among maltreated and non-maltreated youth. *Development and Psychopathology, 10,* 61–85.

Woodward, L. J., Fergusson, D. M., & Horwood, L. J. (2002). Romantic relationships of young people with childhood and adolescent onset antisocial behavior problems. *Journal of Abnormal Child Psychology, 30,* 231–243.

6

THE PSYCHOPHYSIOLOGY OF INTIMATE PARTNER VIOLENCE: ARE THERE PHYSIOLOGICAL MARKERS OF PSYCHOLOGICAL AND PHYSICAL AGGRESSION?

JARED D. MICHONSKI AND JULIA C. BABCOCK

Psychophysiology researchers have long been interested in the relations between autonomic reactivity and emotion in association with adaptive and maladaptive functioning. Applied to psychopathology, psychophysiology research promises to tap into the biological root of emotional dysregulation. Applied to the study of marriage, it promises to uncover biological cues of an unhealthy relationship. In fact, a relatively consistent body of research has shown that relationship dissatisfaction and divorce can be predicted by increased autonomic reactivity during observed marital conflict (Gottman & Levenson, 1992; Roisman, 2007). If relationship satisfaction and stability can be predicted by autonomic reactivity, can changes in heart rate (HR) and skin conductance (SC) also predict which relationships become extremely maladaptive and violent? Although the question posed is a simple one, the answer is not. In this chapter, we detail the circuitous path of the nascent psychophysiology research as it relates to intimate partner violence (IPV) and aggression.

We begin by considering the study that set the stage for examining partner violence physiologically (Gottman et al., 1995), including a review of the criticisms it sparked and subsequent attempts at replication. Next, we turn our attention to two research literatures that have had a longer history of employing physiological methodologies. First, we review the antisocial/psychopathy literature, followed by a discussion of the hostility and cardiovascular literature. Along the way, we offer general conclusions from these areas that appear to hold promise for uncovering physiological underpinnings of IPV. Finally, we integrate these findings with trends in the IPV field to suggest future directions of inquiry.

ORIGINAL PHYSIOLOGICAL TYPOLOGY OF INTIMATE PARTNER VIOLENCE

Gottman et al. (1995) were the first to extend physiological methodologies used in couples research to the study of intimate partner violence. Even though many of the study's conclusions would later be disconfirmed (Babcock, Green, Webb, & Graham, 2004; Meehan, Holtzworth-Munroe, & Herron, 2001), it nonetheless set the stage for subsequent physiological investigations of IPV. Gottman and colleagues sought to differentiate subtypes of batterers on the basis of physiological reactivity. They divided a community-drawn sample of husbands who were violent toward their partners into two groups using the criterion of whether their HR increased or decreased from baseline during a conflict discussion task with their wives. They found that subgroups of batterers could be distinguished using measures of HR reactivity.

Although this typology did not have a clear precedent in the psychophysiology literature, Gottman and colleagues (Gottman et al., 1995; Jacobson, Gottman, & Shortt, 1995) drew on two lines of research to explain their findings: (a) the antisocial and criminality literature and (b) the hostility and cardiovascular disease literature. Reviewing these literatures, Gottman and his coworkers (Gottman, 2001; Gottman et al., 1995; Jacobson et al., 1995) perceived two competing theories of aggression, psychopathology, and physiological responding. The first, based on antisocial and psychopathy research, supported a hypothesis of underarousal. For instance, it has been proposed that abnormally low autonomic arousal levels may underlie the fearlessness exhibited by criminals and psychopaths (Lykken, 1957; Mednick, 1977; Rain, 1997). Following in the tradition of Cleckley (1941), psychopaths are emotionally withdrawn and lacking in empathy.

Alternatively, Gottman and colleagues (Gottman, 2001; Gottman et al., 1995) referred to findings in the Type A personality, cardiovascular disease, and interpersonal hostility literature (e.g., Kaplan, Botchin, & Manuck, 1994; Siegman & Smith, 1994; Smith & Brown, 1991) to support a hypothesis for overarousal. According to this view, offenders commit violent acts in association with high autonomic reactivity. This two-fold hypothesis for aggressive behavior was also consistent with findings in the domestic violence and IPV literature that indicated the existence of subgroups of batterers differentiated by proactive verses reactive uses of violence (e.g., Holtzworth-Munroe & Stuart, 1994; Tweed & Dutton, 1998). Informed by such findings, Gottman et al. explored the differences in their two subgroups of batterers—those who calmed down physiologically based on HR reactivity compared with those who increased physiologically throughout the course of an observed marital conflict. They referred to men whose HRs lowered during the course of the naturalistic conflict interaction task as *Type 1 batterers* and to men whose HRs increased as *Type 2 batterers*.

Gottman and his colleagues observed several differences between these two subtypes. Type 1 batterers exhibited more contempt and belligerence, which the researchers interpreted to mean that Type 1 men were more emotionally abusive than Type 2 men (Jacobson, Gottman, & Shortt, 1995). Type 1 batterers were also more generally violent outside the home, more likely to be drug dependent, and more likely to exhibit antisocial personality traits than were Type 2 batterers (Gottman, 2001; Jacobson et al., 1995). Type 1 men were also more likely to be antisocial and drug dependent (Gottman, 2001; Jacobson et al., 1995). Type 2 men became more emotionally aggressive as the marital interaction progressed. Consequently, Gottman et al. (1995) speculated that Type 2 batterers were more reactively abusive, whereas Type 1 men may have used violence strategically as a means to intimidate their wives. Gottman et al. also reported that the marriages of Type 2 men were more unstable than those of Type 1 men. A 2-year follow-up revealed a separation–divorce rate of 27% for the 48 marriages of Type 2 men, as opposed to a 0% separation–divorce rate for the 12 marriages of Type 1 men (Jacobson et al., 1995).

Gottman (2001) explained these two types by the differential predictions one would make if guided by the criminality/psychopathy versus the hostility/cardiovascular disease literature. The Type 1 batterer was in keeping with hyporeactivity findings associated with the former, whereas the Type 2 batterer was in keeping with hyperreactivity findings associated with the latter. As has been theorized in the antisocial literature (Eysenck, 1964; Quay, 1965; Raine, 1997), Type 1 batterers were thought to be chronically bored and underaroused, leading to sensation seeking. Gottman et al. (1995) and Jacobson et al. (1995) hypothesized further that the lowered HR Type 1 batterers exhibited may serve as a means to focus attention, perhaps to "maximize the impact of their verbal aggression" (Jacobson et al., 1995, p. 275). In contrast, the researchers perceived the physiological responding of Type 2 men as a more reactive form of abuse such that these men, "rather than being conflict avoidant, are the kind of men who confront their partner, restraining their wives from exiting and responding to anger with physical abuse that escalates when the wife tries to withdraw" (Jacobson et al., 1995, p. 275). For Type 2 batterers, then, it appeared that an exaggerated anger–hostility response led to violence.

Gottman et al.'s (1995) use of HR reactivity to typologize batterers had little prior research history, and this novel approach met with criticism (Margolin, Gordis, Oliver, & Raine, 1995; Ornduff, Kelsey, & O'Leary, 1995). Even Jacobson and Gottman acknowledged uncertainty regarding their findings, yet they could not ignore the robustness of their data:

> Even though we do not yet know why heart rate reactivity was such a powerful discriminating variable in our sample, we have seldom dealt with a variable that has accounted for as much. After some reanalyses, we now realize that it does even more than we originally thought. (Jacobson et al., 1995, p. 272)

Criticisms and Popularity of Gottman et al.'s (1995) Typology

The original article by Gottman et al. (1995) was followed by three critiques (Margolin et al., 1995; Ornduff et al., 1995; Walker, 1995). The authors of these critiques raised several concerns that, in light of inconsistent findings in the psychopathy and hostility/cardiovascular disease literatures, were not unfounded. For instance, although acknowledging that there is some support for lower resting HRs among criminals and psychopaths, both Margolin et al. (1995) and Ornduff et al. (1995) questioned Gottman et al.'s interpretation of the criminality literature as being consistent with deceleration in HR. Furthermore, both raised concerns about the baseline HR of the sample of batterers, noting that the mean reported by Gottman et al. (77.05 beats per min, averaged across both types) was higher than the mean resting HR for the average adult reported elsewhere (70 beats per min; see Larsen, Schneiderman, & Pasin, 1986).

Rather than drawing a parallel to the sensation-seeking hypothesis, as Gottman et al. (1995) did, Margolin et al. (1995) suggested that the literature examining findings with respect to anticipatory HR (e.g., Hare, 1978) may be more relevant in explaining Gottman et al.'s results. Margolin et al. also elaborated on Gottman et al.'s findings, especially regarding HR acceleration. They suggested that increased HR may be associated with stress and, therefore, that Type 2 men may exhibit heightened arousal in response to the aversive condition produced by direct confrontation with their wives. This explanation would also account for the increasing levels of aggression throughout the conflict/discussion, given that Type 2 men were unable to disengage from the conflict. Additionally, they noted the complexity of HR reactivity and the associated difficulty in interpreting such findings: "Marital interaction is not a discrete event, is not standardized across couples, and does not carry the same valence for all participants. Each participant simultaneously is both a respondent and an actor in the discussion" (Margolin et al., 1995, p. 257).

Ornduff et al. (1995) elaborated on Gottman's et al.'s (1995) interpretation of hypoarousal, noting that in no instances were Type 1 men found to be more physiologically reactive than Type 2 men. This fact, they stated, is in keeping with the psychopathy literature, which reports normal or hyporeactive autonomic functioning in psychopaths (e.g., Fowles, 1980; Patrick, 1994). Rather than making reference to the stimulation-seeking hypothesis, however, Ornduff et al. discussed these findings with respect to a deficit in behavioral inhibition system functioning, as Fowles (1980) suggested. Specifically, rather than being sensation seekers, Type 1 batterers may be better described as lacking in behavioral inhibition. Additionally, Ornduff et al. proposed that the HR differences between Type 1 and Type 2 batterers may reflect differences in task engagement, suspecting that Type 1 batterers were more withdrawn from the conflict/discussion.

In spite of these criticisms, the popular press, including the *Oprah Winfrey Show* and the *CBS Evening News*, picked up on the Type 1–Type 2 distinction. Jacobson and Gottman (1998) also wrote about their research findings in a book for the lay audience, labeling the Type 1 batterers *cobras* and the Type II batterers *pit bulls*. The cool and methodical cobras are calm when they inflict pain and humiliation on their victims. The pit bulls, on the other hand, whose emotions boil over quickly, are deeply insecure and tend to become stalkers, unable to let go of relationships after they have ended. The descriptions and vignettes are chilling and compelling. The psychophysiological findings were hailed for bringing "insight into the nature of evil" (Loftus, 1998). The book was well written and has influenced many.

Failed Replications

Unfortunately, the science behind the book is not as straightforward as originally thought. Two subsequent attempts (Babcock et al., 2004; Meehan et al., 2001) failed to replicate the Gottman et al. (1995) typology. Meehan et al. (2001) sought to test the Gottman et al. typology of batterers, to elaborate on the distinctions between Type 1 and Type 2 batterers, and to compare Gottman et al.'s typology to their own batterer typology (Holtzworth-Munroe & Stuart, 1994). Like Gottman et al., Meehan et al. found that HR reactivity could be used to separate batterers into two groups: those whose HR decreased and those whose HR increased.

However, the similarities ended there. Meehan et al. (2001) reported finding no evidence that batterers whose HR decreased were more severely violent, emotionally aggressive, likely to exhibit antisocial personalities, drug dependent, or generally violent than Type 2 batterers. Furthermore, they found no parallels between Gottman et al.'s (1995) typology and the

Holtzworth-Munroe typology (Holtzworth-Munroe & Stuart, 1994). Consequently, Meehan et al. suggested that the utility of the Gottman et al. typology using HR reactivity to differentiate subtypes of batterers is suspect.

In a response to Meehan et al.'s (2001) findings, Gottman (2001) questioned first whether the study represented a precise replication of his original study. Specifically, Gottman et al. (1995) assessed interbeat interval with electrocardiogram (EKG) recording, whereas Meehan et al. assessed HR through a finger pulse recording, which is susceptible to distortion under experimental conditions (Giardino, Lehrer, & Edelberg, 2002). Second, Gottman suggested that the replication used a marital interaction task that was milder than the highly conflictual task used in the original study.

The second attempt at replication, however, followed Gottman et al.'s (1995) procedure more closely and also made one important modification: extending the 2-minute baseline period to 4 minutes to ensure a more stable recording of baseline HR (Babcock et al., 2004). In keeping with Gottman et al. and Meehan et al. (2001), Babcock and colleagues (2004) identified a subgroup of batterers whose HR increased and another subgroup whose HR decreased during the conflict discussion. Consistent with Meehan et al., results did not show the expected differences between Type 1 and Type 2 batterers based on HR change. Babcock et al. explained this failure as resulting from unusually high baseline HRs for the Type 1 men in the Gottman et al. (1995) study (M = 82.83 beats per minute). Using EKG during a longer, stable baseline, Babcock et al. did, however, find relations in the expected direction between antisocial spectrum behavior and resting HR. This finding is more compatible with the antisocial literature than is HR reactivity (Raine, 1993).

In light of these findings and Meehan et al.'s (2001) previous failure to replicate, Babcock and colleagues (2004) concluded that the Gottman et al. (1995) dichotomization of batterers on the basis of HR change does not appear to withstand scientific scrutiny. However, HR, as well as other physiological measures, may be a valid risk marker for IPV. Hence, before continuing our discussion of the psychophysiology of IPV, we review relevant findings in the antisocial/criminality and hostility/cardiovascular reactivity literatures. Then we will return to IPV and discuss the utility of a psychophysiological approach to studying partner abuse.

PHYSIOLOGICAL FINDINGS IN THE ANTISOCIAL/ PSYCHOPATHY LITERATURE

The antisocial/criminality literature includes a vast number of studies that have used psychophysiological methodologies. This literature has important and relevant implications for domestic violence researchers, particularly given the small number of IPV studies using physiological measures.

Unfortunately, space does not permit us to review all of the relevant physiological findings within psychopathy and antisocial research (see reviews by Hare, 1978; Lorber, 2004; Patrick & Verona, 2007; Raine, 1993). We summarize several key assumptions and findings that we view as most pertinent to our discussion of IPV.

Antisocial/Psychopathy: Conceptual Differences

The psychopathy and antisocial literatures are replete with mixed findings and differences of interpretation. Many of these differences can be attributed to variations in how researchers both conceptualize and measure antisocial behavior/personality (Lorber, 2004). Presently, two labels of antisocial individuals predominate in the literature (although at times they are used interchangeably)—*psychopathy* and *antisocial personality disorder* (ASPD).

The first and more historic labeling is *psychopathy*. Psychopathy is a personality-laden construct (Lilienfeld, 1994) that is generally associated with a specific pattern of personality traits. The emphasis on a particular constellation of traits dates back to Cleckley's (1941) well-known clinical descriptions in *The Mask of Sanity*. Cleckley described psychopaths as characterized by a set of 16 criteria, among them superficial charm, absence of anxiety, insincerity, lack of remorse, poverty of affect, and inability to form interpersonal relationships. Presently, psychopathy is most often viewed as consisting of two factors, as operationalized by Hare's Psychopathy Checklist—Revised (PCL–R; Hare, 1991, 2003; see Cooke & Michie, 2001, for a three-factor model). Factor 1 captures Cleckley's description and is characterized by emotional detachment (Patrick, 1994). Factor 2 captures antisocial and externalizing behaviors such as impulsivity, irresponsibility, and delinquency.

The second most featured labeling is *antisocial personality disorder*, which appears in the *Diagnostic and Statistical Manual of Mental Disorders* (4th ed., text rev.; American Psychiatric Association, 2000). ASPD is a more behaviorally based construct (Lilienfeld, 1994) and correlates moderately with Factor 2 only (Harpur, Hare, & Hakstian, 1989). ASPD is a broader construct than psychopathy: Whereas estimates suggest that 90% of criminals meeting criteria for psychopathy also meet criteria for ASPD, only 30% of criminals meeting for ASPD also meet criteria for psychopathy (Hart & Hare, 1997). These different conceptualizations are important because they function differently in relation to autonomic arousal.

Psychopathy versus ASPD is not the only distinction that researchers have made when describing antisocial behavior. Specifically, psychopathy is itself often viewed as a heterogeneous construct (e.g., Brinkley, Newman, Widiger, & Lynam, 2004; Lilienfeld, 1994; Lykken, 1995; Newman & Brinkley, 1997). Psychopathy has long been differentiated into primary and secondary forms (Karpman, 1948). Primary psychopaths, like the Cleckleyian description, are emotionally withdrawn, callous, manipulative, and egocentric. Secondary psychopaths are neurotic and impulsive, their antisocial behavior stemming from emotional conflict (Lilienfeld, 1994; Lykken, 1995; Newman & Brinkley, 1997).

Lykken (1995) suggested that primary and secondary forms should be differentiated on the basis of fearlessness; primary psychopaths are characterized by low fear. He argued that researchers should use an additional measure (e.g., Activities Preference Questionnaire; Lykken & Katzenmeyer, 1973) in combination with the PCL–R to capture this low-fear quality. Other researchers (Newman & Brinkley, 1997) asserted that anxiety, namely, neurotic anxiety (as measured by the Welsh Anxiety Scale; Welsh, 1956), is better able to account for differences between primary and secondary psychopaths (Brinkley et al., 2004; Newman & Brinkley, 1997). Such heterogeneity among those who commit antisocial acts is likely also to apply to those who commit IPV and may even exist within subgroups of batterers (e.g., the generally violent Type 1 batterer).

Physiological Arousal

Explanations for the importance of physiological functioning in antisocial outcomes historically have been rooted primarily in two, largely complementary theories: fearlessness and stimulation seeking (Raine, 1997; alternatively, see Blair, Jones, Clark, & Smith, 1997). The fearlessness theory is the more prominent of the two and has undergone more empirical investigation. It is grounded in the notion that low levels of fear manifest in the form of low levels of autonomic arousal (Hare, 1978; Raine, 1993, 1997). Alternatively, proponents of a sensation seeking or reward dependence hypothesis suggest that low arousal represents an aversive state, one that is alleviated through the pursuit of arousing stimuli in order to obtain an optimal level of arousal (Eysenck, 1964; Quay, 1965; Raine, 1993, 1997; Zuckerman, 1978). Raine (1997) suggested that fearlessness and reward dependence may work in complementary fashion, exerting a synergistic effect such that low levels of autonomic arousal may predispose one to engage in antisocial behaviors because it simultaneously produces low levels of fear and promotes sensation seeking. Underarousal may lead to psychopathic outcomes via poor passive-avoidance learning, hypothesized to occur by classical conditioning—that is, those who do not experience appropriate levels of anxious or fearful arousal do not learn to inhibit inappropriate, antisocial behaviors (Eysenck, 1977; Fowles, 1980; Gray, 1987; Lykken, 1957; Mednick, 1977).

Three psychophysiological measures have been most pertinent to the hypotheses of underarousal/stimulation seeking: SC, HR, and eye-blink startle response. Findings on the relations between these specific physiological avenues and antisocial outcomes are varied. Often they depend on the specific experimental paradigm and the inclusion of moderating variables. But generally speaking, the literature does seem to support the importance of physiology in understanding antisocial/psychopathic behavior.

Skin Conductance

The most commonly reported of the physiological measures is electrodermal activity or, more specifically, SC. SC, which essentially reflects changes in perspiration, is useful because it directly corresponds to the sympathetic autonomic nervous system and consequently provides an index of emotional arousal (Raine, 1993). In particular, theorists have viewed SC as an index of fear, anxiety, and behavioral inhibition (Fowles, 1980). Researchers have most commonly reported resting level and reactivity in anticipation of and in response to noxious or novel stimuli (Hare, 1978; Lorber, 2004; Raine, 1993).

Studies examining the relationship between psychopathy and SC provide a good example of the complex state of the physiology and antisocial literature. Findings are often mixed: Some reviews suggest the importance of this relation (Hare, 1978), whereas others are more inconclusive (Raine, 1993; Sutker & Allain, 2004). In a recent meta-analysis, however, Lorber (2004) reported that psychopathy was significantly negatively related both to resting SC and to SC reactivity but found no associations between the broader construct of aggression and SC.

Heart Rate

HR has received less attention in the psychopathy/antisocial literature than has SC (Arnett, 1997), probably because there is less consensus about the significance of HR. HR is more complex than SC in that it reflects both the sympathetic and parasympathetic nervous systems (Raine, 1993). Fowles (1980) proposed that HR serves as an index of the behavioral approach system—a gauge for approach or active-avoidance behaviors—and he further proposed that psychopaths are characterized by a normal or strong behavioral approach system. Hence, psychopaths might be expected to exhibit exaggerated HR accelerations when in pursuit of a reward. There is some support for this view (Arnett, 1997; Arnett, Smith, & Newman, 1997). Other researchers have noted that HR may serve as an index of one's experience of either fear or pleasure (Patrick, 1994). Further, HR decelerations may represent enhanced orienting and attentional processing (Levenston, Patrick, Bradley, & Lang, 2000; Patrick, 1994; Raine, 1993). HR may accelerate or decelerate depending on the context and methodology of the given experimental paradigm (Patrick, 1994).

In adults, neither low resting HR nor HR reactivity appears to be a significant predictor of psychopathy (Hare, 1978; Lorber, 2004; Raine, 1993, 1997). However, when considering antisocial and aggression more generally, the findings have been largely consistent. Developmentally, the results are very clear: Low resting HR in youths is one of the most robust findings in the antisocial literature (Raine, 1993, 1997). For example, a longitudinal investigation revealed that low resting HR at age 3 predicted later aggression at age 11 (Raine, Venables, & Mednick, 1997). In adults, aggression is associated both with low resting HR and with greater HR reactivity (Lorber, 2004).

Eye-Blink Startle Response

More recently, eye-blink startle response has been used to assess the fearlessness attribute of psychopaths (Patrick, 1994; Patrick, Bradley, & Lang, 1993). Using this physiological measure, Patrick and colleagues found that psychopaths displayed inhibited reactions to aversive tones while viewing emotionally explicit slides. Additionally, after more in-depth analysis, these researchers discovered that diminished startle response was more strongly associated with emotional detachment (Factor 1) than with antisocial behavior (Factor 2). Subsequent research has suggested that the association between psychopathy and diminished startle response is consistent (Levenston et al., 2000) and may even extend to noncriminal populations (Flor, Birbaumer, Hermann, Ziegler, & Patrick, 2002). Hence, the relative importance of psychopathic traits in predicting physiological responses may also hold for IPV samples.

Moderators and Mediators

Examining moderating and mediating variables is important because doing so may help clarify the often muddled relations between autonomic arousal and antisocial behavior. Several studies by Raine and colleagues point to the moderating effect of social environment (Brennan et al., 1997; Raine, 2002; Raine & Venables, 1981). For instance, antisocial adolescents from high social classes exhibited reduced SC responsiveness, whereas those from low social classes exhibited enhanced SC responsiveness (Raine & Venables, 1981). More recently, Ishikawa, Raine, Lencz, Bihrle, and LaCasse (2001) found that HR reactivity distinguished "unsuccessful" (i.e., caught/incarcerated) from "successful" (community sample) psychopaths. Unsuccessful psychopaths exhibited reduced HR reactivity in the context of an emotionally stressful task designed to elicit embarrassment and guilt. This finding suggests that conviction status or severity of antisocial behavior may moderate the relationship between psychopathy and autonomic arousal.

Furthermore, Arnett et al.'s (1997) work examining differences between high- and low-anxious psychopaths provides some evidence for reduced SC responding and enhanced HR responding (sensation seeking in pursuit of reward) for low-anxious psychopaths. Thus, it appears that anxiety (namely, neurotic anxiety) may moderate the relation between psychopathy and autonomic functioning. The importance of intervening variables to physiological underarousal also found support in a study of narcissistic individuals (Kelsey, Ornduff, McCann, & Reiff, 2001). Narcissistic personality, characterized by egocentricity and lack of empathy, may be the predominant trait associated with the psychopathic personality (Kernberg, 1989). Results showed that narcissism is associated with low levels of anxiety and reduced SCR (skin conductance response). Perhaps, then, it is the narcissistic personality traits of the psychopath that are responsible for and mediate the association between psychopathy and physiological hyporeactivity.

Implications for Intimate Partner Violence Research

Although physiological findings in the antisocial/psychopathy literature are often difficult to sort out, physiological functioning does appear to be important in understanding antisocial outcomes (Lorber, 2004). By extension, then, psychophysiology must be relevant to domestic violence. Several general conclusions can be drawn from the antisocial/psychopathy literature that have important implications for IPV research. First, the antisocial and psychopathic constructs are heterogeneous. When different researchers investigate antisocial and psychopathic individuals, they often use different conceptualizations of what characterize these individuals. These differing conceptualizations—for example, psychopathy, ASPD, low-anxious psychopathy, high Factor 1—may perform differently under physiological examination. Such variations in how antisocial behavior is conceived may be important to IPV research in that they may correspond to subtypes of batterers (e.g., instrumental vs. impulsive batterers, antisocial/generally violent vs. borderline/dysphoric).

Furthermore, given the muddled state of the antisocial/psychopathy literature, it becomes evident that considering mediating and moderating factors may help to clarify relations between autonomic functioning and antisocial outcomes. This likewise holds true for IPV research. Evidence suggests that conviction status (Ishikawa et al., 2001), other personality disorders (Kelsey et al., 2001), social environment (Raine & Venables, 1981), and anxiety (Arnett, 1997) may act as moderators or mediators.

Just as the antisocial constructs themselves are heterogeneous, so are the methodologies used to assess them, including the physiological measures (e.g., SC, HR, eye-blink startle) and the stimulus used to elicit the affective response (e.g., visual, auditory, olfactory). Regarding the stimulus, there is some evidence that socially meaningful stimuli (Raine, 1993) and vicarious emotional stimuli (Hare, 1978; Verona, Patrick, Curtain, Bradley, & Lang, 2004) may be more efficacious in eliciting hypoarousal among psychopaths. This finding is consistent with the research of Blair and his colleagues, who suggested that psychopaths are particularly insensitive to vicarious distress stimuli (Blair, 1999; Blair et al., 1997). Such research highlights the potential utility of the marital conflict paradigm Gottman et al. (1995) originally used. However, psychopathy researchers generally study psychophysiological responding within the confines of tightly controlled experimental paradigms.

Within the IPV literature, physiological responding has been examined more frequently in the context of naturalistic conflict discussions with one's partner (cf. Babcock, Green, Webb, & Yerington, 2005). Thus, research findings on psychopathy to IPV must be compared cautiously. The cardiovascular disease literature does, however, contain studies in which marital discussion tasks have been used.

PSYCHOPHYSIOLOGICAL FINDINGS IN THE HOSTILITY AND CARDIOVASCULAR LITERATURE

Gottman et al. (1995) referenced findings in the coronary heart disease (CHD) literature to support a hypothesis of hyperarousal among Type 2 batterers. Many studies have attempted to connect Type A personality, and hostility in particular, to CHD (see Siegman & Smith, 1994, for a review). Some of this research has implicated cardiovascular reactivity, namely HR and systolic blood pressure (SBP) reactivity, as mechanisms by which hostility/Type A leads to CHD. Hostility has been the focus of much of this research because it is believed to be the primary component of the Type A construct that leads to CHD (Siegman, 1994). Such research is relevant to IPV because batterers are more hostile, psychologically abusive, and aggressive toward their wives than nonbattering men (Dutton, 1988).

Although most studies examining the relation between hostility and cardiovascular reactivity have not involved marital discussion tasks, in a small number of studies researchers have used such designs. We focus our review on these studies, as they are the most applicable to IPV research. In general, trait hostility has not been consistently associated with exaggerated cardiovascular reactivity, but effects may be more likely in experimental situations involving interpersonal stressors (e.g., harassment, mistrust) or when other personality characteristics are considered (Houston, 1994; Suls & Wan, 1993).

A couples interaction paradigm allows for such interpersonal stressors, and results from studies involving this design have been promising. But just as in the antisocial/psychopathy literature, effects often depend on the methodology used and the moderating variables involved. For instance, "agentic" concerns of the husband, characterized by efforts to assert dominance and control over his partner, may moderate the relation between hostility and physiology or demonstrate a direct effect on physiology apart from hostility (Smith, Gallo, Goble, Ngue, & Stark, 1998).

During a marital discussion task, husbands who were high in trait cynical hostility displayed greater HR reactivity than those who were low in this trait (Smith & Brown, 1991). Similarly, husbands who were trying to influence their wives or who were being evaluated in an achievement task exhibited greater HR and SBP reactivity (Brown & Smith, 1992; Smith et al., 1998). The relation between husband achievement and cardiovascular reactivity was moderated by hostility for SBP but not for HR reactivity (Smith & Gallo, 1999). Miller, Dopp, Myers, Felten, and Fahey (1999) found no significant relations between anger and HR, but anger was significantly related to SBP, and this association was moderated by cynical hostility. In sum, these findings indicate that hostility and achievement or agentic concerns are related to cardiovascular hyperarousal. However, this relation may be more robust for blood pressure than for HR.

Physiological responding may also be related to differences in communication styles, as well as to gender. Although nonviolent couples typically exhibit the communication pattern in which the wife makes demands and the husband withdraws (Eldridge & Christensen, 2002), in violent couples this pattern tends to be reversed: Violent men demand and wives withdraw (Babcock, Waltz, Jacobson, & Gottman, 1993; Berns, Jacobson, & Gottman, 1999). A psychophysiological investigation of nonviolent couples (Denton, Burleson, Hobbs, Von Stein, & Rodriguez, 2001) revealed that initiator (demander) husbands exhibited significantly greater HR reactivity than did avoider (withdrawer) husbands. Additionally, when interacting with withdrawer wives, husbands experienced significantly more BP reactivity than when interacting with demander wives. This relation was especially pronounced for demander husbands. Hence, physiological reactivity may be more a function of the combined interactive style of the couple than of gender itself (Denton et al., 2001). Withdrawers will become physiologically reactive during confrontation with demanders and vice versa, irrespective of gender (Denton et al., 2001). No research to date has examined couples' demand–withdraw communication pattern as it relates to psychophysiological reactivity within couples experiencing IPV.

Hostility is clearly implicated in marital violence (see Norlander & Eckhardt, 2005, for a review). Male batterers are known to be more hostile, more abusive psychologically, and more provocative and aggressive toward their wives than other men (Gottman et al., 1995; Jacobson et al., 1994). We know that IPV men exhibit more provocative anger and contempt (Babcock et al., 2004; Jacobson et al., 1994). However, to date, no psychophysiological research has tried to uncouple the concept of hostility from IPV. Similarly, we know very little about the combined interactive style of the male and female partner within violent relationships as it relates to psychophysiological reactivity.

REVISITING PSYCHOPHYSIOLOGY AND INTIMATE PARTNER VIOLENCE

Given the psychophysiological trends in the antisocial/psychopathy literature, two failed attempts at replication (Babcock et al., 2004; Meehan et al., 2001), and methodological concerns, the question of whether batterers can be dichotomized using HR reactivity to form meaningful subtypes (Gottman et al., 1995) should be put to rest. There are no consistent differences in abuse, general violence, personality, or psychopathy when batterers are differentiated in this way. Does that mean that HR reactivity is irrelevant to the study of IPV? Our review of the psychophysiological literature has shown that autonomic functioning (a) is not typically dichotomized, (b) is task dependent, and (c) is moderated or mediated by other important variables. The story on IPV and psychophysiological reactivity is a complex one and cannot easily be summarized into a sound-bite.

In our lab, we are exploring the psychophysiological functioning of IPV men by keeping physiological variables as continuous measures and exploring possible mediators and moderators. In our first extension of the Gottman et al. (1995) findings (Babcock et al., 2005), we tried to address three problems with the original research. First, we found it necessary to uncouple the construct of partner abuse from the global construct of antisocial behavior. That is, is IPV a construct that is distinct from the antisocial spectrum of behavior or just another variant of it? A measurement model suggests that IPV can be parsed out from the general antisocial spectrum of behavior (Babcock et al., 2005). Additionally, we assessed autonomic reactivity in two different laboratory tasks: a conflict discussion task and a standardized anger induction task. The latter allowed for more a more tightly controlled situation. Further, we used broader selection criteria than did Gottman et al., yielding a wide range of IPV. Doing so, we found that the frequency and severity of IPV moderate the relation between IPV and physiological reactivity.

We hypothesized that hyporeactivity would be associated with partner abuse only within a severely violent sample like that of Gottman et al. (1995). Conversely, hyperreactivity was expected to be associated with partner abuse and antisocial traits with respect to low-level batterers or within couples experiencing situational or "common couple" violence (Johnson & Ferraro, 2000). When we compared nonviolent, low-level violent, and severely violent men on measures of antisocial behavior, IPV, and autonomic reactivity, we found that low resting HR and psychophysiological reactivity were more consistently related to the broad construct of antisocial behavior than to IPV per se. Furthermore, severity of violence moderated the relations of both HR and SC with the antisocial spectrum of behavior. As predicted, HR reactivity and SC change were negatively correlated with antisocial behavior for severely violent men only. However, for low-level batterers, HR reactivity and SC change were positively correlated with antisocial behavior. Findings were similar across the naturalistic conflict discussion and the more tightly standardized anger induction task.

These findings are consistent with Johnson's (1995) notion that men who perpetrate severe IPV may be qualitatively different from those who engage in low levels of abuse. Although a dichotomous typology based on

HR deceleration alone may be questionable, a categorical distinction based on having committed a life-threatening act may be appropriate when examining psychophysiological correlates of IPV. Increased HR and SC reactivity may act to inhibit severe violence perpetration for men with aggressive tendencies.

In keeping with findings in the antisocial literature (Brennan et al., 1997; Raine, Venables, & Williams, 1995, 1996), men who report antisocial traits but are highly physiologically reactive may also be more anxious and fearful, which may serve as protective factors against severely battering their mates. An alternative explanation is that severe battering may lead to autonomic hyporeactivity such that batterers become desensitized to interpersonal conflict. Although antisocial, severely violent men may still act angry, they may have learned to refrain from reacting physiologically in anger-inducing situations. In contrast, antisocial men who perpetrate low levels of violence show the expected pattern of increased cardiovascular and electrodermal responding when angered, suggesting a failure to regulate physiological arousal, also called *flooding* (Gottman, 1994). The most antisocial of the severely violent men, however, display not only low resting HRs but decreases in cardiovascular and electrodermal responding when angered. This suggests a different process of regulating anger for the antisocial, severely violent men. It also suggests that interventions teaching emotional regulation strategies to prevent flooding may not benefit the antisocial, severely violent batterer.

Babcock et al. (2005) examined only one of the many potential moderating variables influencing the relation between psychophysiological responding and IPV. Other directions might include examining psychophysiological reactivity across other extant batterer typologies, including those based on motivation for perpetrating violence (Chase, O'Leary, & Heyman, 2001), personality (Hamberger & Hastings, 1986; Tweed & Dutton, 1998), personality and generality of violence (Holtzworth-Munroe & Stuart, 1994), bilaterality and severity of men's and women's violence, and control (Johnson, 1995). These subtypes of batterers are in keeping with the research on psychopathy/antisocial behavior, as reviewed previously.

Each attempt to typologize batterers yields a subgroup characterized by emotional detachment and a more instrumental form of violence. Although they have assumed various labels, including *Type 1* (Gottman et al., 1995), *generally violent/antisocial* (Holtzworth-Munroe & Stuart, 1994), *narcissistic/psychopathic* (Hamberger & Hastings, 1986), *patriarchal terrorism* (Johnson, 1995), and *instrumental* (Tweed & Dutton, 1998), they are all reminiscent of the callous–unemotional, Factor 1, Cleckleyian conceptualization of the primary psychopath.

A second subgroup of batterers that typically emerges in typology studies is characterized by reactive violence; inclination to experience anger, anxiety, and depression; and a preoccupied attachment style. These batterers have assumed the labels Type 2 (Gottman et al., 1995), *dysphoric/borderline* (Holtzworth-Munroe & Stuart, 1994), *Jekyll & Hyde* (Hamberger & Hastings, 1986), *preoccupied* (Babcock, Jacobson, Gottman, & Yerington, 2000), and *impulsive* (Tweed & Dutton, 1998). They may be nonpsychopathic antisocial, high Factor 2 or secondary, high-anxious psychopaths, and they may have markedly different patterns of psychophysiological responding as compared with the instrumental/GVA/ primary psychopathic batterer. They may have emotional dysregulation problems common to individuals diagnosed with borderline personality disorder.

Inasmuch as hypoarousal is thought to be the hallmark of at least primary psychopaths, affective hyperarousal is thought to be a hallmark of borderline personality disorder (Herpertz, Kunert, Schwenger, Eng, & Sass, 1999; Linehan, 1993). Therefore, comparing and contrasting the psychophysiological arousal of batterers with psychopathic features versus those with borderline personality features may prove fruitful (Babcock, Ross, Canady, & Senior, 2007).

THE BOTTOM LINE

Although Gottman et al.'s (1995) dichotomy based on HR reactivity is unsubstantiated, psychophysiological research does have something to offer the IPV field. Clearly, there are psychophysiological correlates of psychopathy, hostility, and dysfunctional marital interaction. By extension, there necessarily must be psychophysiological correlates of intimate partner aggression, as psychopathic traits, hostility, and dysfunctional relationships are part and parcel of IPV. Exploring the psychophysiological correlates of IPV may represent good basic science, but to what extent are psychophysiological correlates clinically useful in interventions for IPV? Autonomic functioning is not thought to be highly malleable, except perhaps with drug therapies. Psychophysiological reactivity during couples conflict is moderated by culture (Tsai, Levenson, & McCoy, 2006), attachment style (Roisman, 2007), and severity of violence perpetrated (Babcock et al., 2005). Perhaps further exploration of particular moderators or mediators will someday elucidate therapeutic mechanisms of change and treatment targets. The challenge now is to apply existing models or to develop new theories that capture the complexities of psychophysiological responding as it relates to aggression and violence.

REFERENCES

American Psychiatric Association. (2000). *Diagnostic and statistical manual of mental disorders* (4th ed., text rev.). Washington, DC: Author.

Arnett, P. A. (1997). Autonomic responsivity in psychopaths: A critical review and theoretical proposal. *Clinical Psychology Review, 17*, 903–936.

Arnett, P. A., Smith, S. S., & Newman, J. P. (1997). Approach and avoidance motivation in incarcerated psychopaths during passive avoidance. *Journal of Personality and Social Psychology, 72*, 1413–1428.

Babcock, J. C., Green, C. E., Webb, S. A., & Graham, K. H. (2004). A second failure to replicate the Gottman et al. (1995) typology of men who abuse intimate partners . . . and possible reasons why. *Journal of Family Psychology, 18*, 396–400.

Babcock, J. C., Green, C. E., Webb, S. A., & Yerington, T. P. (2005). Psychophysiological profiles of batterers: Autonomic emotional reactivity as it predicts the antisocial spectrum of behavior among intimate partner abusers. *Journal of Abnormal Psychology, 114*, 444–455.

Babcock, J. C., Jacobson, N. S., Gottman, J. M., & Yerington, T. P. (2000). Attachment, emotional regulation, and the function of marital violence: Differences between secure, preoccupied and dismissing violent and nonviolent husbands. *Journal of Family Violence, 15*, 391–409.

Babcock, J. C., Ross, J. M., Canady, B., & Senior, A. (2007). *Psychophysiological reactivity associated with psychopathic, borderline, and antisocial personality features among intimate partner abusers during two emotional tasks.* Manuscript in preparation.

Babcock, J. C., Waltz, J., Jacobson, N. S., & Gottman, J. M. (1993). Power and violence: The relationship between communication patterns, power discrepancies and domestic violence. *Journal of Consulting and Clinical Psychology, 61*, 40–50.

Berns, S. B., Jacobson, N. S., & Gottman, J. M. (1999). Demand–withdraw interaction in couples with a violent husband. *Journal of Consulting and Clinical Psychology, 67*, 666–674.

Blair, R. J. R. (1999). Responsiveness to distress cues in the child with psychopathic tendencies. *Personality and Individual Differences, 27*, 135–145.

Blair, R. J. R., Jones, L., Clark, F., & Smith, M. (1997). The psychopathic individual: A lack of responsiveness to distress cues? *Psychophysiology, 34*, 192–198.

Brennan, P. A., Raine, A., Schulsinger, F., Kirkegaard-Sorensen, L., Knop, J., Hutchings, B., et al. (1997). Psychophysiological protective factors for male subjects at high risk for criminal behavior. *American Journal of Psychiatry, 154*, 853–855.

Brinkley, C., Newman, J., Widiger, T., & Lynam, D. (2004). Two approaches to parsing the heterogeneity of psychopathy. *Clinical Psychology: Science and Practice, 11*, 69–94.

Brown, P. C., & Smith, T. W. (1992). Social influence, marriage, and the heart: Cardiovascular consequences of interpersonal control in husbands and wives. *Health Psychology, 11*, 88–96.

Chase, K. A., O'Leary, K. D., & Heyman, R. E. (2001). Categorizing partner-violent men within the reactive–proactive typology model. *Journal of Consulting and Clinical Psychology, 69*, 567–572.

Cleckley, H. (1941). *The mask of sanity: An attempt to reinterpret the so-called psychopathic personality.* Oxford, England: Mosby.

Cooke, D. J., & Michie, C. (2001). Refining the construct of psychopathy: Towards a hierarchical model. *Psychological Assessment, 13,* 171–188.

Denton, W. H., Burleson, B. R., Hobbs, B. V., Von Stein, M., & Rodriguez, C. P. (2001). Cardiovascular reactivity and initiate/avoid patterns of marital communication: A test of Gottman's psychophysiologic model of marital interaction. *Journal of Behavioral Medicine, 24,* 401–421.

Dutton, D. G. (1988). Profiling of wife assaulters: Preliminary evidence for a trimodal analysis. *Violence and Victims, 3,* 5–29.

Eldridge, K. A., & Christensen, A. (2002). Demand–withdraw communication during couple conflict: A review and analysis. In P. Noller & J. Feeney (Eds.), *Understanding marriage: Developments in the study of couple interaction* (pp. 289–322). New York: Cambridge University Press.

Eysenck, H. J. (1964). *Crime and personality.* London: Methuen.

Eysenck, H. J. (1977). *Crime and personality* (3rd ed.). St. Albans, England: Paladin.

Flor, H., Birbaumer, N., Hermann, C., Ziegler, S., & Patrick, C. J. (2002). Aversive Pavlovian conditioning in psychopaths: Peripheral and central correlates. *Psychophysiology, 39,* 505–518.

Fowles, D. C. (1980). The three arousal model: Implication of Gray's two-factor learning theory for heart rate, electrodermal activity, and psychopathy. *Psychophysiology, 17,* 87–104.

Giardino, N. D., Lehrer, P. M., & Edelberg, R. (2002). Comparison of finger plethysmograph to ECG in the measurement of heart rate variability. *Psychophysiology, 39,* 246–253.

Gottman, J. M. (1994). *Why marriages succeed or fail.* New York: Simon & Schuster.

Gottman, J. M. (2001). Crime, hostility, wife battering, and the heart: On the Meehan et al. failure to replicate the Gottman et al. (1995) typology. *Journal of Family Psychology, 15,* 409–414.

Gottman, J. M., Jacobson, N. S., Rushe, R. H., Shortt, J. W., Babcock, J. C., LaTaillade, J. J., & Waltz, J. (1995). The relationship between heart rate reactivity, emotionally aggressive behavior, and general violence in batterers. *Journal of Family Psychology, 9,* 227–248.

Gottman, J. M., & Levenson, R. W. (1992). Marital processes predictive of later dissolution: Behavior, physiology, and health. *Journal of Personality and Social Psychology, 63,* 221–233.

Gray, J. A. (1987). *The psychology of fear and stress.* New York: Cambridge University Press.

Hamberger, L. K., & Hastings, J. E. (1986). Personality correlates of men who abuse their partners: A cross-validation study. *Journal of Family Violence, 1,* 323–341.

Hare, R. D. (1978). Electrodermal and cardiovascular correlates of psychopathy. In R. D. Hare & D. Schalling (Eds.), *Psychopathic behavior: Approaches to research* (pp. 107–144). Chichester, England: Wiley.

Hare, R. D. (1991). *The Hare Psychopathy Checklist—Revised*. Toronto, Ontario, Canada: Multi-Health Systems.

Hare, R. D. (2003). *Manual for the Hare Psychopathy Checklist—Revised* (2nd ed.). Toronto, Ontario, Canada: Multi-Health Systems.

Harpur, T. J., Hare, R. D., & Hakstian, A. R. (1989). Two-factor conceptualization of psychopathy: Construct validity and assessment implications. *Journal of Consulting and Clinical Psychology, 1*, 6–17.

Hart, S. D., & Hare, R. D. (1997). Psychopathy: Assessment and association with criminal conduct. In D. M. Stoff, J. Breiling, & J. D. Maser (Eds.), *Handbook of antisocial behavior* (pp. 22–35). New York: Wiley.

Herpertz, S., Kunert, H., Schwenger, U., Eng, M., & Sass, H. (1999). Affective responsiveness in borderline personality disorder: A psychophysiological approach. *American Journal of Psychiatry, 156*, 1550–1556.

Holtzworth-Munroe, A., & Stuart, G. L. (1994). Typologies of male batterers: Three subtypes and the differences among them. *Psychological Bulletin, 116*, 476–497.

Houston, B. K. (1994). Anger, hostility, and psychophysiological reactivity. In A. W. Siegman & T. W. Smith (Eds.), *Anger, hostility, and the heart* (pp. 97–116). Hillsdale, NJ: Erlbaum.

Ishikawa, S. S., Raine, A., Lencz, T., Bihrle, S., & LaCasse, L. (2001). Autonomic stress reactivity and executive functions in successful and unsuccessful criminal psychopaths from the community. *Journal of Abnormal Psychology, 110*, 423–432.

Jacobson, N. S., & Gottman, J. M. (1998). *When men batter women: New insights into ending abusive relationships*. New York: Simon & Schuster.

Jacobson, N. S., Gottman, J. M., & Shortt, J. W. (1995). The distinction between Type 1 and Type 2 batterers—Further considerations: Reply to Ornduff et al. (1995), Margolin et al. (1995), and Walker (1995). *Journal of Family Psychology, 9*, 272–279.

Jacobson, N. S., Gottman, J. M., Waltz, J., Rushe, R., Babcock, J., & Holtzworth-Munroe, A. (1994). Affect, verbal content, and psychophysiology in the arguments of couples with a violent husband. *Journal of Consulting and Clinical Psychology, 62*, 982–988.

Johnson, M. P. (1995). Patriarchal terrorism and common couple violence: Two forms of violence against women. *Journal of Marriage and the Family, 57*, 283–294.

Johnson, M. P., & Ferraro, K. J. (2000). Research on domestic violence in the 1990s: Making distinctions. *Journal of Marriage and the Family, 62*, 948–963.

Kaplan, J. R., Botchin, M. B., & Manuck, S. B. (1994). Animal models of aggression and cardiovascular disease. In A. W. Siegman & T. W. Smith (Eds.), *Anger, hostility, and the heart* (pp. 127–148). Hillsdale, NJ: Erlbaum.

Karpman, B. (1948). Myth of psychopathic personality. *American Journal of Psychiatry, 104*, 523–534.

Kelsey, R. M., Ornduff, S. R., McCann, C. M., & Reiff, S. (2001). Psychophysiological characteristics of narcissism during active and passive coping. *Psychophysiology, 38,* 292–303.

Kernberg, O. F. (1989). The narcissistic personality disorder and the differential diagnosis of antisocial behavior. *Psychiatric Clinics of North America, 12,* 553–570.

Larsen, P. B., Schneiderman, N., & Pasin, R. D. (1986). Physiological bases of cardiovascular psychophysiology. In M. G. H. Coles, E. Donchin, & S. W. Porges (Eds.), *Psychophysiology: Systems, processes, and applications* (pp. 122–165). New York: Guilford Press.

Levenston, G. K., Patrick, C. J., Bradley, M. M., & Lang, P. J. (2000). The psychopath as observer: Emotion and attention in picture processing. *Journal of Abnormal Psychology, 109,* 373–386.

Lilienfeld, S. O. (1994). Conceptual problems in the assessment of psychopathy. *Clinical Psychology Review, 14,* 17–38.

Linehan, M. M. (1993). *Cognitive–behavioral treatment of borderline personality disorder.* New York: Guilford Press.

Loftus, E. (1998). [Endorsement on book jacket]. In N. Jacobson & J. Gottman, *When men batter women: New insights into ending abusive relationships.* New York: Simon & Schuster.

Lorber, M. F. (2004). The psychophysiology of aggression, psychopathy, and conduct problems: A meta-analysis. *Psychological Bulletin, 130,* 531–552.

Lykken, D. T. (1957). A study of anxiety in the sociopathic personality. *Journal of Abnormal and Social Psychology, 55,* 6–10.

Lykken, D. T. (1995). *The antisocial personalities.* Hillsdale, NJ: Erlbaum.

Lykken, D. T., & Katzenmeyer, C. (1973). *Manual for the Activity Preference Questionnaire (APQ)* (Report No. PR-68-3). Minneapolis: University of Minnesota.

Margolin, G., Gordis, E. B., Oliver, P. H., & Raine, A. (1995). A physiologically based typology of batterers—Promising but preliminary: Comment on Gottman et al. (1995). *Journal of Family Psychology, 9,* 253–263.

Mednick, S. A. (1977). A bio-social theory of the learning of law-abiding behavior. In S. A. Mednick & K. O. Christiansen (Eds.), *Biosocial bases of criminal behavior* (pp. 1–8). New York: Gardner Press.

Meehan, J. C., Holtzworth-Munroe, A., & Herron, K. (2001). Maritally violent men's heart rate reactivity to marital interactions: A failure to replicate the Gottman et al. (1995) typology. *Journal of Family Psychology, 15,* 394–408.

Miller, G. E., Dopp, J. M., Myers, H. F., Felten, S. Y., & Fahey, J. L. (1999). Psychosocial predictors of natural killer cell mobilization during marital conflict. *Health Psychology, 18,* 262–271.

Newman, J. P., & Brinkley, C. A. (1997). Book review essays on Lykken's *The antisocial personalities. Psychological Inquiry, 8,* 236–260.

Norlander, B. & Eckhardt, C. I. (2005). Anger, hostility, and male perpetrators of intimate partner violence: A meta-analytic review. *Clinical Psychology Review, 25,* 119–152.

Ornduff, S. R., Kelsey, R. M., & O'Leary, K. D. (1995). What do we know about typologies of batterers? Comment on Gottman et al. (1995). *Journal of Family Psychology, 9,* 249–252.

Patrick, C. J. (1994). Emotion and psychopathy: Startling new insights. *Psychophysiology, 31,* 19–30.

Patrick, C. J., Bradley, M. M., & Lang, P. J. (1993). Emotion in the criminal psychopath: Startle reflex modulation. *Journal of Abnormal Psychology, 102,* 82–92.

Patrick, C. J., & Verona, E. (2007). The psychophysiology of aggression: Autonomic, electrocortical, and neuro-imaging findings. In D. J. Flannery, A. T. Vazsonyi, & I. D. Waldman (Eds.), *The Cambridge handbook of violent behavior and aggression* (pp. 111–150). New York: Cambridge University Press.

Quay, H. C. (1965). Psychopathic personality as pathological stimulation-seeking. *American Journal of Psychiatry, 122,* 180–183.

Raine, A. (1993). *The psychopathology of crime: Criminal behavior as a clinical disorder.* San Diego, CA: Academic Press.

Raine, A. (1997). Antisocial behavior and psychophysiology: A biosocial perspective and a prefrontal dysfunction hypothesis. In D. Stoff, J. Breiling, & J. D. Maser (Eds.), *Handbook of antisocial behavior* (pp. 289–304). New York: Wiley.

Raine, A. (2002). Biosocial studies of antisocial and violent behavior in children and adults: A review. *Journal of Abnormal Child Psychology, 30,* 311–326.

Raine, A., & Venables, P. H. (1981). Classical conditioning and socialization—A biosocial interaction. *Personality and Individual Differences, 2,* 273–283.

Raine, A., Venables, P. H., & Mednick, S. A. (1997). Low resting heart rate at age 3 years predisposes to aggression at age 11 years: Evidence from the Mauritius Child Health Project. *Journal of the American Academy of Child & Adolescent Psychiatry, 36,* 1457–1464.

Raine, A., Venables, P. H., & Williams, M. (1995). High autonomic arousal and electrodermal orienting at age 15 years as protective factors against criminal behavior at age 29 years. *American Journal of Psychiatry, 152,* 1595–1600.

Raine, A., Venables, P. H., & Williams, M. (1996). Better autonomic conditioning and faster electrodermal half-recovery time at age 15 years as possible protective factors against crime at age 29 years. *Developmental Psychology, 32,* 624–630.

Roisman, G. I. (2007). The psychophysiology of adult attachment relationships: Autonomic reactivity in marital and premarital interactions. *Developmental Psychology, 43,* 39–53.

Siegman, A. W. (1994). From Type A to hostility to anger: Reflections on the history of coronary-prone behavior. In A. W. Siegman & T. W. Smith (Eds.), *Anger, hostility, and heart* (pp. 1–22). Hillsdale, NJ: Erlbaum.

Siegman, A. W., & Smith, T. W. (1994). *Anger, hostility, and the heart.* Hillsdale, NJ: Erlbaum.

Smith, T. W., & Brown, P. C. (1991). Cynical hostility, attempts to exert social control, and cardiovascular reactivity in married couples. *Journal of Behavioral Medicine, 14,* 579–590.

Smith, T. W., & Gallo, L. C. (1999). Hostility and cardiovascular reactivity during marital interaction. *Psychosomatic Medicine, 61*, 436–445.

Smith, T. W., Gallo, L. C., Goble, L., Ngue, L. Q., & Stark, K. A. (1998). Agency, communion, and cardiovascular reactivity during marital interaction. *Health Psychology, 17*, 537–545.

Suls, J., & Wan, C. K. (1993). The relationship between trait hostility and cardiovascular reactivity: A quantitative review and analysis. *Psychophysiology, 30*, 615–626.

Sutker, P. B., & Allain, A. N. (2004). Antisocial personality disorder. In H. E. Adams & P. B. Sutker (Eds.), *Comprehensive handbook of psychopathology* (3rd ed., pp. 445–490). New York: Springer.

Tsai, J. L., Levenson, R. W., & McCoy, K. (2006). Cultural and termperamental variations in emotional response. *Emotion, 6*, 484–497.

Tweed, R. G., & Dutton, D. G. (1998). A comparison of impulsive and instrumental subgroups of batterers. *Violence and Victims, 13*, 217–230.

Verona, E., Patrick, C. J., Curtin, J. J., Bradley, M. M., & Lang, P. J. (2004). Psychopathy and physiological response to emotionally evocative sounds. *Journal of Abnormal Psychology, 113*, 99–108.

Walker, L. E. (1995). Current perspectives on men who batter women—Implications for intervention and treatment to stop violence: Comment on Gottman et al. (1995). *Journal of Family Psychology, 9*, 264–271.

Welsh, G. (1956). Factor dimensions A and R. In G. S. Welsh & W. G. Dahlstrom (Eds.), *Basic readings on the MMPI in psychology and medicine* (pp. 264–281). Minneapolis: University of Minnesota Press.

Zuckerman, M. (1978). Sensation seeking and psychopathy. In R. D. Hare & D. Schalling (Eds.), *Psychopathic behaviour: Approaches to research* (pp. 165–185). Chichester, England: Wiley.

7

HOW MUCH VARIANCE IN PSYCHOLOGICAL AND PHYSICAL AGGRESSION IS PREDICTED BY GENETICS?

DENISE A. HINES AND KIMBERLY J. SAUDINO

Genetic studies have demonstrated significant heritability of a wide range of psychological characteristics and behaviors (Plomin, DeFries, McClearn, & McGuffin, 2001), including aggression and antisocial behavior. However, few researchers have considered that intimate partner aggression (IPA) may show significant genetic influences, even though there is substantial evidence that IPA passes through the generations, such that children who are exposed to aggression in their families of origin, either through experiencing child abuse or witnessing interparental aggression, are more likely to use aggression in their relationships as adults than children who are never exposed to familial aggression (Egeland, 1993). This intergenerational transmission of IPA is one of the most reliable predictors of IPA in adulthood (e.g., Hotaling & Sugarman, 1986; Stith et al., 2000).

The twin study discussed in this chapter was supported by Grant MH64252-01 from the National Institute of Mental Health and a Twins Days Research Grant.

Because IPA tends to run in families, there is the possibility that it could have genetic influences. This chapter first briefly discusses evidence concerning the intergenerational transmission of IPA and the current dominant perspective, social learning theory, used to explain this transmission. Then we discuss the theoretical rationale and recent empirical evidence suggesting that there may be genetic influences operating on this transmission. Finally, we discuss the clinical implications of these findings, along with avenues for future research.

EVIDENCE FOR THE INTERGENERATIONAL TRANSMISSION OF INTIMATE PARTNER AGGRESSION

Research on several different populations has consistently shown that, for both men and women, exposure to aggression in the family of origin is a significant predictor of the perpetration of physical IPA. This research has examined male batterers (e.g., Corvo & Carpenter, 2000), college students (e.g., Foo & Margolin, 1995), community samples of newlyweds (e.g., Malone, Tyree, & O'Leary, 1989), a longitudinal study of a birth cohort in New Zealand (Magdol, Moffitt, Caspi, & Silva, 1998), a 20-year prospective longitudinal study of a representative sample from upstate New York (Ehrensaft et al., 2003), nationally representative samples (e.g., Straus & Yodanis, 1996), gay and lesbian samples (e.g., Schilit, Lie, Bush, Montagne, & Reyes, 1991), and samples of different racial and ethnic groups within the United States (e.g., Perilla, 1999). The association holds even when controlling for other risk factors, such as age, occupational status, unemployment status (Howell & Pugliesi, 1988), and alcohol use (Straus & Kaufman Kantor, 1994). Moreover, experiencing child abuse and witnessing interparental aggression seem to constitute a "double whammy" risk factor for adult IPA (Kalmuss, 1984; Straus, Gelles, & Steinmetz, 1980)—that is, the combination is worse than either alone. For example, in a nationally representative sample, only 1% to 2% of people who experienced neither form of aggression perpetrated physical IPA. The incidence of IPA perpetrated increased to 3% to 4% for those who experienced only child abuse and to 6% to 8% for individuals who only witnessed IPA in their families of origin. However, for those who both experienced and witnessed family-of-origin aggression, 12% to 17% perpetrated IPA as adults (Kalmuss, 1984).

Several researchers have conducted thorough investigations of the extant literature to investigate whether this intergenerational transmission of IPA applies across different methodologies, definitions, and samples. For example, in a literature review of risk markers for husband-to-wife violence, witnessing interparental aggression and experiencing child abuse were two of only eight risk factors that were consistently predictive of husband-to-wife violence (Hotaling & Sugarman, 1986). In a meta-analysis of 39 studies that addressed the intergenerational transmission of IPA, both witnessing interparental aggression and experiencing child abuse were significantly associated with adult IPA, with a moderate effect size of .18. This association held for both men and women and for clinical and community samples (Stith et al., 2000).

Although the bulk of the research on the intergenerational transmission of IPA has focused on the perpetration of physical aggression, this transmission of physical aggression can have two dependent variables: perpetration and victimization. Several researchers who have studied predictors of victimization have found that not only the perpetration of IPA transmits through families, but also the victimization. Studies of college students (e.g., Marshall & Rose, 1990), high school students (e.g., O'Keefe, 1998), community residents (e.g., Simons, Johnson, Beaman, & Conger, 1993), military families (e.g., Langhinrichsen-Rohling, Neidig, & Thorn, 1995), high-risk samples (e.g., Yates, Ruh, & Egeland, 2001), battered women (e.g., Walker, 2000), and battered men (Bergman & Brismar, 1993) have all found evidence for the intergenerational transmission of intimate partner victimization. Also, a meta-analysis found that for both men and women, those who had witnessed interparental aggression as children and/or were abused by a parent were more likely to be victimized by IPA in adulthood (Stith et al., 2000).

Finally, in comparison with the intergenerational transmission of partner violence victimization, the intergenerational transmission of psychological aggression (victimization and perpetration) is an even less researched area. However, preliminary evidence shows that the perpetration and victimization of this behavior also tend to run in families, in that the more verbal aggression children sustained, the more verbal aggression they perpetrated and sustained in their dating relationships (Hines & Malley-Morrison, 2003; Martin, 1990). Therefore, there is evidence that many forms of IPA pass through the generations.

SOCIAL LEARNING THEORY

The current dominant theory to explain the intergenerational transmission of IPA is social learning theory. According to researchers who subscribe to this perspective, the roots of IPA can be found in the family environment that the parents created. Children who live in families in which parents use aggression to resolve frustrations and conflicts with family members may witness their parents' behavior. If the children observe their parents' aggressive behavior being rewarded, the children will learn that it is appropriate to use aggression to get what they want (Eron, 1997). Through repeated observations of their parents' aggression toward family members, children will learn that aggression in family and love relationships is appropriate and that aggression is a proper means to relieve stress, resolve conflicts, and express anger (Kalmuss, 1984). In many of these families in which aggression is the primary way of resolving family conflicts and stress, children may not be exposed to any prosocial means of solving conflicts and, therefore, may not develop any alternative methods, other than aggression, for resolving disputes (Eron, 1997). Thus, based on the theoretical rationale of Bandura (1979), children may learn patterns of IPA through the process of observational learning.

Parents can model aggression in the family in at least two ways: They can physically punish the child, and/or they can physically assault each other. The physical punishment of children provides children with direct exposure to aggression (Kalmuss, 1984), and they can learn that aggression is a coping mechanism to be used when one is frustrated or angry with someone one cares about (O'Leary, 1988). They may also learn that it is acceptable to use aggression if someone does something they perceive is wrong and that the degree of aggression used is based on one's own interpretation of how serious the wrongdoing was (Herzberger, 1983). When parents physically assault each other in front of the children, the children have a direct model of IPA, and they can learn to reproduce in their adult relationships the specific types of IPA their parents used.

Each type of modeling alone contributes to the intergenerational transmission of IPA, but as indicated previously, the chances of a person engaging in IPA increase exponentially if that person both experienced child abuse and witnessed interparental aggression (Kalmuss, 1984). The combination may lead to this exponential increase in IPA because the aggression in the family of origin is probably so entrenched in the family system that aggression is viewed as a normal and legitimate way of interacting with loved ones (Herzberger, 1983).

A BEHAVIORAL GENETIC PERSPECTIVE

A relatively new perspective to explain the intergenerational transmission of IPA is the behavioral genetic perspective. This perspective points out that social learning theory relies solely on the shared family environment to explain the familial resemblance in IPA (Hines & Saudino, 2002). However, because families share both genes and environments, the pattern of familial resemblance reported in the literature could also be due to shared genes. Although in the past 20 years several researchers have proposed looking at biological and genetic contributors to family aggression (e.g., DiLalla & Gottesman, 1991; Herzberger, 1996; Kaufman & Zigler, 1993; Widom, 1989), only one study has empirically examined possible genetic contributions (Hines & Saudino, 2004).

Behavioral Genetic Methods

A goal of behavioral genetic research is to estimate the extent to which genetic and environmental factors contribute to variations in behavior in a given population. To do this, behavioral genetic researchers decompose the phenotypic variance (i.e., observed variance) of a behavior into its genetic and environmental variance components. Heritability, the genetic effect size, is the proportion of observed variance for a behavior that can be attributed to genetic influences. The remaining variance is attributed to all nonheritable influences and is considered the environmental variance component. This environmental variance component can be further decomposed into shared and nonshared environmental influences. Shared environmental variance (c^2) is familial resemblance in a behavior that cannot be explained by genetic variance. Thus, c^2 includes those environmental influences common to members of a family that enhance familial similarity. Examples of possible shared environmental influences include socioeconomic status, parental education, and the presence of other siblings in the home, to the extent that these variables serve to enhance familial similarity. Nonshared environmental variance (e^2) includes environmental influences that are unique to each individual and serve to make members of the same family different from one another in a behavior. Possible examples of nonshared environmental influences are differential parental treatment, differential extrafamilial relationships with friends and teachers, and nonsystematic factors such as accidents or illness, to the extent that they result in behavioral differences between family members (Plomin, Chipuer, & Neiderhiser, 1994). Nonshared environmental influences also include measurement error.

To disentangle genetic and environmental sources of variance, behavioral genetics researchers study individuals who vary systematically in their genetic and/or environmental similarity. The three basic designs in behavioral genetics research are family, twin, and adoption studies. Although the three designs differ in approach, the assumption underlying them is the same: If genetic influences are important to a behavior, then behavioral similarity should covary with genetic relatedness; that is, individuals who are more genetically similar should be more behaviorally similar (Saudino, 2001).

Family Studies

When conducting a family study, researchers explore a variety of kinship relationships to investigate whether there is familial resemblance for the behavior under study. If a behavior is genetically influenced, then it should "run in families," and the more closely related the family members are, the more similar they should be for that behavior (e.g., first-degree relatives > second-degree relatives > third-degree relatives > unrelated individuals). If family members do not resemble each other in a behavior, then the behavior cannot be genetically influenced (Saudino, 2001). The problem with family studies is that relatives share environments as well as genes. In fact, the more genetically related relatives are, the more similar their environments tend to be (Plomin, 1990), and family studies cannot separate shared environmental from genetic influences.

Nonetheless, such studies are an important first step in examining genetic and environmental influences on behavior because if family studies show no familial resemblance for a behavior, then the behavior must not be influenced by either genetic or familial environmental factors. However, if there is familial resemblance, then family studies provide an upper-limit estimate of genetic influences on a behavior because genetic influences usually cannot exceed the degree of familial resemblance (Plomin et al., 2001). Researchers can then take the next step and conduct more genetically sensitive designs that can disentangle the relative influences of genes and shared environments. These designs include twin and adoption designs.

Twin Studies

To estimate the extent to which genetic, shared, and nonshared environmental factors contribute to behavioral variability in the population, the twin design compares genetically identical (monozygotic, or MZ) twins with fraternal (dizygotic, or DZ) twins who share approximately 50% of their segregating genes. Genetic influences are implied when twin similarity covaries with the degree of genetic relatedness. Thus, if a trait is genetically influenced, then MZ twins should be approximately twice as similar in a behavior as DZ twins because MZ twins shared twice as many genes in common (e.g., if MZ twins are correlated .50 for a behavior and DZ twins are correlated .25, there is evidence for genetic influences on that behavior). DZ twin resemblance that exceeds that predicted by the genetic hypothesis (i.e., resemblance greater than one half the MZ twin resemblance) suggests the presence of shared environmental influences (e.g., if MZ twins are correlated .50 for a behavior and DZ twins are correlated .40, there is evidence of shared environmental influences because DZ twins are more similar than they should be if genes alone were operating). Finally, because MZ twins share all of their genes and all of their shared environments, differences within pairs of MZ twins can only be due to environmental influences that are unique to each member of the twin pair (i.e., nonshared environmental influences; Saudino, 2001).

This classic twin design contains several important assumptions. First, the twin design assumes that the environmental similarity for MZ twins is roughly equivalent to that of DZ twins—the equal environments assumption. It has been argued, though, that any greater similarity observed in MZ twins is due to more similar environments and not just genes. This potential problem could result in inflated heritability estimates. However, many researchers have studied the equal environments assumption in many different ways, and it seems to be a valid assumption for most behaviors (Plomin et al., 2001). For example, one study of twins compared those who were misclassified (i.e., labeled *fraternal* when they were actually identical or vice versa) with those who were correctly labeled. When parents believed their identical twins were fraternal or vice versa, the mislabeled twins' behavior was just as similar as correctly labeled twins' behavior (Scarr & Carter-Saltzmann, 1979). Therefore, it can be argued that identical twins may have more similar experiences than fraternal twins because they are more similar genetically (Plomin et al., 2001).

The twin design also assumes that a given person in the population will have an equal chance of mating with any other person in the population. However, mate choices are not always random, and if people choose their mates on the basis of similarity for the behavior under study, they will necessarily share genes in common for that behavior. This assortative mating will serve to increase the genetic similarity of DZ twins because their parents share genes in common; consequently, estimates of heritability for a behavior that is subject to assortative mating will be underestimated (Plomin et al., 2001).

Adoption Studies

Researchers who conduct adoption studies estimate the relative influence of genes and environments by using one of two methods: the parent–offspring design or the adoptive–nonadoptive sibling design. Both types of adoption studies examine individuals who were adopted at an early age (Saudino, 2001). The parent–offspring design compares the behavioral similarity between adopted children and their biological parents with that between adopted children and their adoptive parents. An adopted child and his or her biological parent share 50% of their segregating genes but do not share environments. By contrast, an adopted child and his or her adoptive parents share environments but not genes. Thus, the resemblance between an adopted child and his or her biological parent reflects genetic influences, whereas resemblance between an adopted child and his or her adoptive parent reflects shared environmental influences.

Likewise, the adoptive–nonadoptive sibling design compares the similarity of adoptive and nonadoptive sibling pairs. Genetic influences are suggested when nonadoptive siblings who, like all first-degree siblings, share approximately 50% of their segregating genes are more similar than adoptive siblings who are not genetically related. The extent to which genetically unrelated adoptive siblings resemble each other is an indicator of shared environmental influences.

Several issues arise through the use of adoption studies, however. First, can the results from families who experience adoption be generalized to families who never experience it? Are adoptive families and families who give up their children for adoption somehow different from the rest of the population? The answers to these questions depend on each adoption study. Some adoption studies show that their sample is representative of the population as a whole, whereas others have questionable representativeness. Another issue concerns the prenatal environment. Genetic mothers share an environment with their adopted-away children during the prenatal period, but by comparing correlations for birth mothers with correlations for birth fathers, the relative contributions of prenatal and postnatal environments can be assessed. Finally, selective placement can pose a problem. In other words, if the adopted-away child is placed in a home that is similar in environment to that of the genetic parents, the relative contributions of genes and environments can be blurred. Although there is some evidence for selective placement for intelligence, there is no evidence for selective placement for other psychological traits (Plomin et al., 2001).

Behavioral Genetics and Intimate Partner Aggression

The many studies that show that IPA tends to transmit through families can be viewed as family studies. Although it is commonly accepted that the intergenerational transmission of IPA is due to environmental factors (e.g., through social learning mechanisms), as indicated earlier, family studies cannot parcel out the relative contributions of shared genes from shared environments. In other words, the intergenerational transmission of IPA may well be due to genetic influences. Therefore, a theoretical explanation that considers only environmental reasons for the intergenerational transmission of IPA cannot be fully accepted if behavioral genetic research shows that the transmission is, at least in part, due to genetic influences (Hines & Saudino, 2004).

As mentioned, family studies can provide an estimate of the upper limit of heritability because heritability cannot exceed the degree of familial resemblance. For IPA, the upper limit of heritability would be twice the correlation between being exposed to aggression in the family of origin and perpetrating IPA in adulthood. Based on Stith et al.'s (2000) meta-analysis, the overall association between growing up in a violent home and perpetrating intimate partner violence is .18. Therefore, the upper limit of heritability for intimate partner violence would be .36. Given this knowledge, researchers should then conduct a more genetically sensitive design to disentangle the relative influences of genes and shared environments.

Behavioral Genetic Studies of General Aggression and Antisocial Behavior

The literature on extrafamilial aggression and antisocial behavior consistently shows that MZ twins are more similar than DZ twins and that adoptees are more similar to their biological relatives than to their adoptive relatives for a broad range of antisocial behaviors and traits, including convictions for felonies (e.g., Raine, 1993), symptom counts for antisocial personality disorder (e.g., Lyons et al., 1995), self-reported aggression (e.g., Miles & Carey, 1997), and personality scales for aggression and hostility (e.g., McGue, Bacon, & Lykken, 1993). A recent meta-analysis of 51 twin and adoption studies on antisocial behavior showed that genetic influences accounted for 41% of the variance in these behaviors, with 43% of the variance accounted for by nonshared environmental influences and 16% accounted for by shared environmental influences (Rhee & Waldman, 2002). These estimates did not differ for men and women, and familial influences tended to decrease with age, whereas nonfamilial influences increased with age.

Recent research with children has found that both bullying and victimization (i.e., experiencing bullying) are substantially heritable. In the Environmental Risk Longitudinal Twin Study, which comprises a large epidemiological sample of twins assessed at 7 and 10 years of age, genetic influences accounted for 61% and 73% of the variance in bullying and victimization, respectively, with the remaining variance due to nonshared environmental influences (Ball et al., 2008). Boys and girls did not significantly differ in the magnitude of genetic effects. Although there were genetic effects specific to bullying and victimization, genetic factors entirely explained the phenotypic correlation between bullying and victimization (i.e., the tendency to be both a bully and victim is due to only genetic factors).

One of the most consistent findings in the literature is that a combination of genetic and environmental risk factors leads to the greatest incidence of adulthood antisocial behavior as measured by criminality (e.g., Cadoret, Yates, Troughton, Woodworth, & Stewart, 1995). That is, in adoption studies, adoptees who had both genetic and environmental risk factors for antisocial traits were the most likely to engage in criminal behavior later in life. Genetic risk factors included biological parents who were convicted of a felony or had a diagnosis of antisocial behavior and/or drug abuse (Cadoret, Cain, & Crowe, 1983; Cadoret et al., 1995), whereas environmental risk factors included divorce in adoptive homes and adoptive parent or sibling psychopathology (Cadoret et al., 1983, 1995). This combination of genetic and environmental influences suggests a genotype–environment interaction— genetic factors play a larger role than environmental factors, but when they are combined, they increase the risk for criminality exponentially (DiLalla & Gottesman, 1991).

One study of Danish adoptees provides an illustrative example of this genotype–environment interaction (Hutchings & Mednick, 1977). The researchers found that when neither the adoptive nor the biological fathers were criminals, 10.5% of the adoptees committed a crime. The next highest prevalence rate (11.5%) was for adoptees who had only a criminal adoptive father. When only the biological father was a criminal, 22.0% of the adoptees committed a crime. The highest prevalence rates by far were among adoptees whose biological *and* adoptive fathers were criminals: Of these, 36.2% committed a crime. These data also suggest the relative nonimportance of an adverse rearing environment in the absence of a genetic predisposition; whether or not the adoptive fathers were criminals did not make a difference when the biological fathers were not criminals (Hutchings & Mednick, 1977). In other words, in the absence of a genetic predisposition for criminality, adverse home environments do not predict adoptees' criminal behaviors, a result that has been replicated in at least one other study (Cadoret et al., 1995). If these results were applied to IPA, it would suggest that growing up in a violent home would not lead to adult IPA if one were not genetically predisposed to engage in IPA.

A TWIN STUDY OF INTIMATE PARTNER AGGRESSION

As stated earlier, there is a need for behavioral genetic studies of IPA. Thus far, however, only one has been conducted (Hines & Saudino, 2004). This investigation was a small twin study that we recently conducted on a sample of 134 MZ and 41 same-sex DZ twins. The twins completed the Revised Conflict Tactics Scales (Straus, Hamby, Boney-McCoy, & Sugarman, 1996), the most widely used measure of IPV, on which participants report whether and how often they used and sustained various acts of physical and psychological aggression in their current or most recent intimate partner relationship. The majority of the participants were women (87%) and White (92%). The average age of the participants was 40.3 years, and the average length of their relationship was 11.8 years. The levels of IPA study participants reported were very similar to population-based studies of IPA; specifically, 82.9% reported using psychological aggression and 22.9% reported using physical aggression, most of which was minor (e.g., slapping, pushing, shoving, grabbing). Similarly, 78.6% and 24.0% reported sustaining psychological and physical aggression, respectively. There were no differences between MZ and DZ twins on any demographic variables associated with IPA or on their reported use or receipt of IPA.

We conducted univariate model-fitting analyses to estimate the extent to which genetic, shared environmental, and nonshared environmental influences contributed to variability in physical and psychological IPA (see Hines & Saudino, 2004). The results consistently showed that the use of IPA was influenced by shared genes and nonshared environments, with little evidence of shared environmental influences. Specifically, genetic influences accounted for 16% of the variance in the use of physical aggression and 22% of the variance in the use of psychological aggression, and nonshared environmental influences accounted for the remaining variance. For victimization, 25% and 15% of the variance for psychological and physical aggression were due to genetic influences, respectively, and the remaining variance was due to nonshared environmental influences.

In addition, our analyses showed that perpetration and victimization were highly intercorrelated: For psychological aggression, the correlation between perpetration and victimization was .85 ($p < .001$), and for physical aggression, the correlation was .59 ($p < .01$). The fact that the two aspects of IPA are correlated suggests that there is some overlap between the factors that influence each. To explore this possibility, we used multivariate model-fitting procedures to evaluate the extent to which the same genetic and environmental factors influenced perpetration and victimization. For psychological aggression, there was almost complete overlap between the genetic and nonshared environmental effects influencing the use and receipt of aggression (i.e., the genetic and nonshared environmental correlations between the use and receipt of aggression were .97 and .82, respectively). Although not quite as strong as for psychological aggression, there were also substantial genetic and nonshared environmental correlations between the use and receipt of physical aggression (genetic correlation = .85; nonshared environmental correlation = .55). Overall, these findings suggest that to a considerable extent, the same genes are responsible for the use and receipt of aggression in interpersonal relationships. Similar nonshared environmental factors influence the use and receipt of aggression, although to a lesser extent.

We also investigated the question of genetic and environmental overlap between types of interpersonal aggression (Hines & Saudino, 2007). That is, do the same genetic and environmental influences operate for physical and psychological aggression? Previous literature has shown that the two are intercorrelated (e.g., Murphy & O'Leary, 1989), and some researchers have suggested that the association may be due to similar etiologies (e.g., Stets, 1990). This was the case in our twin sample. Psychological and physical IPA were significantly correlated at the phenotypic level (r for perpetration = .38; r for victimization = .46), and our multivariate genetic analyses of the genetic and environmental overlap found that the correlations between physical and psychological aggression were largely due to shared genes (for perpetration, the genetic correlation was .74; for victimization, it was 1.00) and partly due to nonshared environments (for perpetration, the nonshared environmental correlation was .30; for victimization, it was .32). Thus, any etiological differences between physical and psychological IPA seem to be due to differences in nonshared environmental influences.

DISCUSSION

Prior research on aggression and antisocial behavior suggests that individual differences in general aggressive tendencies are genetically influenced (e.g., Carey & Goldman, 1997). It seems reasonable, then, to predict that the intergenerational transmission of IPA may also be due to genetic factors. The first behavioral genetic investigation of IPA suggests that familial resemblance in IPA is likely due to shared genes, not shared environments (Hines & Saudino, 2004). This finding runs counter to the dominant theory of intergenerational transmission of IPA (i.e., social learning theory), which posits that it is the shared familial environment that is responsible for the transmission of IPA through the generations (Eron, 1997).

Although it is important to also consider possible genetic and environmental influences on IPA victimization, many researchers do not investigate the etiology of such victimization, probably because of fears of blaming the victim. However, it is an important avenue of research and does not necessarily translate into victim blaming. It is important to make the distinction between causation and blame. Whether a victim's behavior played a causal role in a victimization incident is a scientific question. Whether the victim's behavior is blameworthy is a moral question for the legal system and for public opinion (Felson, 2002). Thus, as social scientists, it is our role to investigate causality in incidents, whereas the determination of blame is a matter for the courts. Interestingly, as is the case for perpetration, studies show that victimization also runs in families (e.g., Stith et al., 2000), and our twin study results suggested that it is the shared genetic effects that influence this familial resemblance (Hines & Saudino, 2004). Similar results have emerged from a recent large-scale study of victimization in middle childhood (Ball et al., 2008); however, genetic effects on victimization were considerably larger in this younger sample.

The fact that there seem to be genetic influences on behaviors performed by individuals other than the respondents may seem paradoxical. How can behaviors performed by others be influenced by the genotype of the receiver? Are not the participants merely victims of the aggressive behaviors that are used by their partners? Although at first genetic influences on IPA victimization may seem illogical, there is consistent evidence that people are not merely passive receivers of their environments. To some extent, people's environments reflect their genetically influenced traits (e.g., Kendler, Neale, Kessler, Heath, & Eaves, 1993). Therefore, events that may seem external to the individual can have genetic influences. For example, there are genetic influences on being assaulted and having marital difficulties (Kendler et al., 1993). Not only is aggression within a marriage symbolic of marital difficulties, but when the aggression is physical, it is also a type of assault. Genetic influences on IPA victimization may be due to evocative or active genotype–environment correlations; in *evocative* correlations, the victimized individuals may experience IPA because they have genetically influenced traits that evoke aggressive reactions from others, and in *active* correlations, the victimized individuals choose aggressive romantic partners because those partners are congruent with certain genetically influenced characteristics of the victims (Scarr & McCartney, 1983).

In fact, there is considerable evidence that individuals with problems such as depression and alcoholism tend to marry partners with such problems at a rate much higher than would be expected by chance (e.g., Agrawal et al., 2006; Mathews & Reus, 2001). In addition, there is evidence for this type of assortative mating for antisocial behaviors in general (Krueger, Moffitt, Capsi, Bleske, & Silva, 1998) and for IPA in particular (e.g., Simons et al., 1993; Straus & Gelles, 1990). Taken together, this research suggests that aggressive people are choosing partners who also tend to be aggressive, which can be considered evidence of both evocative (e.g., one's genetically influenced aggressive behavior evokes aggression in one's partner) and active (e.g., aggressive people actively choose aggressive partners) genotype–environment correlations. Behavioral genetic analyses of the association between the two types of IPA suggest that there is a large overlap between the genetic influences that operate on perpetration and victimization. Thus, it seems that there is a general tendency to get involved in aggressive relationships that is genetically influenced (Hines & Saudino, 2004).

Again, the research on bullying and victimization in children mirrors these findings. Although the covariation between bullying and victimization in childhood is more modest, it is solely due to genetic factors (Ball et al., 2008). This convergence of findings across related phenotypes (i.e., IPV and bullying) and age ranges attests to the robustness of the effects. Research that identifies characteristics that mediate the genetic association between the perpetration and victimization of IPV would inform about causality and could lead to appropriate interventions.

Similarly, there is also substantial overlap in the genetic and environmental influences operating on both psychological and physical IPA (Hines & Saudino, 2007). The high genetic correlations between psychological and physical IPA suggest that to a considerable extent, they are influenced by the same genetic factors. However, the nonshared environmental factors that influence each seem to have some independence, as indicated by the lower nonshared environmental correlations between psychological and physical IPA. Thus, although there was some overlap in the nonshared environmental influences that operate on each type of aggression, the etiological differences between the two are largely a function of nonshared environmental influences. A possible explanation for this finding is that people who have a genetic predisposition toward engaging in aggressive behavior will engage in different types of aggressive behaviors depending on their differences in nonshared environmental influences. That is, there may be a modest genetic predisposition toward aggressive behavior, but what determines whether someone is physically versus psychologically aggressive is primarily due to environmental experiences that are unique to each member of a family (Hines & Saudino, 2007).

Limitations

Before discussing the potential implications of findings of genetic influences on IPA, it is important to address this study's limitations. So far, this is the only behavioral genetic study of IPA, and its results need to be replicated on a larger, more diverse twin sample. The limitations of the sample itself also need to be acknowledged—for example, the sample consisted of mostly White women, and therefore, the generalizability of these results to men and non-White groups is questionable. Unfortunately, the current sample was also too small to investigate differential effects of gender on genetic and environmental influences on IPA. It is possible that men and women may have differential underlying genetic predispositions toward IPA. However, the majority of studies have not provided evidence for sex-specific genetic or environmental influences on extrafamilial aggression (e.g., Jacobson, Prescott, & Kendler, 2002; Rhee & Waldman, 2002), and given that extrafamilial and intrafamilial aggression are at least moderately intercorrelated (e.g., Hotaling, Straus, & Lincoln, 1990), it is unlikely that there will be sex differences in genetic and environmental influences on IPA.

Another caution for generalizability concerns the level of violence in this sample. The majority of the participants who were involved in relationships in which IPA occurred experienced reciprocal minor levels of aggression, what some researchers have termed *common couple violence* (Johnson, 1995). Different results might emerge for more severe spousal abuse (i.e., battering). Nonetheless, the levels of both physical and psychological IPA in this sample were comparable to population-based samples, and the associations between IPA and major demographic variables (e.g., gender and age) were typical. Thus, the results of this study should be viewed as preliminary evidence of genetic influences on IPA, and replication with a larger, more diverse sample is needed to strengthen these preliminary findings.

Clinical Implications

It is important to clarify what we mean when we say that IPA may be genetically influenced. We mean that under the current environmental conditions, certain people, because of their genotype, are more likely to be involved in IPA than people who do not have that same genotype. Thus, genetic influences are probabilistic, not deterministic. Genetic influences on IPA should be seen as a predisposition toward behaving aggressively, not as inevitability (e.g., Raine, 1993). Thus, manipulations in the environment can be very successful in reducing IPA and preventing the full expression of any genetic predisposition (Hines & Saudino, 2004; Raine, 1993).

Although behavioral genetic research suggests that shared familial environmental influences do not contribute to familial resemblance in IPA and related behaviors (i.e., aggression and bullying), this finding does not mean that the environment does not play a role. Environmental influences are important, explaining at least half of the variance in both perpetration and victimization of IPA (Hines & Saudino, 2004); however, the environments found to be important are those that are unique to each member of a family (i.e., not those that family members share). This does not rule out familial influences on IPV. Families may play an important role in individual differences in IPV, but family effects do not appear to operate on a familywide basis. The finding of substantial nonshared environmental influences on IPV suggests that familial influences on IPV are likely to be those that are specific to each family member (e.g., differential parental treatment).

Although such nonshared environmental effects include measurement error, in Hines and Saudino (2004, 2007), the reliabilities of all measures were high (ranging from .75 to .90). Therefore, nonshared environmental influences on IPV do not appear to be simply measurement error. This leaves open more interesting possibilities for nonshared environmental influences on IPV and provides an important focus for researchers interested in environmental influences on IPV. Instead of examining environmental factors that differ across families, this finding suggests that it will be more profitable to focus on environmental factors that differ within families. Not all children raised in the same aggressive family environment go on to engage in IPA as adults. Researchers need to consider why individuals within the same family differ so much with regard to IPA. This will involve studying more than one individual per family and exploring the association of experiential differences within a family with differences in IPA.

By understanding the importance and meaning of genetic influences in these behaviors and by further understanding the impact of the environment, several steps can be taken to reduce the problem of IPA. For example, genetic predispositions for IPA imply that there are certain biological processes that are associated with aggression, and medications might be developed to alter those biological processes. However, a more fruitful avenue of intervention is the environment, specifically those nonshared environments that are responsible for, or conducive to, IPA and that can be modified (Cadoret, Leve, & Devor, 1997). Such environments might include differential peer groups, differential exposure to aggression in the community, or differential exposure to certain traumatic events, such as a head injury, that may influence one to engage in IPA.

Rhee and Waldman (2002) and Harris (1995) suggested focusing on neighborhood and peer influences in the development of aggressive behavior, because both seem to be important environmental influences on antisocial behaviors. Thus, perhaps the social transmission of aggressive behaviors is horizontal and not vertical (Rowe, 1994). In other words, children may inherit the genes that predispose them to engage in IPA from their parents, but their eventual involvement in IPA may not depend on whether their parents behave aggressively, but rather on whether their peers do. Children who inherit genes that predispose them to IPA may seek out peers who behave aggressively, and therefore their use of IPA in adult relationships may be due to their genetic predisposition combined with the aggressive modeling of their peers, not their parents.

At least one study has shown that exposure to aggression in the family of origin no longer predicts one's later use of IPA after controlling for one's association with peers who engage in IPA (e.g., Silverman & Williamson, 1997). This study investigated physical aggression in college dating relationships, and replications and extensions of this type of research are needed. Nonetheless, it is possible that parents provide the genetic predisposition toward involvement in IPA but that aggressive peer groups are the catalyst for genetically predisposed people to become involved with IPA (Hines & Saudino, 2004).

However, assuming that exposure to deviant peer groups and antisocial behavior in the neighborhood is purely environmental is also problematic because it assumes that no peer selection is operating—that is, that the aggressive child is not seeking out aggressive peer groups and aggressive situations (Rowe, Woulbroun, & Gulley, 1994). Studies have shown that there are genetic influences operating on the association between antisocial behavior and association with deviant peers (Rowe & Osgood, 1984). Nonetheless, by investigating these issues using genetically sensitive designs, one can control for genetic influences on the association between peer group influences and the experience of IPA.

Nonshared environmental influences can also include certain family environments that siblings who have different genotypes experience differentially (Turkheimer & Gottesman, 1996). Therefore, the family environment may make siblings dissimilar, rather than similar, in their propensity to experience IPA. To that end, Rhee and Waldman (2002) suggested studying parental supervision as a possible nonshared environmental influence in the development of aggressive behaviors. They pointed to studies showing that coercive parenting cycles can increase children's aggressive behaviors—for example, the child behaves aggressively and the parent reinforces the aggression by backing off (Patterson, Reid, & Dishion, 1992). Parenting classes aimed at altering this behavior by teaching parents to ignore aggressive behavior and reward prosocial behavior have shown promise in reducing children's aggression (e.g., Eddy & Chamberlain, 2000).

Rhee and Waldman (2002) noted, however, that focusing on parenting as an environmental influence may also be misguided because it ignores the fact that both parenting and children's behavior are genetically influenced and that parents may merely be reacting to children's genetically influenced aggressive behavior (e.g., Harris, 1995). As with peer group influences, though, by conducting these studies with genetically sensitive designs, it is possible to control for genetic influences on the effect of parental supervision on the development of IPA (Rhee & Waldman, 2002).

The fact that genotype–environment interactions have been found for aggressive behaviors in general highlights the possibility that they may also be operating on IPA. A genotype–environment interaction may occur if different genotypes are differentially reactive to a given environment (Plomin, DeFries, & Loehlin, 1977). For example, exposure to violent models may be more detrimental to the development of IPA for only those children who are genetically predisposed to behave aggressively. This possibility has been supported by behavioral genetic studies on criminality, which have provided evidence for the existence of genotype–environment interactions. In one such adoption study of antisocial behavior (Hutchings & Mednick, 1977), the researchers found that only adoptees with a criminal biological parent (i.e., a genetic risk) were influenced by adverse adoptive rearing environments (i.e., environmental risk). That is, the adverse rearing environment did not negatively influence those adoptees who did not have genetic risk. Furthermore, having both a genetic and environmental risk led to an exponential increase in the rates of criminality in adoptees (Hutchings & Mednick, 1977).

Similar genotype–environment interactions may be operating for IPA and are suggested by studies showing that conduct disorder is a strong mediator for the association between childhood exposure to family violence and later IPA perpetration (Capaldi & Clark, 1998; Ehrensaft et al., 2003; Simons, Lin, & Gordon, 1998). That is, it could be that children with conduct disorder may be more vulnerable to the environmental impacts of being exposed to violence. By learning more about the genetic and environmental factors that influence IPA, researchers and clinicians will be better able to identify those individuals who are genetically at risk for IPA and alter those environments that are responsible for allowing this genetic predisposition to fully express itself.

REFERENCES

Agrawal, A., Heath, A. C., Grant, J. D., Pergadia, M. L., Statham, D. J., Bucholz, K. K., et al. (2006). Assortative mating for cigarette smoking and for alcohol consumption in female Australian twins and their spouses. *Behavior Genetics*, 36, 553–556.

Ball, H. A., Arseneault, L., Taylor, A., Maughan, B., Caspi, A., & Moffitt, T. E. (2008). Genetic and environmental influences on victims, bullies and bully–victims in childhood. *Journal of Child Psychology and Psychiatry*, 49, 104–112.

Bandura, A. (1979). The social learning perspective: Mechanisms of aggression. In H. Toch (Ed.), *Psychology of crime and criminal justice* (pp. 198–236). New York: Holt, Rinehart & Winston.

Bergman, B., & Brismar, B. (1993). Assailants and victims: A comparative study of male wife-beaters and battered males. *Journal of Addictive Diseases*, 12, 1–10.

Cadoret, R. J., Cain, C. A., & Crowe, R. R. (1983). Evidence for gene–environment interaction in the development of adolescent antisocial behavior. *Behavior Genetics, 13,* 301–310.

Cadoret, R. J., Leve, L. D., & Devor, E. (1997). Genetics of aggressive and violent behavior. *Psychiatric Clinics of North America, 20,* 301–322.

Cadoret, R. J., Yates, W. R., Troughton, E., Woodworth, G., & Stewart, M. A. (1995). Genetic–environmental interaction in the genesis of aggressivity and conduct disorders. *Archives of General Psychiatry, 52,* 916–924.

Capaldi, D. M., & Clark, S. C. (1998). Prospective family predictors of aggression toward female partners for at-risk young men. *Developmental Psychology, 34,* 1175–1188.

Carey, G., & Goldman, D. (1997). The genetics of antisocial behavior. In D. M. Stoff, J. Breiling, & J. D. Maser (Eds.), *Handbook of antisocial behavior* (pp. 243–254). New York: Wiley.

Corvo, K., & Carpenter, E. H. (2000). Effects of parental substance abuse on current levels of domestic violence: A possible elaboration of the intergenerational transmission processes. *Journal of Family Violence, 15,* 123–135.

DiLalla, L. F., & Gottesman, I. I. (1991). Biological and genetic contributors to violence—Widom's untold tale. *Psychological Bulletin, 109,* 125–129.

Eddy, J. M., & Chamberlain, P. (2000). Family management and deviant peer association as mediators of the impact of treatment condition on youth antisocial behavior. *Journal of Consulting and Clinical Psychology, 68,* 857–863.

Egeland, B. (1993). A history of abuse is a major risk factor for abusing the next generation. In R. J. Gelles & D. R. Loseke (Eds.), *Current controversies on family violence* (pp. 197–208). Newbury Park, CA: Sage.

Ehrensaft, M. K., Cohen, P., Brown, J., Smailes, E., Chen, H., & Johnson, J. G. (2003). Intergenerational transmission of partner violence: A 20-year prospective study. *Journal of Consulting and Clinical Psychology, 71,* 741–753.

Eron, L. D. (1997). The development of antisocial behavior from a learning perspective. In D. M. Stoff, J. Breiling, & J. D. Maser (Eds.), *Handbook of antisocial behavior* (pp. 140–147). New York: Wiley.

Felson, R. B. (2002). *Violence and gender reexamined.* Washington, DC: American Psychological Association.

Foo, L., & Margolin, G. (1995). A multivariate investigation of dating aggression. *Journal of Family Violence, 10,* 351–377.

Harris, J. R. (1995). Where is the child's environment? A group socialization theory of development. *Psychological Review, 102,* 458–489.

Herzberger, S. D. (1983). Social cognition and the transmission of abuse. In D. Finkelhor, R. J. Gelles, G. T. Hotaling, & M. A. Straus (Eds.), *The dark side of families: Current family violence research* (pp. 317–329). Thousand Oaks, CA: Sage.

Herzberger, S. D. (1996). *Violence within the family: Social psychological perspectives.* Boulder, CO: Westview Press.

Hines, D. A., & Malley-Morrison, K. (2003, July). *Abusive childhood experiences: Effects in late adolescent boys*. Paper presented at the International Family Violence Conference, Portsmouth, NH.

Hines, D. A., & Saudino, K. J. (2002). Intergenerational transmission of intimate partner violence: A behavioral genetic perspective. *Trauma, Violence, & Abuse, 3*, 210–225.

Hines, D. A., & Saudino, K. J. (2004). Genetic and environmental influences on intimate partner aggression: A preliminary study. *Violence and Victims, 19*, 701–718.

Hines, D. A., & Saudino, K. J. (2007). Etiological similarities between psychological and physical aggression in intimate relationships: A behavioral genetic exploration. *Journal of Family Violence, 22*, 122–129.

Hotaling, G. T., Straus, M. A., & Lincoln, A. J. (1990). Intrafamily violence and crime and violence outside the family. In M. A. Straus & R. J. Gelles (Eds.), *Physical violence in American families: Risk factors and adaptation to violence in 8,145 families* (pp. 431–472). New Brunswick, NJ: Transaction.

Hotaling, G. T., & Sugarman, D. B. (1986). An analysis of risk markers in husband to wife violence: The current state of knowledge. *Violence and Victims, 1*, 101–124.

Howell, M. J., & Pugliesi, K. L. (1988). Husbands who harm: Predicting spousal violence by men. *Journal of Family Violence, 3*, 15–27.

Hutchings, B., & Mednick, S. A. (1977). Criminality in adoptees and their adoptive and biological parents: A pilot study. In S. A. Mednick & K. O. Christiansen (Eds.), *Biosocial bases of criminal behavior* (pp. 127–141). New York: Gardner Press.

Jacobson, K. C., Prescott, C. A., & Kendler, K. S. (2002). Sex differences in the genetic and environmental influences on the development of antisocial behavior. *Development and Psychopathology, 14*, 395–416.

Johnson, M. P. (1995). Patriarchal terrorism and common couple violence: Two forms of violence against women. *Journal of Marriage and the Family, 57*, 283–294.

Kalmuss, D. (1984). The intergenerational transmission of marital aggression. *Journal of Marriage and the Family, 46*, 11–19.

Kaufman, J., & Zigler, E. (1993). The intergenerational transmission of abuse is overstated. In R. J. Gelles & D. R. Loseke (Eds.), *Current controversies on family violence* (pp. 209–221). Newbury Park, CA: Sage.

Kendler, K. S., Neale, M., Kessler, R., Heath, A., & Eaves, L. (1993). A twin study of recent life events and difficulties. *Archives of General Psychiatry, 50*, 789–796.

Krueger, R. F., Moffitt, T. E., Caspi, A., Bleske, A., & Silva, P. A. (1998). Assortative mating for antisocial behavior: Developmental and methodological implications. *Behavior Genetics, 28*, 173–185.

Langhinrichsen-Rohling, J., Neidig, P., & Thorn, G. (1995). Violent marriages: Gender differences in levels of current violence and past abuse. *Journal of Family Violence, 10*, 159–176.

Lyons, M. J., True, W. R., Eisen, S. A., Goldberg, J., Meyer, J. M., Faraone, S. V., et al. (1995). Differential heritability of adult and juvenile antisocial traits. *Archives of General Psychiatry, 52,* 906–915.

Magdol, L., Moffit, T. E., Caspi, A., & Silva, P. A. (1998). Developmental antecedents of partner abuse: A prospective–longitudinal study. *Journal of Abnormal Psychology, 107,* 375–389.

Malone, J., Tyree, A., & O'Leary, D. (1989). Generalization and containment: Different effects of past aggression for wives and husbands. *Journal of Marriage and the Family, 51,* 687–697.

Marshall, L. L., & Rose, P. (1990). Premarital violence: The impact of origin violence, stress, and reciprocity. *Violence and Victims, 5,* 51–64.

Martin, B. (1990). The transmission of relationship difficulties from one generation to the next. *Journal of Youth and Adolescence, 19,* 181–199.

Mathews, C. A., & Reus, V. I. (2001). Assortative mating in the affective disorders: A systematic review and meta-analysis. *Comprehensive Psychiatry, 42,* 257–262.

McGue, M., Bacon, S., & Lykken, D. T. (1993). Personality stability and change in early childhood: A behavioral genetic analysis. *Developmental Psychology, 29,* 96–109.

Miles, D. R., & Carey, G. (1997). Genetic and environmental architecture of human aggression. *Journal of Personality and Social Psychology, 72,* 207–217.

Murphy, C. M., & O'Leary, K. D. (1989). Psychological aggression predicts physical aggression in early marriage. *Journal of Consulting and Clinical Psychology, 57,* 579–582.

O'Keefe, M. (1998). Factors mediating the link between witnessing interparental violence and dating violence. *Journal of Family Violence, 13,* 39–57.

O'Leary, K. D. (1988). Physical aggression between spouses: A social learning theory perspective. In V. B. VanHasselt, R. L. Morrison, A. S. Bellack, & M. Hersen (Eds.), *Handbook of family violence* (pp. 31–55). New York: Plenum Press.

Patterson, G. R., Reid, J. B., & Dishion, T. J. (1992). *Antisocial boys.* Eugene, OR: Castalia.

Perilla, J. L. (1999). Domestic violence as a human rights issue: The case of immigrant Latinos. *Hispanic Journal of Behavioral Sciences, 21,* 107–133.

Plomin, R. (1990). *Nature and nurture: An introduction to human behavioral genetics.* Pacific Grove, CA: Brooks/Cole.

Plomin, R., Chipuer, H. M., & Neiderhiser, J. M. (1994). Behavioral genetic evidence for the importance of nonshared environment. In E. M. Hetherington, D. Reiss, & R. Plomin (Eds.), *Separate social worlds of siblings: Importance of nonshared environment on development* (pp. 1–31). Hillsdale, NJ: Erlbaum.

Plomin, R., DeFries, J. C., & Loehlin, J. C. (1977). Genotype–environment interaction and correlation in the analysis of human behavior. *Psychological Bulletin, 84,* 309–322.

Plomin, R., DeFries, J. C., McClearn, G. E., & McGuffin, P. (2001). *Behavioral genetics* (4th ed.). New York: Worth.

Raine, A. (1993). *The psychopathology of crime: Criminal behavior as a clinical disorder*. San Diego, CA: Academic Press.

Rhee, S. H., & Waldman, I. D. (2002). Genetic and environmental influences on antisocial behavior: A meta-analysis of twin and adoption studies. *Psychological Bulletin, 128*, 490–529.

Rowe, D. C. (1994). *The limits of family influence: Genes, experience, and behavior*. New York: Guilford Press.

Rowe, D. C., & Osgood, D. W. (1984). Heredity and sociological theories of delinquency: A reconsideration. *American Sociological Review, 49*, 526–540.

Rowe, D. C., Woulbroun, E. J., & Gulley, B. L. (1994). Peers and friends as nonshared environmental influences. In E. M. Hetherington, D. Reiss, & R. Plomin (Eds.), *Separate social worlds of siblings: The impact of nonshared environment on development* (pp. 159–173). Hillsdale, NJ: Erlbaum.

Saudino, K. J. (2001). Behavioral genetics, social phobia, social fears, and related temperaments. In S. G. Hofmann & P. M. DiBartolo (Eds.), *Social phobia and social anxiety: An integration* (pp. 200–215). Needham Heights, MA: Allyn & Bacon.

Scarr, S., & Carter-Saltzmann, L. (1979). Twin method: Defense of a critical assumption. *Behavior Genetics, 9*, 527–542.

Scarr, S., & McCartney, K. (1983). How people make their own environments: A theory of genotype–environment effects. *Child Development, 54*, 424–435.

Schilit, R., Lie, G. Y., Bush, J., Montagne, M., & Reyes, L. (1991). Intergenerational transmission of violence in lesbian relationships. *Affilia, 6*, 72–87.

Silverman, J. G., & Williamson, G. M. (1997). Social ecology and entitlements involved in battering by heterosexual college males: Contributions of family and peers. *Violence and Victims, 12*, 147–164.

Simons, R. L., Johnson, C., Beaman, J., & Conger, R. D. (1993). Explaining women's double jeopardy: Factors that mediate the association between harsh treatment as a child and violence by a husband. *Journal of Marriage and the Family, 55*, 713–723.

Simons, R. L., Lin, K., & Gordon, L. C. (1998). Socialization in the family of origin and male dating violence: A prospective study. *Journal of Marriage and the Family, 60*, 467–478.

Stets, J. E. (1990). Verbal and physical aggression in marriage. *Journal of Marriage and the Family, 52*, 501–514.

Stith, S. M., Rosen, K. H., Middleton, K. A., Busch, A. L., Lundeberg, K., & Carlton, R. P. (2000). The intergenerational transmission of spouse abuse: A meta-analysis. *Journal of Marriage and the Family, 62*, 640–654.

Straus, M. A., & Gelles, R. J. (Eds.). (1990). *Physical violence in American families: Risk factors and adaptations to violence in 8,145 families* (pp. 113–132). New Brunswick, NJ: Transaction.

Straus, M. A., Gelles, R. J., & Steinmetz, S. (1980). *Behind closed doors: Violence in the American family*. Garden City, NJ: Anchor Books.

8

APPROACHES TO PREVENTING PSYCHOLOGICAL, PHYSICAL, AND SEXUAL PARTNER ABUSE

VANGIE A. FOSHEE, HEATHE LUZ McNAUGHTON REYES,
AND SARAH C. WYCKOFF

Adult partner abuse has its roots in childhood, adolescence, and young adulthood. Many childhood and adolescent risk factors have been found to predict adult partner violence victimization and perpetration, including exposure to parental domestic violence (Ehrensaft et al., 2003; Magdol, Moffitt, Caspi, & Silva, 1998); exposure to child abuse, physical punishment, and/or harsh discipline (Bank & Burraston, 2001; Ehrensaft et al., 2003; Herrenkohl et al., 2004; Magdol et al., 1998); substance use (Magdol et al., 1998); poor educational achievement and school dropout (Magdol et al., 1998); aggression against peers (Andrews, Foster, Capaldi, & Hops, 2000; Capaldi, Dishion, Stoolmiller, & Yoerger, 2001; Herrenkohl et al., 2004; Magdol et al., 1998); and adolescent association with deviant peers (Capaldi et al., 2001). Furthermore, being a victim of dating abuse during adolescence or during courtship before marriage has been associated with being a victim of partner abuse as an adult (Gayford, 1975; Roscoe & Benaske, 1985; P. H. Smith, White, & Holland, 2003). Thus, efforts to prevent adult partner abuse need to begin early by preventing the psychological, contextual, and behavioral precursors to domestic violence that develop during infancy, childhood, adolescence, and young adulthood.

This chapter describes approaches to the prevention of dating and partner abuse perpetration and victimization targeted at each of these stages in the life span. For each approach, we describe the links to dating or partner abuse prevention, and when available, we provide empirical findings related to efficacy based on randomized trials. The chapter concludes with clinical recommendations.

Dating and partner abuse include psychological abuse, physical violence, and sexual abuse (Saltzman, Fanslow, McMahon, & Shelley, 2002). Because of the interrelatedness of the three types of abuse and their harmful consequences, we describe approaches to preventing each type.

National probability samples (Caetano, Cunradi, Clark, & Schafer, 2000; Sorenson, Upchurch, & Shen, 1996; Straus & Gelles, 1990) and local adult samples (Archer, 2000) have found that women are as likely as or more likely than men to engage in certain forms of physical partner abuse, although men are more likely than women to inflict injury (Archer, 2000; Morse, 1995). Almost all studies have found that the prevalence of dating abuse perpetration among adolescents was either nearly the same for boys and girls or greater for girls than boys (see Foshee & Matthew, 2007, for a review). Therefore, when available, we also describe findings related to the efficacy of each prevention approach for males and females.

PREVENTION EFFORTS TARGETED AT PARENTS

A number of parent- and family-related characteristics have been identified as risk factors for adolescent and adult partner abuse. These factors include corporal punishment (Foshee, Bauman, & Linder, 1999; Magdol et al., 1998; Simons, Lin, & Gordon, 1998); child abuse (Bank & Burraston, 2001; Ehrensaft et al., 2003; Herrenkohl et al., 2004; Magdol et al., 1998; D. Smith, 1999; J. P. Smith & Williams, 1992); child maltreatment (M. Schwartz, O'Leary, & Kendziora, 1997; Wekerle et al., 2001; Wolfe et al., 2001; Wolfe, Wekerle, Reitzel-Jaffe, & Lefebvre, 1998; Wolfe, Wekerle, Scott, Straatman, & Grasley, 2004); domestic violence (Chapple, 2003; Ehrensaft et al., 2003; Foshee et al., 1999; Magdol et al., 1998; Malik, Sorenson, & Aneshensel, 1997; O'Keefe, 1997; O'Keeffe, Brockopp, & Chew, 1986); inadequate parenting, including lack of warmth, inadequate supervision and monitoring, and inconsistent discipline (Bank & Burraston, 2001; Brendgen, Vitaro, Tremblay, & Lavoie, 2001; Capaldi & Clark, 1998; Foshee et al., 1999; Foshee, Linder, MacDougall, & Bangdiwala, 2001; Lavoie et al., 2002; Simons et al., 1998); and poor family functioning (Gorman-Smith, Tolan, Shiedow, & Henry, 2001).

These findings suggest that one approach to preventing adolescent and adult partner abuse is to intervene with parents to decrease the likelihood that children will be exposed to parental and family risk factors associated with partner abuse. Findings from a number of randomized trials suggest that programs targeted at the parents of infants, children, and adolescents have been effective in reducing the family-related risk factors associated with partner violence (Eckenrode et al., 2000; Eddy, Reid, & Fetrow, 2000; Fergusson, Grant, Horwood, & Ridder, 2005; Hawkins, Von Cleve, & Catalano, 1991; Love et al., 2005; Olds et al., 1997, 1999; Olds, Henderson, Chamberlin, & Tatelbaum, 1986; Seitz, Rosenbaum, & Apfel, 1985; Shaw, Dishion, Supplee, Gardner, & Arnds, 2006; Spoth, Redmond, & Shin, 2000; Wagner & Clayton, 1999; Webster-Stratton & Hammond, 1997) and child and adolescent aggression (Fergusson et al., 2005; Hawkins et al., 1991; Love et al., 2005; Martinez & Eddy, 2005; Olds et al., 2004; Spoth et al., 2000; Tremblay et al., 1992).

Despite the evidence that parenting factors are associated with adolescent dating abuse and adult partner abuse, and despite the evidence that programs focused on parents are effective in altering family-related risk factors, there have been no published evaluations of family-based programs for preventing adolescent dating abuse. However, we are currently conducting such a study. In this study, 515 families across the United States with 13- to 15-year-olds were identified via listed telephone numbers, and a caretaker, usually a parent but sometimes a grandmother or foster parent, and the child completed a baseline telephone interview assessing risk factors for dating violence. Parents randomly allocated to the treatment condition participated in the Families for Safe Dates program, which included (a) a series of six booklets mailed one at a time to caretakers with information on dating abuse and interactive activities to do with the adolescent to address risk factors associated with dating abuse and (b) telephone calls from a health educator 2 weeks after mailing each booklet to answer questions and determine whether the family completed the activities before receiving the next booklet. The treatment group families have completed the program, and we are currently conducting 3-month postintervention interviews with parents and adolescents. Preliminary findings are promising, but we must await the final findings to determine whether this approach to preventing adolescent dating violence is effective.

PREVENTION EFFORTS TARGETED AT CHILDREN AND ADOLESCENTS: BEHAVIORAL PRECURSORS TO PARTNER ABUSE

It has been suggested that one way to prevent partner abuse is to intervene with children and adolescents to prevent behavioral precursors of partner and dating abuse such as sexual harassment, bullying, and aggression toward peers (Cascardi & Avery-Leaf, 2000; Cascardi, Avery-Leaf, O'Leary, & Smith Slep, 1999; Connolly, Pepler, Craig, & Taradash, 2000; Wolfe & Jaffe, 1999). However, no studies have examined whether sexual harassment is in fact a precursor to adolescent or adult partner violence, and there have been no evaluations of sexual harassment prevention programs for children and adolescents.

Bullying has been defined as a specific form of violent or aggressive behavior characterized by repeated acts of intentional aggression (including intimidation, harassment, and physical harm) against a vulnerable victim (Vreeman & Carroll, 2007). Although bullying has been proposed as a precursor to dating violence, only one study has directly assessed this association (Connolly et al., 2000). In a sample of adolescents in Grades 5 to 8, Connolly et al. (2000) found that bullies (both boys and girls) started dating earlier than nonbullies; participated in more types of dating activities; spent more time outside of school with other-sex friends; were more likely to have a current boyfriend or girlfriend; perceived their relationship with their boyfriend or girlfriend as less intimate, affectionate, and durable; were more likely to engage in undesirable activities to keep a boyfriend or girlfriend; and perceived dating relationships as less equitable in power. Also, bullies were more likely than nonbullies to be perpetrators and victims of social and physical dating aggression, although the sample for these analyses was very small.

In contrast to the dearth of research on the relationship between bullying and sexual harassment and dating violence, several longitudinal studies have found that aggression toward peers predicted adolescent dating violence (Brendgen et al., 2001; Capaldi & Clark, 1998; Herrenkohl et al., 2004; Lavoie et al., 2002; Simons et al., 1998) and adult partner abuse (Andrews et al., 2000; Capaldi et al., 2001; Herrenkohl et al., 2004).

Several randomized trials have suggested that school-based bullying prevention programs targeting children and early adolescents can reduce bullying behaviors (DeRosier, 2004; Fekkes, Pijpers, & Verloove-Vanhorick, 2006; Frey et al., 2005). In a review of both experimental and quasi-experimental studies of school-based bullying prevention programs, however, Vreeman and Carol (2007) found that effects are sometimes modest and have been inconsistent across outcomes and intervention types. For example, the reviewers found that three of four interventions targeted at children involved in bullying (primarily teaching social skills training) did not reduce bullying and that 6 of 10 programs implemented in classrooms (mostly implementing curricula or using videotapes) were not effective in reducing bullying. Seven of 10 programs that took a "whole-school approach" (a combination of schoolwide rules and sanctions, classroom curriculum, conflict resolution training, and individual counseling), however, were effective in reducing bullying behaviors (Vreeman & Carroll, 2007).

Numerous studies have assessed the effects of programs targeted at children and adolescents to prevent aggression against peers, and there have been a number of outstanding reviews of these studies (see Mihalic, Fagan, Irwin, Ballard, & Elliott, 2004; Mytton, DiGuiseppi, Gough, Taylor, & Logan, 2006; Thorton, Craft, Dahlberg, Lynch, & Baer, 2000; U.S. Department of Health and Human Services, 2001; D. B. Wilson, Gottfredson, & Najaka, 2001; S. J. Wilson, Lipsey, & Derzon, 2003). These reviews suggest that effective strategies for preventing aggression include parent and teacher training in behavior monitoring, appropriate reinforcement of behaviors, classroom management, early home visitation programs to build and promote positive family interaction and communication (as described earlier), building of school capacity (e.g., by reorganizing grades or classes, training administrators and teachers in discipline management), alterations in school climate or culture (e.g., establishing norms and expectations for behavior), and promotion of cooperative learning and children's social competencies. Ineffective strategies included boot camps and alternative schools for aggressive youths, peer counseling, firearm training and gun buyback programs, individual counseling, and zero-tolerance policies at school with regard to weapons, unless these strategies also attended to school climate or promoted feelings of safety.

Although programs for preventing behavioral precursors to partner violence such as bullying and aggression toward peers have been effective in preventing these precursors, their effectiveness in preventing dating and partner abuse has not been assessed. However, as the children in the intervention studies previously described become older, assessments of the impact of bullying prevention or general aggression prevention programs on dating abuse may become available.

PREVENTION EFFORTS TARGETED AT CHILDREN AND ADOLESCENTS EXPOSED TO FAMILY VIOLENCE

As indicated earlier, children who have been exposed to domestic violence or child abuse are at increased risk of becoming perpetrators and victims of dating and partner abuse, and therefore it is particularly important to target these children for dating and partner abuse prevention programs. However, only one dating abuse prevention program evaluated in a randomized trial has targeted adolescents exposed to family violence (Wolfe et al., 2003). In fact, despite substantial evidence that children exposed to family violence experience a number of negative outcomes, including depression, anxiety, aggression, and social relationship problems (for reviews, see Graham-Bermann, 2001; Graham-Bermann & Hughes, 2003; Jouriles et al., 2001; Rossman, 2001; Sullivan, Bybee, & Allen, 2002), very few prevention programs addressing these issues have been evaluated.

This lack of evaluation research reflects the challenges of doing such research. Such challenges include the location and recruitment of adolescents who have been exposed to domestic violence or child abuse into studies, high family stress levels that can interfere with study participation, diffi-culties locating families for follow-up if mothers have left an abuser, diffi-culty in finding high enough numbers of participants for adequate power given recruitment options (e.g., shelters, community agencies, advertisements, social services), social services reporting requirements if child abuse is de-tected, and ethical considerations in allocating children in such need for intervention to a control group (Ammerman, 1998; Christopoulos et al., 1987; Graham-Bermann, 2001; Hughes & Luke, 1998; Moore & Pepler, 1998; Wolfe, Zak, Wilson, & Jaffe, 1986).

Probably because of these obstacles, we could identify only five ran-domized trials of programs for preventing problematic behaviors and attributes in children exposed to domestic violence (Graham-Bermann & Hughes, 2003; Graham-Bermann, Lynch, Banyard, DeVoe, & Halabu, 2007; Jouriles et al., 2001; McDonald, Jouriles, & Skopp, 2006; McFarlane, Groff, O'Brien, & Watson, 2005a, 2005b; Sullivan et al., 2002; Wagar & Rodway, 1995). Three of the five studies evaluated programs that included both a psychoeducational component for the child and a component intended to provide support to the mother. These studies reported significant treatment effects in the ex-pected directions on child conduct problems, internalizing problems, happi-ness, self-worth, physical appearance, perceptions of athletic competence, and witnessing of abuse against the mother (Graham-Bermann et al., 2007; Jouriles et al., 2001; McDonald et al., 2006; Sullivan et al., 2002), as well as on mother measures of child management skills, self-esteem, depression, and victimization from abuse (Jouriles et al., 2001; McDonald et al., 2006; Sullivan et al., 2002).

Of the two remaining trials, one assessed the effectiveness on child out-comes of a program that included an intervention component only for the abused mothers (McFarlane et al., 2005a, 2005b), and the other assessed the effectiveness of a program that included an intervention component only for the child (Wagar & Rodway, 1995). In the former, there were no effects of the program (nurse case management) on child internalizing and externaliz-ing behaviors. In the latter, significant group differences in the expected di-rections were found in the child's attitudes and responses to anger and sense of responsibility for their parent's violence, but there were no differences in knowledge or problem-solving abilities related to safety skills and support. Aggressive behaviors were not assessed.

In a meta-analysis of psychological interventions for maltreated chil-dren, Skowron and Reinemann (2005) included a total of 21 evaluations of programs targeted at these children and adolescents to improve cognitive, emotional, and behavioral outcomes. Only 11 of the studies included were experimental. The overall effect size across the 21 studies was .54, which is considered a medium effect; the analyses indicated that exposure to programs increased average improvement across multiple outcomes for participants by 28%. Effect sizes were larger for studies that had a no-treatment control group than studies with a placebo treatment condition; effect sizes also increased as the duration of the intervention increased, although these findings were confounded by the type of intervention (nonbehavioral programs, which were longer, had larger effect sizes than behavioral interventions, which were shorter). Mandated and volunteer programs were equally effective.

Wolfe and colleagues (2003) conducted the only evaluation of a dating violence prevention program for maltreated adolescents, but Skowron and Reinemann (2005) did not include the study in their meta-analysis. The program, titled the Youth Relationship Project (Wolfe et al., 1996), consisted of 18 two-hour sessions with small groups of participants ages 14 to 16 years who had been identified through child protective services. A man and a woman cofacilitated all sessions and modeled positive relationship skills. The program included skills for communication, conflict negotiation, and help-seeking, as well as activities designed to educate participants about partner abuse, gender inequalities, gender stereotypes, power dynamics in intimate relationships, and community resources for seeking help for dating violence.

Data were collected at baseline and 4 months later after an intervention/control period, then bimonthly for a total of seven waves of data (treatment group $n = 96$; control group $n = 62$). The treatment significantly reduced physical dating abuse perpetration, emotional dating abuse victimization, and victimization from threatening behaviors. It was more effective for boys than for girls in reducing victimization from physical abuse and more effective in reducing physical victimization for boys with higher levels of maltreatment. There was no effect on perpetration of emotional abuse or threatening behaviors. Wolfe et al. (2003) also examined the effects of the program on proposed mediating variables, including trauma symptoms, hostility, and communication and problem-solving skills. Treatment reduced trauma symptoms but had no effects on hostility or communication and problem-solving skills. However, formal mediation was not tested statistically.

Children exposed to family violence are clearly in need of programs to prevent negative outcomes that can affect the quality of their entire lives, including the likelihood of being perpetrators or victims of partner abuse. Those interested in conducting such research may want to refer to the literature on mediators and moderators of the relationships between exposure to family violence and dating and partner violence as a guide for developing interventions. Studies examining mediators have identified the causal processes through which family violence influences use of violence against a partner, and those mechanisms can become the targets for change in treatment programs. For example, studies have identified dating abuse norms, aggressive conflict response style (Foshee et al., 1999; Lewis & Fremouw, 2001), participation in various deviant actions (Swinford, DeMaris, Cernkovich, & Giordano, 2000), hostility (Wolfe et al., 1998, 2004), and trauma symptomatology (Wekerle et al., 2001; Wolfe et al., 2004) as mediators of exposure to family violence and dating violence, and each of these could be targeted for change in prevention programs offered to children exposed to family violence.

A consistent mediator between witnessing domestic violence and other child outcomes is the mental health and stress level of the mother, and that is why many prevention programs for children who have witnessed domestic violence also provide support and resources to the mother (Graham-Bermann & Hughes, 2003). Graham-Bermann and Hughes (2003) and Wolfe and Jaffe (1999) reviewed studies of mediators between exposure to family violence and other problematic child outcomes, such as conduct disorder, aggression, anxiety, and depression.

Studies examining moderators have identified conditions under which family violence does and does not lead to partner violence; prevention programs can attempt to alter these conditions so that the impact of family violence on partner violence is weakened. Only two studies, however, have assessed moderators of the associations between exposure to family violence and dating violence; they found that attachment style (Wekerle & Wolfe, 1998), race, family structure, and socioeconomic status (Foshee et al., 2007) moderated associations in the expected directions. Although not strictly a moderation analysis, O'Keefe's (1998) study found that for boys who had witnessed domestic violence, lower socioeconomic status, exposure to school and community violence, acceptance of dating abuse, and lower self-esteem distinguished perpetrators of dating abuse from nonperpetrators. For girls who had witnessed domestic violence, exposure to school and community violence, poor school performance, and the experience of child abuse distinguished perpetrators of dating abuse from nonperpetrators.

PREVENTION EFFORTS TARGETED AT ADOLESCENTS: DATING ABUSE

National surveys have reported that from 9% to 12% of adolescents have been physically abused by a date in the previous year (Centers for Disease Control and Prevention, 2000, 2002, 2004; Halpern, Oslak, Young, Martin, & Kupper, 2001) and that 29% have been psychologically abused (Halpern et al., 2001). These victimization prevalence rates are lower than those from local samples, possibly because the national studies assessed victimization with only one or two limited questions, whereas local samples typically assessed victimization with more extensive scales such as the Conflict Tactics Scale (Straus, Hamby, Boney-McCoy, & Sugarman, 1996).

No nationally representative studies have been conducted on adolescent dating abuse perpetration, but localized studies suggest that between 11% and 41% of adolescents report using some form of physical violence against their dating partners (Foshee & Matthew, 2007). Prevalence rates for sexual dating violence victimization range widely depending on gender and the measure used (i.e., forced sex only or other types of sexual coercion). For forced sex, rates range from 1% to 13% (Ackard & Neumark-Sztainer, 2002; O'Keefe & Treister, 1998; Poitras & Lavoie, 1995; Rickert, Wiemann, Vaughan, & White, 2004), and for other types of forced sexual activity or unwanted contact among girls, they range from 15% to 77% (Bennett & Fineran, 1998; Bergman, 1992; Foshee, 1996; Gagne, Lavoie, & Hebert, 2005; Jackson, Cram, & Seymour, 2000; Jezl, Molidor, & Wright, 1996; Poitras & Lavoie, 1995; Rhynard, Krebs, & Glover, 1997; Rickert et al., 2004).

Dating abuse during adolescence has been hypothesized to predict abuse against adult partners, although prospective studies have not empirically tested this assertion. Because of this hypothesized link and the prevalence of dating abuse during adolescence, many of the efforts at preventing adult partner abuse have focused on preventing dating abuse by adolescents. Several reviews have described in detail the limitations of these program evaluations (Cascardi & Avery-Leaf, 2000; Foshee & Matthew, 2007; Hickman, Jaycox, & Aronoff, 2004; O'Leary, Woodin, & Timmons Fritz, 2005; Wekerle & Wolfe, 1999). Of the evaluations of adolescent dating abuse prevention programs, we were able to find only five randomized trials. We summarize the findings from four of these trials. (One trial, the Youth Relationship Project, was described in the previous section; see also Wolfe et al., 2003.)

The Dating Violence Intervention and Prevention for Teenagers (Kraizer & Larson, 1993) and Building Relationships in Greater Harmony Together (BRIGHT; Avery-Leaf, Cascardi, O'Leary, & Cano, 1997) each consisted of five 1-hour long sessions taught in school by trained teachers. The five sessions of the first program included discussion on

- violence in society and relationships;
- the role of self-esteem in interpersonal violence;
- how to recognize physical, sexual, and emotional abuse;
- the role of power and control in abusive relationships;
- how to build healthy relationships, including problem-solving and communication skills; and
- identifying resources for getting help.

The five sessions in the BRIGHT program included discussion of

- how gender inequality may foster violence,
- individual and societal attitudes toward violence, and
- constructive communication skills and support resources for victims of abuse who seek help.

Evaluations of these two programs found that the treatment group showed significant favorable changes in attitudes toward dating violence from pretest to posttest, whereas there was no change in scores in the control group (Avery-Leaf et al., 1997; Macgowan, 1997). Gender did not moderate program effects in either study, but Macgowan found that in the treatment group, male students with the highest academic ability showed the greatest changes in attitudes. Although these findings are promising, in both studies the posttest assessments were conducted immediately after the intervention was completed, and therefore lasting effects of the intervention are not known. Also, it is not known whether changes in attitudes resulted in changes in behavior. Additionally, both studies had limited generalizability. Macgowan's study was conducted in a single, primarily African American urban school in Florida, and the analyses included about half of the initial sample. BRIGHT was evaluated in one large New York high school. Although there were significant program effects on one of the scales measuring justification of dating aggression, there were no effects on justification for dating jealousy or on a second scale measuring justification for dating abuse. Despite random allocation of classrooms in both studies, analyses did not account for clustering by classroom.

Ending Violence: A Curriculum for Educating Teens on Domestic Violence and the Law was a three-session school-based curriculum taught by attorneys that focused on legal aspects of dating violence and was designed to alter knowledge and norms about dating abuse, promote favorable attitudes toward seeking help for dating violence, and decrease the prevalence of dating violence perpetration and victimization. In the location of the evaluation, public schools are overcrowded, and to address this issue, the schools are composed of multiple educational groups that attend school at different times during the calendar year. For the evaluation, 40 educational groups that attended 10 schools whose student bodies were more than 80% Latino were randomly allocated to treatment and control condition (Jaycox et al., 2006). There were significant treatment effects, in the expected directions, on knowledge of the laws related to dating violence, acceptance of female-on-male violence, and likelihood of help seeking for dating violence, but there were no differences between treatment and control groups in acceptance of male-on-female violence, abusive/fearful dating experiences, or dating violence perpetration or victimization. All program effects had dissipated at the 6-month follow-up except for knowledge of laws and perceived helpfulness of speaking with a lawyer about dating abuse. Program effects were not moderated by gender, but some of the effects on the perceived helpfulness of others (like doctors and nurses) were stronger for those with lower English proficiency.

The Safe Dates program included a 45-minute theater production, a 10-session school-based curriculum, and a poster contest (Foshee & Langwick, 2004). Content was designed to improve norms related to dating abuse, gender-based expectations, anger and conflict management skills, and help seeking as ways of preventing dating abuse perpetration and victimization. For the randomized trial, 14 schools with eighth and ninth grades in a primarily rural county were randomly allocated to the treatment or control condition. Students were assessed at baseline, 1 month after activities ended, and then yearly thereafter for 4 years.

Positive program effects were noted in all four evaluation papers that have been published (Foshee et al., 1998, 2000, 2004, 2005). Here we summarize the findings from the most recent and comprehensive paper, which used random coefficient models to examine the effects of Safe Dates in preventing or reducing perpetration and victimization over time using four waves of follow-up data. Treatment significantly reduced psychological, moderate physical, and sexual dating violence perpetration at all four follow-up periods (Foshee et al., 2005). Treatment also significantly reduced severe physical dating abuse perpetration over time but only for adolescents who reported no or average prior involvement in severe physical perpetration at baseline. The program also significantly reduced moderate physical dating violence victimization, but it did not prevent or reduce psychological ($p = .17$), severe physical ($p = .14$), or sexual ($p = .07$) dating abuse victimization. Treatment effects were not moderated by gender or race and were mediated primarily by changes in dating violence norms, gender role norms, and awareness of community services. The program did not affect conflict management skills or belief in the need for help.

PREVENTION EFFORTS TARGETED AT YOUNG ADULTS

J. Schwartz, Magee, Griffin, and Dupuis (2004) conducted the only published randomized trial of a program specifically designed to prevent dating violence by young adults. Conducted with college students, the program included four sessions, each 90 minutes long, that incorporated didactic activities and skills development activities designed to decrease gender role stereotyping and conflict, affect entitlement attitudes, and improve skills in managing anger. At follow-up, treatment group students were significantly less accepting of stereotypical and traditional gender roles, had more confidence in communicating needs and emotions to others, had more healthy entitlement attitudes (i.e., were more willing to stand up for themselves and had more confidence), and had better anger management skills. These findings are promising, though abusive dating behaviors were not measured, and the study was limited by the small sample size ($n = 65$), precluding examination of program effects by gender.

For her dissertation research, Woodin (2007) conducted the first randomized trial of a couples-based motivational interviewing intervention for the prevention of partner violence among a sample of college student couples who had experienced some mild physical aggression in their relationship. Findings are promising in that the treatment group couples had significant reductions in mild physical aggression, harmful alcohol use, and acceptance of female psychological aggression compared with the control group.

A number of randomized trials have been conducted of programs developed for young adult couples to improve partner communication skills, problem-solving skills, and marital satisfaction and to decrease marital distress, marital conflict, and divorce (Halford, Moore, Wilson, Farrugia, & Dyer, 2004; Halford, Sanders, & Behrens, 2001; Laurenceau, Stanley, Olmos-Gallo, Baucom, & Markman, 2004; Markman, Floyd, Stanley, & Storaasli, 1988; Markman, Renick, Floyd, Stanley, & Clements, 1993; Stanley et al., 2001; Van Widenfelt, Hosman, Schaap, & van der Staak, 1996). Although these programs were not designed specifically to prevent partner violence, they have been shown to influence relationship-related outcomes that may buffer a couple against domestic violence. These types of programs have demonstrated some effectiveness in improving couple communication (Halford et al., 2001; Laurenceau et al., 2004; Markman et al., 1988, 1993; Stanley et al., 2001), preventing divorce (Markman et al., 1988, 1993), and improving relationship satisfaction (Halford et al., 2001, 2004; Markman et al., 1988, 1993). For some studies, however, positive program effects were found only for high-risk couples (Halford et al., 2001), and some iatrogenic (negative) effects of programs have been noted (Halford et al., 2001; Van Widenfelt et al., 1996).

Only one trial evaluated the effects of such programs on the prevention of domestic violence; Markman and colleagues (1993) found fewer instances of physical abuse being reported in the treatment group than in the control group 4 years after the treatment group was exposed to their Prevention and Relationship Enhancement Program. However, it is important to note that the sample size for this study was very small, and the 21 couples who completed treatment represented only 40% of those initially assigned to treatment condition; therefore, there was probably substantial selection bias that could have affected the results of the study. For a meta-analysis of 11 experimental studies of premarital education and counseling programs, see Carroll and Doherty (2003).

With the high prevalence of sexual assault, particularly acquaintance sexual assault, among young adults on college campuses, many college-based sexual assault prevention programs have been developed. Randomized trials have assessed the effectiveness of such programs in altering risk factors for sexual assault victimization, preventing sexual assault victimization, altering various attitudes supportive of rape, and preventing sexual assault perpetration.

A number of studies have found that problematic cognitions such as acceptance of rape myths, cognitive distortions justifying rape and male dominance ideology, poor heterosocial skills such as an inability to perceive negative cues from partners, and an inability to feel empathy for sexual assault victims are associated with sexual offending and rape (Koss, Leonard, Beazley,

& Oros, 1985; Rickert & Wiemann, 1998; Schewe & O'Donohue, 1993, 1996). Several meta-analyses have been conducted of studies evaluating the effectiveness of programs in altering these precursors to sexual violence. Flores and Hartlaub (1998) reviewed studies examining effects on rape-myth attitudes; Brecklin and Forde (2001) reviewed studies examining effects on rape attitudes; and Anderson and Whiston (2005) reviewed studies examining effects on rape attitudes, rape empathy, rape-related attitudes, rape knowledge, behavioral intent, awareness behavior, and incidence.

The review by Anderson and Whiston (2005) is, to date, the most recent and comprehensive of these reviews. They included 69 studies in their analysis, 68% (n = 49) of which used random assignment to a treatment condition; the rest had some type of comparison group, and all included pretests so that comparability of groups at baseline could be assessed. In addition to calculating effect sizes for outcomes, they analyzed a variety of methodological and content-related factors that could influence program effectiveness. They found that effect sizes were strongest when the outcome was rape knowledge (d = .57—a medium effect size) and next strongest when the outcome was rape attitudes (d = .21—a small effect size; Cohen, 1988). Effect sizes were significantly different from 0 for rape-related attitudes (.125), behavioral intent (.136), and incidence of rape (.101), but not for rape empathy or awareness. Effect sizes were smaller in experimental than in quasi-experimental studies.

Thus, this meta-analysis suggests that the effectiveness of sexual assault prevention programs depends on the outcomes measured and that when significant effects are found, they tend to be small (except on rape knowledge). The longer the duration of the program, the stronger the effects, and thus Anderson and Whiston (2005) suggested that sexual assault prevention programs should be a semester long or be a multisession workshop (as opposed to the 1-hour sexual assault prevention programs commonly conducted on college campuses). Effect sizes were also stronger when presenters were professionals rather than graduate students or peers, and programs that covered gender role socialization, provided general information about rape, discussed rape myths and facts, and addressed risk-reduction strategies tended to be more effective in altering rape and rape-related attitudes than other approaches. Also, focused programs were more effective than those covering many different topics, and greater effects were observed on rape-related attitudes when the program targeted fraternity and sorority members than for other types of population.

CLINICAL IMPLICATIONS FOR PREVENTION EFFORTS

This chapter described a number of approaches to the primary prevention of partner abuse, including the following:

- intervening with parents to decrease the likelihood that children will be exposed to parental and family-based risk factors for adolescent dating abuse and adult partner abuse;
- preventing and reducing behavioral precursors to dating and partner abuse, such as bullying and aggression toward peers;
- intervening with children who have been exposed to family violence and are at increased risk for dating and partner abuse by attempting to alter factors that mediate and moderate the association between exposure to family violence and partner abuse;
- delivering dating abuse prevention programs to adolescents;
- offering to young couples premarital education and counseling programs designed to improve couple communication, problem-solving skills, and marital satisfaction and to decrease marital distress and conflict; and
- offering sexual assault prevention programs on college campuses because many of the cognitions, attitudes, and behaviors altered by these programs have been associated with the use of sexual violence against partners.

For each approach, results from experimental studies were presented to direct the reader to evidence-based programs.

There are examples of evidence-based programs in all categories. The parenting programs with the strongest evidence of effectiveness are home visiting programs targeting parents of infants and children. The most widely known and comprehensively evaluated home visitation program is the Nurse Home Visitation Program developed by Olds and colleagues (1999), but there are a number of others as well, including Early Start (Fergusson et al., 2005), Early Head Start (Love et al., 2005), Parents as Teachers and Teen Parents as Teachers (Wagner & Clayton, 1999), and the Prenatal/Early Infancy Project (Seitz et al., 1985). These programs have resulted in significant changes in many risk factors for later dating violence that lasted many years after program exposure. The Bullying Prevention Program developed by Olweus and Limber (1999) has served as the basis for many effective whole-school approaches to bullying and is an example of an evidence-based program for preventing and reducing behavioral precursors to dating and partner abuse. Project Support (Jouriles et al., 2001), a program developed for mothers of children exposed to domestic violence, has resulted in decreases in many child risk factors for later dating violence. Adolescent dating abuse prevention programs with particularly strong evidence of effectiveness are the Safe Dates program (Foshee & Langwick, 2004) and the Youth Relationship Project (Wolfe et al., 1996). The line of research on the Prevention and Relationship Enhancement Program developed by Markman and colleagues (1988) has made important strides in identifying ways to intervene and not to intervene with young adult couples to prevent partner violence. Finally, programs developed by Gilbert, Heesacker, and Gannon (1991) and Schewe and O'Donohue (1996) have demonstrated effectiveness in changing attitudes supportive of sexual aggression in college men.

CONCLUSION

Although we described potential approaches for preventing partner abuse, it is clear that mental and public health professionals have a long way to go in understanding how to prevent partner abuse. As noted throughout, the effectiveness of many of the approaches in preventing dating or partner violence has not yet been established. We strongly recommend that evaluators of these types of programs include dating abuse as a measured outcome. The field has also been hampered by the paucity of randomized trials evaluating the programmatic approaches described. Even among the randomized trials reviewed, many were limited by small sample sizes, short follow-up periods, substantial attrition, and limited generalizability; in addition, measurement of attitudes, knowledge, and intentions rather than actual behaviors, such as dating or sexual violence, limits confidence in the efficacy of a number of programs.

The programmatic approaches described are almost all community- or school-based interventions. We recommend developing strong community and school partners when conducting evaluations of such programs as a way of enhancing the quality of future randomized designs. For example, close collaboration with schools will be essential to obtain the necessary permission for including questions about psychological, physical, and sexual dating abuse on in-school surveys, and community agencies that know their targeted populations well can be invaluable in helping with recruitment and retention of study subjects.

Research on the prevention of partner abuse has been a priority for the Centers for Disease Control and Prevention for some time, and recently a number of other agencies, including the World Health Organization, the Robert Wood Johnson Foundation, and the National Institute of Justice, have made the prevention of partner abuse a priority. We hope that these commitments will facilitate growth in the science base for the primary prevention of partner abuse.

REFERENCES

Ackard, D. M., & Neumark-Sztainer, D. (2002). Date violence and date rape among adolescents: Associations with disordered eating behaviors and psychological health. *Child Abuse & Neglect, 26,* 455–473.

Ammerman, R. T. (1998). Methodological issues in child maltreatment research. In J. R. Lutzker (Ed.), *Handbook of child abuse research and treatment* (pp. 117–132). New York: Plenum Press.

Anderson, L., & Whiston, S. C. (2005). Sexual assault education programs: A meta-analytic examination of their effectiveness. *Psychology of Women Quarterly, 29*, 374–388.

Andrews, J. A., Foster, S. L., Capaldi, D., & Hops, H. (2000). Adolescent and family predictors of physical aggression, communication, and satisfaction in young adult couples: A prospective analysis. *Journal of Consulting and Clinical Psychology, 68*, 195–208.

Archer, J. (2000). Sex differences in aggression between heterosexual partners: A meta-analytic review. *Psychological Bulletin, 126*, 651–680.

Avery-Leaf, S., Cascardi, M., O'Leary, K. D., & Cano, A. (1997). Efficacy of a dating violence prevention program on attitudes justifying aggression. *Journal of Adolescent Health, 21*, 11–17.

Bank, L., & Burraston, B. (2001). Abusive home environments as predictors of poor adjustment during adolescence and early childhood. *Journal of Community Psychology, 29*, 195–217.

Bennett, L., & Fineran, S. (1998). Sexual and severe physical violence among high school students—Power beliefs, gender, and relationship. *American Journal of Orthopsychology, 68*, 645–652.

Bergman, L. (1992). Dating violence among high school students. *Social Work, 37*, 21–27.

Brecklin, L. R., & Forde, D. R. (2001). A meta-analysis of rape education programs. *Violence and Victims, 16*, 303–321.

Brendgen, M., Vitaro, F., Tremblay, R. E., & Lavoie, F. (2001). Reactive and proactive aggression: Predictions to physical violence in different contexts and moderating effects of parental monitoring and caregiving behavior. *Journal of Abnormal Child Psychology, 29*, 293–304.

Caetano, R., Cunradi, C. B., Clark, C. L., & Schafer, J. (2000). Intimate partner violence and drinking patterns among White, Black and Hispanic couples in the U.S. *Journal of Substance Abuse, 11*, 123–138.

Capaldi, D. M., & Clark, S. (1998). Prospective family predictors of aggression toward female partners for young at-risk males. *Developmental Psychology, 34*, 1175–1188.

Capaldi, D. M., Dishion, T. J., Stoolmiller, M., & Yoerger, K. L. (2001). Aggression toward female partners by at-risk young men: The contribution of male adolescent friendships. *Developmental Psychology, 37*, 61–73.

Carroll, J. S., & Doherty, W. J. (2003). Evaluating the effectiveness of premarital prevention programs: A meta-analytic review of outcome research. *Family Relations, 52*, 105–118.

Cascardi, M., & Avery-Leaf, S. (2000). *Violence against women: Synthesis of research for secondary school officials* (Report No. NCJ 201342). Unpublished report submitted to the U.S. Department of Justice, Washington, DC.

Cascardi, M., Avery-Leaf, S., O'Leary, K. D., & Smith Slep, A. M. (1999). Factor structure and convergent validity of the Conflict Tactics Scale in high school students. *Psychological Assessment, 14*, 546–555.

Centers for Disease Control and Prevention. (2000). Surveillance summaries. *Morbidity and Mortality Weekly Report, 49*(SSO5), 1–96.

Centers for Disease Control and Prevention. (2002). Surveillance summaries. *Morbidity and Mortality Weekly Report, 51*(SSO4), 1–64.

Centers for Disease Control and Prevention. (2004). Surveillance summaries. *Morbidity and Mortality Weekly Report, 53*(SS-2), 1–100.

Chapple, C. (2003). Examining intergenerational violence: Violent role modeling or weak parental controls? *Violence and Victims, 18*, 143–162.

Christopoulos, C., Cohn, D. A., Shaw, D. S., Joyce, S., Sullivan-Hanson, J., Kraft, S. P., et al. (1987). Children of abused women: Adjustment at time of shelter residence. *Journal of Marriage and the Family, 49*, 611–619.

Cohen, J. (1988). *Statistical power analysis for the behavioral sciences.* Mahwah, NJ: Erlbaum.

Connolly, J., Pepler, D. J., Craig, W. M., & Taradash, A. (2000). Dating experiences of bullies in early adolescence. *Child Maltreatment, 5*, 299–310.

DeRosier, M. E. (2004). Building relationships and combating bullying: Effectiveness of a school-based social skills group intervention. *Journal of Clinical Child and Adolescent Psychology, 33*, 196–201.

Eckenrode, J., Ganzel, B., Henderson, C. R., Jr., Smith, E., Olds, D. L., Powers, J., et al. (2000). Preventing child abuse and neglect with a program of nurse home visitation: The limiting effects of domestic violence. *JAMA, 284*, 1385–1391.

Eddy, J. M., Reid, R. J., & Fetrow, R. A. (2000). An elementary school-based prevention program targeting modifiable antecedents of youth delinquency and violence: Linking the Interests of Families and Teachers (LIFT). *Journal of Emotional and Behavioral Disorders, 8*, 165–176.

Ehrensaft, M. K., Cohen, P., Brown, J., Smailes, E., Chen, H., & Johnson, J. G. (2003). Intergenerational transmission of partner violence: A 20-year prospective study. *Journal of Consulting and Clinical Psychology, 71*, 741–753.

Fekkes, M., Pijpers, F. I., & Verloove-Vanhorick, S. P. (2006). Effects of antibullying school program on bullying and health complaints. *Archives of Pediatric and Adolescent Medicine, 160*, 638–644.

Fergusson, D. M., Grant, H., Horwood, L. J., & Ridder, E. M. (2005). Randomized trial of the Early Start program of home visitation. *Pediatrics, 116*, e803–e809. doi: 10.1542/peds.2005-0948

Flores, S. A., & Hartlaub, M. G. (1998). Reducing rape-myth acceptance in male college students: A meta-analysis of intervention studies. *Journal of College Student Development, 39*, 438–448.

Foshee, V. A. (1996). Gender differences in adolescent dating abuse prevalence, types, and injuries. *Health Education Research, 11*, 275–286.

Foshee, V. A., Bauman, K., Arriaga, X., Helms, R., Koch, G., & Linder, G. (1998). An evaluation of Safe Dates, an adolescent dating violence prevention program. *American Journal of Public Health, 88*, 45–50.

Foshee, V. A., Bauman, K. E., Ennett, S. T., Linder, G. F., Benefield, T., & Suchindran, C. (2004). Assessing the long-term effects of the Safe Dates program and a booster in preventing and reducing adolescent dating violence victimization and perpetration. *American Journal of Public Health, 94*, 619–624.

Foshee, V. A., Bauman, K. E., Ennett, S. T., Suchindran, C., Benefield, T., & Linder, G. F. (2005). Assessing the effects of the dating violence prevention program "Safe Dates" using random coefficient regression modeling. *Prevention Science, 6*, 245–258.

Foshee, V. A., Bauman, K. E., Greene, W. F., Koch, G. G., Linder, G. F., & MacDougall, J. E. (2000). The Safe-Dates program: 1-year follow-up results. *American Journal of Public Health, 90*, 1619–1622.

Foshee, V. A., Bauman, K. E., & Linder, G. F. (1999). Family violence and the perpetration of adolescent dating violence: Examining social learning and social control processes. *Journal of Marriage and the Family, 61*, 331–342.

Foshee, V. A., Ennett, S. E., Bauman, K., Granger, D. A., Benefield, T., Suchindran, C., et al. (2007). A test of biosocial models of adolescent cigarette and alcohol involvement. *The Journal of Early Adolescence, 27*, 1–36.

Foshee, V. A., & Langwick, S. (2004). *Safe Dates: An adolescent dating abuse prevention curriculum* [Program manual]. Center City, MN: Hazelden Publishing and Educational Services.

Foshee, V. A., Linder, F., MacDougall, J. E., & Bangdiwala, S. (2001). Gender differences in the longitudinal predictors of dating violence. *Preventive Medicine, 32*, 128–141.

Foshee, V. A., & Matthew, R. (2007). Adolescent dating abuse perpetration: A review of findings, methodological limitations, and suggestions for future research. In D. Flannery, A. Vazonsyi, & I. Waldman (Eds.), *The Cambridge handbook of violent behavior* (pp. 431–449). New York: Cambridge University Press.

Frey, K. S., Hirschstein, M. K., Snell, J. L., Edstrom, L. V., MacKenzie, E. P., & Broderick, C. J. (2005). Reducing playground bullying and supporting beliefs: An experimental trial of the Steps to Respect program. *Developmental Psychology, 41*, 479–490.

Gagne, M. H., Lavoie, F., & Hebert, M. (2005). Victimization during childhood and revictimization in dating relationships in adolescent girls. *Child Abuse & Neglect, 29*, 1155–1172.

Gayford, J. (1975, January 25). Wife battering: A preliminary survey of 100 cases. *BMJ, 1*, 194–197.

Gilbert, B. J., Heesacker, M., & Gannon, L. G. (1991). Changing the sexual aggression supportive attitudes of men: A psychoeducational intervention. *Journal of Counseling Psychology, 38*, 197–203.

Gorman-Smith, D., Tolan, P. H., Shiedow, A. J., & Henry, D. B. (2001). Partner violence and street violence among urban adolescents: Do the same family factors relate? *Journal of Research on Adolescence, 11*, 273–295.

Graham-Bermann, S. A. (2001). Designing intervention evaluations for children exposed to domestic violence: Applications of research and theory. In S. A. Graham-Bermann & J. L. Edelson (Eds.), *Domestic violence in the lives of children* (pp. 237–267). Washington, DC: American Psychological Association.

Graham-Bermann, S. A., & Hughes, H. M. (2003). Intervention for children exposed to interparental violence (IPV): Assessment of needs and research priorities. *Clinical Child and Family Psychology Review, 6*, 189–204.

Graham-Bermann, S. A., Lynch, S., Banyard, V., DeVoe, E. R., & Halabu, H. (2007). Community-based intervention for children exposed to intimate partner violence: An efficacy trial. *Journal of Consulting and Clinical Psychology, 75*, 199–209.

Halford, W. K., Moore, E., Wilson, K., Farrugia, C., & Dyer, C. (2004). Benefits of flexible delivery relationship education: An evaluation of the Couple CARE Program. *Family Relations, 53*, 469–476.

Halford, W. K., Sanders, M. R., & Behrens, B. C. (2001). Can skills training prevent relationship problems in at-risk couples? Four-year effects of a behavioral relationship education program. *Journal of Family Psychology, 15*, 750–768.

Halpern, C. T., Oslak, S. G., Young, M. L., Martin, S. L., & Kupper, L. L. (2001). Partner violence among adolescents in opposite-sex romantic relationships: Findings from the National Longitudinal Study of Adolescent Health. *American Journal of Public Health, 91*, 1679–1685.

Hawkins, J. D., Von Cleve, E., & Catalano, R. F., Jr. (1991). Reducing early childhood aggression: Results of a primary prevention program. *Journal of the American Academy of Child & Adolescent Psychiatry, 30*, 208–217.

Herrenkohl, T. I., Mason, W. A., Kosterman, R., Lengua, L. J., Hawkins, J. D., & Abbott, R. D. (2004). Pathways from physical childhood abuse to partner violence in young adulthood. *Violence and Victims, 19*, 123–136.

Hickman, L. J., Jaycox, L. H., & Aronoff, J. (2004). Dating violence among adolescents: Prevalence, gender distribution, and prevention program effectiveness. *Trauma, Violence, & Abuse, 5*, 123–142.

Hughes, H. M., & Luke, D. A. (1998). Heterogeneity in adjustment among children of battered women. In G. W. Holden, R. Geffner, & E. N. Jouriles (Eds.), *Children exposed to marital violence* (pp. 185–221). Washington, DC: American Psychological Association.

Jackson, S. M., Cram, F., & Seymour, F. W. (2000). Violence and sexual coercion in high school students' dating relationships. *Journal of Family Violence, 15*, 23–35.

Jaycox, L. H., McCaffrey, D., Eiseman, B., Aronoff, J., Shelley, G. A., Collins, R. L., et al. (2006). Impact of a school-based dating violence prevention program among Latino teens: Randomized controlled effectiveness trial. *Journal of Adolescent Health, 39*, 694–704.

Jezl, D. R., Molidor, C., & Wright, R. L. (1996). Physical, sexual and psychological abuse in high school dating relationships: Prevalence rates and self-esteem issues. *Child Adolescent Social Work Journal, 13*, 69–87.

Jouriles, E. N., McDonald, R., Spiller, L., Norwood, W. D., Swank, P. R., Stephens, N., et al. (2001). Reducing conduct problems among children of battered women. *Journal of Consulting and Clinical Psychology, 69*, 774–785.

Koss, M., Leonard, H., Beazley, D., & Oros, C. (1985). Nonstranger sexual aggression: A discriminant analysis of the psychological characteristics of undetected offenders. *Sex Roles, 12*, 981–992.

Kraizer, S., & Larson, C. L. (1993). *Dating violence: Intervention & prevention for teenagers* [Program manual]. Tulsa: University of Oklahoma, College of Continuing Education, National Resource Center for Youth Services.

Laurenceau, J. P., Stanley, S. M., Olmos-Gallo, A., Baucom, B., & Markman, H. J. (2004). Community-based prevention of marital dysfunction: Multilevel modeling of a randomized effectiveness study. *Journal of Consulting and Clinical Psychology, 72*, 933–943.

Lavoie, F., Hebert, M., Tremblay, R. E., Vitaro, F., Vezina, L., & McDuff, P. (2002). History of family dysfunction and perpetration of dating violence by adolescent boys: A longitudinal study. *Journal of Adolescent Health, 30*, 375–383.

Lewis, S. F., & Fremouw, W. (2001). Dating violence: A critical review of the literature. *Clinical Psychology Review, 21*, 105–127.

Love, J. M., Kisker, E. E., Ross, C., Raikes, H., Constantine, J., Boller, K., et al. (2005). The effectiveness of Early Head Start for 3-year-old children and their parents: Lessons for policy and programs. *Developmental Psychology, 41*, 885–901.

Macgowan, M. J. (1997). An evaluation of a dating violence prevention program for middle school students. *Violence and Victims, 12*, 223–235.

Magdol, L., Moffitt, T. E., Caspi, A., & Silva, P. A. (1998). Developmental antecedents of partner abuse: A prospective–longitudinal study. *Journal of Abnormal Psychology, 107*, 375–389.

Malik, S., Sorenson, S. B., & Aneshensel, C. S. (1997). Community and dating violence among adolescents: Perpetration and victimization. *Journal of Adolescent Health, 21*, 291–302.

Markman, H. J., Floyd, F. J., Stanley, S. M., & Storaasli, R. D. (1988). Prevention of marital distress: A longitudinal investigation. *Journal of Consulting and Clinical Psychology, 56*, 210–217.

Markman, H. J., Renick, M. J., Floyd, F. J., Stanley, S. M., & Clements, M. (1993). Preventing marital distress through communication and conflict management training: A 4-year and 5-year follow-up. *Journal of Consulting and Clinical Psychology, 61*, 70–77.

Martinez, C. R., Jr., & Eddy, J. M. (2005). Effects of culturally adapted parent management training on Latino youth behavioral health outcomes. *Journal of Consulting and Clinical Psychology, 73*, 841–851.

McDonald, R., Jouriles, E. N., & Skopp, N. A. (2006). Reducing conduct problems among children brought to women's shelters: Intervention effects 24 months following termination of services. *Journal of Family Psychology, 20*, 127–136.

McFarlane, J. M., Groff, J. Y., O'Brien, J. A., & Watson, K. (2005a). Behaviors of children exposed to intimate partner violence before and 1 year after a treatment program for their mother. *Applied Nursing Research, 18,* 7–12.

McFarlane, J. M., Groff, J. Y., O'Brien, J. A., & Watson, K. (2005b). Behaviors of children following a randomized controlled treatment program for their abused mothers. *Issues in Comprehensive Pediatric Nursing, 28,* 195–211.

Mihalic, S., Fagan, A., Irwin, K., Ballard, D., & Elliott, D. (2004). *Blueprints for violence prevention.* Boulder: University of Colorado.

Moore, T. E., & Pepler, D. J. (1998). Correlates of adjustment in children at risk. In G. W. Holden, R. Geffner, & E. N. Jouriles (Eds.), *Children exposed to marital violence: Theory, research, and applied issues* (pp. 157–184). Washington, DC: American Psychological Association.

Morse, B. J. (1995). Beyond the Conflict Tactics Scale: Assessing gender differences in partner violence. *Violence and Victims, 10,* 251–272.

Mytton, J., DiGuiseppi, M. J., Gough, D., Taylor, R., & Logan, S. (2006). School-based secondary prevention programmes for preventing violence. *Cochrane Database of Systemic Reviews, 3.* Available from http://www.cochrane.org

O'Keefe, M. (1997). Predictors of dating violence among high school students. *Journal of Interpersonal Violence, 12,* 546–568.

O'Keefe, M. (1998). Factors mediating the link between witnessing interparental violence and dating violence. *Journal of Family Violence, 13,* 39–57.

O'Keefe, M., & Treister, L. (1998). Victims of dating violence among high school students: Are predictors different for males and females? *Violence Against Women, 4,* 195–223.

O'Keeffe, N. K., Brockopp, K., & Chew, E. (1986). Teen dating violence. *Social Work, 31,* 465–468.

Olds, D. L., Eckenrode, J., Henderson, C. R., Jr., Kitzman, H., Powers, J., Cole, R., et al. (1997). Long-term effects of home visitation on maternal life course and child abuse and neglect: Fifteen-year follow-up of a randomized trial. *JAMA, 278,* 637–643.

Olds, D. L., Henderson, C. R., Jr., Chamberlin, R., & Tatelbaum, R. (1986). Preventing child abuse and neglect: A randomized trial of nurse home visitation. *Pediatrics, 78,* 65–78.

Olds, D. L., Henderson, C. R., Jr., Kitzman, H. J., Eckenrode, J. J., Cole, R. E., & Tatelbaum, R. C. (1999). Prenatal and infancy home visitation by nurses: Recent findings. *The Future of Children, 9,* 44–65.

Olds, D. L., Kitzman, H., Cole, R., Robinson, J., Sidora, K., Luckey, D. W., et al. (2004). Effects of nurse home-visiting on maternal life course and child development: Age 6 follow-up results of a randomized trial. *Pediatrics, 114,* 1550–1559.

O'Leary, K. D., Woodin, E. M., & Timmons Fritz, P. A. (2005). Can we prevent the hitting? Recommendations for preventing intimate partner violence between young adults. *Journal of Aggression, Maltreatment and Trauma, 13*(3/4), 125–181.

Olweus, D., & Limber, S. (1999). *Blueprints for violence prevention: Bullying Prevention Program.* Boulder: Institute of Behavior, University of Colorado.

Poitras, M., & Lavoie, F. (1995). A study of the prevalence of sexual coercion in adolescent heterosexual dating relationships in a Quebec sample. *Violence and Victims, 10,* 299–313.

Rhynard, J., Krebs, M., & Glover, J. (1997). Sexual assault in dating relationships. *Journal of School Health, 67,* 89–93.

Rickert, V. I., & Wiemann, C. M. (1998). Date rape among adolescents and young adults. *Journal of Pediatric and Adolescent Gynecology, 11,* 167–175.

Rickert, V. I., Wiemann, C. M., Vaughan, R. D., & White, J. W. (2004). Rates and risk factors for sexual violence among an ethnically diverse sample of adolescents. *Archives of Pediatric and Adolescent Medicine, 158,* 1132–1139.

Roscoe, B., & Benaske, N. (1985). Courtship violence experienced by abused wives: Similarities in patterns of abuse. *Family Relations, 34,* 419–424.

Rossman, B. B. R. (2001). Longer term effects of children's exposure to domestic violence. In S. A. Graham-Bermann & J. L. Edelson (Eds.), *Domestic violence in the lives of children* (pp. 35–65). Washington, DC: American Psychological Association.

Saltzman, L., Fanslow, J., McMahon, P., & Shelley, G. (2002). *Intimate partner violence surveillance: Uniform definitions and recommended data elements, Version 1.0.* Atlanta, GA: National Center for Injury Prevention and Control, Centers for Disease Control and Prevention.

Schewe, P., & O'Donohue, W. (1993). Rape prevention: Methodological problems and new directions. *Clinical Psychology Review, 13,* 667–682.

Schewe, P., & O'Donohue, W. (1996). Rape prevention with high-risk males: Short-term outcome of two interventions. *Archives of Sexual Behavior, 25,* 455–471.

Schwartz, J., Magee, M., Griffin, L., & Dupuis, C. (2004). Effects of a group preventive intervention on risk and protective factors related to dating violence. *Group Dynamics: Theory, Research, and Practice, 8,* 221–231.

Schwartz, M., O'Leary, S. G., & Kendziora, K. T. (1997). Dating aggression among high school students. *Violence and Victims, 12,* 295–305.

Seitz, V., Rosenbaum, L. K., & Apfel, N. H. (1985). Effects of family support intervention: A ten-year follow-up. *Child Development, 56,* 376–391.

Shaw, D. S., Dishion, T. J., Supplee, L., Gardner, F., & Arnds, K. (2006). Randomized trial of a family-centered approach to the prevention of early conduct problems: 2-year effects of the family check-up in early childhood. *Journal of Consulting and Clinical Psychology, 74,* 1–9.

Simons, R. L., Lin, K., & Gordon, L. C. (1998). Socialization in the family of origin and male dating violence: A prospective study. *Journal of Marriage and the Family, 60,* 467–478.

Skowron, E., & Reinemann, D. H. S. (2005). Effectiveness of psychological interventions for child maltreatment: A meta-analysis. *Psychotherapy: Theory, Research, Practice, Training, 42,* 52–71.

Smith, D. (1999). *Intergenerational transmission of courtship violence: A meta-analysis.* Falls Church: Virginia Polytechnic Institute.

Smith, J. P., & Williams, J. G. (1992). From abusive household to dating violence. *Journal of Family Violence, 7,* 153–165.

Smith, P. H., White, J. W., & Holland, L. J. (2003). A longitudinal perspective on dating violence among adolescent and college-age women. *American Journal of Public Health, 93,* 1104–1109.

Sorenson, S. B., Upchurch, D. M., & Shen, H. (1996). Violence and injury in marital arguments: Risk patterns and gender differences. *American Journal of Public Health, 86,* 35–40.

Spoth, R. L., Redmond, C., & Shin, C. (2000). Reducing adolescents' aggressive and hostile behaviors: Randomized trial effects of a brief family intervention 4 years past baseline. *Archives of Pediatric and Adolescent Medicine, 154,* 1248–1257.

Stanley, S. M., Markman, H. J., Prado, L., Olmos-Gallo, A., Tonelli, L., St. Peters, M., et al. (2001). Community-based premarital prevention: Clergy and lay leaders on the front lines. *Family Relations, 50,* 67–76.

Straus, M. A., & Gelles, R. J. (1990). How violent are American families? Estimates from the National Family Violence Resurvey and other studies. In M. A. Straus & R. J. Gelles (Eds.), *Physical violence in American families: Risk factors and adaptations to violence in 8,145 families* (pp. 341–363). New Brunswick, NJ: Transaction.

Straus, M. A., Hamby, S. L., Boney-McCoy, S., & Sugarman, D. B. (1996). The Revised Conflict Tactics Scales (CTS2): Development and preliminary psychometric data. *Journal of Family Issues, 17,* 283–316.

Sullivan, C. M., Bybee, D. I., & Allen, N. E. (2002). Findings from a community-based program for battered women and their children. *Journal of Interpersonal Violence, 17,* 915–936.

Swinford, S. P., DeMaris, A., Cernkovich, S. A., & Giordano, P. (2000). Harsh discipline in childhood and violence in later romantic involvements: The mediating role of problem behaviors. *Journal of Marriage and the Family, 62,* 508–519.

Thorton, T. N., Craft, C. A., Dahlberg, L. L., Lynch, B. S., & Baer, K. (2000). *Best practices of youth violence prevention: A sourcebook for community action.* Atlanta, GA: National Center for Injury Prevention and Control, Centers for Disease Control and Prevention.

Tremblay, R. E., Vitaro, F., Bertrand, L., LeBlanc, M., Beauchesne, H., Bioleau, H., et al. (1992). Parent and child training to prevent early onset of delinquency: The Montreal Longitudinal Study. In J. McCord & R. E. Tremblay (Eds.), *Preventing antisocial behaviour: Interventions from birth through adolescence* (pp. 117–138). New York: Guilford Press.

U.S. Department of Health and Human Services. (2001). *Youth violence: A report of the Surgeon General*. Rockville, MD: Author.

Van Widenfelt, B., Hosman, C., Schaap, C., & van der Staak, C. (1996). The prevention of relationship distress for couples at risk: A controlled evaluation with nine-month and two-year follow-ups. *Family Relations, 45*, 156–165.

Vreeman, R. C., & Carroll, A. E. (2007). A systematic review of school-based interventions to prevent bullying. *Archives of Pediatric and Adolescent Medicine, 161*, 78–88.

Wagar, J. M., & Rodway, M. R. (1995). An evaluation of a group treatment approach for children who have witnessed wife abuse. *Journal of Family Violence, 10*, 295–306.

Wagner, M. M., & Clayton, S. L. (1999). The Parents as Teachers program: Results from two demonstrations. *The Future of Children, 9*, 91–115, 179–189.

Webster-Stratton, C., & Hammond, M. (1997). Treating children with early-onset conduct problems: A comparison of child and parent training interventions. *Journal of Consulting and Clinical Psychology, 65*, 93–109.

Wekerle, C., & Wolfe, D. A. (1998). The role of child maltreatment and attachment style in adolescent relationship violence. *Development and Psychopathology, 10*, 571–586.

Wekerle, C., & Wolfe, D. A. (1999). Dating violence in mid-adolescence: Theory, significance, and emerging prevention initiatives. *Clinical Psychology Review, 19*, 435–456.

Wekerle, C., Wolfe, D. A., Hawkins, D. L., Pittman, A., Glickman, A., & Lovald, B. E. (2001). Child maltreatment, posttraumatic stress symptomatology and adolescent dating violence: Considering the value of adolescent perceptions of abuse and a trauma mediational model. *Development and Psychopathology, 13*, 847–871.

Wilson, D. B., Gottfredson, D. C., & Najaka, S. S. (2001). School-based prevention of problem behaviors: A meta-analysis. *Journal of Quantitative Criminology, 17*, 247–272.

Wilson, S. J., Lipsey, M. W., & Derzon, J. H. (2003). The effects of school-based intervention programs on aggressive behavior: A meta-analysis. *Journal of Consulting and Clinical Psychology, 71*, 136–149.

Wolfe, D. A., & Jaffe, P. G. (1999). Emerging strategies in the prevention of domestic violence. *The Future of Children, 9*, 133–144.

Wolfe, D. A., Scott, K., Reitzel-Jaffe, D., Wekerle, C., Grasley, C., & Straatman, A. L. (2001). Development and validation of the Conflict in Adolescent Dating Relationships Inventory. *Psychological Assessment, 13*, 277–293.

Wolfe, D. A., Wekerle, C., Gough, R., Reitzel-Jaffe, D., Grasley, C., Pittman, A., et al. (1996). *The Youth Relationships Manual: A group approach with adolescents for the prevention of woman abuse and the promotion of healthy relationships*. Thousand Oaks, CA: Sage.

Wolfe, D. A., Wekerle, C., Reitzel-Jaffe, D., & Lefebvre, L. (1998). Factors associated with abusive relationships among maltreated and nonmaltreated youth. *Developmental Psychopathology, 10*, 61–85.

Wolfe, D. A., Wekerle, C., Scott, K., Straatman, A. L., & Grasley, C. (2004). Predicting abuse in adolescent dating relationships over 1 year: The role of child maltreatment and trauma. *Journal of Abnormal Psychology, 113*, 406–415.

Wolfe, D. A., Wekerle, C., Scott, K., Straatman, A. L., Grasley, C., & Reitzel-Jaffe, D. (2003). Dating violence prevention with at-risk youth: A controlled outcome evaluation. *Journal of Consulting and Clinical Psychology, 71*, 279–291.

Wolfe, D. A., Zak, L., Wilson, S., & Jaffe, P. (1986). Child witnesses to violence between parents: Critical issues in behavioral and social adjustment. *Journal of Abnormal Child Psychology, 14*, 95–104.

Woodin, E. M. (2007). *Motivational interviewing as a targeted prevention approach for physically aggressive dating couples.* Unpublished doctoral dissertation, Stony Brook University, Stony Brook, NY.

9

GROUP INTERVENTIONS FOR INTIMATE PARTNER VIOLENCE

ALAN ROSENBAUM AND TRACII S. KUNKEL

From the outset, the modal approach to batterer intervention has been psychoeducational group treatment. Programs based on cognitive behavioral strategies delivered in gender specific groups ranging in length from 6 weeks to a year or more, predominate. In this chapter, we briefly describe the history of group batterer intervention programs (BIPs). At this writing, the majority of states in the United States have enacted standards for BIPs, and these standards frequently dictate the structure, content, leadership, and philosophy of programs within the respective states. We use the standards as a framework for characterizing the various elements of the group intervention approach for intimate partner violence (IPV).

The intervention model that has received the most attention is the Domestic Abuse Intervention Program (DAIP), more commonly known as the Duluth model (Pence & Paymar, 1993). Many published descriptions of batterer intervention programs and much of the research examining the outcome of batterer intervention involve Duluth model programs. DAIP exemplifies a management and control approach that includes a coordinated community response. There are, however, alternative approaches, many of which are more therapeutically based than is DAIP. In order to familiarize the reader with these different types of programs, we invited Ellen Pence and Martha McMahon, developers of the DAIP program, and Steven Stosny, developer of the Compassion Power program to provide descriptions of their programs to be included in the chapter. Finally, we examine the issue of the effectiveness of batterer intervention as well as the existing outcome research.

HISTORY OF BATTERER INTERVENTION PROGRAMS: GRASSROOTS AND THERAPEUTIC APPROACHES

The earliest programs, such as Emerge and RAVEN (i.e., Rape and Violence End Now), began in the late 1970s and were closely aligned with the battered women's movement. They espoused a profeminist philosophy and were intentionally nontherapeutic. Batterers attended voluntarily or, more likely, because they were "spouse mandated," as it would take another decade for state legislatures to empower courts to mandate batterers into intervention programs. Understandably, these early programs treated few batterers, and because participants were self-selected, those most in need of treatment were probably not well served.

During the 1980s, largely through the efforts of the battered women's movement, intimate partner violence increasingly became criminalized. States instituted proarrest police policies, and prosecutors pursued cases more aggressively. Vigorous prosecution led to more convictions and pleas, as well as the need for appropriate penalties. The courts quickly embraced BIPs as the disposition of choice for several reasons. In many cases, incarceration is not a viable option, whether because of the terms of the plea, the level of violence (e.g., misdemeanor), or the status of the offender (e.g., first offense). As Davis and Taylor (1999) pointed out, many victims choose to remain with their partners and would suffer negative consequences (e.g., loss of income, social stigma) if the batterer is incarcerated. Even if a jail sentence is imposed, it is brief, and there remains little evidence that incarceration serves a rehabilitative function. In addition, given the prevalence of IPV, there is insufficient jail space to accommodate the volume of offenders. The courts have considered mandated intervention to hold out the possibility of curtailing further violence by the offender.

Since the early 1990s, most states have enacted legislation empowering the courts to require batterers to attend BIPs either as a term of probation or as a diversion in lieu of prosecution. Anticipating an influx of mandated clients paying fees enforced by the courts, the number of BIPs in the United States increased dramatically. Gelles (2001), extrapolating from the exponential growth of BIPs in Rhode Island from 1980 to 1996, suggested that "it is reasonable to assume that there are thousands of treatment programs treating tens, if not hundreds of thousands of men each year" (p. 13). As of 2006, there were more than 450 registered programs in California alone, serving more than 25,000 batterers (California State Auditor, 2006). Even in the much smaller state of Massachusetts, more than 3,000 men were served annually (Massachusetts Department of Public Health, 2001).

Although there is no national register of batterer intervention programs, a recent survey (Price & Rosenbaum, 2007) found 1,750 programs nationwide. This undoubtedly is an underestimate, as the researchers counted only certified programs referenced in state directories and there is no practical mechanism for identifying uncertified programs. Additionally, the survey counted only freestanding programs; thus, programs and practitioners operating under other auspices (e.g., as part of a clinic or practice) were included only if they were listed in their state directory or were identified by a participating program.

Unfortunately, the rate of growth in BIPs outstripped the development of effective interventions and the supply of experienced facilitators. Two types of intervention developed simultaneously. The larger and better known involved grassroots programs and developed within the battered women's movement. According to Mederos (2002), early programs focused on protecting female victims, stopping men's violence, resocializing men toward equality with women, and getting perpetrators to take responsibility for their behavior. These programs were facilitated by social advocates, battered women's advocates, substance abuse counselors, and master's-level mental health counselors. Their expertise came from listening to the voices of battered women, whom they considered to be the true experts on battering. The developers of many of these programs regarded their mission as management and control of batterers, viewing themselves as extensions of the courts and probation departments. Few, if any, of these programs collected outcome data, so the effectiveness of these approaches is unknown.

The second type of intervention developed within the mental health professions. It approached batterers as a client or patient population, used modifications of existing therapy approaches, was informed by research illuminating the characteristics of batterers and the dynamics of battering relationships, and sought to assess the outcome of intervention efforts. This so-called therapeutic approach, however, was no less motivated by, or invested in, the protection of victims and the reduction of violence against women.

Although these intervention types, known as *grassroots* and *therapeutic* approaches, respectively, have shared common objectives, there has always been a tension between them. Of concern to the former group is the possibility that viewing batterers as suffering from some psychological condition would diminish responsibility for their behavior both in their own eyes and before society at large, negating hard-fought efforts to criminalize violence against women. The fact that in most jurisdictions referral to a BIP is the disposition of choice in IPV cases would appear to validate this fear. Such concerns have led to the preference for the term *batterer intervention* over *batterer treatment*. In Massachusetts, for example, the first revision of the standards specified the semantic change from "treatment" to "intervention" (Commonwealth of Massachusetts, 2001).

Although the grassroots and therapeutic approaches have been contrasted with each other, there are, in fact, many similarities in their structure and content. Almost all programs, for example, focus on power and control issues and use some form of the power and control wheel (Pence & Paymar, 1993), which remains the core of the Duluth model (described later in this chapter). Three out of four state standards, in fact, specify that BIPs address power and control issues. Programs differ with respect to the centrality of power and control and the amount of time spent dealing with this issue. However, these differences occur within, as well as across, the different types of programs. Similarly, the majority of programs utilize some form of the time-out procedure and anger management strategies (Price & Rosenbaum, 2007).

Protection of confidentiality is an important issue on which the grassroots and therapeutic programs diverge. Grassroots programs readily share information with both the courts and the victim. Such information might include group attendance, drinking behavior, noncompliance, and even opinions regarding progress or lack thereof. Therapeutic programs, in contrast, are typically bound by the ethical guidelines of a specific mental health profession (e.g., the American Psychological Association), which restrict violations of confidentiality to threats made by the client against a specified target. In the mental health professions, confidentiality is regarded as essential to the therapeutic process, and there is justifiable concern that if it is not protected, clients will not freely report behavior that the therapist must be aware of if the client is to make progress. For example, if the batterer is unable to report that he got so angry that he almost hit his partner because of fear that he may be reported, how can the group leaders help him to identify the chain of events leading up to that point and suggest alternative ways of responding at each step along the way? Behavior change requires the disclosure of the behaviors that need to change.

Differences between therapeutic and grassroots programs aside, there is substantial diversity even among programs within the same genre. Although the majority of programs may identify the primary goals of victim safety (Austin & Dankwort, 1999) and batterer accountability (Healy, Smith, & O'Sullivan, 1998), they may differ on critical variables such as treatment model, structure, curriculum, and the credentials and training of group facilitators. As Healy and colleagues noted, there is great variance even between programs claiming to follow the same model. This observation may be particularly true with respect to the Duluth model, as it is now common to see BIPs referred to as "Duluth-based" or "Duluth-type." Bennett and Vincent (2001) noted in their evaluation of the Illinois protocol that "half of the programs [surveyed] say they utilize some variation of the Duluth approach" (p. 190).

Although the literature providing descriptions of individual programs is expanding, the number of published reports remains small compared with the estimated volume of agencies in operation. Furthermore, such descriptions often occur in the context of studies evaluating the efficacy of a particular model of intervention. In many cases, the logistics of the research necessitate a focus on more time-limited programs.

STATE STANDARDS

Given the dearth of descriptions, one way to get an idea of program content and structure is by examining the established state standards. Although several states have yet to adopt established criteria for batterer intervention programs, that number has dwindled over the past decade. In 1997, Austin and Dankwort cited only 24 states as having existing certification standards, with seven more in draft form. As of 2007, the number of states with established standards had risen to 42. Assuming that the majority of programs in states with standards are adhering at least reasonably to the established protocols, these standards may provide a picture of what is happening in large numbers of these programs. With this in mind, we review the established standards for these 42 states, comparing and contrasting across several pertinent variables.

Program Length

All but three of the states with established standards set criteria for program length, ranging from a low of 12 sessions (Utah) to a high of 52 sessions (Santa Monica County, California,[1] Idaho, and New Mexico). San Diego County, California; Oregon; and Washington State each required regular attendance at 24 to 48 weekly sessions, then once monthly for the remainder of a full year from admission. Michigan and New York required only 26 sessions but recommended 52. Perhaps the most complicated standards were in Arizona. A decade ago, Arizona required only 12 sessions minimum, the lowest at that time (Austin & Dankwort, 1997). At the time of our review, Arizona had three tiers—26 weeks for first offenses, 36 weeks for second offenses, and 52 weeks for any subsequent offenses. Nearly all of the remaining states specified approximately 6 months (24–26 weeks) of intervention.

Currently, relatively little is known about the impact of program length. In a comparison of four batterer intervention programs, Gondolf (1999) found a slight trend for lower rates of severe and repeated reassault for the longest

---

[1]California allows the probation departments in each county to set specific standards; hence, in most cases we cannot refer to California as an entity.

program. Rosenbaum, Gearan, and Ondovic (2001) found a slight effect on recidivism rate for program length among batterers placed in programs of 7, 10, and 20 sessions. The recidivism rate for the 20-week program (2.4%) was lower than that reported for the 10-week program (4.2%), although not significantly. However, both rates were significantly lower than that reported for the 7-week program (15.6%). Edleson and Syers (1990) reported lower rates of recidivism for batterers participating in 12-session groups than for those participating in 32-session groups.

These studies suggest that longer treatment duration is not necessarily better. We are not aware, however, of studies examining long-term groups (i.e., 52 sessions and longer). It is also possible that treatment duration interacts with treatment type (therapeutic or management/control), though this possibility has not as yet been empirically demonstrated. Regarding the length of each session, the standards show far more consistency: Disregarding the eight state standards not addressing session length, 91% of the standards required 1.5 to 2 hours per group session.

Group Versus Individual Session Format

All states that had standards were in agreement that group treatment was the preferred mode. Although the majority of program standards (78%) allowed for individual therapy under special circumstances, not a single state regarded individual therapy as an equal, or near-equal, treatment option. Illinois and Indiana both allowed for individual counseling to be offered in conjunction with group treatment, but at a maximum of four sessions and two sessions, respectively.

Group size also varied across standards, with a majority of states setting a maximum number of members per group at 15. The smallest maximum number of members per group was 12 (Colorado, Idaho, Vermont, and Washington). In Florida, the maximum number of group members was capped at 15 when there was a single facilitator, increasing to 24 for the recommended two-facilitator configuration. Delaware similarly set limits based on the number of facilitators.

Facilitator Requirements

Training requirements, the gender makeup of the cofacilitator team, the acceptability of former batterers or victims as group leaders, and even the required number of group leaders for any one group varied from state to state. The majority of states (60%) specified a required number of facilitators necessary to lead a group. Of these, 76% mandated that groups be run by at least two facilitators, regardless of group size. The remaining 24% set limits on the size of groups run by a single facilitator but cited no other concerns for single-facilitator-led groups and stated no preference for single or dual facilitators.

A distinct advantage of the dual-facilitator model is that it allows for male–female coleadership. This coleadership can serve to demonstrate equality, cooperation, shared power and respect, and even respectful disagreement. The Ohio Domestic Violence Network (2002), in an addendum to its standards for batterer intervention programs, stated, "If we can't, won't, don't model shared power, clients will not believe our words or value what we say about shared power" (p. 11).

At the time of our review, only four states (Alabama, Iowa, Ohio, and Maine) required a mixed-sex cofacilitator team, although nearly half of state standards addressed the issue of mixed-sex facilitator teams. Although many states either required or recommended a male–female (or female–male) coleadership format, mixed-sex coleadership is not without problems (Nosko & Wallace, 1997). The New Hampshire standards noted that "a disadvantage of group co-leadership is that if the male is more experienced (e.g., is training a female intern) or assumes a dominant role, this model could reinforce damaging stereotypes" (New Hampshire Batterers Intervention Subcommittee, 2002, p. 20). Several state standards that recommended mixed-sex coleadership pointed out that the facilitators must take great care to ensure that facilitator contribution is coequal.

The credentials and training of treatment providers have also been identified as a topic of concern (e.g., Dutton, 2006; Maiuro, Hagar, Lin, & Olson, 2001). According to Maiuro et al. (2001), in their survey of the 30 states with standards in place, only 20% required a minimum education level of a bachelor's degree. By the time of our review, that percentage had doubled. However, in 47% of those states, this requirement could be offset by 1 to 2 years of group facilitator experience or "the equivalent." Alabama required that at least one member of a dual-facilitator team have at minimum a bachelor's degree. Although many states required facilitators to attend specialized training in domestic violence (e.g., Illinois required 60 hours[2]), no state required a specific counseling degree. Wisconsin's standards addressed this issue as follows: "The possession or attainment of a formal degree or formal education is viewed as neither necessary nor sufficient for educational qualifications to facilitate batterers' treatment groups" (State of Wisconsin, 1996, § IV-D).

Most state standards required group facilitators, regardless of their degree or educational background, to have training in domestic violence issues. Oregon, for example, required 200 hours of training, although a large portion of that could be offset by a bachelor's degree or relevant experience. Michigan required 80 hours of training in addition to a bachelor's degree or 2 years of experience. The majority of remaining states varied from 24 to 60 hours of required training, and virtually all required some amount of observation with a fully trained facilitator. Some states (e.g., Delaware) required facilitators to

---

[2]This training consists of 40 hours of a feminist-based domestic violence protocol and 20 hours of batterer intervention training.

observe a number of domestic violence court hearings before providing treatment. Additionally, the majority (64%) of states required or recommended continuing education beyond the initial training requirements. The amount of this training ranged from 8 hours (Arizona and Maine) to 24 hours (San Diego County, California) annually, but most commonly was between 12 and 16 hours per year.

In many states, former batterers were allowed to become group facilitators. We identified only one state that explicitly prohibited such practice. Washington specified that facilitators must be "free of criminal convictions involving moral turpitude" (Washington State Legislature, 2001, § 388-60-0315). Although Nevada had a moral turpitude clause as well, it went on to state that such convictions should not necessarily exclude former batterers in recovery programs. In all states that allowed batterers to lead groups, there were strict regulations in place that involved having successfully completed a batterer intervention program and being free of violence for a minimum of 1 year. Some states (e.g., Illinois) required that if one cofacilitator was a former batterer, the history of the other must be violence free. Only two states (Alabama and New Mexico) specifically mentioned former victims of domestic violence becoming facilitators.

Attendance Requirements

Poor batterer attendance can be a problem for BIPs and can represent a safety concern for victims. Although most states set a maximum number of allowable absences, programs were typically required to set their own limit on absences. The program maximum could be more stringent than the state limits. However, few states mandated that a client be terminated once the maximum number of allowed absences was exceeded. For example, Santa Clara County, California, allowed only five absences in its 52-week program. Furthermore, each absence must be made up with a group covering the same content. If a client was absent a sixth time, he was automatically terminated. However, Santa Clara County did provide for a "leave of absence" to cover missed group sessions because of health or family emergencies, employment obligations, or military duty. Colorado, which had a 36-week program, allowed three absences. The fourth absence was considered a "non-negotiable violation of the offender contract" (Colorado Domestic Violence Offender Management Board, 2007, § 6-2), and the appropriate criminal justice agency had to be notified within 24 hours. In addition, after each absence, the program contacted both the appropriate criminal agency and the victim advocate within 24 hours.

Program Fees

Client fees are another topic of concern for various reasons. First, many individuals referred into BIPs are of lower socioeconomic status (Aldarondo,

1998; Holtzworth-Munroe, Bates, Smutzler, & Sandlin, 1997) and may not be able to afford the standard program fee. For this reason, the vast majority of programs have established sliding fee scales and indigence policies. However, many of the state standards specified that even if a batterer is determined to fall under the indigence criteria, he still has to pay something. In these standards, the argument was made that by having to pay for services, the batterer would attach value to them. As stated in the Vermont standards, "An assigned fee places value on the program and a participant's payment is associated with his taking personal responsibility for his need for the program and literal ownership of the solution" (Vermont Coalition of Batterer Intervention Services, 2002, p. 34). A second reason the majority of states cited for mandating at least a minimal fee was that at no time should a batterer intervention program receive funding that would otherwise be distributed to victims' services.

With the need to provide their own funding through client fees and the suggested association between fees and accountability, there can be pressure on programs to set higher fees. However, there are cautions against doing so. One such caution is that often the batterers in treatment are still living with their families and/or supporting them financially, and fees can place increased financial hardship on those whom the programs are most trying to help. Also, there is the potential that the batterer's victim may be coerced into paying for his treatment.

Victim Contact

Whether the BIP should contact victims is one of the more controversial issues. Although virtually every state standard at least recommended that the BIP contact the victim both when a batterer was admitted into a program and when he was discharged (after either successfully completing the program or being terminated), there are victim safety issues to be considered (the Illinois protocol included a discussion of these considerations). For this reason, in most standards victim contact was left up to the discretion of the individual BIP. Although all states recommended some sort of victim contact, they differed on the information to be shared and who would make the contact.

In general, the objectives of victim contact cited in the standards were to assess victim safety and provide referral information. In some cases, victims were to be contacted to ensure that they did not interpret batterer participation in a program as an indication that they were safer or able to return to the batterer. In Maine, following admission into a program, program personnel were required to meet with the victim face to face to discuss details of the program (e.g., purpose, limitations, victim services). In many cases, victims do not desire contact with the program, fearing that this will lead to threats, coercion, or increased violence if, for example, the batterer fears she will be reporting on his behavior or that her reports will be used in group or in decisions regarding his length of treatment. Information obtained from victims is, in fact, rarely usable in group, and group leaders must be especially careful to protect the victim's confidentiality.

Curriculum

BIP curricula vary greatly from state to state and even from program to program. With the exceptions of those of Maryland and Utah, all state standards reviewed provided some level of curriculum description, although that description ranged from a broad overview (as in the case of Arizona) to a week-by-week road map (e.g., Nevada). Regardless, there were a few themes found in a majority of protocols. Batterer accountability was found in every one, due in large part to the relationship between BIPs and the legal system, which is responsible for 80% of referrals (Healy et al., 1998).

Education on the effects of violence on women and children was included in the mandatory curriculum in 79% of state standards, followed closely by sociocultural attitudes toward gender roles and male dominance (76%). Discussion of the effects of violence on women and children may be particularly effective, as it has been suggested that many batterers witnessed interparental IPV in their own homes as children (National Coalition Against Domestic Violence, 2007). Along these lines, teaching appropriate parenting techniques was mentioned in 29% of standards.

Beliefs associated with violence and the oppression of women were a mandatory content area in 57% of programs. Education regarding the association between alcohol/substance abuse and domestic violence was found in 55% of standards. However, different programs addressed different aspects of this issue. Some programs focused on batterers not using substance abuse as an excuse for abusive behavior, whereas others addressed the often comorbid problem of substance abuse in more depth. For batterers deemed to have an alcohol or substance abuse problem, most states required referral for treatment if necessary either prior to, or in conjunction with, batterer intervention.

Although most of the content areas identified thus far may be thought of as awareness and insight building, a few more "practical" topics were listed in a significant number of standards and deserve mention. Stress and anger management were found in nearly half. However, several states cautioned that anger and stress management were appropriate only with the caveat that abuse is not an anger response, but a controlled behavior. In fact, many states that did allow anger and stress management included it only among listings of inappropriate content, stating that these topics could be used as appropriate material only under specific conditions. Other states prohibited anger management on the basis that anger could be used as an excuse for abuse (e.g., Arizona) or that batterers would be able to satisfy the requirement of completing a program by attending anger management programs without specific IPV content.

Roughly a quarter of the state standards mentioned specific techniques used to address some of the curricula areas or to provide group members with tools to reduce the risk of violence. Of those that did so, the time-out was identified in every instance. Colorado required sufficient demonstration of the use of time-outs before discharge. Both Nevada and San Diego County, California, outlined steps for an effective, nonabusive time-out that involved planning, attention to anger cues, an established signal between partners, and cognitive exercises.

Finally, although perhaps not a specific tool, several states (e.g., Colorado, Georgia, Kentucky) required that a batterer complete a "responsibility" or "control" plan before being discharged. These plans were to include recognition of anger cues, antecedent thoughts and/or feelings, and time-out or "bailout" plans. These plans may be very specific, detailing a friend who may be called (in some cases, a group peer), where exactly a time-out may be taken, and specific de-escalation techniques to be used.

Nearly three quarters of the state standards identified prohibited content. Consistent with goals of batterer accountability, anything that could be regarded as victim blaming was universally prohibited. Likewise, addiction counseling models that identify the violence as an addiction and the victim and children as enabling or codependent in the violence, models that attribute the violence to poor impulse control, and psychodynamic models were prohibited in nearly half of the states that identified disallowed content. "Fair fighting," which is listed as an appropriate focus area in a very limited number of states, was prohibited by 23% of states identifying prohibited content.

Finally, couples therapy was not considered appropriate treatment in 74% of state standards that identified disallowed content. Colorado allowed a limited number of couples meetings for specific purposes, including to elicit information, set behavioral goals, arrange for a separation, or teach anger management skills such as the time-out. In other states, couple counseling was permitted, but not as a primary treatment for IPV, and only after the batterer had completed a BIP and it had been determined that the woman was choosing to remain in the relationship.

PROGRAM DESCRIPTIONS

As previously noted, BIPs can be roughly divided into two groups, grassroots programs and therapeutic programs. We asked the developers of two well-known program exemplars (one representing each approach) to write a brief description following these guidelines: "We are asking each of you to briefly describe the philosophy of your program, the structure, curriculum highlights, evidence for efficacy/effectiveness, and any other comments regarding why your program is unique/different/superior to other approaches." We should note that the Duluth model is the most widely known and emulated program. Though far less popular, we selected the Core Value Workshop as representative of a more humanistic, therapeutic approach.

In recent years, the number of programs using a more therapeutic approach to batterers has increased, and there is empirical support for this development. For example, Taft, Murphy, King, Musser, and DeDeyn (2003) evaluated the effective components of BIPs and found that the therapeutic alliance and group cohesion were the most important contributors to reducing physical and psychological aggression following group treatment.

The Core Value Workshop, Described by Steven Stosny, PhD

In developing the Core Value Workshop in 1990, I believed that the differences in approaches to intervention groups with batterers were not substantive, and certainly not in the goals of safety and protection of victims. The primary differences came down to ways of engaging abusers in the change process, which are merely differences in motivational and educational beliefs. Underlying the Core Value Workshop is the belief that you cannot change abusers by confronting them with your superior values. Rather, change comes from appeal to the abuser's own deepest values.

Drawing on principles of attachment, affect, and individuation theories, the Core Value Workshop provides skill-building treatment for spouse, child, and parent abusers. The treatment targets the affective motivation for abusive behavior through self-regulation strategies that help abusers develop internally regulated, prosocial forms of self-empowerment through compassion for their loved ones.

A basic assumption of the treatment is that human beings use various modes of self-empowerment both to avoid and relieve paralyzing feelings of powerlessness, self-doubt, and weakened or diminished sense of self. States of powerlessness can be triggered within the self (self-denigration, presumed inadequacy) or externally (perceived criticism, disrespect, rejection, or attack by others). Modes of self-empowerment can be achieved from within (enhancing the sense of self or changing the meaning of the disempowering trigger), from without (manipulating the environment), and through avoidance or dismissal (denial, alcoholism, workaholism, or a "Who needs this!" attitude). They can be asocial (personal meaning with no intended interaction), antisocial (coercive, domineering, and violent), and prosocial (compassionate, cooperative, empowering of others). Because asocial forms of self-empowerment are not sustainable in attachment relationships (they inadvertently communicate disregard and rejection in intimate contexts), internally regulated, prosocial self-empowerment skills seem necessary for nonabusive intimate relationships.

Pursuit of self-empowerment predominantly through manipulation of the environment motivates controlling behavior. Until abusers learn to internalize personal power, mediated by compassion for self and loved ones, they are unlikely to stop controlling and abusing others, although they may learn more subtle forms of control and abuse that entail no legal consequences.

Unlike interventions derived from sociocultural explanations of family abuse that rely on education to change the content of attitudes and belief systems, the Core Value Workshop addresses the content-free process of self-empowerment. Psychologically charged content provided by culture is seen as a habitual set of signals to activate learned patterns of self-empowerment. Self-empowerment is always the end, regardless of the strength of the particular sociocultural signal and the degree of reinforcement for it. On the deeper processing level, new activating signals can supersede entrenched sociocultural cues if associated with more perdurable, successful, or satisfying forms of self-empowerment.

For example, consider the abusive husband who slaps his wife because she did not make his dinner. It may seem to him that he did so because she failed to defer to him as the "head of the household." He learns in the Core Value Workshop that his interpretation of her behavior created a diminished sense of self (he felt rejected and unlovable) and that his aggression was a doomed attempt to relieve his state of powerlessness—doomed because hurting a loved one can only make him feel more unlovable. He can enjoy an enduring mode of self-empowerment by understanding that his sense of self cannot be diminished by someone else's behavior (only by his own) and that his inherent importance and value as a human being (what we call *core value*) is completely unaffected by anyone else's behavior. (If his core value seems threatened, it must be reinstated internally by appeal to his deepest values, which include protection of loved ones.) The abuser's problem is not his wife's behavior, but his own feeling of unworthiness of love.

In blaming his feelings of unworthiness on his wife, he renders himself powerless to correct them. What's more, he now understands that he cannot feel more worthy of love by hurting someone he loves. With his personal boundaries reinstated through awareness that his emotions reflect his own, deeper sense of self, he can understand that his wife's behavior reflects her own, deeper sense of self—in this instance, her feeling of devaluation and powerlessness at having to make his dinner. He can now enhance his sense of self by validating her feelings of powerlessness and respectfully negotiating behaviors that empower both of them. Now his sense of self depends on his own compassionate behavior, not on her response to him; he is self-regulating.

In contrast, merely confronting the irrationality of his belief about "male privilege" increases his feelings of powerlessness (until he learns to tell the group leader what he or she wants to hear) without helping him develop internal, prosocial forms of self-empowerment. Such approaches fail to understand (and to teach) that the compassionate self is the empowered, proactive, autonomous self, as opposed to the reactive, dependent, powerless, confrontational self of the abuser. In the Core Value Workshop, the abuser understands that compassion is power.

The Duluth Model, Described by Ellen Pence, PhD, and Martha McMahon, PhD

The Duluth model of intervention in cases of battering is the most replicated model of intervention in the United States. Hundreds of communities use some version of the model of intervention that began in Duluth in 1980. The Duluth approach to intervention in cases of battering requires a tremendous commitment on the part of intervening agencies to work collaboratively to identify specific ways current interventions compromise or centralize safety. Through interagency meetings and work groups that take on correcting specific practices that compromise victim safety, agencies analyze the complex sources of poor case outcomes and change problematic practices as a group of intervening agencies rather than operating within silos untouched by each others' policies and practices.

The model requires agencies to make changes in the infrastructure of case management in five ways:

1. examining their intervention goals,
2. articulating each worker's functions in a case,
3. examining the allocation of scarce resources in these cases (jail space, probation surveillance, intervention time),
4. correcting philosophical assumptions that do not reflect what is actually going on (e.g., fix the communication patterns of the couple and the battering will stop, or all domestic violence is battering), and
5. collectively agree on policies and case management procedures that will centralize victim safety and offender accountability.

Doing this work can be tedious, requiring discussions and reviews of more than 100 intervention actions, from the time the dispatcher takes the initial call for help to the closing of a case almost 2 years later. More than 10 agencies and dozens of workers will touch the case, and five distinct levels of government will be involved in resolving the case. Coordination does not mean holding a monthly meeting; it means organizing each one of those workers, across disciplines, time, and institutional function, to operate as an orchestra, doing different things but reading from the same sheet of music. And so a key feature of the model has been to limit practitioners' discretion to act on personal beliefs. The model attempts to do this without making responses so rote that the practitioner does not use his or her skills, experience, and training to evaluate each case and act in ways that fit the situation and people before them. Thus, the model involves extensive training designed to help practitioners apply intervention policies and procedures to very different cases. For example, police use a series of 22 videotaped case scenarios to learn how to apply the arrest policy; the predominant aggressor and self-defense clauses in it; the interview techniques for suspects, victims, and child witnesses; and so forth. The model puts into place a system of information gathering and sharing to help individual practitioners act on cases and to enable the evaluation of compliance and program impact on continued abuse and victim safety.

Batterers groups are incorporated into this multiagency response. Just as dispatcher, police, and probation officer responses have been standardized, so have rehabilitation counselor responses. A curriculum was created that standardizes the content of the batterers groups and encourages a process that embraces certain assumptions and values about group work. All of the mental health and education practitioners facilitating groups receive training and participate in a monthly meeting to discuss their work. Judges order most defendants convicted of assault to the DAIP, which conducts an intake and assigns the offender to a community-based educational group or to a counseling agency. The DAIP monitors attendance and keeps in touch with victims. If the offender fails to regularly attend groups or continues to harass or abuse the victim, the DAIP brings the case back to court and facilitates communication among the court, the group leader, and other interveners familiar with the case.

Most offenders who are battering are placed in groups that use a cognitive–behavioral approach to changing intimidating, coercive, and violent behavior. (Offenders who use violence but are not battering the victim are funneled to different rehabilitation services.) The curriculum frames batterers groups so that when members leave, they are able to

- understand which of the behaviors they are using are abusive;
- recognize the intents they have when they use these behaviors;
- explore the belief systems that underlie these intents and behaviors;
- identify the relationship of their negative feelings and emotions to these belief systems;
- identify alternative ways of thinking about situations that would not give rise to such negativity and its corresponding actions;
- acknowledge and name the impact of these behaviors on their victims, children, and themselves; and
- explore and practice nonabusive options to situations in which they are using violence or intimidation.

The model promotes a process in groups that recognizes the social nature of this crime and its roots in the historic separation of roles and power between men and women in society and marriage. The program walks a fine line of challenging members to do the personal work it takes to change without demonizing members as somehow different from the community at large. Members of the group learned these belief systems, latched onto them because of certain circumstances in their lives, and now act from them in ways that cause a tremendous amount of harm. Their change process is linked to how a community acts to limit batterers' opportunities to do more harm and how group facilitators challenge them to rethink their patterns of behavior and make different choices about how to be in relationship to their partners and children.

Although these programs take somewhat different paths to the same goal of eliminating intimate partner violence and promoting the safety of women and children, there are a number of commonalities. Both recognize that to some extent, IPV is rooted in the batterer's internal feelings of unhappiness, inadequacy, and powerlessness. They also recognize the primacy of helping batterers accept responsibility for their behavior and make prosocial changes in their attitudes and belief systems (especially with regard to women, relationships, and the unacceptability of aggression).

EFFECTIVENESS OF GROUP INTERVENTIONS FOR BATTERERS

There remains the question of whether BIPs are an effective intervention for IPV. A thorough discussion of this issue is beyond the scope of this chapter, and the reader is referred to several reviews, meta-analyses, and provocative commentaries for a lengthier presentation of the results and the many issues and controversies (see, e.g., Babcock, Green, & Robie, 2004; Davis & Taylor, 1999; Dutton & Corvo, 2006; Levesque & Gelles, 1998). In brief, meta-analytic studies of the effects of participation in BIPs consistently demonstrate a small effect for intervention over and above the effects of arrest alone. Furthermore, as Babcock et al. (2004) noted, the various treatment modalities that have been examined appear to be equally effective in achieving very small demonstrated gains.

These findings must be considered, however, in the context of several methodological issues and limitations. For example, a very limited number of treatment modalities, most commonly the Duluth model, were represented in the outcome evaluations included in the meta-analytic studies. Therapeutic approaches and lengthier (more than 36 weeks) programs are underrepresented, and it is unclear whether these types of programs might produce better results. Despite the cautions against applying the same program to diverse types of batterers, few, if any, of the included programs used a prescriptive strategy of matching program content to batterer type. Additionally, as others have pointed out, legal system interventions alone do have some violence reduction effect (Dutton, 1987), IPV shows a substantial "spontaneous violence cessation rate" (O'Leary et al., as cited in Babcock et al., 2004, p. 1048), and the phases of the cycle of violence (e.g., the honeymoon phase) can be sufficiently long, even in untreated samples, that the bar for showing a substantial treatment effect might be so high as to preclude anything more than a modest effect even in the instance of an effective intervention.

In contrast to the very modest effects reported in these meta-analyses, Stosny (1995) reported some very encouraging results for his Core Value Workshop. Stosny described his sample as being in the 99th percentile in physical aggression and in the 97th percentile in psychological aggression. He obtained outcome data from the female victims and compared his 12-week workshop with the 24-week treatment program provided by agencies in the same area. Despite being half as long, the results for the Core Value Workshop were substantially better than for the standard agency approach. At 12-month follow-up, 87% of the graduates of the Core Value Workshop were violence free, compared with 41% of the agency-treated men. He also reported that they were substantially lower in anxiety and anger and hostility than agency-treated men. Controlled studies comparing management/control approaches (as exemplified by the Duluth and Emerge models) with more therapeutic/humanistic approaches are clearly warranted. Unfortunately, very restrictive state standards and certification requirements, as well as the reluctance of judges to randomly assign perpetrators to the various treatment groups, are impediments to this important work.

The gold standard for treatment outcome research, randomized clinical trials, is almost nonexistent in the evaluation of BIPs for a number of reasons. Most BIP participants are court-ordered into treatment, and courts are usually reluctant to use random assignment in sentencing. It has been suggested that to do so would be a violation of a batterer's 14th Amendment rights. The equal protection clause requires that all persons similarly situated be treated equally. Furthermore, assigning batterers either to no-treatment or wait-list control groups might place victims at even greater risk.

CONCLUSION

This chapter has provided an overview of group interventions for batterers. To that end, we have identified some of the controversies and issues surrounding batterer intervention, described some of the program parameters, and had the providers of two contrasting examples of batterer intervention programs briefly describe their programs in their own words. The unfortunate exclamation point at the end of this chapter is that there is little empirical support for the effectiveness of batterer intervention. For years, we have heard the mantra that in batterer intervention "one size doesn't fit all" and that we need different approaches for different types of batterers. Yet the reality is that specialized programs based on batterer subtype or stage of readiness for change do not exist in actual practice (Price & Rosenbaum, 2007). Specialized programs for the purported subtypes of batterer have not been developed, and even if they were, the likelihood is low that BIPs would have sufficient financial resources to implement them.

An alternative to evaluating existing programs would be to deconstruct batterer intervention to identify the component strategies that are the most effective (i.e., what works and what does not work). Taft et al. (2003), for example, looked at the process rather than the content and found that the therapeutic alliance and group cohesion were important components of effective batterer intervention, a promising development in this regard. Also necessary are flexible state standards that recognize the current state of ignorance in the field regarding the most effective ways to treat batterers and that permit experimentation aimed at developing more effective approaches. The programs described in this chapter take different approaches to dealing with batterers; however, both contributors are convinced of the value and effectiveness of their program, and both believe that their approach protects victims.

It is also clear that batterer intervention can succeed only in the context of a coordinated community response to IPV that includes the police, courts, probation departments, and battered women's advocacy groups, including shelters. Batterer intervention is a work in progress, and there may be many ways to effectively intervene to end intimate partner violence.

REFERENCES

Aldarondo, E. (1998). Perpetrators of domestic violence. In A. Bellack & M. Hersen (Eds.), *Comprehensive clinical psychology* (pp. 432–452). New York: Pergamon Press.

Austin, J., & Dankwort, J. (1997). *A review of standards for batterer intervention programs*. Retrieved August 24, 2007, from http://www.vaw.umn.edu/Vawnet/standard.htm

Austin, J., & Dankwort, J. (1999). Standards for batterer programs: A review and analysis. *Journal of Interpersonal Violence, 14*, 152–168.

Babcock, J. C., Green, C. E., & Robie, C. (2004). Does batterers' treatment work? A meta-analytic review of domestic violence treatment. *Clinical Psychology Review, 23*, 1023–1053.

Bennett, L. W., & Vincent, N. V. (2001). Standards for batterer programs: A formative evaluation of the Illinois protocol. *Journal of Aggression, Maltreatment & Trauma, 5*, 181–197.

California State Auditor. (2006). *Batterer intervention programs: County probation departments could improve their compliance with state law, but progress in batterer accountability also depends on the courts*. Sacramento, CA: Author.

Colorado Domestic Violence Offender Management Board. (2007). *Standards for treatment with court ordered domestic violence offenders*. Lakewood, CO: Author.

Commonwealth of Massachusetts, Department of Public Health. (2001). *Guidelines and standards for the certification of batterer intervention programs*. Boston: Author.

Davis, R. C., & Taylor, B. G. (1999). Does batterer treatment reduce violence? A synthesis of the literature. *Women and Criminal Justice, 10*(2), 69–93.

Dutton, D. G. (1987). The criminal justice response to wife assault. *Law and Human Behavior, 11*, 189–206.

Dutton, D. G. (2006). *Rethinking domestic violence*. Vancouver, British Columbia, Canada: UBC Press.

Dutton, D. G., & Corvo, K. (2006). Transforming a flawed policy: A call to revive psychology and science in domestic violence research and practice. *Aggression and Violent Behavior, 11*, 457–483.

Edleson, J. L., & Syers, M. (1990). Relative effectiveness of group treatments for men who batter. *Social Work Research and Abstracts, 26*(2), 10–17.

Gelles, R. J. (2001). Standards for programs for men who batter? Not yet. *Journal of Aggression, Maltreatment & Trauma, 5*, 11–20.

Gondolf, E. W. (1999). A comparison of four batterer intervention systems: Do court referral, program length, and services matter? *Journal of Interpersonal Violence, 14*, 41–61.

Healy, K., Smith, C., & O'Sullivan, C. (1998). *Batterer intervention: Program approaches and criminal justice strategies* (Report No. NCJ 168638). Washington, DC: U.S. Department of Justice.

Holtzworth-Munroe, A., Bates, L., Smutzler, N., & Sandin, E. (1997). A brief review of the research on husband violence: Part 1. Maritally violent versus nonviolent men. *Aggression and Violent Behavior, 2*, 65–99.

Levesque, D., & Gelles, R. (1998). *Does treatment reduce violence recidivism in men who batter? Meta-analytic evaluation of treatment outcome research*. Paper presented at Program Evaluation and Family Violence Research conference, Durham, NH.

Maiuro, R. D., Hagar, T. S., Lin, H., & Olson, N. (2001). Are current state standards for domestic violence perpetrator treatment adequately informed by research? A question of questions. *Journal of Aggression, Maltreatment & Trauma, 5*, 21–44.

Massachusetts Department of Public Health. (2001). *Batterer intervention program services annual program report data*. Boston: Bureau of Family and Community Health, Department of Violence Prevention and Intervention Program Services.

Mederos, F. (2002). Changing our visions of intervention—The evolution of programs for physically abusive men. In E. Aldarondo & F. Mederos (Eds.), *Pro-*

grams for men who batter: Intervention and prevention strategies in a diverse society (pp. 1–26) Kingston, NJ: Civic Research Institute.

National Coalition Against Domestic Violence. (2007). *Children and domestic violence fact sheet.* Washington, DC: Author.

New Hampshire Batterers Intervention Subcommittee. (2002). *Governor's commission on domestic and sexual violence batterer intervention standards.* Concord: New Hampshire Department of Justice.

Nosko, A., & Wallace, R. (1997). Female/male co-leadership in groups. *Social Work with Groups, 20,* 3–16.

Ohio Domestic Violence Network. (2002). *Addendum to ODVN standards for batterers intervention.* Columbus, OH: Author.

Pence, E., & Paymar, M. (1993). *Education groups for men who batter: The Duluth model.* New York: Springer.

Price, B., & Rosenbaum, A. (2007, July). *A national survey of perpetrator intervention programs.* Paper presented at the International Family Violence and Child Victimization Research Conference, Portsmouth, NH.

Rosenbaum, A., Gearan, P. J., & Ondovic, C. (2001). Completion and recidivism among court- and self-referred batterers in a psychoeducational group treatment program: Implications for intervention and public policy. *Journal of Aggression, Maltreatment & Trauma, 5,* 199–220.

State of Wisconsin. (1996). *Male batterers treatment standards for state funded domestic abuse batterers treatments grants/contracts.* Madison: Wisconsin Batterers Treatment Providers.

Stosny, S. (1995). *Treating attachment abuse: A compassion approach.* New York: Springer.

Taft, C. T., Murphy, C. M., King, D. W., Musser, P. H., & DeDeyn, J. M. (2003). Process and treatment adherence factors in group cognitive–behavioral therapy for partner violent men. *Journal of Consulting and Clinical Psychology, 71,* 812–820.

Vermont Coalition of Batterer Intervention Services. (2002). *Vermont statewide standards for domestic abuse intervention.* Waterbury: Vermont Department of Corrections.

Washington State Legislature. (2001). *Domestic violence perpetrator treatment program standards.* Olympia, WA: Author.

10

INDIVIDUALIZED SERVICES AND INDIVIDUAL THERAPY FOR PARTNER ABUSE PERPETRATORS

CHRISTOPHER M. MURPHY, LAURA A. MEIS,
AND CHRISTOPHER I. ECKHARDT

Increasingly, research and theory indicate that those who abuse intimate partners are heterogeneous in clinically important ways (Holtzworth-Munroe & Stuart, 1994; O'Leary, 1993). Diversity in readiness to change, motivations for abusive behavior, personality problems, and comorbid difficulties such as substance abuse and trauma symptoms can pose substantial challenges to the use of standardized "one size fits all" treatment protocols and the group treatment format for perpetrators of intimate partner violence (IPV). Nevertheless, standardized group treatments for abusive partners are almost exclusively recommended by U.S. state program guidelines (Austin & Dankwort, 1999; Maiuro, Hagar, Lin, & Olson, 2002). Virtually all research on abuser interventions to date has been conducted using standardized group formats (Babcock, Green, & Robie, 2004; Feder & Wilson, 2005). Recently, we proposed an alternative treatment that uses motivational and cognitive–behavioral therapy (CBT) strategies within a case formulation approach to address the individual treatment needs of abusive clients (Murphy & Eckhardt, 2005). This chapter outlines the rationale, basic principles, and implications of this treatment model.

BASIC CONCEPTS AND DEFINITIONS

Whereas *individual therapy* refers to a one-on-one treatment format that contrasts with group or couples therapy, the term *individualized services* refers to intervention strategies tailored to meet the specific needs of each client. There are a number of ways in which therapists might adapt abuser interventions to the individual case. The first is by adopting risk management strategies from forensic psychology. The therapist identifies risk factors for reassault through a careful assessment of each abusive client and enacts a risk management plan to alter relevant processes (Kropp, 2004; Kropp & Hart, 2000). Another approach is to screen clients into alternative interventions on the basis of their presenting problems and clinical profiles. For example, IPV programs might offer distinct interventions to those with co-occurring substance dependence or those with extensive trauma histories. Programs might similarly use readiness to change profiles to assign clients to stage-appropriate interventions. As is obvious from these examples, individualized service planning is not inconsistent with the use of standard group interventions but may require additional assessment, service adaptations, and case management.

Another strategy to address specific client issues involves the use of the individual therapy format. One-on-one treatment facilitates individualized service delivery insofar as the therapist is able to select and adapt intervention strategies on the basis of specific case information. Tailoring of intervention strategies requires a high level of clinical knowledge and skill, including the ability to formulate the specific problems and strengths of each abusive client and to deliver relevant interventions in a coherent and flexible fashion.

Given that individual therapy is likely to be more expensive and time consuming than standard group approaches, a hybrid model could be used in which particularly challenging clients, or those who have failed to benefit from standard group services, are selected to receive individual services, whereas more typical and less difficult clients receive a standard group intervention. Unfortunately, at the current time no empirical criteria are available to predict differential responsiveness to individual versus group intervention, but the development of a rational decision process to allocate such services may be a prudent goal for future research.

RATIONALE FOR USING INDIVIDUAL SERVICES AND/OR INDIVIDUAL THERAPY

Group interventions have a number of potentially important benefits. In non-IPV areas of mental health research, groups are often equal in efficacy to individual interventions (McRoberts, Burlingame, & Hoag, 1998) and are highly cost-effective (Dies, 1995). The group environment can provide a "microcosm of society" for directly observing and addressing participants' interpersonal difficulties (Dies, 1995). For partner-abusive clients, group facilitators can use peer social influence to model appropriate behavior and motivate change (Daniels & Murphy, 1997). Some IPV offenders may respond better to peers than to therapists.

Despite these benefits, group interventions for IPV may have several specific and potentially important limitations relative to individual treatment. Most notable is the inherent challenge in addressing multiple and varied treatment needs presented by partner-violent individuals. For example, members of a group may vary substantially in the severity and frequency of partner violence, forms and patterns of emotional abuse, and extent of generalized problems with anger and aggression (Holtzworth-Munroe, Meehan, Herron, Rehman, & Stuart, 2000; Holtzworth-Munroe, Rehman, & Herron, 2000; Saunders, 1992). A significant minority of abusive clients have problems that predict poor response to treatment, including substance abuse or dependence (Fals-Stewart, 2003; Jones & Gondolf, 2001); antisocial, borderline, or narcissistic personality traits (Hamberger & Hastings, 1991; Hart, Dutton, & Newlove, 1993); or severe anger dysregulation (Murphy, Taft, & Eckhardt, 2007). Other potential complications include mood disorders (Ehrensaft, Cohen, & Johnson, 2006; Kessler, Molnar, Feurer, & Applebaum, 2001) and histories of childhood trauma.

Given this variable constellation of presenting concerns, interventions that are highly relevant or necessary for one individual may be irrelevant, distracting, or counterproductive for others. Efforts to address comorbid difficulties through multiple referrals create challenges for service coordination and may increase noncompliance rates. Careful case management may promote safety and compliance in these complex cases, but such efforts can become unmanageable with large treatment groups. Individual approaches, in contrast, provide enhanced opportunities to facilitate and monitor adjunctive service referrals, flexibility in sequencing interventions, and the ability to address multiple treatment targets with a primary therapist.

Variations in patterns of abusive behavior and the factors that motivate it pose further challenges to the group format. Many state treatment standards are based on the assumption that all abuse emerges from men's patriarchal socialization, which may lead providers to overlook or dismiss information about the specific contextual factors and consequences that precede or maintain abuse in the individual case (Dutton & Corvo, 2006). By relying on a singular explanation of abuse, treatment staff may become entrenched in lexical battles as clients report on what they see as the causes of an abusive incident (e.g., "She's always nagging me and putting me down, and I couldn't take it any more") and facilitators offer stock interpretations (e.g., "You believe it is within your rights to control your partner through abuse"). These disparities may activate client resistance and defensiveness (e.g., "You just don't get it; I didn't say that"), short-circuiting the collaborative change process.

Alliance formation and motivation are better facilitated by reflective listening and reframing focused on the relationship challenges the client faces, emotional reactions to the partner's requests and demands, and wishes for better communication and problem solving. Greater sensitivity to individual differences in the nature of abusive behavior and the contexts in which it occurs also help to avoid the pitfalls of single-variable explanations of abuse. Although general assumptions often serve as a starting point (e.g., that most abusive individuals display hostile cognitive biases toward their partners), individualized treatment offers flexibility to modify these assumptions as a function of specific case information.

IPV offenders also vary considerably in their readiness for change (Alexander & Morris, 2008; Begun et al., 2003; Eckhardt et al., 2008; Levesque, Gelles, & Velicer, 2000). Interventions designed to enhance motivation to change and facilitate movement through the stages of change are effective in reducing addictive behaviors and promoting health behaviors (Burke, Arkowitz, & Menchola, 2003). Translating these treatment principles into the group context, however, can be quite challenging. Interventions geared toward active change may be lost on those who are not yet prepared to change, and interventions geared toward raising problem awareness and resolving ambivalence may alienate those who are already committed to change. In the individual format, the therapist can attempt to meet the client where he or she is in the change process. As necessary, therapeutic efforts can focus on raising awareness of abuse and its effects, resolving ambivalence and making a commitment to change, devising and selecting appropriate change strategies, refining change efforts, and maintaining change over time.

Other challenges arise from variation in relationship status and functioning. Some IPV perpetrators are separated from their partners at the time of intervention, some have legal no-contact orders, and some remain in a committed relationship. Some reunite or separate during treatment, and some have multiple ongoing relationships. It can be very challenging in a traditional group format to respond to this range of relationship scenarios, and highly scripted interventions may impede alliance formation if they do not correspond to the client's personal situation (Cadsky, Hanson, Crawford, & Lalonde, 1996). In addition, although most abusive clients can benefit greatly from training in active listening and other communication skills, they vary considerably in the degree and nature of communication deficits and the speed with which they can improve in these areas. Some clients may require many weeks of intense focus to improve their listening skills. Unfortunately, standard group interventions place serious limitations on the ability to adapt session focus or time allocated to specific treatment targets.

Finally, the degree to which all IPV offenders are appropriate candidates for group intervention remains in question. Most notably, those with antisocial and narcissistic personality styles may present risk for self-aggrandizing or deviance-promoting engagement with other group members and would not likely be recommended for traditional group therapy (Yalom, 2005). Some group members may impede others' progress by promoting blame of the partner or system, encouraging subtly abusive or controlling solutions to relationship problems, or modeling rejection of the therapist's influence. Research with antisocial teens indicates that increased contact with other delinquent youths can reduce the effectiveness of treatment (Ang & Hughes, 2002; Gifford-Smith, Dodge, Dishion, & McCord, 2005) and exacerbate delinquent behavior (Dishion, McCord, & Poulin, 1999; Fo & O'Donnell, 1975) through mutual reinforcement of deviant talk and actions (Handwerk, Field, & Friman, 2000).

Although these deviance-reinforcing processes have yet to be studied with partner-violent men, a qualitative analysis of poor outcome cases provided evidence for the interplay between individual risk factors and negative group dynamics (Lynch, DeDeyn, & Murphy, 2003). In this small-scale investigation, almost all of the poor responders (i.e., those whose partners reported multiple, severe, and/or injurious acts of physical aggression in the 6 months following treatment) had multiple risk factors for unfavorable outcome, including evidence of personality disorders, substance abuse, extensive arrest histories, serious trauma exposure, and/or mood disorders. Additionally, several poor responders were clustered in specific treatment groups. Review of session videotapes revealed that some of these groups were characterized by general disengagement and persistent negative interactions between the group members and therapists. Although more extensive quantitative studies are needed to confirm these observations, it appears that the aggregation of hostile and resistant clients may produce negative group dynamics that confer risk for poor treatment outcome.

EFFICACY OF GROUP TREATMENTS VERSUS INDIVIDUAL TREATMENT FOR ABUSERS

The previously discussed possible benefits of individual treatment are reason enough to investigate the efficacy of individual treatment, particularly in comparison with group treatment. Unfortunately, almost no research has been conducted on the efficacy of individual treatment for IPV. But research does exist on the efficacy of group interventions for IPV, and meta-analytic comparisons have been made between group and individual treatment for non-IPV problems. Despite considerable variability across studies, these literature reviews have concluded that group interventions for IPV are associated with small average reductions in IPV (e.g., Babcock et al., 2004; Davis & Taylor, 1999). In a review of 22 studies that used quasi- or true experimental designs and police or partner reports of violence recidivism, effect sizes for IPV intervention on violence cessation, expressed in standard deviation units separating treated participants from controls (d), ranged from .09 to .34 (Babcock et al., 2004). In randomized experiments, men assigned to batterer intervention programs had average violence recidivism rates about 5% lower than men assigned to control conditions.

From a meta-analysis with more restrictive criteria for study inclusion, Feder and Wilson (2005) drew equally pessimistic conclusions. In randomized experiments, IPV intervention had no overall effect on subsequent physical assault according to victim reports ($d = .01$) and a small effect according to official criminal reports ($d = .26$).

Meta-analytic investigations comparing the efficacy of group to individual treatment approaches across a wide array of clinical problems have demonstrated mixed results, with some investigations finding no significant differences in treatment outcome (e.g., R. C. Miller & Berman, 1983; Robinson, Berman, & Niemeyer, 1990; Smith, Glass, & Miller, 1980; Tillitski, 1990) and others supporting the superiority of individual approaches (Dush, Hirt, & Schroeder, 1983; Nietzel, Russell, Hemmings, & Gretter, 1987; Shapiro & Shapiro, 1982). A meta-analysis examining 23 studies that directly compared group with individual therapy in randomized designs found no overall significant difference in effect sizes (McRoberts et al., 1998). However, group interventions were superior when studies examined circumscribed problems or were conducted before 1981, whereas individual treatment performed better in research published after 1987 or when cases were evaluated using a formal diagnostic system. Differences favoring individual therapy also approached significance for studies examining the treatment of depression.

More recent reviews examining specific disorders have found that individual therapy tends to produce larger treatment effects than group therapy for bulimia nervosa (Thompson-Brenner, Glass, & Westen, 2003), but no significant differences have been apparent for substance use disorders (Weiss, Jaffee, de Menil, & Cogley, 2004). In brief, the overall differences between group and individual therapy formats appear to be modest, but advantages for individual therapy may arise when group contagion effects can promote problematic beliefs such as excessive concern with weight and appearance or pessimistic thinking. It is also important to note that the available reviews focus on therapy formats, rather than the issue of individualized, case-tailored services.

PRINCIPLES OF INDIVIDUALIZED TREATMENT FOR INTIMATE PARTNER VIOLENCE

The following is a proposed cognitive–behavioral model for individualized treatment of IPV perpetrators. The approach is informed by empirical research on the psychological characteristics of IPV perpetrators and treatments for similar and related conditions. Empirical research is needed, however, to examine the efficacy of this approach and its specific components.

Address Adjunctive and Concomitant Service Needs

Individual treatment should address presenting clinical problems other than IPV with adjunctive and/or concomitant services. *Adjunctive services* refers to treatment for clinical problems provided by professionals other than the IPV service provider because of limitations in professional competence or constraints of the IPV treatment context. *Concomitant services* refers to efforts by the IPV service provider to address clinical problems other than IPV within the context of individualized IPV services. Problems with employment, literacy and education, and parenting are commonly identified. The most challenging professional service needs generally involve substance abuse and major psychiatric disorders, which are discussed next.

Substance Abuse

Any individualized service planning process should address participants' use and abuse of substances associated with risk for partner violence, most notably alcohol and stimulant drugs such as amphetamines and cocaine (Brookoff, O'Brien, Cook, Thompson, & Williams, 1997; Murphy, O'Farrell, Fals-Stewart, & Feehan, 2001). Using a daily diary method, Fals-Stewart (2003) found that men in treatment for partner violence were 8 times more likely to reassault their partners on a day of drinking than on a sober day and 17 times more likely on a day of heavy drinking. Similarly, Jones and Gondolf (2001) found that recidivism rates were roughly 3 times higher for men who drank alcohol during a quarterly follow-up period than for men who did not drink and 16 times higher for those who were drunk nearly every day. Although the specific mechanisms whereby alcohol is associated with increased risk for reassault are largely unknown, research indicates that stable remission of problem drinking is associated with dramatic reductions in partner violence (O'Farrell, Fals-Stewart, Murphy, & Murphy, 2003; O'Farrell & Murphy, 1995).

Major Psychiatric Disorders

The following anecdote illustrates a common problem in addressing psychological disorders within abuser intervention:

At a meeting with abuser intervention program directors, the topic of offenders with psychotic or manic symptoms came up. When asked how the programs handled such cases, all the directors noted that these individuals were inappropriate for standard abuser services and were therefore either sent back to the referring source or referred elsewhere for services. By their account, most of those with serious psychopathology spent weeks or months in limbo awaiting other services, and many fell through the cracks, receiving no further services or appropriate referrals.

This is a classic example of a situation in which some of the highest risk offenders receive the lowest levels of monitoring and intervention. A similar problem exists in many locales (especially highly populated areas with overloaded court systems) when highly antisocial offenders fail to appear for court-ordered intervention services yet elude further detection or sanctions.

Other Comorbid Difficulties

Practical constraints in personnel and resources may influence whether adjunctive services can be delivered in the abuser program context or whether a referral and monitoring process is needed. In either event, it is incumbent on service providers to conduct basic mental health assessments, including screening for alcohol and drug problems, psychosis, and mood disorders. In working with court-mandated populations, it can be very helpful to distinguish between required and recommended services for comorbid problems. With conditions that are likely to impede the success of IPV counseling—for example, psychotic symptoms, mania, or alcohol dependence—it is prudent to require that individuals receive services for these problems to remain eligible for participation in IPV intervention. Providers should either offer such services directly or be very active in facilitating appropriate referrals and monitoring compliance and progress. With conditions that may impede functioning but are not likely to render IPV intervention ineffective, adjunctive services can be recommended but not required. Examples include social anxiety conditions, posttraumatic stress disorder, nonpsychotic mood disorders, and subclinical problems with alcohol or other drugs. The use of a case formulation approach often links such difficulties to eliciting conditions for abuse (e.g., abuse while under the influence of alcohol or other drugs) or consequences of abuse (e.g., depression as a result of relationship separation).

Services for comorbid difficulties can also vary in intensity. Some individuals may benefit from a modest degree of clinical attention for problems that are not presenting serious risk for violence recidivism or severely impairing personal functioning. For example, when unhealthy or risky patterns of substance use are present, yet the individual does not meet criteria for substance abuse or dependence, a brief intervention designed to stimulate change may invoke less resistance than a more extensive treatment program. Mild to moderate depression arising from a recent relationship separation may resolve with standard IPV intervention without adjunctive services.

Provide Individual Cognitive–Behavioral Therapy for Abusive Clients

Traditional behavioral and cognitive theories emphasize that similar problem behaviors in different individuals may be associated with unique learning histories, unique patterns of thought and emotion, and unique behavioral functions. By implication, unique solutions may also be needed. In this section, we propose an individual CBT approach for abusive clients. As discussed previously, empirical support for individual treatment of IPV perpetration is sorely lacking. Therefore, our primary goal in devising this individual CBT approach for abusive clients is to stimulate further research, given that there has been almost no research to date on individual treatment for abusive clients. Further details about the conceptual formulation and intervention strategies are available in a more extensive treatment manual (Murphy & Eckhardt, 2005).

Develop Intervention Goals and Strategies for Each Individual Case

CBT case formulation for partner-abusive individuals uses a detailed assessment of problem behaviors, associated cognitions, and personal strengths and resources to develop hypotheses involving key intervention targets and change strategies. For mandated clients, the personal goal of avoiding further legal complications is consistent with the goals of the legal system to reduce reoffense on similar charges and promote public safety. A detailed analysis of problem behaviors focuses on their specific forms and patterns, the life contexts and situations in which they occur, associated emotions and cognitions, and behavioral consequences. The provider uses this assessment to develop hypotheses about the associations among various presenting problems, the functions of abusive behavior, and relevant underlying cognitive themes. In turn, these hypotheses, in concert with an evaluation of the individual's strengths and resources, guide the formulation of intervention targets and the selection of strategies to promote change.

The case formulation approach not only focuses the provider on relevant targets and change strategies but can also be used to promote a strong client–provider alliance. Angry and abusive clients often have a difficult experience in treatment because the factors that they perceive as being the cause of their problems (e.g., "stupid and annoying people") often conflict with the treatment provider's perceived causes (e.g., the client's hostile attitudes; DiGiuseppe, Tafrate, & Eckhardt, 1994). The process of case formulation creates many opportunities to review and discuss the client's assumptions about the nature and causes of their difficulties and to provide new perspectives on these issues from the therapist's point of view. When executed with appropriate levels of empathy and skill, these efforts promote mutual understanding, trust in the therapist, and agreement on intervention goals and strategies (Murphy & Eckhardt, 2005).

Attend to Different Phases of Treatment

Individual treatment for IPV proceeds through a series of phases. These should be seen more as a useful heuristic than as a hard-and-fast plan for the progress of treatment. Flexible movement between phases is both common and necessary. Concerns regarding the safety of potential victims and others who might be negatively affected by the client's abusive behavior must always be paramount in treatment planning and implementation.

Motivation to Change

The first phase involves enhancement of motivational readiness to change. This aspect of treatment is essential for those individuals who arrive at treatment not yet ready to commit to an active plan for behavior change. The motivational phase of treatment may be relatively brief for those who recognize that they have a problem and want to resolve it, but this phase can take up many sessions for those who are in early stages of change. Although periodic attention to motivational issues is helpful throughout treatment, the motivational phase can be thought to end when the individual has clearly articulated goals for change and, together with the therapist, has committed to a plan for working on these change goals.

Motivational interviewing (MI) offers an excellent conceptual framework and set of clinical techniques for these aspects of treatment (W. R. Miller & Rollnick, 2002), particularly for individuals who have not yet recognized their difficulties with abusive behavior or other relationship problems or who are ambivalent about the need for personal change. MI relies largely on reflective listening strategies, with judicious use of change-relevant advice, exploration of factors that encourage or limit change, and use of structured change-planning strategies. Resistance is conceptualized as a two-person dynamic in which the therapist is moving faster than the client, and techniques for "rolling with resistance" are an important feature of the MI approach.

In addition to providing strategies for early-stage clients, MI provides a spirit in which more directive treatment techniques can be delivered. Paying attention to client ownership of the change process, affirming client autonomy, and eliciting permission from the client before offering advice are examples of MI-consistent therapist behaviors that can be profitably used throughout treatment.

Two recent investigations have examined motivational interviewing, delivered in a one-on-one format, as a method to enhance treatment engagement and stimulate the change process among partner-violent men. Kistenmacher and Weiss (2008) randomly assigned 33 court-mandated partner-abusive men to a two-session of MI intervention or a no-MI control. They found a significantly greater decrease in externalizing attributions for abuse and enhanced readiness to change by self-report for those receiving MI treatment. Musser, Semiatin, Taft, and Murphy (2008) assigned 108 men presenting for services at a community domestic violence agency to receive an intake process that included two MI sessions or a structured intake control. In the subsequent group CBT program, those in the MI condition displayed significantly more constructive behavior in early sessions by observer report, higher CBT homework compliance, stronger working alliance as rated by therapists late in treatment, and more outside help seeking during treatment. They also had lower posttreatment violence rates than those in the standard intake condition, but this effect only approached statistical significance. In general, these investigations provide encouraging initial support for the value of MI in increasing receptivity to change among partner-violent men.

Safety and Stabilization

As IPV clients become aware of the prospects for change and less resistant to the therapist's influence, initial goals usually emphasize promotion of safety and efforts to address life or relationship instabilities. Therapist and client undertake a careful examination of specific abuse incidents, difficult relationship scenarios, and/or other violent situations outside the family to develop hypotheses about the eliciting conditions and functions of abusive and violent behavior. They address and work on nonviolent alternatives, particularly for crisis or emergency situations with the potential to escalate to physical violence. They also identify and address attitudes and beliefs that support the use of violence. These efforts typically meld into more general relationship skills training and relationship enhancement, characterized as the next phase of treatment.

In the early phases of treatment, many abusive clients present with a range of life instabilities that, if not addressed, may seriously impede subsequent treatment efforts. Some have recently separated from a long-term relationship and are struggling with housing issues, mounting financial stress, child support arrangements, or difficulties with custody or visitation. Some have extreme ambivalence about whether to remain in the current relationship, complications from ongoing or recent affairs, or confusion resulting from multiple ongoing relationships. Job instabilities, negative life complications from incarceration, or severe educational limitations may also be present. As trust develops in the treatment relationship, clients may disclose substance abuse problems or mental health disorders in one or both partners. The competent therapist is able to promote personal stability through support and focused problem solving without becoming totally derailed from the predominant change agenda that focuses on relationship and interpersonal functioning and cessation of abuse.

Relationship Skills Training and Relationship Enhancement

Ideally, the majority of treatment is devoted to the enhancement of relationship skills and interpersonal functioning. These treatment targets represent the predominant strategies to prevent escalation to abusive and violent relationship behaviors. Case formulation helps the therapist identify the specific problematic relationship beliefs each client holds, along with his or her predominant limitations in interpersonal and relationship skills. From clinical impressions, the areas of relationship skills training that we have found most helpful involve active listening, assertive and respectful self-expression, negotiation and compromise, and acceptance. For clients who are not currently in an intimate relationship, skills training typically focuses on communication with ex-partners regarding child visitation and related issues, communication difficulties that arose in previous relationships, and helpful skills and attitudes to use in establishing and maintaining healthier relationships in the future.

In virtually every case, relationship skills training proceeds at the level of both cognition and behavior. After identifying key relationship skills to work on, the therapist typically describes and discusses the skill and its potential usefulness, discusses how and when the client may benefit from its use (relating it to the client's explicit goals and the general case formulation whenever possible), provides a written handout with information about the skill, role models good (and sometimes bad) examples of its use, and then shapes the client's use of the skill through repetitive role-plays. Almost invariably, these exercises reveal prominent beliefs that severely impede abusive clients' communication and problem solving. Therefore, the focus typically shifts back and forth between skills training and the cognitive restructuring interventions. Homework is used judiciously, particularly at the outset, with a consistent focus on safety. Ironically, many abusive clients are highly conflict avoidant in their relationships and must proceed slowly given that avoidance is their primary strategy for preventing escalation to abusive behavior. The therapist encourages clients to experiment with active listening and acceptance (of the partner) during no-conflict or low-conflict interactions, addressing more significant problems only after they have success with these less threatening applications.

For the vast majority of partner-abusive clients, problematic assumptions and beliefs emerge consistently throughout assessment and intervention. The skillful therapist is attuned to evidence of these beliefs, often reflecting the client's words and phrases explicitly as a means of highlighting problematic assumptions. The most obvious and destructive distortions often involve the partner. Extreme examples include the notion that the partner wants to be abused; provokes abuse; benefits from being abused; or is somehow deficient, disturbed, or "crazy." Many examples involve distortions of the partner's intentions and emotions—for example, distorting the partner's expressions of concern as attempts to control or punish, or seeing continued reactions to past abuse as a willful effort to undermine change efforts. Abusive clients often catastrophize about the partner's friends and relatives, child-rearing practices, housekeeping, spending habits, or desire for independence.

Communication skills training often reveals problematic assumptions— for example, that the client is always right (and the partner is always wrong). Abusive clients often confuse matters of taste and preference with matters of fact. Many have trouble distinguishing between minor everyday relationship concerns, significant disagreements that warrant problem solving, and major betrayals of trust. Some believe that all relationships are abusive and violent, that one person always has to be in control, or that there is always a victim and a perpetrator. Some have destructive gender beliefs—for example, all women are deceptive, women only want men for a paycheck, and the man should have the final say in all decisions. Problematic assumptions about the usefulness of aggression are also common. Many abusive clients have histories of witnessed or experienced abuse, and some grew up in neighborhoods or families where being tough and violent were important survival strategies. These individuals may believe that violence will resolve conflicts, even the score, and set things straight. Some abusive clients present a moral fervor in wanting to teach others a lesson and make sure that they "get what is coming to them." The depth of these convictions is revealed by confusion and distress clients experience when reconciling the negative effects of their aggressive outbursts with the belief that such behaviors should have positive interpersonal consequences.

Finally, many abusive clients have problematic beliefs about themselves involving depressive or anxious thinking and/or distortions associated with personality disorders. In exploring situations that arouse distress and anger, underlying inadequacies and insecurities are often apparent. Some clients respond well to the idea that anger "buttons" reflect their own limitations and insecurities. With entrenched cognitive distortions, the most difficult task is to help the client separate or disengage from powerful beliefs that are seen as reality rather than personal assumptions about reality. In addition, some distorted self-beliefs, such as narcissistic grandiosity, are extremely difficult to challenge because they have self-protective and self-enhancing benefits.

Trauma Recovery and Relapse Prevention

The final phase of treatment focuses on trauma recovery and relapse prevention. Abusive clients with histories of witnessed or experienced abuse in childhood or those with other serious traumatic exposures may benefit from clinical attention to trauma issues at the later stages of therapy. Such interventions can include trauma exposure (Foa & Rothbaum, 1998) as well as cognitive interventions targeted at understanding and changing the ways in which childhood experiences have shaped expectations and views of the self and relationships using strategies derived from cognitive processing therapy (Resick & Schnicke, 1993) and schema therapy (Young, Klosko, & Weishaar, 2003). At the current time, trauma recovery as a last phase of treatment remains largely aspirational, as very few of our clients have progressed to this work. Some have failed to engage in trauma recovery as a function of persistent life difficulties and chaos. Others have outwardly and explicitly declined to address their trauma histories despite careful and supportive efforts by clinicians to encourage such work. Some remain unconvinced that their childhood experiences had a negative impact on their relationship functioning, despite what appears to the clinician as quite convincing evidence to the contrary.

Relapse prevention is relevant to all who undergo a change process, given the propensity to return to earlier patterns of problematic behavior. Although no empirical support is yet available for such practices with abusive clients, we recommend that treatment be phased out slowly, that booster sessions to maintain changes be provided, and that clients be encouraged to return in the future for check-ups or to address new difficulties that may emerge. Some partner-violent individuals slide back into old patterns of controlling and abusive behavior after making initial changes and may benefit greatly from ongoing support and encouragement.

Relapse prevention sessions should focus on helping the client identify potentially challenging situations and "relapse cues" for abusive behavior, understand his or her own personal pattern of lapse and relapse to old ways of acting, and prepare for these challenges. Careful review of changes and gains made in the course of treatment is important during the final phase, and many clients benefit from deriving a specific plan for continued change efforts at the end of treatment. We recommend loose adoption of three key ideas from Marlatt and Gordon's (1985) relapse prevention model for addictive behaviors: (a) examining the role of lifestyle imbalance and stress in stimulating a return to problematic behavior, (b) helping clients appreciate the distinction between a temporary lapse (e.g., verbal aggression, controlling behavior) and a more complete relapse to problematic behavior (e.g., more extensive forms of abuse or physical assault), and (c) understanding and addressing the cognitive and emotional features that precipitate relapse through the analysis of potentially high-risk situations.

FUTURE PROSPECTS AND CHALLENGES

It is becoming increasingly difficult to make the case for preserving abuser intervention programs in their current state. At best, the effectiveness literature suggests that men who complete traditional group programs are only slightly more likely to refrain from IPV than men assigned to minimal interventions. At worst, a near majority of men mandated to attend such groups do not complete them, and in some studies treatment completers fare no better or even slightly worse than men assigned to minimal interventions. These conclusions have led many in the field to question whether intervention programs for partner violence waste valuable resources and create a false sense of security among victims who expect the abusive partner to change (Jackson et al., 2003).

The time is ripe to develop, evaluate, and disseminate alternative intervention programs for partner-abusive individuals to enhance victim safety. But is the system ready for new intervention models? Assuming that new, empirically supported interventions become available, will the relevant criminal justice and social service agencies adopt such approaches? To the extent that intervention programs are instituted and maintained for reasons that have nothing to do with empirical justification, the answer may well be no (for additional discussion, see Eckhardt, Murphy, Black, & Suhr, 2006).

One major challenge involves state-mandated guidelines and standards for batterer intervention programs. For example, programs based on an individualized risk assessment and intervention model may be explicitly or implicitly countermanded in some states. In their review of state standards for batterer programs, Austin and Dankwort (1999) reported that 86% of states identified group intervention as the preferred format and that more than two thirds (68%) of states indicated that one-on-one interventions were inappropriate as a primary format, with some indicating that exceptions may be necessary in special circumstances.

Our more current Web search of state standards revealed a similar outcome. Of the 43 states with existing standards or guidelines for abuser intervention programs, 89% listed group as the preferred intervention format, and 32% required group interventions. Forty-one percent of states allowed individual interventions only in "special circumstances," with most standards listing active psychosis, language problems, adolescent status, or significant cultural differences as exemplars of such circumstances. Only four states (Arizona, Kentucky, Maryland, and Utah) did not list a preference for individual versus group formats. Thus, despite the fact that there are almost no data available concerning the relative effectiveness of individual interventions for abusive individuals and that the majority of data do not provide strong support for the efficacy of existing group interventions, standards or guidelines are nevertheless in place across in a majority of states that severely restrict the implementation of individual intervention services.

Many state guidelines include very strong statements, with little or no empirical support, about the causes of IPV, the effectiveness or ineffectiveness of various interventions, and the process of abusive behavior change (Maiuro et al., 2002). Why is this the case? One reason involves suspicions about any intervention that may suggest or imply a medical model approach to IPV under the assumption that abusers will blame their actions on a mental disorder or psychological problem. In addition, there is concern that an individual approach will be exclusively focused on some unitary issue such as childhood experiences, addiction, or anger and that such focus will derail attention from personal responsibility or social influences that contribute to IPV. The veracity of these claims awaits clinical and empirical verification. But it is also critical to note that as of this writing, there is scant empirical support for group intervention effectiveness, there is no evidence to suggest that the group format uniquely contributes to behavior change, and there is little evidence to suggest that the presumed mechanisms of change in group abuser interventions are actually responsible for change among men mandated to such programs. In short, although state coalitions against domestic violence and policymakers have the safety of women as their top priority, most state guidelines continue to restrict intervention offerings to models that may actually do little to prevent women from continued abuse.

Another often-stated objection to individualized services and individual therapy for partner abusive men is cost-effectiveness. Can such services be offered at rates that are affordable for agencies and clients? Cost-cutting measures, however, can be taken too far if programs fail to conduct a competent assessment of problems that are associated with substantial risk for continued violence (e.g., substance abuse), do not perform adequate outreach to victims, or are unable to provide basic individual case management to handle referrals and adjunctive service needs of high-risk offenders. Competent intervention programs, regardless of whether the primary intervention is an individual or group format, necessitate some degree of individual assessment, outreach, and case management. At this point, the cost-effectiveness of more extensive individual services remains an empirical question. A key consideration, however, is whether interventions with low front-end costs, such as traditional group programs, are truly cost-effective relative to more intensive service delivery formats, given the high rates of recidivism and criminal reinvolvement.

We are not arguing that all abusive individuals should be given individual therapy or that individual treatment should supplant group approaches. To make such claims in the absence of compelling empirical data would recapitulate the problems in existing state guidelines that require or prohibit various interventions in the absence of supporting research. Rather, our point is that the time is ripe to develop and test alternative interventions, given that available group approaches have modest effects and potential limitations. To ignore the need for new intervention approaches would be a grave disservice to victims and may lead to the erosion of community support for court-mandated abuser counseling.

Given this state of affairs, the material presented in this chapter reflects our recent efforts to provide a clear conceptual rationale for individualized services and individual therapy with abuse perpetrators that uses motivational and CBT strategies to address their varied treatment needs. This approach has been described in more detail in a treatment manual that was designed to promote research on the efficacy of individual CBT for partner abuse perpetrators (Murphy & Eckhardt, 2005). Initial research efforts have provided support for the efficacy of motivational interviewing in enhancing engagement into abuser counseling (Musser et al., 2008). Ongoing studies are comparing individual to group CBT for this population and exploring aspects of group interactions that may promote or discourage abuse-promoting attitudes and behaviors. It is our sincere hope that the treatment technology in this field will advance considerably in upcoming years and that programs and state guidelines will be able to adapt to accommodate empirically supported intervention strategies.

REFERENCES

Alexander, P. C., & Morris, E. (2008). Stages of change in batterers and their response to treatment. *Violence and Victims, 23,* 476–492.

Ang, R., & Hughes, J. (2002). Differential benefits of skills training with antisocial youth based on group composition: A meta-analytic investigation. *School Psychology Review, 31,* 164–185.

Austin, J. B., & Dankwort, J. (1999). Standards for batterer programs: A review and analysis. *Journal of Interpersonal Violence, 14,* 152–168.

Babcock, J. C., Green, C. E., & Robie, C. (2004). Does batterers' treatment work? A meta-analytic review of domestic violence treatment. *Clinical Psychology Review, 23,* 1023–1053.

Begun, A. L., Murphy, C. M., Bolt, D., Weinstein, B., Strodthoff, T., Short, L., & Shelley, G. (2003). Characteristics of the Safe at Home instrument for assessing readiness to change intimate partner violence. *Research on Social Work Practice, 13,* 80–107.

Brookoff, D., O'Brien, K., Cook, C. S., Thompson, T. D., & Williams, C. (1997). Characteristics of participants in domestic violence: Assessment at the scene of domestic assault. *JAMA, 227,* 1369–1373.

Burke, B., Arkowitz, H., & Menchola, M. (2003). The efficacy of motivational interviewing: A meta-analysis of controlled clinical trials. *Journal of Consulting and Clinical Psychology, 71,* 843–861.

Cadsky, O., Hanson, R., Crawford, M., & Lalonde, C. (1996). Attrition from a male batterer treatment program: Client–treatment congruence and lifestyle instability. *Violence and Victims, 11,* 51–64.

Daniels, J. W., & Murphy, C. M. (1997). Stages and processes of change in batterers' treatment. *Cognitive and Behavioral Practice, 4,* 123–145.

Davis, R. C., & Taylor, B. G. (1999). Does batterer treatment reduce violence? A synthesis of the literature. *Women and Criminal Justice, 10,* 69–93.

Dies, R. R. (1995). Group psychotherapies. In A. S. Gurman & S. B. Messer (Eds.), *Essential psychotherapies: Theory and practice* (pp. 488–522). New York: Guilford Press.

DiGiuseppe, R., Tafrate, R., & Eckhardt, C. (1994). Critical issues in the treatment of anger. *Cognitive and Behavioral Practice, 1,* 111–132.

Dishion, T., McCord, J., & Poulin, F. (1999). When interventions harm: Peer groups and problem behavior. *American Psychologist, 54,* 755–764.

Dush, D. M., Hirt, M. L., & Schroeder, H. (1983). Self-statement modification with adults: A meta-analysis. *Psychological Bulletin, 94,* 408–422.

Dutton, D. G., & Corvo, K. (2006). Transforming a flawed policy: A call to revive psychology and science in domestic violence research and practice. *Aggression and Violent Behavior, 11,* 457–483.

Eckhardt, C. I., Holtzworth-Munroe, A., Norlander, B., Sibley, A., Togun, I., & Cahill, M. (2008). Readiness to change, partner violence subtypes, and treatment outcomes among men in treatment for partner assault. *Violence and Victims, 23,* 446–475.

Eckhardt, C. I., Murphy, C., Black, D., & Suhr, L. (2006). Intervention programs for perpetrators of intimate partner violence: Conclusions from a clinical research perspective. *Public Health Reports, 121,* 369–381.

Ehrensaft, M., Cohen, P., & Johnson, J. (2006). Development of personality disorder symptoms and the risk for partner violence. *Journal of Abnormal Psychology, 115,* 474–483.

Fals-Stewart, W. (2003). The occurrence of partner physical aggression on days of alcohol consumption: A longitudinal diary study. *Journal of Consulting and Clinical Psychology, 71,* 41–52.

Feder, L., & Wilson, D. (2005). A meta-analytic review of court-mandated batterer intervention programs: Can courts affect abusers' behavior? *Journal of Experimental Criminology, 1,* 239–262.

Fo, W. S., & O'Donnell, C. R. (1975). The buddy system: Effect of community intervention on delinquent offenses. *Behavior Therapy, 6,* 522–524.

Foa, E. B., & Rothbaum, B. O. (1998). *Treating the trauma of rape: Cognitive–behavioral therapy for PTSD.* New York: Guilford Press.

Gifford-Smith, M., Dodge, K. A., Dishion, T. J., & McCord, J. (2005). Peer influence in children and adolescents: Crossing the bridge from developmental to intervention science. *Journal of Abnormal Child Psychology, 33,* 255–265.

Hamberger, L. K., & Hastings, J. E. (1991). Personality correlates of men who batter and nonviolent men: Some continuities and discontinuities. *Journal of Family Violence, 6,* 131–147.

Handwerk, M. L., Field, C. E., & Friman, P. C. (2000). The iatrogenic effects of group intervention for antisocial youth: Premature extrapolations? *Journal of Behavioral Education, 10,* 223–238.

Hart, S. D., Dutton, D. G., & Newlove, T. (1993). The prevalence of personality disorder among wife assaulters. *Journal of Personality Disorders, 7,* 329–341.

Holtzworth-Munroe, A., Meehan, J. C., Herron, K., Rehman, U., & Stuart, G. L. (2000). Testing the Holtzworth-Munroe and Stuart (1994) batterer typology. *Journal of Consulting and Clinical Psychology, 68,* 1000–1019.

Holtzworth-Munroe, A., Rehman, U., & Herron, K. (2000). General and spouse-specific anger and hostility in subtypes of maritally violent men and nonviolent men. *Behavior Therapy, 31,* 603–630.

Holtzworth-Munroe, A., & Stuart, G. L. (1994). Typologies of male batterers: Three subtypes and the differences among them. *Psychological Bulletin, 116,* 476–497.

Jackson, S., Feder, L., Forde, D. R., Davis, R. C., Maxwell, C. D., & Taylor, B. G. (2003). *Batterer intervention programs: Where do we go from here?* (Report No. NCJ 195079). Washington, DC: U.S. Department of Justice.

Jones, A. S., & Gondolf, E. W. (2001). Time-varying risk factors for reassault among batterer program participants. *Journal of Family Violence, 16,* 345–359.

Kessler, R. C., Molnar, B. E., Feurer, I. D., & Applebaum, M. (2001). Patterns and mental health predictors of domestic violence in the United States: Results from the National Comorbidity Study. *International Journal of Law and Psychiatry, 24,* 487–508.

Kistenmacher, B. R., & Weiss, R. L. (2008). Motivational interviewing as a mechanism for change in men who batter: A randomized controlled trial. *Violence and Victims, 23,* 558–570.

Kropp, P. R. (2004). Some questions regarding spousal assault risk assessment. *Violence Against Women, 10,* 676–697.

Kropp, P. R., & Hart, S. D. (2000). The Spousal Assault Risk Assessment (SARA) guide: Reliability and validity in adult make offenders. *Law and Human Behavior, 24,* 101–118.

Levesque, D. A., Gelles, R. J., & Velicer, W. F. (2000). Development and validation of a stages of change measure for men in batterer treatment. *Cognitive Therapy and Research, 24,* 175–199.

Lynch, L. A., DeDeyn, J. M., & Murphy, C. M. (2003, November). *A qualitative case analysis of partner violent men who respond poorly to cognitive–behavioral group treatment.* Poster session presented at the annual meeting of the Association for the Advancement of Behavior Therapy, Boston, MA.

Maiuro, R. D., Hagar, T. S., Lin, H., & Olson, N. (2002). Are current state standards for domestic violence perpetrator treatment adequately informed by research? A question of questions. *Journal of Aggression, Maltreatment & Trauma, 5,* 21–44.

Marlatt, G. A., & Gordon, J. R. (Eds.). (1985). *Relapse prevention: Maintenance strategies in the treatment of addictive behaviors.* New York: Guilford Press.

McRoberts, C., Burlingame, G. M., & Hoag, M. J. (1998). Comparative efficacy of individual and group psychotherapy: A meta-analytic perspective. *Group Dynamics: Theory, Research, and Practice, 2,* 101–117.

Miller, R. C., & Berman, J. S. (1983). The efficacy of cognitive behavior therapies: A quantitative review of the research evidence. *Psychological Bulletin, 94*, 39–53.

Miller, W. R., & Rollnick, S. (2002). *Motivational interviewing: Preparing people to change addictive behavior* (2nd ed.). New York: Guilford Press.

Murphy, C. M., & Eckhardt, C. I. (2005). *Treating the abusive partner: An individualized, cognitive–behavioral approach.* New York: Guilford Press.

Murphy, C. M., O'Farrell, T. J., Fals-Stewart, W., & Feehan, M. (2001). Correlates of intimate partner violence among male alcoholic patients. *Journal of Consulting and Clinical Psychology, 69*, 528–540.

Murphy, C. M., Taft, C. T., & Eckhardt, C. I. (2007). Anger problem profiles among partner violent men: Differences in clinical presentation and treatment outcome. *Journal of Counseling Psychology, 54*, 189–200.

Musser, P. H., Semiatin, J. N., Taft, C. T., & Murphy, C. M. (2008). Motivational interviewing as a pre-group intervention for partner violent men. *Violence and Victims, 23*, 539–557.

Nietzel, M. T., Russell, R. L., Hemmings, K. A., & Gretter, M. L. (1987). Clinical significance of psychotherapy for unipolar depression: A meta-analytic approach to social comparison. *Journal of Consulting and Clinical Psychology, 55*, 156–161.

O'Farrell, T. J., Fals-Stewart, W., Murphy, M., & Murphy, C. M. (2003). Partner violence before and after individually-based alcoholism treatment for male alcoholic patients. *Journal of Consulting and Clinical Psychology, 71*, 92–102.

O'Farrell, T. J., & Murphy, C. M. (1995). Marital violence before and after alcoholism treatment. *Journal of Consulting and Clinical Psychology, 63*, 256–262.

O'Leary, K. D. (1993). Through a psychological lens: Personality traits, personality disorders, and levels of violence. In R. J. Gelles & D. Loseke (Eds.), *Current controversies on family violence* (pp. 7–29). Newbury Park, CA: Sage.

Resick, P. A., & Schnicke, M. K. (1993). *Cognitive processing therapy for rape victims: A treatment manual.* Newbury Park, CA: Sage.

Robinson, L. A., Berman, J. S., & Niemeyer, R. A. (1990). Psychotherapy for the treatment of depression: A comprehensive review of controlled outcome research. *Psychological Bulletin, 108*, 30–49.

Saunders, D. G. (1992). A typology of men who batter: Three types derived from cluster analysis. *American Journal of Orthopsychiatry, 62*, 11–22.

Shapiro, D. A., & Shapiro, D. (1982). Meta-analysis of comparative therapy outcome studies: A replication and refinement. *Psychological Bulletin, 92*, 581–604.

Smith, M. L., Glass, G. V., & Miller, T. I. (1980). *The benefits of psychotherapy.* Baltimore: Johns Hopkins University Press.

Thompson-Brenner, H., Glass, S., & Westen, D. (2003). A multidimensional meta-analysis of psychotherapy for bulimia nervosa. *Clinical Psychology: Science and Practice, 10*, 269–287.

Tillitski, C. J. (1990). A meta-analysis of estimated effect sizes for group versus individual versus control treatments. *International Journal of Group Psychotherapy, 40*, 215–224.

Weiss, R. D., Jaffee, W. B., de Menil, V. P., & Cogley, C. B. (2004). Group therapy for substance use disorders: What do we know? *Harvard Review of Psychiatry, 12*, 339–350.

Yalom, I. (2005). *The theory and practice of group psychotherapy* (5th ed.). New York: Basic Books.

Young, J. E., Klosko, J. S., & Weishaar, M. E. (2003). *Schema therapy: A practitioner's guide*. New York: Guilford Press.

11

COUPLES TREATMENT FOR PSYCHOLOGICAL AND PHYSICAL AGGRESSION

SANDRA M. STITH AND ERIC E. McCOLLUM

THE CHANGING FACE OF INTIMATE PARTNER VIOLENCE

When we began working with female victims of intimate partner violence (IPV) in the early 1980s, our beliefs about the issue were clear and unequivocal. We thought that all IPV offenders and victims were the same, that men were always the assailants (i.e., the primary aggressors), and that men used violence to gain power and control over women. We thought that women hit only in self-defense. When we spoke about IPV, we told audiences, "If he hits you once, he *will* hit again." We believed that women who stayed in abusive relationships stayed because they were experiencing "learned helplessness." We believed that group treatment for male offenders was safe for victims and generally effective and that couples treatment was never appropriate for couples in which IPV was occurring.

Since then, our knowledge and understanding about IPV has grown exponentially. We now know that all IPV is not the same, nor is it all solely based on male power and control (Gondolf, 1988; Holtzworth-Munroe & Stuart, 1994; Johnson & Ferraro, 2000). Although variations exist, most

233

typologies now recognize at least two types of IPV, one that is characterological and one that is situational (Babcock, Canady, Graham, & Schart, 2007). The characterological form of IPV tends to be more asymmetrical (there is a clear perpetrator and victim) and is used in a context of control and domination. In addition, the perpetrator may have diagnosable psychopathology or a personality disorder.

The situational form of IPV is not just a less frequent or severe form of characterological violence. Situational violence is usually sustained by interactive factors, and bilateral violence (partners assaulting each other) is its most common form (Dutton & Corvo, 2006; Rosen, Stith, Few, Daly, & Tritt, 2005). It is different from the violence committed by characterological batterers (Leone, Johnson, Cohan, & Lloyd, 2004). Situational violence tends to be more reciprocal and symmetrical (there is not a clear perpetrator and victim) and does not involve a context of control and fear. In situational IPV, women are violent at least as often as men, although they usually do less physical damage. Situational violence is likely to be part of a negative cycle that includes a pattern of ongoing psychological abuse, negative reciprocity, rapid escalation, and lack of procedures to escape from the escalating arguments (Babcock et al., 2007; Jacobson & Gottman, 1998). In other words, it is characterized by habitual patterns of conflict that these couples do not know how to break.

We have also learned that the traditional form of treatment for male IPV offenders does not work as well as we first hoped. Most programs designed to treat offenders use all-male psychoeducational groups focusing on changing attitudes toward women and violence. However, these groups tend to have at least a 50% dropout rate (O'Leary, 2002), and they have a minimal impact on reducing recidivism beyond the effect of being arrested (Babcock, Green, & Robie, 2004). Male-only treatment may also elicit negative male bonding (Hart, 1988), which can tend to support violence. In our own work, some women whose partners had participated in a male-only batterer program before beginning our couples program reported that the most dangerous time of the week for them was the evening after their husbands came home from the batterer program. The husbands were often angry that they were mandated to treatment and sometimes felt criticized and belittled in the confrontational programs they attended.

We have also learned that there are many reasons couples stay together after experiencing violence in their relationship and that a primary reason is because they care about each other and want to try to make their relationship work. We have also learned from our work and from the work of many others that violence can end and relationships can improve.

As we came to realize that some of our most widely accepted assumptions about IPV and its treatment were not valid, we began to develop and test a treatment program for couples experiencing situational IPV. Our initial development of the program was met with strong reactions from some who continued to believe that conjoint treatment was never appropriate if there had ever been IPV in a relationship. Some reaction against couple-level interventions for IPV occurs because these types of interventions seem to suggest that the victim is at least in part to blame or otherwise coresponsible for the abuse (Schechter, 1987). Another concern is that conjoint treatment may increase danger for victims of abuse by forcing them to confront their abusers directly (Stith, Rosen, & McCollum, 2003). Alternatively, victims may be reluctant to speak freely in front of their partner for fear of retaliatory abuse. Because of these concerns, in 2005, 68% of the 44 states with IPV offender standards expressly prohibited the funding of any program that offered couples or family counseling as a primary mode of intervention when there had been IPV (Maiuro & Eberle, 2008). We believe, however, that the case against couples therapy is not nearly so straightforward.

Our belief is that in cases of characterological violence, couples-level treatments may not be appropriate and may increase danger to partners. However, in cases of situational violence, couples treatment may be indicated. In cases of situational, reciprocal violence, treating men without treating women is not likely to stop the violence (Stith, McCollum, Rosen, Locke, & Goldberg, 2005). Although men's treatment groups address men's role in IPV, they do not always address underlying relationship dynamics that may influence each partner's decision to remain in the violent relationship despite the violence or that may play a part in maintaining the violence. In fact, research has shown that cessation of partner violence by one partner is highly dependent on whether the other partner also stops the violence (Capaldi, Shortt, & Crosby, 2003; Feld & Straus, 1989; Gelles & Straus, 1988). Furthermore, an estimated 21% to 80% of battered women remain with their abusive partner (Ferraro & Johnson, 1983; Sullivan & Rumptz, 1994). Failing to provide services to both parties in an ongoing relationship may inadvertently disadvantage the female partner who chooses to stay. With situationally violent couples, the violence (both psychological and physical) may stop when the partners enter new relationships with less volatile partners (Capaldi et al., 2003; Moffit, Robins, & Caspi, 2001) or when they learn to adopt better communication strategies, suggesting that a change in relationship dynamics leads to change in violent behavior.

Finally, despite the controversy and proclamations against couples therapy in cases of domestic violence, couples therapists routinely treat violent couples. Approximately 67% of couples seeking outpatient couples therapy (not for domestic violence) report some IPV if they are asked systematically about the frequency of their use of physically aggressive acts (O'Leary, Vivian, & Malone, 1992), although they generally do not mention that any form of physical aggression is a problem in their relationship. In early research at our clinic (Stith, Rosen, Barasch, & Wilson, 1991), we found that although only 12% of 262 families initially reported partner violence as the presenting problem, when interviewed carefully, at least 40% of the families reported some type of partner violence. Therefore, another reason to develop couples treatment models for IPV is that abusive couples are being treated in standard couples therapy regularly. Specific models for this group may increase effectiveness and safety.

RESEARCH ON THE EFFECTIVENESS OF COUPLES TREATMENT WITH INTIMATE PARTNER VIOLENCE

To date, three groups of studies have used experimental designs (i.e., couples randomly assigned to two or more treatment conditions) in examining the effectiveness of conjoint treatment for IPV (see McCollum & Stith, 2007, for further discussion). These studies include

- research conducted by the Families and Addiction Program, Harvard Medical School, and the Research Institute on Addictions, University at Buffalo, the State University of New York;
- studies examining a version of the Domestic Conflict Containment Program (DCCP) or the revised Physical Aggression Couples Treatment (PACT) conducted at the State University of New York, Stony Brook; and
- studies examining the Domestic Violence Focused Couples Treatment (DVFCT) program.

In this section, we briefly review this research.

Behavioral Couples Therapy for Substance Abuse

A variety of studies documenting the effectiveness of behavioral couples therapy (BCT) for substance abuse on reducing IPV have demonstrated the efficacy of BCT in reducing IPV for substance-abusing couples (Fals-Stewart, Kashdan, O'Farrell, & Birchler, 2002; O'Farrell, Fals-Stewart, Murphy, Stephan, & Murphy, 2004). For example, a study by Fals-Stewart and colleagues (2002) randomly assigned 80 drug-abusing couples to either individual treatment or BCT. The overall dropout rate was 14% in both individual substance abuse treatment and in BCT couples treatment. Although IPV was reduced in both conditions, couples attending BCT were significantly less likely to be violent in the year after treatment than were couples in which only the male partner attended treatment. Fals-Stewart and Kennedy (2005) suggested that conjoint treatment may be more effective in reducing IPV because when both partners are in treatment, not only does the substance-abusing partner increase his or her likelihood of becoming abstinent, but the non-substance-abusing partner learns coping skills and measures to increase safety when faced with a situation where the likelihood of violence increases. Fals-Stewart and Kennedy were so convinced of the value of conjoint treatment that they stated that "providers should use partner-based interventions, particularly BCT, for the majority of substance-abusing patients who have engaged in IPV prior to program entry" (p. 8).

Neidig, O'Leary, and Heyman Models

A variety of studies have examined the effectiveness of Neidig's (1985) Domestic Conflict Containment Program and various revisions of it (Brannen & Rubin, 1996; Heyman, Brown, Feldbau-Kohn, & O'Leary, 1999; O'Leary, Heyman, & Neidig, 1999). These treatment programs are delivered by male–female professional cotherapy teams to multicouple groups. The treatment focuses on anger management skills and couples' issues such as communication, fair fighting, gender differences, sex, and jealousy. Studies have examined the efficacy of DCCP or Physical Aggression Couples Treatment using samples of military couples (Neidig, 1985), court-ordered civilians (Brannen & Rubin, 1996), and couples seeking help voluntarily (O'Leary et al., 1999). Both Brannen and Rubin (1996) and O'Leary et al. (1999) randomly assigned couples to either multicouple groups or gender-specific groups. O'Leary et al. indicated that the overall dropout rate for their study was 47% (45% for the multicouple group and 50% for the gender-specific groups), and Brannen and Rubin reported dropout rates of 27% for the gender-specific group and 4% for the couples group. Both of these studies reported that the treatment program was effective in helping men reduce their level of violence. In addition, the studies that compared DCCP or PACT with a gender-specific treatment reported no significant differences between the groups in dropout or violent recidivism rates.

In discussing their findings, O'Leary et al. (1999) also addressed some of the concerns about conjoint treatment. The authors observed that

> compared to wives in the [gender-specific treatment], wives in the conjoint treatment were not fearful of participating with their husbands; were not fearful during the sessions; did not blame themselves for the violence; and were not put at an increased risk for violence during the program. (p. 494)

They further suggested that

> at this point, both conjoint treatment and [gender-specific treatments] for wife abuse appear to be equally viable modes of intervention. There were significant reductions in men's psychological aggression (i.e., approximately a 50% reduction) that were associated with reductions in physical aggression. (p. 501)

Domestic Violence Focused Couples Treatment

Stith, McCollum, and Rosen at Virginia Tech in Falls Church, Virginia, developed and tested a couples treatment for IPV, DVFCT, which is based on a solution-focused treatment approach (Rosen, Matheson, Stith, McCollum, & Locke, 2003; Stith, McCollum, Rosen, & Locke, 2002; Stith, Rosen, McCollum, & Thomsen, 2004). They compared the outcome of clients randomly assigned to participate in a multicouple version of their program with couples randomly assigned to participate in a single-couple version and with a nonrandom group of comparison couples (Stith et al., 2004). The dropout rates (30% for the single-couple condition and 27% for the multicouple condition) did not vary between groups. Six months after completing treatment, the scores of participants in the multicouple group decreased on acceptability of wife beating and increased on marital satisfaction significantly over time, whereas the scores of participants in the single-couple therapy and the comparison group did not. Furthermore, levels of marital aggression (both physical and psychological) decreased significantly among individuals who participated in the multicouple group but not among participants in the single-couple treatment and the comparison group. This pattern was similar for men and women.

Stith et al. (2004) also assessed male physical violence recidivism rates at the 6-month follow-up. Recidivism rates were significantly lower for the multicouple group (25%) than for the comparison group (66%). In contrast, men in the single-couple condition were not significantly less likely to recidivate (43%) than those in the comparison group. Despite a small sample size, the results of the study were clear: The multicouple treatment had significant effects in reducing subsequent partner violence. Couples who completed the multicouple treatment were less likely to believe that violence was appropriate in intimate relationships and had the largest increases in relationship satisfaction and the lowest recurrence of IPV.

Summary of Research

In each of the published studies, the couples treatment condition was at least as effective in ending violence as the comparison approach, and in none of the studies was there any evidence that a dyadic intervention increased danger to either partner. Furthermore, the reported dropout rates from the couples programs in all but one program was lower than the overall dropout rate of 50% reported by O'Leary (2002) for batterer programs. Thus, evidence supports the idea that a couple-based intervention is appropriate and safe for some couples once violence has occurred. However, we believe that such treatment is different from regular outpatient marital therapy; thorough screening of participants and structural changes to therapy to promote continued monitoring of safety and the appropriateness of conjoint interventions are necessary. In the next section, we discuss the procedures we use in the DVFCT program.

PROTOCOL OF DOMESTIC VIOLENCE
FOCUSED COUPLES TREATMENT

For the past 10 years, we have developed and refined a model of treatment for IPV called DVFCT. A quasi-experimental outcome evaluation of the approach has been published (Stith et al., 2004) and was discussed earlier in this chapter. We have also published a series of articles on the clinical procedures we use in the treatment (Rosen et al., 2003; Stith, McCollum, et al., 2002; Stith, Rosen, & McCollum, 2002; Stith et al., 2005; Tucker, Stith, Howell, McCollum, & Rosen, 2000). In this section, we describe the program's basic protocol.

Treatment Goals and Format

The overall treatment model is solution focused. The goals of the treatment include (a) ending of all forms of violence (e.g., psychological, sexual, physical), (b) increasing positive affect and experience between partners, and (c) increasing partners' responsibility for their own behavior. DVFCT is designed to be delivered in 18 weeks through either a multicouple group format or a single-couple format. Regardless of format, the preferred delivery of the program is through cotherapy teams. Because the treatment lasts only 18 weeks, the primary goal of DVFCT is to end all forms of violence between partners. Some couples who complete the program continue in an alumni group that meets every other week or monthly, depending on the needs of the group, and some participate in further therapy to address addiction, trauma, and other serious issues that may get in the way of the couple having the type of relationship they prefer. We believe the program is successful if the physical and psychological violence has been eliminated or markedly reduced, but we do not expect all individual and relationship issues to be resolved in 18 weeks.

Assumptions Guiding Domestic Violence Focused Couples Treatment

A number of assumptions guide our program. A primary one is that violence is a choice. Although the treatment we provide is based on a systemic understanding of relationships, we do not believe that any behavior of a partner is a justification for violence. Each person makes choices about how to respond to provocations from his or her partner, and we work to encourage both partners to take responsibility for their choices.

The second assumption that guides our work is that safety is paramount. As we will describe, we have instituted a number of safeguards to enhance safety, and we encourage clinicians who deliver the program to disregard the treatment manual if they have any concerns that the protocol will compro-

mise the safety of a particular couple. For example, if the manualized protocol indicates that the couple should be seen together in a particular session
but the couple comes in angry, the cotherapists may choose to see each partner individually.

The final assumption that guides our work is that different treatments
fit different types of violence. We do not believe that couples treatment is
appropriate for all types of IPV. This treatment is designed for couples experiencing situational violence.

Screening Criteria

We use a variety of criteria to determine whether a couple is appropriate for the treatment program. We always interview the man and woman
separately so that we can gather accurate data and not endanger either partner who might disclose difficult material. We ask the man and woman to
complete the same set of assessment tools, including the Revised Conflict
Tactics Scale (CTS2; Straus, Hamby, Boney-McCoy, & Sugarman, 1996).
The CTS2 asks the man to report about the frequency and seriousness of his
own abusive behavior (physical, psychological, and sexual) directed toward
his female partner and also asks him to report the frequency and seriousness
of the woman's abusive behavior directed toward him. The woman fills out
the same questionnaire and reports her abusive behavior directed at the man
and his abusive behavior directed at her.

We meet with each partner separately to find out why they are interested in the program and if they are feeling coerced into participating. We
also ask whether they have any fear for their continued safety if they speak
honestly about their concerns in front of their partner.

Many couples may be afraid that confronting their partner may hurt
their partner's feelings or may make him or her angry, but most couples do
not think that speaking freely will lead their partner to be violent. We exclude couples who are fearful about speaking freely. We also exclude couples
with serious untreated mental health or substance abuse issues. Because substance abuse is often associated with IPV, we do address substance abuse
issues in our treatment program, but we do not provide primary substance
abuse treatment or have the ability to deal with untreated abuse or dependence. Couples included in the program must have some desire to try to
maintain the relationship and must have experienced at least one act of physical aggression in the past year or ongoing psychological violence.

To help us determine whether couples should be excluded from the
program, we compare each potential participant's responses on the CTS2
with his or her partner's responses. At one time, we automatically excluded
couples if either partner reported receiving any acts of severe violence (e.g.,
choking, using a weapon, hitting with a fist). Although we continue to be
very concerned about severe violence, we are now more concerned if there is

a significant discrepancy between what one partner reports about his or her own perpetrating behavior compared with the other partner's reports of abusive behavior received from that partner.

For example, if a wife reports that her husband raped her and beat her up, and the husband reports that he shoved and pushed his wife in the past year but does not admit to beating her up or sexually assaulting her, we would probably exclude the couple. We would be concerned both that the level of violence perpetrated by the husband had been too high to safely begin treatment with a couples intervention and that the husband was not admitting to a very high level of violence. In this case, we could not directly address the extent of violence occurring in the relationship without potentially endangering the wife. But if both partners report independently that the husband choked the wife and that this incident was what led them to know they needed help, we may decide to allow them to begin treatment.

Gender-Specific 6-Week Program

DVFCT begins with a 6-week gender-specific treatment program. During the first 6 weeks of the program, five of the sessions are delivered separately to the male and female clients, either individually or in a men's or women's group. The goals of the 6-week program are to (a) provide psychoeducation about domestic violence, (b) increase participants' comfort level, (c) screen for safety of conjoint interventions, and (d) increase participants' sense of individual responsibility for their own behavior. If, at the end of the 6-week program, therapists are concerned that a participant continues to blame the partner, takes no responsibility for his or her own violence, and behaves aggressively in the session, the couple will be referred to individual treatment or to a community batterer intervention and victims' assistance program before beginning couples treatment.

The 6-week gender-specific treatment program has a set agenda for each session. In the first session, one cotherapist meets with the man and one with the woman (or men's and women's groups). The purpose of the 1st week is to listen to the participant's story and begin to build the alliance between therapist and client. It is important that each partner feels respected and supported in their commitment to develop a relationship free of psychological and physical violence. Previous research has found that the formation of a positive alliance between the therapist and each member of the couple is related to decreases in husband-to-wife psychological aggression and in mild and severe physical aggression (Brown & O'Leary, 2000).

The second session is the only session in the first 6 weeks that is conjoint. Couples meet together with the cotherapists to develop a vision of their preferred outcome. In the single-couple condition, the cotherapists spend the entire session using the miracle question, a solution-focused brief therapy (SFBT) intervention designed to help clients envision their lives without the problems that brought them to therapy and to anchor that vision in specific and concrete aspects of daily life (for a more extensive description, see de Shazer et al., 2007). The general form of the miracle questions is as follows:

> Now I want to ask you a strange question. Suppose that while you are sleeping tonight and the entire house is quiet, a miracle happens. The miracle is that the problem that brought you here is solved. However, because you are sleeping, you don't know that the miracle has happened. So, when you wake up tomorrow morning, what will be different that will tell you a miracle has happened and the problem that brought you here is solved? (De Jong & Berg, 1998, p. 77–78)

As couples answer this question, they begin to describe—in specific detail, because the miracle must be discovered in the routines of daily life—what would happen in the absence of the problem they are struggling with. This helps clients define their preferred outcome, sets the stage for exploring in therapy exceptions to the problem—that is, times when the problem did not happen and something positive happened instead—and begins to shift the clients toward progressive descriptions of change and improvement rather than descriptions of static states of dysfunction. As each member of the couple answers this question (and the answers may be different for each), the therapist also weaves in reflexive questions—how the occurrence of one partner's miracle would change the interaction between the two. This process makes the miracle interactional as well as individual and sets the stage for a joint exploration of ways the miracle could occur in real life.

In the multicouple group, the cotherapists work with the group to define their vision of a healthy relationship. This discussion can be very difficult for clients who are used to focusing on problems. We ask them, instead of focusing on problems, to focus on what they would like to see in their relationships, and we use focused questions to help them describe these qualities as specifically and clearly as they can. We schedule this visioning session early in the treatment so that we can let the clients' goals and visions guide the rest of treatment.

During the third session, we provide psychoeducation on IPV. One cotherapist meets with the man and one with the woman (or men's and women's groups). We give clients handouts on the different types of abuse and discuss examples of each. In the multicouple group, we use a version of an activity "The House of Abuse," developed by the Wilder Foundation, (Matthews, 1995). In this activity, we draw a house with many rooms on the blackboard. We label each room with a different type of abuse—for example, *gender privilege* (e.g., men shouldn't have to wash dishes, women know what's best for children), *physical abuse, psychological abuse, power* and *control,* intimidation—and ask group members to offer examples of these types of behaviors. Both men and women are often surprised at the types of behaviors that can be considered abusive. A woman in one of our groups commented, "You mean it's abusive when I throw a chair at my husband?" After labeling all the rooms in the house, we erase the *physical abuse* label and ask participants if this is a house they would want to live in and would want their child to live in. This activity helps them consider how abuse is much more than physical abuse and how creating a healthy home environment means eliminating more than physical abuse. In both single-couple and multicouple groups, the therapists use this exercise to help clients take responsibility for their own abusive behavior.

Week 4 focuses on two issues, mindfulness and safety planning. The therapists teach clients a basic form of mindfulness meditation using a word or phrase (see Carrington, 1998, for instructions on teaching this approach). Mindfulness is used to promote increased physiological awareness of escalation signals and of the need for self-soothing during time-outs or other times of emotional intensity. Clients are encouraged to practice meditation regularly at home. After Week 4, we begin each session with a brief (e.g., 10-minute) period of meditation by therapists and clients together to reinforce this practice and begin the session in a relatively calm atmosphere.

During Week 4, we also work with clients to develop clear safety plans for keeping themselves safe if tension increases when they begin conjoint work. We ensure that female clients have information about local victim advocate and shelter services. We talk with them about where they might go if violence escalates and how they can be prepared. We ask each client to develop a plan with strategies they can use to keep increases in tension in their relationship from escalating into violence.

Week 5 focuses on the development of a negotiated time-out (for details, see Rosen et al., 2003). This time-out is different from what is normally taught in a men's group, because each couple works together to develop a plan that works for them.

The final week of the 6-week pretreatment program involves motivational interviewing regarding substance abuse. This program is optional, depending on whether substance use is a problem for either partner. In this session, we use motivational interviewing techniques to talk about alcohol and drug use and its consequences for clients. We make a clear recommendation that people in abusive relationships abstain from alcohol and drug use; however, they are the only ones who can choose whether or not that fits for them. This session is designed to help them think about the pros and cons of their own substance use and decide what, if anything, they want to do about it.

We begin by giving clients (in separate-gender sessions) information about the relationship between IPV and substance abuse. Research on alcohol abuse and domestic violence makes it clear that people with drinking problems are at high risk to be abusive toward their partners. However, it is also clear that many people who have drinking problems do not abuse their partners and that some people who do not have drinking problems abuse their partners. We recommend abstinence because alcohol and drug use is known to impair thinking and judgment, produce changes in mood and behavior, reduce inhibition, and increase aggression. We recommend the "better safe than sorry" route. We give them information about how much alcohol use represents problem drinking and ask them to think about (and/or talk about) the impact of drinking or drug use on their lives. We also ask them to think about the good and not-so-good things about drinking. Finally, we ask them to make plans for their future regarding their drug and alcohol use. We ask them to seal their plans in an envelope, and we give them back their plans at the end of treatment.

12-Week Conjoint Treatment

The next 12 weeks consist of primarily conjoint sessions. Although many couples are eager to begin this phase of treatment, there is often some anxiety about changing the format. To enhance safety and to continue the support from the single-gender groups and/or the one-one-one therapy, we use a specific format.

Each session begins with a 15-minute separate-gender session that includes a 10-minute centering meditation and a review of the good things that happened in the past week. Therapists use this time to check whether any physical or psychological violence occurred during the preceding week.

After the separate-gender session, the cotherapists meet privately to finalize plans for the session. If violence has recurred and both partners reported the same incident, the cotherapists may decide to use the session to talk about improving the time-out plan or to brainstorm other strategies to reduce escalation. If the violence recurred but the perpetrator did not report the violence and the victim is fearful about the perpetrator knowing he or she reported the violence, the cotherapists may decide to hold separate sessions. Successes are highlighted in the couples session. If couples face challenges, such as not being successful with using time-outs, guidelines are revisited and/or challenges are addressed.

At the end of the conjoint session, the couple meets again in separate-gender sessions. The purpose of the postsession meeting is to ensure that both partners are calm and that any difficult issues addressed in the conjoint session have not led either partner to begin to escalate. If a partner is angry, the cotherapist working with that partner may have him or her use the centering meditation again or may simply review the strategies developed earlier to increase the partner's feeling of calm.

The conjoint session is guided by an SFBT framework (de Shazer et al., 2007). SFBT is a future- and goal-oriented approach that asks clients to define what life would be like for them in the absence of the problem (work already begun in our model through the asking of the miracle question in Week 2) and then helping couples move toward this vision. It assumes that no problem occurs all the time and that the times when problems do not occur (known as *exceptions*) provide clues to how solutions can be constructed. Thus, therapists carefully examine successes the couples report to tease out the ingredients of change that can be reproduced.

SFBT further assumes that small steps can have a large impact and that the future is both created and negotiable. A created and negotiable future orients therapists toward seeing clients and their relationships as works continually in progress, even when they appear to be stuck. This mind-set casts the future as a hopeful place where people are not defined by an unchangeable past or immutable psychological problem that will lead only to further poor functioning. The therapist's task is to help clients find the courage to trust this vision. SFBT work involves careful and thoughtful questions, turning attention to exceptions when the client is tempted to describe problems in great detail, punctuating and complimenting successes, and maintaining the stance that the client is the expert on his or her life.

Although we prefer to work from the solution-focused stance, we are also aware that IPV presents situations in which there is genuine risk. In dealing with this reality, we have embraced Wile's (1993) idea that therapists have primary and secondary "pictures," or operating stances. When constraints arise that prevent the use of the primary stance, the therapist moves to a secondary picture—one that may contain actions or interventions seemingly at odds with the primary stance. Thus, when a constraint such as a heightened risk of violence arises in our work, we temporarily abandon our preferred, solution-focused picture in favor of a more directive and expert stance that may involve direct teaching of skills, directives to separate temporarily, recommendations to use police or court intervention, or other actions that will help to ensure safety. It is not uncommon for us to move to a more expert stance that involves direct teaching of skills, such as active listening or revisiting time-outs, but it is much more uncommon for us to recommend that individuals take such actions as filing a protective order. When safety is restored, we can then return to our preferred, solution-focused model.

Describing the conjoint portion of this work in a step-by-step form is difficult because this stage of treatment relies on helping clients develop their own vision and work toward that vision. In general, this is a process of noticing exceptions, encouraging more of what works, and punctuating and emphasizing movement toward the goal. Therapists are more active in the early stages of conjoint work, when evidence of change can be minimal. However, as successes mount, clients become more and more convinced of the possibility of a different life and feel more and more ownership of the progress they have made.

BEST PRACTICES IN COUPLES TREATMENT OF INTIMATE PARTNER VIOLENCE

From our work and the work of others, we have developed six recommendations for best practices in couples treatment of IPV, regardless of the model used:

1. *Coordinated community response.* Clinicians working with couples who have experienced psychological or physical violence need to work in the context of a coordinated community response. They need to become familiar with the victim support, batterer intervention, substance abuse treatment, and legal and criminal justice services in their community and be prepared to work with different entities to provide comprehensive services to their clients.

2. *Screening to ensure safety.* If therapists are going to safely treat a couple who has experienced violence, they need to carefully screen each participant. Couples should be assessed individually for level of violence received and perpetrated and for the presence of fear, substance abuse, and serious mental health difficulties. Couples treatment is probably not appropriate for all couples, and therapists need to determine if the couple they are seeing is appropriate for this type of treatment.

3. *Couples treatment to address domestic violence.* Although there are no data on the relative effectiveness of couples treatment with no modifications to address IPV versus couples treatment that has been modified to address IPV, we believe that when there has been substantial physical and/or psychological abuse, couples treatment needs to be adapted to address these issues.

4. *Need to ensure safety.* Therapists working with couples experiencing IPV need to ensure that conjoint treatment does not increase the risk for ongoing violence. We have used separate check-in sessions, individual screening, and IPV interventions such as time-outs to enhance safety for couples who are addressing difficult issues.

5. *Ongoing monitoring of level of violence throughout program.* Therapists may decide to proceed with conjoint treatment based on the initial screening, but we believe that it is important to monitor ongoing violence by meeting separately with clients and/or using screening instruments to assess for violence throughout the treatment.

6. *Need for therapist skills in both domestic violence and systemic couples therapy.* Therapists must be skilled in working with high-intensity couples and need a solid knowledge of IPV.

They may believe that a couple is experiencing situational violence, but as more information is obtained, they may find that power and control is a key dynamic. Without understanding IPV, they may miss cues that the situation is more dangerous than they initially thought.

CONCLUSION

There is general consensus from members of the three different research groups that have evaluated treatment programs for individuals with IPV that couples approaches definitely have a place in the reduction of IPV. Fals-Stewart and his colleagues, who have worked with substance abusers, provide documentation in chapter 12 of this volume that a couples-based approach can clearly lead to a reduction in physical aggression against a partner. O'Leary and Cohen (2007 provided their own recommendations about the types of clients that appear to be best suited for a couples-based intervention when physical aggression is evident. And we have provided our own perspective in this chapter on a couples-based approach to reduce psychological and physical aggression in a relationship.

We have only minimal data about the predictors of success and failure in such programs, and different proponents of a couples approach have slightly different qualifications about the types of clients that may best profit from such interventions. Given the relatively poor outcomes that have been found with batterers programs (Babcock et al., 2004), however, it seems prudent to keep our minds open to new perspectives and approaches to reduce psychological and physical aggression in relationships.

REFERENCES

Babcock, J. C., Canady, B., Graham, K. H., & Schart, L. (2007). The evolution of battering interventions: From the Dark Ages into the Scientific Age. In J. Hamel & T. Nicholls (Eds.), *Family therapy for domestic violence: A practitioner's guide to gender-inclusive research and treatment* (pp. 215–246). New York: Springer.

Babcock, J. C., Green, C. E., & Robie, C. (2004). Does batterers' treatment work? A meta-analytic review of domestic violence treatment. *Clinical Psychology Review, 23,* 1023–1053.

Brannen, S. J., & Rubin, A. (1996). Comparing the effectiveness of gender-specific and couples groups in a court-mandated spouse abuse treatment program. *Research on Social Work Practice, 6,* 405–424.

Brown, P. D., & O'Leary, K. D. (2000). Therapeutic alliance: Predicting continuance and success in group treatment for spouse abuse. *Journal of Consulting and Clinical Psychology, 68,* 340–345.

Capaldi, D. M., Shortt, J. W., & Crosby, L. (2003). Physical and psychological aggression in at-risk young couples: Stability and change in young adulthood. *Merrill-Palmer Quarterly, 49*, 1–27.

Carrington, P. (1998). *The book of meditation: The complete guide to modern meditation.* Boston: Element Books.

De Jong, P., & Berg, I. K. (1998). *Interviewing for solutions.* Pacific Grove, CA: Brooks/ Cole.

de Shazer, S., Dolan, Y., Korman, H., Trepper, T., McCollum, E., & Berg, I. (2007). *More than miracles: The state of the art of solution-focused brief therapy.* New York: Haworth Press.

Dutton, D. G., & Corvo, K. (2006). Transforming a flawed policy: A call to revive psychology and science in domestic violence research and practice. *Aggression and Violent Behavior, 11*, 457–483.

Fals-Stewart, W., Kashdan, T. B., O'Farrell, T. J., & Birchler, G. R. (2002). Behavioral couples therapy for drug abusing patients: Effects on partner violence. *Journal of Substance Abuse Treatment, 22*, 87–96.

Fals-Stewart, W., & Kennedy, C. (2005). Addressing intimate partner violence in substance abuse treatment: Overview, options, and recommendations. *Journal of Substance Abuse Treatment, 29*, 5–17.

Feld, S. L., & Straus, M. A. (1989). Escalation and desistance of wife assault in marriage. *Criminology, 27*, 141–161.

Ferraro, K., & Johnson, J. (1983). How women experience battering: The process of victimization. *Social Problems, 30*, 325–339.

Gelles, R. J., & Straus, M. A. (1988). *Intimate violence: The causes and consequences of abuse in the American family.* New York: Simon and Schuster.

Gondolf, E. W. (1988). Who are those guys? Toward a behavioral typology of batterers. *Violence and Victims, 3*, 187–203.

Hart, B. (1988). *Safety for women: Monitoring batterers' programs* [Manual]. Harrisburg: Pennsylvania Coalition Against Domestic Violence.

Heyman, R. E., Brown, P. D., Feldbau-Kohn, R. R., & O'Leary, K. D. (1999). Couples communication behaviors as predictors of dropout and treatment response in wife abuse treatment programs. *Behavior Therapy, 30*, 165–189.

Holtzworth-Munroe, A., & Stuart, G. L. (1994). Typologies of male batterers: Three subtypes and the differences among them. *Psychological Bulletin, 116*, 476–497.

Jacobson, N. S., & Gottman, J. M. (1998). *When men batter women: New insights into ending abusive relationships.* New York: Simon and Schuster.

Johnson, M. P., & Ferraro, K. J. (2000). Research on domestic violence in the 1990s: Making distinctions. *Journal of Marriage and the Family, 62*, 948–963.

Leone, J. M., Johnson, M. P., Cohan, C. L., & Lloyd, S. E. (2004). Consequences of male partner violence for low-income minority women. *Journal of Marriage and Family, 66*, 472–491.

Maiuro, R. D., & Eberle, J. A. (2008). State standards for domestic violence perpetrator treatment: Current status, trends, and recommendations. *Violence and Victims, 23*, 133–155.

Matthews, D. (1995). *Foundations for violence-free living: A step-by-step guide to facilitating men's domestic abuse groups*, St. Paul, MN: Amherst H. Wilder Foundation.

McCollum, E. E., & Stith, S. M. (2007). Conjoint couple's treatment for intimate partner violence: Controversy and promise. *Journal of Couple and Relationship Therapy*, 6(1/2), 71–82.

Moffit, T. E., Robins, R.W., & Caspi, A. (2001). A couples analysis of partner abuse with implications for abuse-prevention policy. *Criminology & Public Policy*, 1, 5–36.

Neidig, P. H. (1985). Domestic Conflict Containment: A spouse abuse treatment program. *Social Casework: The Journal of Contemporary Social Work*, 66, 195–204.

O'Farrell, T. J., Fals-Stewart, W., Murphy, C. M., Stephan, S. H., & Murphy, M. (2004). Partner violence before and after couples-based alcoholism treatment for male alcoholic patients: The role of treatment involvement and abstinence. *Journal of Consulting and Clinical Psychology*, 72, 202–217.

O'Leary, K. D. (2002). Conjoint therapy for partners who engage in physically aggressive behavior: Rationale and research. *Journal of Aggression, Maltreatment & Trauma*, 5, 145–164.

O'Leary, K. D., & Cohen, S. (2007). Treatment of psychological and physical aggression in a couple context. In J. Hamel & T. Nicholls (Eds.), *Family therapy for domestic violence: A practitioner's guide to gender-inclusive research and treatment* (pp. 363–380). New York: Springer.

O'Leary, K. D., Heyman, R. E., & Neidig, P. H. (1999). Treatment of wife abuse: A comparison of gender-specific and conjoint approaches. *Behavior Therapy*, 30, 475–505.

O'Leary, K. D., Vivian, D., & Malone, J. (1992). Assessment of physical aggression against women in marriage: The need for multimodal assessment. *Behavioral Assessment*, 14, 5–14.

Rosen, K. H., Matheson, J. L, Stith, S. M., McCollum, E. E., & Locke, L. D. (2003). Negotiated time-out: A de-escalation tool for couples. *Journal of Marital & Family Therapy*, 29, 291–298.

Rosen, K. H., Stith, S. M., Few, A. L., Daly, K. L., & Tritt, D. R. (2005). A qualitative investigation of Johnson's typology. *Violence and Victims*, 20, 319–334.

Schechter, S. (1987). *Guidelines for mental health practitioners in domestic violence cases*. Washington, DC: National Coalition Against Domestic Violence.

Stith, S. M., McCollum, E. E., Rosen, K. H., & Locke, L. D. (2002). Multicouple group treatment for domestic violence. In F. Kaslow (Ed.), *Comprehensive textbook of psychotherapy* (Vol. 4, pp. 499–520). New York: Wiley.

Stith, S. M., McCollum, E. E., Rosen, K. H., Locke, L., & Goldberg, P. (2005). Domestic violence focused couples treatment. In J. Lebow (Ed.), *Handbook of clinical family therapy* (pp. 406–430). New York: Wiley.

Stith, S. M., Rosen, K. H., Barasch, S. G., & Wilson, S. M. (1991). Clinical research as a training opportunity: Bridging the gap between theory and practice. *Journal of Marital & Family Therapy*, 17, 349–353.

Stith, S. M., Rosen, K. H., & McCollum, E. E. (2002). Developing a manualized couples treatment for domestic violence: Overcoming challenges. *Journal of Marital & Family Therapy, 28*, 21–26.

Stith, S. M., Rosen, K. H., & McCollum, E. E. (2003). Effectiveness of couples treatment for spouse abuse. *Journal of Marital & Family Therapy, 29*, 407–426.

Stith, S. M., Rosen, K. H., McCollum, E. E., & Thomsen, C. J. (2004). Treating intimate partner violence within intact couple relationships: Outcomes of multicouple versus individual couple therapy. *Journal of Marital & Family Therapy, 30*, 305–318.

Straus, M. A., Hamby, S. L., Boney-McCoy, S., & Sugarman, D. B. (1996). The Revised Conflict Tactics Scales (CTS2): Development and preliminary psychometric data. *Journal of Family Issues, 17*, 283–316.

Sullivan, C. M., & Rumptz, M. H. (1994). Adjustment and needs of African-American women who utilized a domestic violence shelter. *Violence and Victims, 9*, 275–286.

Tucker, L. L., Stith, S. M., Howell, L. W., McCollum, E. E., & Rosen, K. H. (2000). Meta dialogues in solution-oriented domestic violence focused couples treatment. *Journal of Systemic Therapy, 19*, 56–72.

Wile, D. B. (1993). *After the fight: Using your disagreements to build a stronger relationship*. New York: Guilford Press.

12

SUBSTANCE ABUSE AND INTIMATE PARTNER VIOLENCE

WILLIAM FALS-STEWART, KEITH KLOSTERMANN,
AND MONIQUE CLINTON-SHERROD

Although historically considered a private family matter, intimate partner violence (IPV) is now widely recognized as a pervasive public health problem requiring the concerted and coordinated attention of the criminal justice, treatment, prevention, public policy, and research communities. The reasons for the extensive societal focus on IPV are compelling; a large and accumulating body of evidence now clearly reveals that IPV exacts an enormous toll on its victims (e.g., Anderson, 2002), other adult and child family members in homes where it occurs (e.g., Kitzmann, Gaylord, Holt, & Kenny, 2003), and society more broadly (e.g., in terms of societal economic burden; National Center for Injury Prevention and Control, 2003).

As with many of today's most pressing social ills (e.g., obesity, HIV), the etiology and maintenance of IPV appear to be influenced by many interrelated and interacting factors, including those that operate at the genomic, biological, individual, dyad, family, and community levels (see Stith, Smith, Penn, Ward, & Tritt, 2004). Among the many factors that have been implicated in the occurrence of IPV, few have stirred more controversy or heated debate than the role of alcohol consumption and other drug use. Although there is now little debate that drinking and drug use are very often elements of IPV episodes, there is far less agreement as to whether substance use and abuse plays a facilitative causal role in partner aggression, provides an excuse or is otherwise a mitigating factor for its occurrence, or is simply a spurious correlate. Given the controversy surrounding the role of substance use in IPV, it is, in turn, not clear whether to address the substance use and IPV sequentially or concurrently.

In this chapter, we explore various aspects of the link between substance use and IPV and their implications for intervention. We highlight (a) the nature and reasons for the controversy regarding the link between IPV and substance use, (b) competing theoretical explanations regarding why there appears to be such a robust association between these behaviors, (c) evidence for and against the causal role substance use may play in IPV, (d) factors that moderate this relationship, and (e) the role of substance use in IPV victimization. We also provide an overview of intervention approaches for co-occurring IPV and substance use, including ones that are most commonly used (i.e., those that focus singularly on only one of these problems), as well as available treatments that focus on both IPV and substance abuse. Conclusions and recommendations for future directions are also briefly discussed.

LINK BETWEEN INTIMATE PARTNER VIOLENCE AND SUBSTANCE USE

The occurrence of violence between intimate partners is thought to be the consequence of several interrelated and interacting factors operating at different levels (e.g., contextual, social, biological, psychological, personality), which exert their influence at different times, under different circumstances, acting in a probabilistic fashion (Crowell & Burgess, 1996). Among the various factors that have been delineated in conceptual and predictive models of IPV, drinking and drug use are among the most controversial and widely debated. Although the preponderance of evidence clearly reveals that those who engage in IPV are often intoxicated or have problems with alcohol or drug abuse (e.g., Foran & O'Leary, 2008), there is considerable debate as to whether substance use simply covaries with partner violence, is inherently facilitative or a contributing cause of IPV, or is simply an excuse for aggression. The implications of the debate are important; if intoxication is causally implicated in IPV, it would follow that interventions that are successful in reducing substance use could reduce or eliminate the occurrence of partner violence.

Theoretical Conceptualizations

Leonard and Quigley (1999) captured the essential elements of the debate when they described three explanatory models that have been used to explain the fairly high co-occurrence of substance use in episodes of IPV. In the *spurious effects model*, the relationship between substance use and IPV appears to exist but disappears when another variable or variables are controlled. As an example, individuals who are young may have a general propensity to solve conflict by using violence and aggression and also have a tendency to drink and use other drugs; thus, substance use and violence may appear to be directly related in these individuals when, in fact, they are not. More specifically, the relationship between substance use and violence is spurious because it would disappear if age was controlled.

According to the *indirect effects model*, chronic drinking and other drug use are viewed as being deleterious to intimate relationships, but the discordant intimate relationship leads directly to IPV. Thus, long-term substance use helps create a dyadic and familial context conducive to conflict, thereby increasing the likelihood of partner violence. This model suggests that any relationship between substance use and violence would be fully mediated by relationship quality and satisfaction.

In the *proximal effects model*, intoxication is a causal agent of IPV. Therefore, individuals who consume alcohol or other drugs are more likely to engage in partner violence because intoxication facilitates violence, which may be mediated through psychopharmacologic effects of these psychoactive agents on cognitive processing (e.g., Chermack & Taylor, 1995) or expectancies associated with intoxication (Critchlow, 1983). It follows from this theory that substance use should precede episodes of IPV and, moreover, that episodes of IPV should occur close in time to consumption (i.e., when the perpetrator is intoxicated).

Each model has its proponents and, to some extent, empirical support. However, even when controlling for factors that may account for spurious effects (sociodemographics, personality) or relationship satisfaction as a mediational factor, the association between substance use and violence remains robust among alcoholics and batterers (e.g., Fals-Stewart, 2003). However, it cannot thus be concluded, simply by default, that the proximal effects model is correct; determining causality between variables such as IPV and substance use is complicated by the nature of these behaviors and the methods used to explore the relationship.

Evaluation of the Causal Connection

Randomized clinical trials have evolved as the definitive approach for evaluating causal connections between potential causal factors and behavioral outcomes. However, as with other research endeavors exploring the links among variables implicated in certain disease and harmful behavioral processes (e.g., tobacco use, cancer), ethical considerations and other barriers make it necessary to rely largely on information gathered from observational studies to ascertain potential causal connections.

In his now classic article, Hill (1965) outlined several conditions needed to establish a causal relationship between two variables in observational and epidemiological research: (a) consistency of association across multiple studies using different methods, (b) strength of association, (c) evidence of a dose–response relationship, (d) coherence (i.e., is the association consistent with a currently accepted theoretical understanding of the relationship between social and biological processes?), (e) evidence of the correct temporal precedence (i.e., the causal variable occurs before the response), (f) experimental evidence indicating that changes in the proposed causal variable yield changes in the outcome, and (g) rejection of plausible alternative explanations. Using these criteria prompts the question, What is the evidence that alcohol and other drug use are causal factors in IPV?

Consistency of Association

Results of multiple investigations reveal consistency in the relationship between the occurrence of IPV episodes and substance use by the male partner, the female partner, or both. In a national sample of 5,159 families, Kaufman Kantor and Strauss (1990) found that more than 20% of men and 10% of women were drinking before the most recent and severe act of violence. In the National Crime Victimization Survey (Bureau of Justice Statistics, 1998), 43% of the victims of IPV reported that the perpetrator had been under the influence of drugs. Studies of college populations, which often focus on sexual violence forms of IPV, have found that 50% of assaults involve alcohol (Abbey, 2002). Among prisoners convicted of murdering an intimate partner, 45% reported that they were drinking at the time of the incident, with an average blood alcohol concentration of 3 times the legal limit. For married or cohabiting patients entering treatment for alcoholism and other drugs of abuse, the proportion of dyads reporting at least one episode of IPV in the previous year is 4 to 6 times higher than observed in national samples (Fals-Stewart, 2003; O'Farrell & Murphy, 1995). In addition, the strong relationship between alcohol use and perpetration of IPV has been found in primary health care settings (McCauley et al., 1995), family practice clinics (Oriel & Flemming, 1998), prenatal clinics (Muhajarine & D'Arcy, 1999), and rural health clinics (Van Hightower & Gorton, 1998).

Although most studies to date have focused largely on men and their substance use, it also appears that substance use is associated with increased partner aggression among women. Cunradi, Caetano, Clark, and Schafer (1999) found that couples in which the female partner had alcohol-related problems were 6 times more likely to experience episodes of female-to-male IPV than couples who reported no female alcohol problems. In a sample of 126 female patients entering substance abuse treatment, more than half reported instances of IPV in the previous year (Chermack, Walton, Fuller, & Blow, 2001).

Research examining the link between use of drugs other than alcohol and IPV is not as well developed. However, recent studies reveal associations between drug use and partner aggression similar to those found with alcohol. As an example, Brookoff, O'Brien, Cook Thompson, and Williams (1997) reported that 92% of partners who engaged in IPV used alcohol or drugs on the day of the episode. Additionally, available evidence indicates that roughly half of substance-abusing men entering treatment have engaged in IPV (e.g., Easton, Swan, & Sinha, 2000).

Strength of Association

The link between substance use and IPV appears to be very robust. Fals-Stewart (2003) found that for men entering a domestic violence treatment program, the odds of any male-to-female physical aggression were more than 8 times higher on days when men drank than on days of no alcohol consumption. The odds of severe male-to-female physical aggression were more than 11 times higher on days of men's drinking than on days of no drinking. In the same report, similar results were found in a sample of men entering alcoholism treatment. The findings of the study were replicated with another sample of those who primarily abused drugs other than alcohol, with cocaine use also being implicated in episodes of IPV (Fals-Stewart, Golden, & Schumacher, 2003).

Dose–Response Relationship

There is also evidence supporting a dose–response relationship between substance use and IPV. Schumacher, Felbau-Kohn, Smith Slep, and Heyman (2001) reviewed five studies examining the association between men's drug use and male-to-female IPV and found effect sizes ranging from .22 to .65, all in the direction of increased drug dependence being associated with greater risk of IPV. O'Leary and Schumacher (2003) analyzed this relationship in data collected as part of two nationally representative samples, the National Family Violence Survey and the National Survey of Families and Households. Men in both samples were classified into similar drinking groups ranging from abstainers to heavy and binge drinkers. For both samples, there was a significant positive linear association between percentage of men who had engaged in any IPV and drinking classification. However, the associated effect sizes were small, and distinctions in drinking patterns may be more important than incremental increases in quantity or frequency when evaluating the alcohol–IPV link.

Theoretical Coherence

The relationship between substance use and IPV is theoretically coherent. This association is consistent with what has sometimes been described as a multiple threshold model (Fals-Stewart, Leonard, & Birchler, 2005), which assumes that aggression occurs when the strength of a given provocation exceeds the strength of inhibitions against aggression. There are multiple thresholds in operation because aggressive inhibitions are assumed to be greater for severe violence than for less severe violence. The psychopharmacological effects of drug intoxication are viewed as leading to a lowering of inhibition against aggression and to impairment of cognitive processes (Chermack & Taylor, 1995).

Temporal Sequence

Perhaps the key argument against the proximal effects model is that studies have generally failed to demonstrate the temporal precedence of alcohol or drug use in episodes of IPV (e.g., Gelles, 1993). Recently, however, several longitudinal studies of alcohol use and IPV have indeed established the appropriate temporal ordering and have shown that episodes tend to occur close in time to drinking. Fals-Stewart (2003) collected detailed diaries from male partners with a history of IPV entering either an alcoholism or a domestic violence treatment program, as well as their female partners, over an extended follow-up period (i.e., 15 months). The diaries contained information not only about the occurrence of male-to-female aggression but also about (a) the time of day these episodes happened, (b) whether the male partner drank alcohol during the same day the violence occurred, and (c) what time of day the drinking occurred. This information allowed for a detailed examination of the daily temporal relationship between male-to-female physical aggression and alcohol consumption. In both samples, more than 60% of all IPV episodes occurred within 2 hours of drinking by the male partner. The findings of the study were recently replicated in a separate investigation that used a sample of men entering treatment for drug abuse (Fals-Stewart et al., 2003).

Experimental Evidence

Although there is little experimental evidence that directly addresses the role of substance use in the occurrence of IPV, the results of available experimental studies exploring substance use and aggressive behavior in different contexts provide support for this relationship. Several laboratory investigations have found that drug use by study participants led to increased aggression as measured by levels of shock administered to a confederate participant (Bushman, 1997; Richardson, 1981). These results provide important evidence for the link between alcohol use and aggression.

Marital interaction experiments have also been conducted to explore the effects of alcohol on negative verbal behavior. Leonard and Roberts (1998) asked intimate partners about an important conflict and then asked them to discuss their most serious area of conflict after the male partner received (a) no alcohol, (b) an active placebo, or (c) an intoxicating dose of alcohol. The intoxicating dose of alcohol led to increased negativity over baseline sessions. Neither the no-alcohol nor the placebo condition led to increased negativity. Although there are exceptions (Frankenstein, Hay, & Nathan, 1982), studies in this area support the hypothesis that the administration of alcohol in the context of marital conflict seems to increase negative interactions (Jacob & Leonard, 1988; Jacob, Leonard, & Haber, 2001). Many limitations of laboratory aggression studies noted earlier are not shared by the marital interaction experiments. The conflicts in the marital interaction studies occurred between intimate partners who used a range of responses they were likely to use in other dyadic conflict situations.

Plausible Alternative Explanations

Perhaps the weakest element of the argument supporting the causal relationship between substance use and IPV is the rejection of plausible alternative explanations. In particular, it may be difficult to reject the hypothesis that an individual who—for various preexisting reasons—wishes to engage in violence against his partner may subsequently use drugs to facilitate such an event. Thus, as opposed to the physiological disinhibition that is assumed in the multiple threshold model described earlier, this conceptualization assumes that individuals consciously use substances in order to be violent and that intoxication provides an excuse for the behavior.

Some investigators have explored this explanation for the relationship between alcohol use and violence; overall, the results have been mixed. In most of the studies, college students were provided short scenarios describing episodes of IPV and then were asked to assign responsibility for the violence. Although some investigators have found that an intoxicated man was assigned less blame than a sober one (e.g., Richardson & Campbell, 1980), others have found the opposite effect (e.g., Leigh & Aramburu, 1994), and still other studies have found no effect of intoxication on the blame assigned to the perpetrator (e.g., Dent & Arias, 1990).

Senchak and Leonard (1994) examined blame attributions for actual male-to-female aggression episodes among IPV perpetrators and victims. They found that husbands who had engaged in more severe violence were more likely to assume responsibility for the episode when drinking than when they were sober. Interestingly, wives did not alter their view of who was responsible for the IPV regardless of whether or not their husbands were drinking.

Several studies have also explored the effect of alcohol use on the actions of treatment providers and representatives of the criminal justice system (e.g., police officers, prosecutors). If alcohol is viewed as an excuse or mitigating factor in episodes of violence, drinking by a husband or wife in an episode of IPV might influence such decisions as referral for treatment or likelihood of arrest. The results of investigations exploring this issue have concluded that alcohol is not viewed as an excuse for violence; in fact, intoxication among perpetrators of IPV was more likely to result in punitive actions by treatment providers (e.g., Stewart & Maddren, 1997) and was associated with an increased likelihood of arrest (Hoyle, 1998). Similarly, drinking by a victim of IPV also appears to increase blame directed toward her (e.g., Home, 1994).

When cases of IPV are prosecuted, the fact that violence was committed under the influence of alcohol or other drugs does not appear to mitigate punishment; rather, intoxication leads to an increased likelihood of prosecution (Buzawa & Buzawa, 1990). It has been speculated this is due to a "get tough" attitude toward substance-abusing individuals or a general belief by prosecutors that the recidivism rate of IPV among substance abusers is comparatively high (Leonard, 2001).

Collectively, these findings provide little support for the notion that alcohol is associated with IPV because it is viewed as a factor excusing the behavior. This finding was consistent across several different samples, including college students, perpetrators, victims, and those who interact with offenders and victims of violence. However, it is also important to highlight that although drinking by a perpetrator does not appear to be an excuse for violence, the responsibility appeared to be mitigated when it was the victim who consumed the alcohol.

Summary of Evidence

Given ethical and pragmatic constraints, there is no design that will definitively demonstrate causality between substance use and IPV; the cross-sectional and longitudinal studies could not eliminate the possibility that spurious variables accounted for the observed substance use–IPV link. The available experimental laboratory studies yielded results that may not generalize to natural settings. As Leonard (2005) suggested, the convergence of evidence drawn from many (although individually flawed) sources suggests that intoxication is one of many causes of IPV.

Factors Moderating the Relationship Between Substance Use and Intimate Partner Violence

Evidence indicates that substance use (particularly alcohol) is associated with IPV, yet only a subset of individuals who consume alcohol and other drugs are aggressive, suggesting that certain factors may moderate the IPV–substance use link. Although there might be a variety of potential moderators of the relationship between substance use and IPV, the most consistent moderator appears to be the presence of other factors that are causally implicated in IPV. For example, several studies have found that alcohol consumption is associated with marital violence only among hostile or maritally discordant couples (Leonard & Blane, 1992). Leonard and Quigley (1999) examined factors that moderate the longitudinal relationship between heavy drinking and relationship violence. Findings revealed that heavy drinking predicted subsequent aggression only among couples high in verbally aggressive conflict styles. Collectively, the results of these studies suggest a synergistic effect of alcohol and aggression-provoking factors, an effect that would be consistent with many of the observations and much of the theorizing in the experimental alcohol and aggression research (Steele & Josephs, 1990).

Conversely, there are at least two other studies indicating somewhat different interactions. Blane, Miller, and Leonard (1988) investigated the relationship between alcohol problems and partner violence among men on parole from prison. Current alcohol problems were associated with current partner abuse among men with lower levels of self-reported criminal violence but not among men with high levels of criminal violence. Similarly, Rice and Harris (1995) conducted a longitudinal evaluation of a large sample of violent offenders to determine the factors associated with recidivism to violent behavior. Findings indicated that alcohol abuse was associated with violent recidivism among those who did not have psychopathic personalities but not among those characterized as psychopathic.

To reconcile the aforementioned findings, Fals-Stewart et al. (2005) applied the multiple threshold model described earlier, integrating the main and interactive effects of substance use and antisocial personality characteristics to predict the occurrence of IPV among male partners with a history of male-to-female physical aggression. As noted previously, the multiple threshold model predicts that aggression occurs when the strength of the provocation exceeds the strength of aggressive inhibitions. As such, aggressive inhibitions, in general, are assumed to be higher for severe violence than for nonsevere violence. However, aggressive inhibitions are assumed to be lower for men with antisocial personality characteristics than for men without these personality traits; the role of intoxication in facilitating violence among men with antisocial traits may be reduced because they may have a natural propensity toward aggressive responding even when sober.

Recently, Foran and O'Leary (in press) used the multiple threshold model to explain the relationship between alcohol use and partner violence in a community sample of 453 couples. The investigators found that men with jealousy problems (but not anger control problems) were the most likely to show the strongest association between problem drinking and IPV. In accord with the multiple threshold model, specific combinations of risk factors appeared to represent different thresholds in which problem drinking influenced the likelihood of IPV.

Role of Intoxication in Victimization

A review of the substance use and violence literature concluded the following: (a) Drinking is involved in roughly 50% of all homicides and assaults, (b) alcohol use before a violent episode is high among both perpetrators and victims, and (c) homicide victims are more likely than their assailants to have been intoxicated if they provoked the altercation (Murdoch, Pihl, & Ross, 1990). An overview of studies on IPV and alcohol consumption estimated that the men were drinking when the violence occurred in nearly 50% of the cases, and the women were drinking in about 20% of the cases (Roizen, 1993).

To date, most of the extant literature examining the relationship of IPV and alcohol intoxication has focused on the perpetration of male-to-female physical aggression. Understanding the role of women's alcohol use in occurrences of IPV is complicated by several issues. Because there is a strong relationship between husbands' and wives' drinking patterns (Leonard & Eiden, 1999), it is difficult to disentangle the effects of wives' drinking independent of husbands' drinking. Although some studies have found an association between wives' drinking and IPV after controlling for husbands' drinking (e.g., Kaufman Kantor & Straus, 1990), the results of other investigations indicate that the alcohol–victimization link is negated when husbands' drinking is controlled (e.g., Kaufman Kantor & Asdigian, 1997). In a study of newlywed couples (Leonard & Senchak, 1996), wives' premarital alcohol use was associated with violence during the follow-up period, but this association was attenuated significantly when husbands' alcohol use was controlled. More research is needed in this area; at present, the extent to which wives' alcohol use may increase their vulnerability to victimization remains unclear. It is important to gain a greater understanding of alcohol's role in both perpetration and victimization of IPV to guide intervention policies and treatment programs for IPV.

INTERVENTION CONSIDERATIONS

Given the fairly robust link between substance use and IPV, it begs the question, "How can these co-occurring problems be treated most effectively?" There is, of course, no single correct answer; treatment plans appropriately vary on the basis of the needs of patients, the context where they receive treatment, and the expertise of the care providers. As such, a range of approaches are used in clinical practice, with varying degrees of empirical support.

Substance Abuse Treatment as an Intervention for Intimate Partner Violence

If drinking and drug use are contributing factors in the occurrence of IPV, it would follow that interventions specifically designed to reduce or eliminate substance use might lead to reductions in IPV. Results of recent investigations provide support for this notion. O'Farrell, Fals-Stewart, Murphy, and Murphy (2003) examined IPV among alcoholic men ($N = 301$) entering a typical outpatient substance abuse treatment program that did not focus on IPV. In the year before treatment, 56% of the alcoholic patients had been violent toward their female partners, compared with 14% in a demographically matched nonalcoholic comparison sample. In the year after treatment, IPV decreased to 25% among all treated patients, including only 15% among remitted alcoholics and 32% among relapsed patients.

Although far less research has been done in this area with women alcoholic patients, available results are similar to those obtained with male alcoholic patients. Stuart and colleagues (2002) examined the effect of intensive alcoholism outpatient treatment on IPV perpetration and victimization among female patients. Results revealed a decrease in the prevalence and frequency of partner violence after treatment. Women who relapsed during the 1-year follow-up period were more likely to engage in IPV than those who had not relapsed.

Thus, IPV does appear to decrease after standard alcoholism treatment, especially among patients who did not relapse in the posttreatment period. These findings suggest (but do not prove) that patients who have problems with alcohol or other drugs should receive substance abuse treatment, at least as a component of an overall intervention for IPV. Unfortunately, the primary limitation of standard substance abuse treatment as a stand-alone intervention for IPV is that the violence reductions appear to rely on alcohol or drug abstinence (Fals-Stewart & Kennedy, 2005). Other factors that may contribute to IPV are, for the most part, ignored in standard substance abuse treatment. Given the high relapse rates typically reported for patients after substance abuse treatment, coupled with the manyfold increase in the likelihood of IPV on days of alcohol or other drug use after standard treatment for alcoholism and drug abuse, standard substance abuse treatment may best be viewed as a necessary, but not sufficient, intervention for patients seeking help for alcoholism or drug abuse who have also engaged in IPV.

Despite evidence linking substance use and IPV, many domestic violence treatment programs do only cursory assessments of substance use and abuse by their clients and rarely provide any treatment designed for substance use disorders (Fals-Stewart & Stappenbeck, 2003). This general lack of attention to drinking appears to evolve from a general philosophy that perpetrators use intoxication to eschew responsibility for their actions (e.g., Zubretsky & Knights, 2001). Because interventions in these programs require that clients assume complete responsibility for their behavior and consider that alcohol use is largely or completely irrelevant, highlighting the facilitative role of substance use in partner violence may be viewed as inconsistent with these programs' core philosophies. Such a stance not only denies the potential causal role of drug and alcohol use in IPV but also ignores the fact that material learned during the course of a batterers program when a client is sober may not be readily available in his or her cognitive stores when he or she is intoxicated. More specifically, if there has been no attempt to address alcohol or other drug use, any of the positive effects from lessons learned in treatment may be eliminated if substance use occurs. Thus, it would seem that any intervention that focused exclusively on IPV in cases in which alcohol and other drug use is also part of the clinical presentation would be incomplete.

Integrated Intimate Partner Violence and Substance Abuse Treatment

Although it would seem to follow from the evidence indicating a robust link between substance use and violence that use of integrated interventions designed to address both would be optimal, such approaches are comparatively rare in community practice and in research settings. Those that have been described in the literature, however, have yielded promising results. For example, a partner-involved treatment for alcoholism and substance abuse that has received extensive empirical support for its effectiveness is behavioral couples therapy (BCT). BCT teaches skills that promote partner support for abstinence and also emphasizes amelioration of common relationship problems in these couples (for a review, see Fals-Stewart, O'Farrell, & Birchler, 2004). With respect to partner violence, non-substance-abusing partners are taught certain coping skills and measures to increase safety when faced with a situation where the likelihood of IPV is increased. In particular, this treatment places emphasis on using behaviors that reduce the likelihood of aggression when a partner is intoxicated (e.g., leaving the situation, avoiding conflictual and emotionally laden discussion topics).

A series of studies have examined the effects of BCT on prevalence and frequency of IPV among substance-abusing men and their non-substance-abusing female partners. O'Farrell, Murphy, Stephan, Fals-Stewart, and Murphy (2004) examined partner violence before and after BCT for 303 married or cohabiting male alcoholic patients and used a demographically matched nonalcoholic comparison sample. In the year before BCT, 60% of alcoholic patients had been violent toward their female partners (based on female partners' reports), 5 times the comparison sample rate of 12%. In the year after BCT, violence decreased significantly to 24% in the BCT group but remained higher than the comparison group. Among remitted alcoholics after BCT, violence prevalence reduced to 12%, identical to the comparison sample and less than half the rate among relapsed patients (30%). Results for the 2nd year after BCT yielded similar findings. Chase, O'Farrell, Murphy, Fals-Stewart, and Murphy (2003) reported similar findings with married or cohabiting alcoholic women and their non-substance-abusing male partners who engaged in BCT.

Fals-Stewart, Kashdan, O'Farrell, and Birchler (2002) examined changes in IPV among 80 married or cohabiting drug-abusing patients and their non-substance-abusing female partners randomly assigned to receive either BCT or individual treatment. Although nearly half of the couples in each condition reported male-to-female IPV during the year before treatment, the number reporting violence in the year after treatment was significantly lower for

BCT (17%) than for individual treatment for the male partner only (42%). Mediation analyses indicated that BCT led to greater reductions in IPV because participation in BCT reduced drug use, drinking, and relationship problems to a greater extent than individual treatment.

Importantly, BCT is designed to reduce partner violence even when relapse occurs (i.e., as noted earlier, non-substance-abusing partners develop safety plans, are taught strategies to interact with their intoxicated partners, and so forth). In contrast to traditional individual treatment for substance abuse, BCT does not rely exclusively on abstinence as the mechanism of action for nonviolence. In turn, we would expect differences between traditional substance abuse treatment and BCT in the likelihood of IPV on days of substance use.

Results of a recent study provide initial support for this hypothesis. Fals-Stewart and Clinton-Sherrod (in press) randomly assigned couples with an alcoholic male partner and recent history of IPV to either BCT or individual-based alcoholism treatment for the male partner only. During the year after treatment, the likelihood of IPV on days of substance use for couples in the two conditions was compared. Both treatments were equally effective in reducing male-to-female physical aggression on days in which the male partner did not drink. However, on days of male partner drinking, the likelihood of male-to-female physical aggression was significantly reduced for couples who received BCT compared with individual-based treatment.

It is important to note that the use of partner-involved treatments for IPV is highly controversial and has not received wide acceptance in the treatment community. In much of the IPV literature, marital and family therapies for IPV are most often viewed as not only inappropriate but also ineffective, ethically questionable, and potentially dangerous (e.g., Zubretsky & Knights, 2001). The controversy is derived, in part, from certain assumptions: first, that conjoint therapy models implicitly or explicitly highlight participants' shared responsibility for the behavior, with the victim assuming she is at least partially responsible for her partner's violence and the abuser thus able to conclude he is not fully responsible for his own aggressive behavior and, second, that conjoint counseling encourages honest and open disclosure, which could lead to conflict in therapy sessions that could escalate to violence outside the confines of therapy. As a consequence of these concerns, most states set standards and guidelines that discourage the use of or prohibit funding for any program that offers couples or family therapy as an intervention modality for IPV (e.g., Healey, Smith, & O'Sullivan, 1998).

Thus, despite some solid evidence supporting the use of conjoint treatments for IPV among patients who also abuse alcohol or other drugs, there is certainly a need for community-friendly individual-based treatments that address both IPV and substance abuse. Although such approaches are rare, there are two nationally recognized examples of such programs: the Integrated Domestic Violence Model in Dade County, Florida (Goldkamp,

Weiland, Collins, & White, 1996), and Yale's Substance Abuse Treatment Unit's Substance Abuse—Domestic Violence (SATU-SADV) program (Easton & Sinha, 2002). The Dade County program is a specialized treatment that addresses substance-abusing behaviors and issues of aggression and anger directed at intimate partners as resulting from the need for power and control. Goldkamp and colleagues (1996) compared treatment outcomes and same-victim reoffending for participants attending the integrated program with those of participants attending a program that was not dual focused. Results showed the integrated treatment program was more successful in maintaining attendance in treatment and obtained lower rates of same-victim reoffending.

Yale's SATU-SADV program is also an integrated approach to treating partner violence and substance abuse that uses a cognitive–behavioral coping skills approach that also incorporates specific interventions that target violent behavior. The SATU-SADV program is delivered in a 12-session group format and teaches coping skills that promote abstinence (e.g., dealing with cravings, negative moods, stress) and nonaggressive responses to conflict (e.g., healthy communication skills, negotiation methods, problem-solving strategies). Preliminary data indicate that this model increases patients' motivation to engage in positive behavior change, improves compliance with treatment, and decreases both anger and alcohol consumption.

CONCLUSION

Across a variety of different studies using samples drawn from both clinical and community populations, substance use and abuse (particularly that of alcohol) have been found to be significantly related to partner violence. Despite what is now a large body of consistent evidence, there nonetheless remains great reluctance among many to acknowledge the causal role drinking and other drug use may play in IPV (e.g., see Minnesota Advocates for Human Rights, 2003). This reluctance appears to be the result of fear that acknowledging the role of substance use in IPV will allow perpetrators to use intoxication as an excuse for their behavior and thus avoid responsibility for their actions. This concern notwithstanding, ignoring what is now very strong evidence of a role for substance use in IPV is likely to result in the use of intervention approaches that are not fully informed by available evidence.

Philosophical and other considerations aside, it would appear that integrated treatment for substance abuse and IPV would lead to improved IPV outcomes in many instances. However, it is also important to emphasize that substance use is only one of many factors that may contribute to IPV among couples and, depending on its degree and severity, may not be a substantial contributor in many cases. Thus, it would seem that a comprehensive assessment of potential factors (including alcohol and other drug use) that may contribute to IPV in a given client or couple is necessary to devise a comprehensive and tailored treatment plan. Depending on the circumstances, this plan may or may not include treatment for substance abuse. But to ignore this factor is likely to lead to suboptimal intervention strategies for a subset of patients and partners whose alcohol and other drug use contributes to episodes of IPV in their relationships.

REFERENCES

Abbey, A. (2002). Alcohol-related sexual assault: A common problem among college students. *Journal of Studies on Alcohol, 14*(Suppl.), 118–128.

Anderson, K. L. (2002). Perpetrator or victim: Relationships between intimate partner violence and well-being. *Journal of Marriage and the Family, 64*, 851–863.

Blane, H. T., Miller, B. A., & Leonard, K. E. (1988). *Intra- and inter-generational aspects of serious domestic violence and alcohol and drugs* (Final Rep., Grant No. 86-IJ-CX-0035, National Institute of Justice). Buffalo, NY: Research Institute on Alcoholism.

Brookoff, D., O'Brien, K. K., Cook, C. S., Thompson, T. D., & Williams, C. (1997). Characteristics of participants in domestic violence: Assessment at the scene of domestic assault. *JAMA, 277*, 1369–1373.

Bureau of Justice Statistics. (1998). *Alcohol and crime: An analysis of national data on the prevalence of alcohol involvement in crime* (Report No. NCJ 168632). Washington, DC: U.S. Department of Justice.

Bushman, B. J. (1997). Effects of alcohol on human aggression: Validity of proposed explanations. *Recent Developments in Alcoholism, 13*, 227–243.

Buzawa, E. S., & Buzawa, C. G. (1990). *Domestic violence: The criminal justice response*. Newbury Park, CA: Sage.

Chase, K. A., O'Farrell, T. J., Murphy, C. M., Fals-Stewart, W., & Murphy, M. (2003). Factors associated with partner violence among female alcoholic patients and their male partners. *Journal of Studies on Alcohol, 64*, 137–149.

Chermack, S. T., & Taylor, S. P. (1995). Alcohol and human physical aggression: Pharmacological versus expectancy effects. *Journal of Studies on Alcohol, 56*, 449–456.

Chermack, S. T., Walton, M. A., Fuller, B. E., & Blow, F. C. (2001). An examination of partner and non-partner violence and victimization among individuals in substance abuse treatment: General and gender-specific correlates. *Psychology of Addictive Behaviors, 15*, 140–151.

Critchlow, B. (1983). Blaming the booze: The attribution of responsibility for drunken behavior. *Personality and Social Psychology Bulletin, 9*, 451–473.

Crowell, N. A., & Burgess, A. W. (1996). *Understanding violence against women*. Washington, DC: National Academies Press.

Cunradi, C. B., Caetano, R., Clark, C. L., & Schafer, J. (1999). Alcohol-related problems and intimate partner violence among White, Black, and Hispanic couples in the U.S. *Alcoholism: Clinical and Experimental Research, 23,* 1492–1501.

Dent, D., & Arias, I. (1990). Effects of alcohol, gender and role of spouses on attributions and evaluations of mental violence scenarios. *Violence and Victims, 5,* 185–193.

Easton, C. J., & Sinha, R. (2002). Treating the addicted male batterer: Promising directions for dual-focused programming. In C. Wekerle & A. Wall (Eds.), *The violence and addiction equation: Theoretical and clinical issues in substance abuse and relationship violence* (pp. 275–292). New York: Brunner-Routledge.

Easton, C. J., Swan, S., & Sinha, R. (2000). Prevalence of family violence entering substance abuse treatment. *Journal of Substance Abuse Treatment, 18,* 23–28.

Fals-Stewart, W. (2003). The occurrence of partner physical aggression on days of alcohol consumption: A longitudinal diary study. *Journal of Consulting and Clinical Psychology, 71,* 41–52.

Fals-Stewart, W., & Clinton-Sherrod, M. (in press). Treating intimate partner violence among substance-abusing dyads: The effect of couples therapy. *Professional Psychology: Research and Practice.*

Fals-Stewart, W., Golden, J., & Schumacher, J. (2003). Intimate partner violence and substance use: A longitudinal day-to-day examination. *Addictive Behaviors, 28,* 1555–1574.

Fals-Stewart, W., Kashdan, T. B., O'Farrell, T. J., & Birchler, G. R. (2002). Behavioral couples therapy for drug-abusing patients: Effects on partner violence. *Journal of Substance Abuse Treatment, 22,* 87–96.

Fals-Stewart, W., & Kennedy, C. (2005). Addressing intimate partner violence in substance abuse treatment. *Journal of Substance Abuse Treatment, 5,* 5–17.

Fals-Stewart, W., Leonard, K. E., & Birchler, G. R. (2005). The occurrence of male-to-female intimate partner violence on days of men's drinking: The moderating effects of antisocial personality disorder. *Journal of Consulting and Clinical Psychology, 73,* 239–248.

Fals-Stewart, W., O'Farrell, T. J., & Birchler, G. R. (2004). Behavioral couples therapy for substance abuse: Rationale, methods, and findings. *Science and Practice Perspectives, 2,* 30–41.

Fals-Stewart, W., & Stappenbeck, C. A. (2003). Intimate partner violence and alcohol use: The role of drinking in partner violence and implications for intervention. *Family Law Psychology Briefs, 4*(4). Retrieved December 16, 2008, from http://www.jmcraig.com/subscribers/archives.htm

Foran, H., & O'Leary, K. D. (2008). Alcohol and intimate partner violence: A meta-analytic review. *Clinical Psychology Review, 28,* 1222–1234.

Foran, H., & O'Leary, K. D. (in press). Problem drinking, jealousy, and anger control: Variables predicting physical aggression against a partner. *Journal of Family Violence.*

Frankenstein, W., Hay, W. H., & Nathan, P. E. (1982). Alcohol intoxication effects on alcoholics' marital communication and problem solving. *Journal of Studies on Alcohol, 46,* 1–9.

Gelles, R. J. (1993). Alcohol and other drugs are associated with violence—They are not its cause. In R. Gelles & D. R. Loseke (Eds.), *Current controversies in family violence* (pp. 154–196). Newbury Park, CA: Sage.

Goldkamp, J. S., Weiland, D., Collins, M., & White, M. (1996). *The role of drug and alcohol abuse in domestic violence and its treatment: Dade County's domestic violence court experiment* [Executive summary] (Report No. NCJ 163411). Washington, DC: U.S. Department of Justice.

Healey, K., Smith, C., & O'Sullivan, C. (1998). *Batterer intervention: Program approaches and criminal justice strategies* (Report No. NCJ 168638). Washington, DC: U.S. Department of Justice.

Hill, A. B. (1965). The environment and disease: Association or causation? *Proceedings of the Royal Society of Medicine, 58,* 295–300.

Home, A. M. (1994). Attributing responsibility and assessing gravity in wife abuse situations: A comparative study of police and social workers. *Journal of Social Service Research, 19,* 67–84.

Hoyle, C. (1998). *Negotiating domestic violence: Police, criminal justice and victims.* Oxford, England: Clarendon Press.

Jacob, T., & Leonard, K. E. (1988). Alcoholic-spouse interaction as a function of alcoholism subtype and alcohol consumption interaction. *Journal of Abnormal Psychology, 97,* 231–237.

Jacob, T., Leonard, K. E., & Haber, J. R. (2001). Family interactions of alcoholics as related to alcoholism type and drinking condition. *Alcoholism: Clinical and Experimental Research, 25,* 835–843.

Kaufman Kantor, G., & Asdigian, N. (1997). When women are under the influence: Does drinking or drug use by women provoke beatings by men? In M. Galanter (Vol. Ed.), *Recent developments in alcoholism: Vol. 13. Alcoholism & violence* (pp. 315–336). New York: Plenum Press.

Kaufman Kantor, G., & Straus, M. A. (1990). The "drunken bum" theory of wife beating. In M. A. Straus & R. J. Gelles (Eds.), *Physical violence in American families: Risk factors and adaptations to violence in 8,145 families* (pp. 203–224). New Brunswick, NJ: Transaction.

Kitzmann, K., Gaylord, N., Holt, A., & Kenny, E. (2003). Child witness to domestic violence: A meta-analytic review. *Journal of Consulting and Clinical Psychology, 71,* 339–352.

Leigh, B. C., & Aramburu, B. (1994). Responsibility attributions for drunken behavior: The role of expectancy violation. *Journal of Applied Social Psychology, 24,* 115–135.

Leonard, K. E. (2001). Domestic violence: What is known and what do we need to know to encourage environmental interactions? *Journal of Substance Use, 6,* 235–247.

Leonard, K. E. (2005). Alcohol and intimate partner violence: When can we say that heavy drinking is a contributing cause of violence? *Addiction, 100,* 422–425.

Leonard, K. E., & Blane, H. T. (1992). Alcohol and marital aggression in a national sample of young men. *Journal of Interpersonal Violence, 7,* 19–30.

Leonard, K. E., & Eiden, R. D. (1999). Husbands and wives drinking: Unilateral or bilateral influences among newlyweds in a general population sample. *Journal of Studies on Alcohol, 13,* 130–138.

Leonard, K. E., & Quigley, B. M. (1999). Drinking and marital aggression in newlyweds: An event-based analysis of drinking and the occurrence of husband marital aggression. *Journal of Studies on Alcohol, 60,* 537–545.

Leonard, K. E., & Roberts, L. J. (1998). The effects of alcohol on the interactions of aggressive and nonaggressive husbands and wives. *Journal of Abnormal Psychology, 107,* 602–615.

Leonard, K. E., & Senchack, M. (1996). Prospective prediction of husband marital aggression within newlywed couples. *Journal of Abnormal Psychology, 105,* 369–380.

McCauley, J., Kern, D. E., Kolodner, K., Dill, L., Schroeder, A. F., Dechant, H. K., et al. (1995). The battering syndrome: Prevalence and clinical characteristics of domestic violence in primary care internal medicine practices. *Annals of Internal Medicine, 123,* 737–746.

Minnesota Advocates for Human Rights. (2003). *Myths about alcohol and domestic violence.* Retrieved December 16, 2008, from http://www.stopvaw.org/Myths_About_Alcohol_and_Domestic_Violence.html

Muhajarine, N., & D'Arcy, C. (1999). Physical abuse during pregnancy: Prevalence and risk factors. *Canadian Medical Association Journal, 160,* 1007–1011.

Murdoch, D., Pihl, R. O., & Ross, D. (1990). Alcohol and crimes of violence: Present issues. *International Journal of the Addictions, 25,* 1065–1081.

National Center for Injury Prevention and Control. (2003). *Cost of intimate partner violence against women in the United States.* Atlanta, GA: Centers for Disease Control and Prevention.

O'Farrell, T. J., Fals-Stewart, W., Murphy, M., & Murphy, C. M. (2003). Partner violence before and after individually based alcoholism treatment for male alcoholic patients. *Journal of Consulting and Clinical Psychology, 71,* 92–102.

O'Farrell, T. J., & Murphy, C. M. (1995). Marital violence before and after alcoholism treatment. *Journal of Consulting and Clinical Psychology, 63,* 256–262.

O'Farrell, T. J., Murphy, C. M., Stephan, S. H., Fals-Stewart, W., & Murphy, M. (2004). Partner violence before and after couples-based alcoholism treatment for male alcoholic patients: The role of treatment involvement and abstinence. *Journal of Consulting and Clinical Psychology, 72,* 202–217.

O'Leary, K. D., & Schumacher, J. A. (2003). The association between alcohol use and intimate partner violence: Linear effect, threshold effect, or both? *Addictive Behaviors, 28,* 1575–1585.

Oriel, K. A., & Fleming, M. F. (1998). Screening men for partner violence in a primary care setting: A new strategy for detecting domestic violence. *Journal of Family Practice, 46,* 493–498.

Rice, M. E., & Harris, G. T. (1995). Psychopathy, schizophrenia, alcohol abuse, and violent recidivism. *International Journal of Law and Psychiatry, 18*, 333–342.

Richardson, D. C. (1981). The effect of alcohol on male aggression toward female targets. *Motivation and Emotion, 5*, 333–343.

Richardson, D. C., & Campbell, J. L. (1980). Alcohol and wife abuse: The effect of alcohol on attributions of blame for wife abuse. *Personality and Social Psychology Bulletin, 6*, 51–56.

Roizen, J. (1993). Issues in the epidemiology of alcohol and violence. In S. E. Martin (Ed.), *Alcohol and interpersonal violence: Fostering multidisciplinary perspectives* (NIAAA Research Monograph No. 24, pp. 3–36). Bethesda, MD: National Institute on Alcohol Abuse and Alcoholism.

Schumacher, J. A., Felbau-Kohn, S., Smith Slep, A. M., & Heyman, R. E. (2001). Risk factors for male–female physical abuse. *Aggression and Violent Behavior, 6*, 281–352.

Senchak, M., & Leonard, K. E. (1994). Attributions for episodes of marital aggression: The effects of aggression severity and alcohol use. *Journal of Family Violence, 9*, 371–381.

Steele, C. M., & Josephs, R. A. (1990). Alcohol myopia: Its prized and dangerous effects. *American Psychologist, 45*, 921–933.

Stewart, A., & Maddren, K. (1997). Police officers' judgments of blame in family violence: The impact of gender and alcohol. *Sex Roles, 37*, 921–933.

Stith, S. M., Smith, D. B., Penn, C. E., Ward, D. B., & Tritt, D. (2004). Intimate physical abuse perpetration and victimization risk factors: A meta-analytic review. *Aggression and Violent Behavior, 10*, 65–98.

Stuart, G. L., Ramsey, S. E., Moore, T. M., Kahler, C. W., Farrell, L. E., Recupero, P. R., & Brown, R. A. (2002). Marital violence victimization and perpetration among women substance abusers: A descriptive study. *Violence Against Women, 8*, 934–952.

Van Hightower, N. R., & Gorton, J. (1998). Domestic violence among patients at two rural health care clinics: Prevalence and social correlates. *Public Health Nursing, 15*, 355–362.

Zubretsky, T. M., & Knights, C. L. (2001). *Basic information about domestic violence.* Rensselaer: New York State Office for the Prevention of Domestic Violence.

AFTERWORD

ERICA M. WOODIN AND K. DANIEL O'LEARY

This book represents a synthesis of state-of-the-art research related to psychological and physical aggression in couples and of the clinical implications of these findings. Many of the foremost experts in the field have discussed key evidence and issues related to the prevalence, etiology, and treatment of partner aggression from a variety of theoretical perspectives. Several key themes that appeared throughout the book are worth noting. Uniting these themes is the emerging understanding that the construct of "partner aggression" is a multifaceted concept.

KEY THEMES AND RESEARCH IMPLICATIONS

The first notable theme of this book is the recognition that aggression toward a partner takes many forms. Physical aggression is perhaps the most documented form in terms of prevalence, etiology, and intervention implications. Physical aggression rarely exists, however, in the absence of at least mild forms of psychological aggression, and it appears to be most dangerous when accompanied by high levels of psychologically controlling and abusive behaviors. In addition, sexual aggression, although less common, does co-occur frequently with male physical aggression and is another important component in understanding violence against women, particularly cross-culturally.

Looking forward, it is crucial that researchers more fully consider the implications of these different forms of partner aggression in tandem and pay attention to the ways in which the various forms interact at the levels of prevalence, etiology, and prevention and intervention implications. Aggression may take many forms at different points in a relationship, and it is likely that only by recognizing and targeting multiple forms concurrently can true aggression cessation be achieved.

271

The second theme evident in this book is that physical and psychological forms of aggression are common in adolescent and young adult couples. Unfortunately, psychological and physical aggression in teens and young adults is quite stable over time and can clearly have adverse consequences. Prevention of serious forms of aggression must consider the relatively high prevalence of aggression in steadily dating teen relationships, particularly given that such aggression is often considered inconsequential by the teens themselves.

The third theme apparent in several chapters of this book relates to the increased importance placed on understanding aggression by women. There is now a relatively large literature regarding the prevalence of aggression by women in community samples in the United States, with evidence that women engage in slightly higher levels of physical and psychological aggression, but far lower levels of sexual aggression, than men. Recent findings also suggest that female aggression in community samples can occur for reasons other than self-defense and is often an expression of anger toward the partner. Furthermore, although female aggression seems to have less impact on partners' physical and mental health than male aggression, male and female aggression are highly correlated within couples and are predictive of marital discord and divorce, as well as of child adjustment problems.

Far less research exists regarding the etiological and contextual factors that account for female aggression, and few current intervention models adequately address the role of nondefensive female aggression. A coherent theoretical model of partner aggression must take into account the behavior of both partners, while also acknowledging the possibility for different etiological explanations based on differing gender role development and expectations.

The fourth theme to emerge from these chapters relates to the concept of "one size fits all" models of partner aggression. Early conceptualizations that relied wholly on one or two constructs, such as male gender role ideology or patriarchal cultural beliefs, to explain and provide structure for batterers interventions failed to take into account the multifaceted nature of partner aggression. More recent theories, including several presented in this book, take the perspective that aggression against partners varies in terms of biological, psychological, and sociocultural influences and that both theory and intervention approaches must address this heterogeneity if clinicians are to successfully understand and intervene with clients.

This theme is controversial and runs counter to many existing protocols that use a standardized treatment approach for all individuals. We believe, however, that the field of partner aggression will continue to progress only through careful exploration of the limits and caveats of existing models as well as the development of more flexible and adaptable intervention approaches.

Furthermore, although this book focuses primarily on research and interventions in the United States and other developed countries, there is still a considerable need to investigate partner aggression as an international phenomenon. A range of studies now suggest that physical aggression against women is nearly universal cross-culturally; physical aggression against men has been much less studied around the world. Socioculturally sanctioned forms of aggression against women tend to be much more widespread and have more serious health consequences than the most common forms of aggression against women in the United States.

CLINICAL IMPLICATIONS

Throughout this book, the chapter authors have extended their analysis of the empirical evidence by commenting on how these findings might be translated to clinical settings. Many of these commentaries echo some of the overarching themes of this book—namely, that aggression is present in various forms and with various functions and impact in a wide variety of intimate relationships and that assessment and treatment approaches must be cognizant of this variation.

Given that physical aggression is so common in many treatment facilities, with about half of all couples seeking marital therapy reporting physical aggression in their relationships, it is important that all clinicians be aware of the phenomenon. Clinicians are encouraged to conduct a thorough assessment of previous and ongoing psychological, physical, and sexual aggression victimization for any individual within a current or previous intimate relationship, regardless of whether they are presenting for couple, family, or individual treatment. An important component of such an assessment is a focus on the mental and physical health impact of aggressive incidents, as well as any impact on the relationship or on other family members. Similarly, for individuals with a history of aggression perpetration, an in-depth and individualized assessment, with a focus on the types and impact of past aggressive behaviors in both former and current relationships, is important. Further, clinicians should assess aggressors for factors such as the reasons for engaging in aggressive behaviors, the level of motivation to change such behaviors, and any co-occurring psychopathology or substance use that might also need concurrent intervention.

In terms of intervention options, ideally these will be tailored to the needs and motivations of the aggressive individual. If couples are experiencing less damaging forms of psychological and physical aggression, such as frequent yelling or occasional pushing and shoving, if neither partner is afraid of the other or overly controlled by the other, and if both are committed to the relationship, couples therapy with a focus on aggression cessation may be considered. In cases where couples therapy is not yet warranted because of concerns for safety, past incidents of serious injury, or lack of commitment to the relationship, individual or group treatment approaches may be preferable.

CONCLUSION

In sum, this book represents an exciting synopsis of the field of partner aggression research. The past 30 years have witnessed a proliferation of increasingly sophisticated theory and empirical work dedicated to understanding and ameliorating a problem many couples face. Emergent themes from this book include (a) the trend toward understanding partner aggression as encompassing a range of psychologically, physically, and sexually aggressive behaviors; (b) a greater awareness of the prevalence and consequences of aggression in young adult relationships; (c) the attempt to document and understand nondefensive female aggression; and (d) the development of multifaceted conceptualizations of partner aggression that draw from a range of biological, psychological, and sociocultural perspectives. The insights provided by the contributors to this book will likely continue to move the field forward for many years to come.

INDEX

in intimate partner violence research, 129–130

moderating and mediating variables for, 128–129

and physiological arousal, 126–128

physiological markers of, 124–130

and sexual aggression, 49–50

Psychopathy Checklist—Revised, 51

Psychophysiology of aggression, 119–134

and antisocial/psychopathy literature, 124–130

current research in, 131–134

and Gottman et al.'s typology, 119–124

and hostility/cardiovascular literature, 130–131

Psychotherapeutic change processes, 81

Psychotic symptoms, 218

PTSD. *See* Posttraumatic stress disorder

Public health, 71, 251

Puntos de Encuentro program, 72

Quigley, B. M., 252–253

Race, as moderating effect, 172

Raine, A., 122–123

Randomized clinical trials, 207

Random national samples, 42, 43. *See also* Representative samples

Rape

acquaintance or date, 38

legal definition, 38, 39

of men by women, 44

and problematic cognitions, 176–177

as term, 9

Rates of injury, 28–29, 31

RAVEN (Rape and Violence End Now) program, 192

Reactive use of violence, 121–122

Readiness for change, of offenders, 214

Rearing environments, adverse, 150, 157

Recidivism

and alcohol use, 92, 217, 259

for Domestic Violence Focused Couples Treatment, 238

and group interventions, 216

of psychopathic offenders, 50

psychopathology as predictor of, 91–92

and traditional treatment, 93, 234

and treatment duration, 196

Reciprocal violence, 235. *See also* Common couple violence

Reflective listening, 214, 220

Reframing, 214

Reinemann, D. H. S., 170–171

Reitzel-Jaffe, D., 171

Rejection

avoidance of, 103

concerns about, 86

Relapse, 262, 263

cues for, 224

prevention of, 224

Relapse prevention model for addictive behaviors, 224

Relational aggression, 107

Relationship risk factors. *See also* Family and relationship predictors of aggression

from family, 100

for psychological and physical aggression, 107–109

for sexual aggression, 50

Relationships

dynamics of, 235

enhancement of, 221

functioning of, 104–105, 214

status of, 214

Relationship satisfaction

mediating effect of, 253

predicted by autonomic reactivity, 119

programs to improve, 176

Relationship skills training, 221–222

Renick, M. J., 176

Reporting

and methodology, 62

of physical and psychological aggression, 16

of sexual aggression, 40

study variables affecting, 60

and terminology of survey, 69–70

Representativeness, of adoption studies, 148

Representative samples

alcohol in, 83–84

as basis for prevention programs, 80

community samples, 41–44, 143

female-to-male violence in, 19, 22–24, 30

male-to-female violence in, 18–22, 24, 30

physical aggression in, 18–23

predicting violent behavior from, 89–90

psychological aggression in, 23, 24

random national samples, 42, 43

Research Institute on Addictions, 236

Resentment, 87

Typologies of perpetrators, 84–88

Underarousal, 120, 126
Undercontrolled behavior, 100
Undercontrolled hostility, 82
Unintended victims, children as, 17
Unity theory, 39
Unsuccessful psychopaths, 128
Unworthiness, 203
Urban location, as prevalence factor for victimization, 70
U.S. Agency for International Development, 62
Utah, intervention programs in, 195, 200, 225

Verbal aggression, 23n1, 143
Verbal behavior, negative, 256–257
Verbally aggressive conflict styles, 258
Verification, of violence reports, 68
Vermont, intervention programs in, 199
Vicarious distress stimuli, 129
Victim blaming, 152, 201, 235
Victimization
    childhood and adolescent risk factors for, 165
    and corporal punishment/child maltreatment, 103
    correlation of perpetration and, 151
    and dating abuse prevention programs, 175
    following alcoholism treatment, 261
    genetic and environmental influences on, 150, 152–153
    heritability of, 149
    intergenerational transmission of, 143, 152
    and intoxication, 259–260
    of maltreated children, 171
Victims
    contacting, 199–200
    family risks for. See Family and relationship predictors of aggression
    as group facilitators, 198
    and health care systems, 79
    intoxication of, 258

safety of, 204, 220, 235, 239
of sexual aggression, 48
tolerance of violent behavior by, 70
Violence
    beliefs associated with, 200
    bilateral, 234
    as choice, 239
    severity of, 89, 132–133, 240, 257
    as term, 10
Violence Against Women Act, 18
Violence profiles, 84
Visioning, 242
Vivian, D., 43

Waltz, J., 120–124
Washington, intervention programs in, 195, 198
Webb, S. A., 124
Weiss, R. L., 220–221
Wekerle, C., 171
Welsh Anxiety Scale, 126
Whiston, S. C., 177
WHO. See World Health Organization
WHO study. See Multi-Country Study on Women's Health and Domestic Violence
Widom, C. S., 104–105
Wilder Foundation, 242
Wile, D. B., 245
Wisconsin, intervention programs in, 197
Wolfe, D. A., 171
Women
    aggression by, 44–45, 254, 272. See also Female-to-male violence
    empowerment of, 72
    violence against, 59–72
Women's movement, 79
Woodin, E. M., 175
World Health Organization (WHO), 60–62, 179
Worldsafe study, 61, 64

Yllo, K., 43
Young adults, prevention of aggression in, 175–177
Youth Relationship Project, 171, 178

ABOUT THE EDITORS

K. Daniel O'Leary, PhD, is Distinguished Professor of Psychology and past chairman of the Psychology Department at Stony Brook University in Stony Brook, New York. Dr. O'Leary was among the top 100 cited psychologists in the English-speaking world (*American Psychologist*, December 1978). He received the Distinguished Scientist Award from the clinical division of the American Psychological Association in 1985, and he was installed to the National Academies of Practice in Psychology in 1986.

Dr. O'Leary is the author or coauthor of 10 books. The most recent include *Depression in Marriage* (1990, with S. R. H. Beach and E. E. Sandeen), *The Couples Psychotherapy Treatment Planner* (1998, with R. E. Heyman and A. E. Jongsma Jr.), and *Psychological Abuse in Violent Domestic Relations* (2001, with R. D. Maiuro). He has shown how marital problems can lead to depression, and his research with S. R. H. Beach showed that marital therapy for clinically depressed and maritally discordant women leads to both increases in marital satisfaction and decreases in depression.

Since 1980, Dr. O'Leary has conducted research on the etiology, prevention, and treatment of partner aggression. In 2007, with A. M. Smith Slep and S. G. O'Leary, he evaluated the relative predictive power of socioeconomic, family history, personality, physiological, and relationship variables as predictors of partner aggression.

Erica M. Woodin, PhD, is an assistant professor in the Department of Psychology at the University of Victoria in British Columbia, Canada. She received her graduate training in clinical psychology at Stony Brook University and is a licensed clinical psychologist in British Columbia.

Her work examines the causes of psychological and physical aggression in couples, the impact of these behaviors on family functioning, the effectiveness of treatment efforts to reduce aggressive behaviors, and the use of prevention efforts to avert aggression in early adulthood. She is also interested in the links between partner aggression and substance abuse and is affiliated with the Centre for Addictions Research of British Columbia. She has received funding from the U.S. National Institute of Mental Health, the Melissa Institute for Violence Prevention, and the British Columbia Mental Health and Addictions Research Network.